William Hazlitt: Critic of Power

Maidstone Museum and Art Gallery

1. WILLIAM HAZLITT AT ABOUT AGE 30. A COPY BY JAMES STEWART
OF AN OIL PAINTING BY JOHN HAZLITT.

William Hazlitt

Critic of Power

JOHN KINNAIRD

COLUMBIA UNIVERSITY PRESS

New York   1978

LIBRARY OF CONGRESS CATALOGING IN PUBLICATION DATA

KINNAIRD, JOHN WILLIAM, 1924–
    WILLIAM HAZLITT: CRITIC OF POWER.

    INCLUDES BIBLIOGRAPHICAL REFERENCES AND INDEX.
    1. HAZLITT, WILLIAM, 1778–1830.   2. HAZLITT,
WILLIAM, 1778–1830—KNOWLEDGE—LITERATURE.   3. CRITI-
CISM—ENGLAND—HISTORY.   4. AUTHORS, ENGLISH—19TH
CENTURY—BIOGRAPHY.   I. TITLE.
PR4773.K5   824'.7   78-14523
ISBN 0-231-04600-6

COLUMBIA UNIVERSITY PRESS
NEW YORK   GUILDFORD, SURREY

COPYRIGHT © 1978 COLUMBIA UNIVERSITY PRESS
ALL RIGHTS RESERVED
PRINTED IN THE UNITED STATES OF AMERICA

*In memory
of
⚜ my mother and father ⚜*

Preface

THERE ARE now several biographies of Hazlitt but none that can properly be called a biography of his mind. Herschel Baker's *William Hazlitt* (1962) and Ralph M. Wardle's *Hazlitt* (1971) are both intimately involved at times with their subject's ideas; but both studies concentrate on the man as he lived, or as he pursued a career, through the contingencies of time—on the record of his "life" in the conventional sense. There is always another life going forward in the case of a thinker and writer like Hazlitt—the life of a mind grappling with enigmatic issues of understanding and conscience, struggling to penetrate the relationships between one act or experience and another, trying to resolve his own conflicts intellectually or bring them to conscious—always to more fully conscious—definition. This is the life of Hazlitt, the journey of a self-exploring mind, revealed only through his *works,* and perhaps most clearly revealed in those works where he is not writing autobiography, or not talking about himself only (or primarily) but about the minds of others as well—in his works, namely, of *criticism.*

To speak of "criticism" in Hazlitt's case is to refer to much more than literature, for his critical intelligence played over almost the entire range of human concerns in his time: philosophy, politics and society, painting and theater, manners and morality and religion—in short, culture generally, or the condition of what he called "the public mind" (20.136). To encompass this diverse terrain would be unthinkable without a unifying theme, and not the least novel among the premises of my study is the assumption that such a theme does indeed exist, with recognizable variations, through the twenty volumes of Hazlitt's prolific achievement. Hence my subtitle, *Critic of Power;* for it is, I believe, his vision of the continuity of "power" and its motives—of "power" both as *kratos* and *dynamis,* both in the political (that is, societal) sense as ruling force or authority, and in the natural, or broadly philosophical, sense as active, creative, or generative energy—that is the informing vision of all his criticism, whatever the immediate subject, whether he is formulating a theory of poetic imagination, or describing the art of Titian, or analyzing the career of Napoleon Buonaparte. "It is important to know in all circumstances," Hazlitt wrote in his *Life of Napoleon,* "what it is that gives power over the human mind" (13.128).

My opening chapter introduces this theme, by showing the root of its dialectic in the conflicts of his upbringing and youthful experience. Subsequent chapters than show his vision of "power" growing in range and complexity, first in his philosophical criticism (chapter 2), then in his political, literary, and art criticism (chapters 3–7), and at last in the darkly paradoxical, dramatically modulated criticism of his last decade, at once "personal" and broadly cultural (chapters 8–10), when his vision of both life and art becomes the expression of an ironic, yet not finally despairing, sense of inescapable "contradiction and anomaly in the mind and heart of man" (11.9).

What emerges from this study will be, I hope, a more informed awareness of Hazlitt's centrality in English Romanticism. This seems to be the main direction of emphasis in Hazlitt studies over the past forty or fifty years—away from the sense of Hazlitt as an important but rather impulsive and eccentric essayist toward a sense of this writer as principally a theorist and critic whose thought, if not his style, flows directly out of the mainstream of English literary culture at the end of the eighteenth century. We now recognize that Hazlitt performs a crucially mediating role in the intellectual life of his time—mediating between Enlightenment and Apocalypse, between the values of tradition and revolt, between earlier and later generations of Romanticism, between the old prose of "sense" and the new poetry of imagination. Scholars of the period, therefore, have good reason to congratulate themselves as they take note of the present occasion—the second centenary of Hazlitt's birth in 1778—for scholarship has at last established the significance of a literary life that begins in the interval between the American and the French Revolutions, and of a mind that grows up, and that would always remain, half in the shadow of one century and half in the shadow of its successor. But an occasion like the present, devoted to honoring past accomplishment as future inspiration, might also move us to some major reconsiderations—to reappraisals not only of this writer's achievement but of our own working assumptions as scholars—and we might begin by asking whether we have not been conceiving of the centrality of Hazlitt's criticism in too simple a sense. Mediator between old and new he certainly is, but we might consider whether Hazlitt could have performed this function so well if his mind had not been central to Romanticism in quite another way—central as the heart is to an organism's energy, or as the brain is to the nervous system. As I read his work, Hazlitt does not assimilate all experience to certain fixed attitudes, or view things from the same vantage point in time, his mind returning forever to the dawn phase of the French Revolution. Rather, his thought moves with the advancing storm center of Romantic creativity: in his mind, as in no other prose writer of the time, the great issues of Romanticism meet, intersect, and interpenetrate, or are joined in battle, converging either toward resolution or toward perpetual conflict. That confrontation of issues—issues mainly, as I see them, of "power"—is what this book is finally about: it is the study of a mind that is, only because it becomes, central to its age in history. And on the basis of this reorientation I shall venture to offer, in my conclusion, some reasons for granting Hazlitt new respect not only as a Romantic critic but as a mind whose insights and judgments still have exemplary value for modern criticism.

One last word of caution may be in order. Although I have added some new biographical material, and although I depart from earlier biographies in my sense of the major turning points in Hazlitt's life, this book is in no sense a substitute for reading a full-scale biography, especially one or the other of the two comprehensive biographies I have mentioned. Similarly, in order to make room for analysis of the structure of Hazlitt's argument in certain works, especially in his lectures on literature and *The Spirit of the Age*, I have had to minimize consideration of sources, parallels, and influences; but I am the less pained at this deficiency by the knowledge that many of these matters have already been investigated in the thorough studies of Walter Jackson Bate, W. P. Albrecht, Elisabeth Schneider, Roy Park, and other scholars to whose able work I stand indebted, as my notes sufficiently indicate.

This study has been in preparation for many years, and I cannot hope to acknowledge here by name the numerous but not forgotten obligations that I have incurred among students, colleagues, and librarians at several institutions. I thank first Jacques Barzun, Professor Emeritus of History and former Provost of Columbia University, for reading the manuscript in an earlier version and for offering much helpful advice and encouragement at a time when it was particularly needed. The late Professor Lionel Trilling of Columbia continued to offer guidance and his special brand of inspiration long after serving, now two decades ago, as director of my dissertation on Hazlitt—but this bald statement cannot begin to suggest how much I owe to his teaching and to his work as a critic. I must also record one other indebtedness of long ago—to the late A. Humphry House of Wadham College, Oxford, whose student I had the brief good fortune to be (while on a Fulbright Fellowship to Jesus College) in the year before his death in 1955; his astonishingly detailed knowledge of the nineteenth century led to certain lines of inquiry whose results are reflected at several points in the following pages. More recently, Steven Marcus, John Andrews, Wallace Jackson, Richard Schoeck, and the late Gordon Pitts of the University of Maryland have read parts of the manuscript and made helpful suggestions. I am indebted to the American Council of Learned Societies for a six-months Grant-in-Aid which enabled me to continue work on this study in 1965, and to the General Research Board of the University of Maryland for a series of summer grants at intervals since 1966. Parts of several chapters have appeared as articles in *Criticism, Shakespeare Quarterly, The Wordsworth Circle, Studies in Romanticism,* and *Partisan Review;* and I am grateful to the editors of these journals for permission to reprint and adapt material. Lastly, my wife has assisted this enterprise in all possible capacities—as

critic, editor, researcher, typist—and, not least, as cheerful sufferer
and true believer.

University of Maryland, College Park   J. K.
March 1978

Short Forms of
Titles Most Frequently Cited

UNLESS otherwise indicated, all references to Hazlitt's writings are to *Complete Works*, Centenary Edition, ed. P. P. Howe, 21 vols. (London: J. M. Dent, 1930–34). Whenever feasible, references to this edition appear parenthetically in the text: the first number given refers to the volume, the second (and any subsequent numbers) to the page or pages, e.g., 12.104–06. For the location of specific titles in the volumes of the Centenary Edition, see the table at the end of this book. (In the list that follows, I include names of publishers only for twentieth-century titles.)

Abrams, *Mirror*	M. H. Abrams. *The Mirror and the Lamp: Romantic Theory and the Critical Tradition.* New York: Norton, 1958.
Albrecht, *HCI*	W. P. Albrecht. *Hazlitt and the Creative Imagination.* Lawrence: University of Kansas Press, 1965.
Baker	Herschel Baker. *William Hazlitt.* Cambridge: Harvard University Press, 1962.
Bate, *Criticism*	*Criticism: The Major Texts.* Ed. Walter Jackson Bate. New York: Harcourt, Brace and World, 1952.
Blake	*The Poetry and Prose of William Blake.* Ed. D. V. Erdman. Garden City, N.Y.: Doubleday, 1965.
Coleridge, *BL*	Samuel Taylor Coleridge. *Biographia Literaria; with his Aesthetical Essays.* Ed. J. Shawcross. London: Clarendon Press, 1907.

Coleridge, *SC* *Samuel Taylor Coleridge: Shakespearean Criticism.* Ed. Thomas Middleton Raysor. 2d ed. 2 vols. New York: Dutton (Everyman's Library), 1960.

ELH *Journal of English Literary History.*

Godwin, *PJ* William Godwin. *An Enquiry concerning Political Justice.* Photographic Facsimile of the Third Edition. Ed. F. E. L. Priestley. 3 vols. Toronto: University of Toronto Press, 1946.

Haydon Benjamin Robert Haydon. *Autobiography and Journals.* Ed. Malcolm Elwin. London: Macdonald, 1950.

Howe P. P. Howe. *The Life of William Hazlitt.* Harmondsworth: Penguin Books, 1949.

Hunt, *LC* *Leigh Hunt's Literary Criticism.* Ed. L. H. Houtchens and C. W. Houtchens. New York: Columbia University Press, 1956.

JAAC *Journal of Aesthetics and Art Criticism.*

Keats, *Letters* *The Letters of John Keats.* Ed. Hyder E. Rollins. 2 vols. Cambridge: Harvard University Press, 1958.

Keats, *Poems* *The Poems of John Keats.* Ed Ernest de Selincourt. London: Methuen, 1905.

Lamb *The Works of Charles and Mary Lamb.* Ed. E. V. Lucas. 5 vols. London: Methuen, 1903.

Landseer Thomas Landseer. *Life and Letters of William Bewick.* 2 vols. London, 1871.

Maclean Catherine M. Maclean. *Born under Saturn: A Biography of William Hazlitt.* London: Collins, 1943.

MLQ *Modern Language Quarterly.*

Moyne *The Journal of Margaret Hazlitt.* Ed. Ernest J. Moyne. Lawrence: University of Kansas Press, 1967.

MP *Modern Philology.*

Park Roy Park. *Hazlitt and the Spirit of the Age: Abstraction and Critical Theory.* Oxford: Clarendon Press, 1971.

PMLA [Publications of the Modern Language Association of America].

Political Tracts *Political Tracts of Wordsworth, Coleridge and Shelley.* Ed. R. J. White. Cambridge: Cambridge University Press, 1953.

Robinson *Henry Crabb Robinson on Books and Their Writers.* Ed. Edith J. Morley. 3 vols. London: J. M. Dent, 1938.

Schneider Elisabeth Schneider. *The Aesthetics of William Hazlitt.* Philadelphia: University of Pennsylvania Press, 1933.

SIR *Studies in Romanticism.*

TWC *The Wordsworth Circle.*

Wardle	Ralph M. Wardle. *Hazlitt.* Lincoln: University of Nebraska Press, 1971.
Watson	George Watson. *The Literary Critics.* Baltimore: Penguin Books, 1962.
Wellek	René Wellek. *A History of Modern Criticism, 1750–1950.* Vol. 2: *The Romantic Age.* New Haven: Yale University Press, 1955.
Wordsworth, *Po W*	*The Poetical Works of William Wordsworth.* 2nd ed. Ed. Ernest de Selincourt, rev. Helen Darbishire. 5 vols. Oxford: Clarendon Press, 1952–59.
Wordsworth, *Pr W*	*The Prose Works of William Wordsworth.* Ed. W. J. B. Owen and Jane Worthington Smyser. 3 vols. Oxford: Clarendon Press, 1974.
Wordsworth, *Prelude*	William Wordsworth. *The Prelude.* 2nd ed. Ed. Ernest de Selincourt, rev. Helen Darbishire. Oxford: Clarendon Press, 1959.

Contents

Illustrations

Chapter One

Puritan Fathers,
Unitarian Sons

HAZLITT once remarked to a friend, "I do not seem to have altered any of my ideas since I was sixteen years old"—whereupon the friend replied, "Why then, you are no wiser now than you were then!" (17.22–23). The reproof has had many, though less genial, echoes ever since. "Hopelessly impenetrable," was Leslie Stephen's comment as he contemplated the anomaly of a thinker who could "claim to have learnt nothing" through the first three decades of the nineteenth century. The only "explanation," Stephen decided, is "that what Hazlitt called his opinions were really his feelings." And Lord David Cecil concludes that while experience could "disturb," it "could not alter" this writer who in his forties was "as full of zest as a boy of twenty"—and who remained "to the end of his life immature," incapable of achieving "a defined, consistent philosophy of life," or even "a consistent point of view."[1]

Today we are no longer quite so ready to equate Hazlitt's boyish "enthusiasm" with intellectual incoherence. We have learned to look with genuine philosophical respect on a theoretic idea that Hazlitt first "discovered" (although it took another ten years to articulate fully) at the age of sixteen (9.51). This is the thesis, which indeed conditions all his thinking thereafter, of "the natural disinterestedness of the human mind," or the doctrine (to give its more familiar cognomen, which scholarship prefers as suggesting its derivations and its literary bearing) of "the sympathetic imagination"; and we shall examine later in this chapter the genesis and logic of his "discovery." But in thus correcting the traditional legend of Hazlitt in one way, we may only have confirmed it in another. For we still seem to be taking for granted, or have left unquestioned, the major premise of the legend—that Hazlitt's thought was unalterably fixed in his youth. He is still being pictured as the incurably young, if always more sour than sanguine, radical: an unrepentant "Jacobin," an enthusiast for "Liberty" so intoxicated by the French Revolution that he became its uncompromising champion—or, if one's politics run the other way, its unforgiving, avenging bigot. And this image has its clear, if seldom recognized, parallel in the assumption that continues to dominate studies of his literary theory, where Hazlitt is assumed to be a thinker who develops a philosophy of imagination in his youth and then, in his practical criticism, holds, or simply extends, this position to the end of his life, altering only his prose style and the emotional tenor of his thought, as the obscure "metaphysician" becomes the popular lecturer and journalist. Now this indeed is "consistency," but it is, I suspect, a coherence gained for Hazlitt's mind at the expense of that cogency we rightly expect from a critic whose work has been recommended to posterity: a cogency of growth, of steadily maturing and balanced wisdom, a flexibly dialectical awareness of those ironies and other complexities of the human condition which cannot be illuminated or resolved by a single logic of doctrine or from a single perspective in judgment. And is it possible that our new reading of Hazlitt's intellectual consistency, like the old legend of the nostalgic emotionalist, still depends less on hard evidence—or on a clearly defined sense of his limitations—than on certain predilections of our own most consistent habits in looking back on the literary past? Would not the landscape of English Romanticism in our minds have a gaping emptiness at its very center if there were not at least one literary figure in the period who would represent unswerving loyalty to the French Revolution, to its attendant ideas and ideals—a symbol of constancy against which we may measure and define the many changes of mind and heart in his less stable contemporaries? We have always been ready to cast Hazlitt in this role, and have seldom been willing to ask whether the record of his criticism really does confirm this contrast with the vicissitudes of Romantic thought in general. We see—indeed strain to see—elaborate crises of will and conscience in all the other leading Romanticists; only Hazlitt, it would seem, is to remain immune from intellectual change in an age of change.[2]

He could not, it is true, have performed his role so long and so successfully in our minds had he not seemed cast for the part by both nature and history—to be born and bred for it as (in his own sardonic description) an "incorrigible" Dissenter (4.102). But again the evidence for this sense of his intellectual identity comes mainly from his own testimonials, and that, by strict courtroom standards, is germane but highly questionable evidence. Hazlitt is a generally reliable autobiographer, but all that we may honestly infer from his many professions of intellectual constancy is that he willed to believe in his constancy—willed, that is, to overlook the significance of some manifest departures from his cherished "first principles." To accept his avowals as literal fact is to defy reasonable probability: for every thinking man, if he does not abandon or expressly deny the heritage of his upbringing, has to repossess it—has to make it his own, assimilate it to his own consciousness and experience. Hazlitt recognizes, in part, this necessity even as he elaborates on his boast of loyalty: "By adhering to the same principles you do not remain stationary. You enlarge, correct and consolidate your reasonings without contradicting or shuffling about in your conclusions" (17.33). But again a sceptical investigator may ask whether there may not be more truth left unspoken than stated in this highly abstract defense. There is no hint here—as there is elsewhere in Hazlitt's confessional prose—of the pain that attends true growth and development, of the shame and grim courage of self-correction, or of "consolidation" as, in proportion to its depth, a resolution of elements in conflict. We may be led to wonder whether the one necessary condition of Hazlitt's intellectual growth was that he never admit to himself how much he was, or had been, "altering" his "ideas"—whether, in short, the condition for adaptive change, for mature self-development, was that he continually protest to the world, and thus assure himself, that he would not or could not change his original "principles" and "conclusions."

His boyhood and adolescence will thus retain in this study all the importance with which the Hazlitt legend has endowed them—though not as the period which shaped a lasting bondage to the past, but as the focal point of his life-long struggle against all that was lethal or stultifying to the self in that bondage. This is why a study of his criticism, if it is to be comprehensive, must begin with, and must then continually look back to, the world of his beginnings. The legend of his uncontrolled emotionality is not misleading in its emphasis on "passion" and boy-like "zest" but in its assumption that these qualities preclude clear thought and a receptivity to novel experience, just as the twentieth-century corrective to the legend has gone wrong, by reaction, in its determination to rescue his thought from his politics and restore it to some emotionally pure realm of literary-aesthetic discourse—with the inevitable result that the true "consistency" of his criticism has been stripped of its richly existential complexity as the expression and resolution of a profound passional conflict in himself. True, detecting this error in our habits does not clear up but only leaves more acute the problem at the center: for now we must acknowledge the paradox of a thinker in conflict with something in himself but who never seems to quarrel with himself intellectually. Yet the paradox is more apparent than real; for its recognition becomes but another way of reminding ourselves that Hazlitt continually sought, even in the familiar essays, to "go out of" himself (a favorite phrase; e.g., 20.170) into the "character" of others, whether living, historical, or imaginary—to go from self-consciousness to "disinterested" sympathy or contemplation, where he could project and master his own conflicts in their generic form, as "contradiction and anomaly in the mind and heart of man" (11.9). If, nevertheless, we should still insist that his testimonials of unwavering loyalty to his past can be credibly refuted only on the basis of cognate evidence of the same kind, that is, in his own words, we may find symptomatic revelation of the conflict in the very statement of constancy that we began by quoting. "I do not seem [and we should not undervalue that honestly tentative *seem*] to have altered any of my ideas since I was sixteen years old": is there not a suggestion here, once we are disposed to look for it, that *before* the age of sixteen he *had* significantly "altered" his ideas—had already learned to challenge some of the beliefs and "principles" of his education as a Dissenter? And evidence of precocious change is what we do find, as we turn now to a brief inspection of his boyhood years: the struggle of his sense of self with his identity in the world does not begin at or after the age of sixteen, but well before that pivotal year of his adolescence.

꿈

Our first clear glimpse of Hazlitt as a boy is at the age of eight or nine in his happy years at Wem, the small market village in Shropshire where his father was minister to the Presbyterian congregation. Margaret Hazlitt remembered her younger brother at Wem as "the most active, lively, and happiest of boys . . . beloved by all for his amiable temper and manners, pleasing above his years." Yet a child loved as "the delight and pride of his family" (Moyne, p. 106) might not have been so thoroughly amiable—and perhaps because of that delight and pride—to other observers. Some letters written at intervals between the ages of ten and twelve reveal a boy of astonishing precocity, and one who already writes with something of the lively emphasis of *Table-Talk,* but who also seems well on his way to becoming an officious prig. A few random fragments will be enough to suggest that Billy's conversation could be at once endearing and ominous: "I can teach a boy of sixteen already who was ciphering eight months before me; is he not a great dunce?" "I spent a very agreeable day yesterday, as I read 160 pages of Priestley, and heard two good sermons." "We were all glad to hear that you were well, and that you have so much business to do. We cannot be happy without being employed." And this (after an argument with another boy on the question of an established Church): "The Presbyterian is better than that, said I. I told him I thought so for certain reasons, not because I went to Chapel. But at last, when I had overpowered him with my arguments, he said he wished he understood it as well as I did." And perhaps the most revealing passage comes in a letter home to his father, written on a visit to Liverpool in 1790:

> I now sit down to spend a little time in an employment, the productions of which I know will give you pleasure. . . . Happy indeed, unspeakably happy, are those people who, when at the point of death, are able to say, with a satisfaction which none but themselves can have any idea of: "I have done with this world, I shall now have no more of its temptations to struggle with, and praise be to God I have overcome them; now no more sorrow, now no more grief, but happiness for evermore!"

We may smile at this as unconscious parody, but when we read the minister's reply ("The piety displayed . . was a great refreshment to me. Continue to cherish those thoughts which then occupied your mind, continue to be virtuous, and you will finally be that happy being whom you describe . . ."),[3] then our smile fades and we begin to understand what it was to be the son of a "Rational Dissenter." Hazlitt was later in no doubts about the artificial maturities of his early adolescence, as he confesses in the essay "On the Conduct of Life"—a public letter of advice to his son that stands in marked contrast to the paternal counsel he himself received at nearly the same age. He is confident that his son, "from the difference of education," has escaped "the spiritual pride and intellectual coxcombry" of his own upbringing, and he seems almost to be recalling the priggishness of his early letters when he confesses: "Those who . . . did not belong to the class of *Rational Dissenters* I was led erroneously to look upon as hardly deserving the name of rational beings" (17.88). And this boy's sense of "spiritual" merit rested on something more stubbornly rooted than pride in his gifts of reason—as we learn from the same letter of 1790, in a passage that immediately follows the one quoted above:

> But how unspeakably miserable is that man, who, when his pleasures are going to end, when his lamp begins to grow dim, is compelled to say: Oh, that I had done my Duty to God and man, oh that I had been wise. . . . But it [life] is now gone, I cannot recall time, nor can I undo all my wicked actions. I cannot seek that mercy which I have so often despised. I have no hope remaining. I must do as well as I can, but, who can endure everlasting fire? Thus does the wicked man breathe his last, and without being able to rely upon his good, with his last

breath, in the anguish of his soul, says, have mercy upon me a
sinner, O God! (qu. in Wardle, p. 33)

Perhaps this is no more than a schoolboy exercise in pious rhetoric, but it indicates unmistakably that our bright young scion of Rational Dissent was also the son and heir of Presbyterian Puritans, still
taught to believe in hellfire and the deadly sin of pleasures unredeemed by a life of obedience to God and His Gospel. Nothing
shows us more emphatically the darker emotions beneath Hazlitt's
remark that by "temperament and education" he was inclined to
"puritanism," with a belief in "the practical efficacy and *saving grace*
of first principles" (20.283; italics mine). Calvinist theology had disappeared from his father's religion but many of its metaphysical and
moral predispositions had not, and these were destined to reappear,
although modified almost beyond recognition, in the acute sense of
evil and the rigorous commitment to "excellence" that Hazlitt would
bring to his critical polemics in the Regency decade. This is not to
suggest, though, that Hazlitt grew up in an atmosphere of morbid
piety: there is almost no resemblance between the grim Nonconformity of the early Victorian towns—the world of the Chadbands and
Roebucks, forever damned in the brilliant satire of Dickens and Arnold—and the Georgian world of an old Presbyterian family like the
Hazlitts, still untouched by, or consciously resisting, the Methodist-
Evangelical movement, and at war with the Prayer Book but seldom
with the literary culture of the Establishment. Lucy Aikin, another
child of "Rational Dissent," recalled that life in her childhood home
was not without such amusements and amenities as once were customary only in families that conformed to the Church; her parents
had freed themselves from "the chains and darkness of Calvinism"
and "their manners softened with their system."[4] A similar liberality
prevailed in the Hazlitt household, although more severely limited
by a devout minister's discipline and the constraints of genteel poverty. Budget permitting, John and Peggy and William were denied
neither novels nor the theater; they were encouraged (as was then
fashionable) to indulge in painting and sketching (both boys would
aspire to be painters, and John grew up to become a professional
miniaturist); Mrs. Hazlitt was known for her handsomeness and the

easy grace of her manners; and the minister himself, true to the streak of "monkish, indolent pleasantry" (17.111) in his disposition, was a fond reader of Horace, Steele, and Sterne as well as a dutiful student of Milton and the Gospels.[5] Henry Crabb Robinson, calling on the family of his friend William in 1799, noted an undertone of "sober earnestness," but he found them "an amusing and agreeable group," and he liked especially "the good old man and his wife, who had all the solidity (I do not mean stolidity) . . . of the more respectable Non-Cons" (Robinson, 1.7).

It was, however, this very "solidity," a strong sense of family identity compounded equally of affection and militant doctrinal conscience, which threatened to deprive the young Hazlitt of his own will to expressive freedom. And if we ask what saved the "amiable" prig from the compulsions of his "rational" piety, we discover that we can be thankful, after all, for the one great love of Hazlitt's youth—which some observers deplore as his most "immature" passion—his "intransigeance," as Cecil calls it (p. 246), about the French Revolution, whose "cause" soon became distinct in the boy's imagination, although not yet in his consciousness of "principle," from the "Liberty" of Puritan Christianity. It was perhaps the happiest accident of his life that the Revolution should break out just as he was entering adolescence; and indeed, without that coincidence we may doubt whether the exuberant Shropshire lad of his sister's description would have rebelled so successfully against the minister's dutifully imitative son. It is always to the time of this "new impulse," and only rarely to the childhood preceding it—as if his experience had only at this juncture properly begun—that Hazlitt returns in his reminiscences: "Youth was then doubly such. It was the dawn of a new era, a new impulse had been given to men's minds, and the sun of Liberty rose upon the sun of Life in the same day, and both were proud to run their race together" (17.197).

The echoes here of Psalm 19 should remind us again that Hazlitt would, in retrospect, never willingly acknowledge a rift between his Puritan heritage and his identification with the Revolution. Indeed, viewed wholly as a matter of abstract political "principle," there was no discontinuity between the ideal of independent will espoused by his religious tradition and his hopes for a regenerated

Maidstone Museum and Art Gallery

2. HAZLITT AT AGE 13. MINIATURE BY JOHN HAZLITT.

"humanity." His father exulted in the Fall of the Bastille as he had in the American Revolution—as another augury of the long-awaited triumph of Christian Liberty over the princely Powers of the World.[6] But the Liberty of Puritan Scripture could not be so happily equated with the rising "sun of Life" in the imagination of a boy who was supposed to be preparing himself for the Dissenting ministry. As the pious young letter writer from Liverpool knew only too well, his own future would have to be dedicated to the happiness of this world only insofar as such happiness confirms and reveals the Glory of the immortal world hereafter. And not long after the Liverpool sojourn we witness the first signs of revolt from his appointed destiny.

It is now that we have our first premonitory glimpse of the shy, brooding, unpredictably volatile young man whom Coleridge would meet and describe—"brow-hanging, shoe-contemplative, *strange*."[7] According to a report from a friend of the family, William now begins to shut himself up in his room for hours at a time; on moonlit nights he roams about the fields "like any wild thing"; he often fails to appear for the family devotions and even for Chapel services, and when he does show his face he assumes a "sullen" manner or displays a "talent for satire, mimicry and caricature." The report is too melodramatic to be entirely reliable, and it is not easy to reconcile this rebellious behavior with reports of the same boy's "over-exertion" in his studies two or three years later, at the age of fifteen—unless we are willing to regard the bouts of "over-study" as being, in part, a guilty reaction from the earlier, and perhaps still recurring, spells of wildness and truculence.[8] There is, however, nothing inherently improbable in the general character of this defiance, which conforms to a familiar adolescent pattern—the acting-out of fantasies from poems or novels devoured in an inviolable upstairs (or outdoors) sanctuary, the sense of the familiar present as confining and unreal, the rehearsing of new life roles in preparation for some unknown but dimly glorious future. We can only speculate as to how conscious the revolt now, or ever, became; but it seems to me clear from a letter that William would write home soon after his arrival at Hackney College in 1793—in which he assures his father that his "past behaviour . . . did not proceed from any real disaffection, but

merely from the nervous disorders" (Howe, p. 39)—that most of his
aberrant conduct, especially in its "sullen" and its satirically exhibi-
tionist aspects, was intended for the father's eyes. Just as the verbally
precocious prodigy of the Liverpool letters was intent on letting the
minister hear what he wished to hear, so this William—mindful that
the soul must exhibit gracious signs of being "called" to preach the
Gospel—seems engaged in demonstrating to his father, or to the paternal conscience in himself, his entire unfitness for the pulpit.

Not until 1795, when Hazlitt would resign from his ministerial
studies and withdraw from the Unitarian New College at Hackney,
does the revolt issue in conscious intellectual independence. This is,
I think, the deeper meaning of that "altering" of "ideas" at the age
of sixteen of which Hazlitt speaks: this is *change* in the fundamental
sense, indeed in the revolutionary sense—that is, the overthrow or
replacement of one set of ideas or governing beliefs by, and for,
another. Intellectually, this change is to become the "discovery" and
formulation of a theory of "natural disinterestedness," which re-
places the egocentric psychology present, either explicitly or implicitly, in the ethics he had been taught. And this change in turn
implies the abandonment not only of the Unitarian ministry but of
Unitarian theology for a humanist ethic independent of traditional
Christian faith. Given the inspiration of the Revolution and his emotional need for its "impulse," it is tempting to see this change as coming about almost wholly through the influence of the new radicalism
fermenting in the years after 1792, and in a moment we shall be
considering what that impact was on Hazlitt. But it should be clear
by now that the son of a "Rational Dissenter" could identify with this
new "truth" only if he could firmly identify its promise with the "first
principles" of the family heritage—only if he could convince the paternal Reason in himself that the advent of a new dispensation for
the world had always inhered in those very doctrines that his father
had preached from the pulpit and had so studiously sought to im-
plant in the conscience of his brightest child and chosen heir.

To arrive at a just assessment of the father's character and his
abiding influence on his son, we would do well to set aside for the

moment the abstract label "Unitarian" (a term that Hazlitt himself seldom uses in speaking of his father) and learn to recognize the paternal tradition in its historical lineage, as "Presbyterian." Hazlitt's seventeenth-century ancestors, staunch "Parliament men" in Ulster, belonged to that stubborn breed of Scots (or Scots-English) emigrants to Ireland who were destined to become perhaps the most dissident Dissenters in the kingdom. To these origins we may ascribe the militant hue and temper of Hazlitt's politics, and most of his lasting prejudice against kings and prelates. But it was less the heritage of the old Scots Covenanters that he was taught to revere than that of English Presbyterianism, which became the family tradition when his father, a convert to Socinian theology in his years (1756–60) at the University of Glasgow, turned his back upon the Calvinism of his Irish parents and chose to launch his ministerial career in England.[9]

By the mid-eighteenth century, the word "Presbyterian" had become almost synonymous in England with "liberty of opinion."[10] Even in its authoritarian days, Presbyterianism had set a premium on faith through learning; and the new ministers of "Rational Dissent" in a more consciously rational age again became England's most adventurous educators—importing new ideas from the Continent, establishing the most advanced academies, publishing the most cosmopolitan journals. As the elder Hazlitt summed up the accord the "Free Dissenters" had reached with the Enlightenment: "Literature advances knowledge . . . knowledge increases virtue. . . . virtue diffuses happiness."[11] Unlike the Independents, the English Presbyterians had never been willing schismatics; they saw themselves as Dissenters upon compulsion, having been forced into Nonconformity by the Act of Uniformity in 1662, when the famous "two thousand" ministers (that was the over-generous number fixed by legend) were ejected from their parishes after refusing to acknowledge the authority of the Crown to establish doctrine. From this encroachment of temporal power the Presbyterians learned to distrust all authority; and their sons and grandsons gradually extended the attack on "subscription" to further Articles in the Prayer Book, until at last they came to challenge the First—the doctrine of the Trinity. This meant, of course, that the Westminster Catechism of their fathers had also to be repudiated; and by the end of the eigh-

teenth century nearly all English churches and chapels which still bore the Presbyterian name had openly disavowed their original Calvinism. Strangely, the name "Presbyterian" refused to vanish with its doctrines, and one of Hazlitt's contemporaries helps us to understand why: "The title was chiefly gloried in by our fathers because it indicated their union with a body of Protestant Dissenters, bound by no fetters with regard to church fellowship, and left, by their trust deeds, at perfect liberty to search for truth wherever it could be found." [12]

In this confidence in the "open trust" we find, I think, the source of that strange blend of traditionalism and faith in "progress" which would remain—until, as we shall see, his very last years—Hazlitt's sense of history. A sermon of the elder Hazlitt's emphatically reaffirms the family covenant: "After the manner some call heresy, so worship we the God of our fathers." [13] And the minister made sure that his son understood the continuity of the Presbyterian "trust" by giving him in his early years at Wem a heavy diet of what his pupil would later call "tiresome ecclesiastical history" (12.222): Foxe's *Book of Martyrs,* Calamy's *Account of the Two Thousand Ejected Ministers,* Daniel Neal's *History of the Puritans* (7.241–42). These books, along with the Bible itself and Bunyan's *Pilgrim's Progress,* shaped Hazlitt's imagination of the long drama of Truth destined to culminate in the Apocalypse of the French Revolution. Calvinism, he was taught, was the "Old Light" of Protestant faith, Unitarian doctrine the "New Light"; and the Light that was common to both was the Truth of the Scriptures emerging ever more clearly, in progressively purer forms of "reason," from the darkness of "Popery and arbitrary power." His reading of Foxe firmly implanted in the boy's mind a lasting vision of the union of throne and altar as Anti-Christ, the Beast of the Book of Revelation—and precisely this image Hazlitt would invoke in denouncing post-Waterloo "Legitimacy" (7.153). From Calamy and Neal he learned to see English history after the Commonwealth as continuing essentially the same struggle for Liberty—the court of the Stuart Restoration having then succeeded to the tyranny of the Papacy as the Power that "united the Church and State into one body under one head." And Hazlitt's youthful optimism about the outcome of this struggle was first learned from the same historians—from their assurances that Providence itself had secured "the Protestant Establishment" through the "wonderful Revolution" of 1688, when at last "the royal prerogative" was confined, though still imperfectly, "within the limits of the law." [14]

Out of this faith, then, in "the progress of truth and its power to crush error" (3.133), Hazlitt would forge both his ritual of filial piety and his revolt from filial bondage. For this myth of history could be reconceived as warranting any honest search for truths of universal "nature," provided that one paid homage in the process (as Hazlitt's style always would) to the spirit of "good sense" in traditional reason, and provided that the new truth prove its "trust" by being directed against the immemorial enemy—the tyranny of Error that was also the error of Tyranny. Just as Hazlitt's father had abandoned Calvinism at Glasgow and had then been reconciled with the God of his fathers by directing his theological rebellion against the Trinitarian Establishment, so this later son of Dissent would abandon at Hackney College the creed of his childhood tutelage and rededicate his conscience politically and philosophically to what the elder Hazlitt called "the great work of reformation." [15] The difficulty now, however, was that the breach with the past could no longer be healed by an appeal to the same modes or standards of judgment: once the sovereign authority of God or Scripture had come into question, or had ceased to be implicit, "reason" no longer connoted a necessary continuity of knowledge with values; "truth," religious and "rational" truth, need no longer be regarded as necessarily "one." In later years Hazlitt was always ready to intimate, if not to declare outright, his religious scepticism, but he was otherwise reluctant to acknowledge that the alteration of "ideas" in his adolescence was a change in the mode of conceiving "truth": he preferred to believe that the rift with his father was reducible to a prejudicial misunderstanding —and, specifically, to theological pedantry. Looking back on the vicissitudes of belief in his family, he wrote: "The grandfather is a Calvinist, who never gets the better of his disappointment at his son's going over to the Unitarian side of the question. The matter rests here, till the grandson, some years after, in the fashion of the day and 'infinite agitation of men's wit,' comes to doubt certain points in the creed in which he has been brought up, and the affair is all abroad again. Here are three generations made uncomfortable, and in a manner set at variance, by a veering point of theology, and the officious meddling Biblical critics!" (8.312).

Once we recognize his fundamental motive in this scorn for theology and Biblical criticism—namely, his need to reject intellectual obedience to his father while at the same time affirming a soundly "rational" fidelity to the same cause—we are better able to penetrate the ambivalence in his reminiscences of the minister and to discover the true nature of his indebtedness to the paternal "creed." In the essay "On Court-Influence," his father is indirectly praised as a specimen of the old Nonconformist clergy, men of steadfast "principle" whose "love of truth" enabled them to keep their faith "as the stars keep their courses" (7.242). But in "My First Acquaintance with Poets" the aging minister at Wem appears rather differently: here he is a recluse poring "from morn to night" over musty theological folios, "worn to the last fading thinness of the understanding," and the portrait closes with the comment, "My father's life was comparatively a dream" (17.110). One would never suspect from this sketch of a retiring, book-enthralled, feckless idealist, the life of militant energy that the first William Hazlitt had actually led for most of his days. He was, in fact, as his obituarist said in 1820, "one of the fathers of the modern Unitarian Church,"[16] and it is with something of this eulogistic emphasis that our sense of his character needs to be corrected.

Born when his father was already turning forty, Hazlitt never knew this dedicated man of God in full mid-career vigor; he never really saw the pioneering reformer who impressed his contemporaries with "a figure tall and commanding," matched with an equally "strong mind,"[17] and who was judged, by prevailing standards, "a sensible fine preacher." In 1780, during his ministry at Bandon, County Cork, he discovered that some American prisoners of war at a nearby prison were being cruelly abused—denied beds and blankets in midwinter—and the minister's sermons and protests to a newspaper succeeded, despite threats upon his life, in forcing the authorities to institute more humane treatment.[18] And it took even greater courage to embark soon after with his family for America—determined "to plant Unitarianism" in the New World.[19] Three years followed of disillusioned but resolute wandering—of "preaching the Divine Unity from Maryland to Kennebec"—through a republic more firmly Calvinist than ever after "The Great Awakening." A proselyte's dream did not go entirely unrealized: his lectures in

Maidstone Museum and Art Gallery

3. THE REVEREND WILLIAM HAZLITT. MINIATURE BY JOHN HAZLITT.

Philadelphia and Boston sowed Unitarian seeds that would ripen in the next generation; but his repeated refusals to compromise his doctrines kept him from gaining a haven for himself. "I would rather die in a ditch," he told the trustees of one Yankee congregation, "than submit to human authority in matters of faith."[20] It is this stubborn integrity—or obstinacy—which forced him to return to England in 1786 and to bring his career to its lonely close in the solitudes of Wem, "far from the only converse that he loved, the talk about disputed texts of Scripture and the cause of civil and religious liberty" (17.110). Hazlitt adds that his father was now "repining but resigned," but Margaret may be correcting this language (and silently rebuking her brother) when, in her recollections, she writes that the minister "did not repine but applied himself to the duties of his ministry and to the education of his youngest son . . . whom it was his fervent wish to train up in the way he should go . . . and in these duties he found his great consolation and reward" (Moyne, p. 105).

Margaret might also have mentioned that her father continued to serve the Unitarian cause with his pen; and his writings in the Wem years afford us our best clues to the doctrinal education that he gave his son. How strong, if always benign, a patriarch the elder Hazlitt could be is suggested by the image of God that emerges from these pages: the universe for this escaped Calvinist is still ruled by a Sovereign demanding absolute obedience, although His rule has now become, as if by analogy with Hanoverian England, domesticated and secure, governed less by stern monarchical decree than by Providential law, communicated to His "one great family" by both Nature and the Gospel. Both Nature and Scripture are here being illumined by "the candle of the Lord"—the indwelling light of human reason and conscience which needs only to be released from the dark bondage of worldly error to find its way back to its divine source. The genealogy of this belief, although never specified in the minister's writings, is obvious: the premise of an innate, intuitional "light" in the mind goes back, through his Glasgow education, to Hutcheson and Shaftesbury (Hazlitt once painted his father reading *Characteristics:* see 8.12 and Fig. 5) and, ultimately, to the Cambridge Platonists.[21] The divine "goodness"—and here is the Shaftesburyan note—has "implanted in us" various "kind affections," the "tender sympathies of our nature"; and it is the task of reason to "grow in grace" through "knowledge of our duty" and a "thorough conviction" of God's "benevolent dispensation." All this is indistinguishable

PURITAN FATHERS, UNITARIAN SONS

from Deism, and the minister is willing to concede to the Deists that Scripture reveals no universal truth that human reason might not have divined: the order of Nature itself, as some ancient philosophers had recognized, manifests the government of One God and portends the immortality of the soul. But Greek, Roman, and Jew alike had "darkened the candle of the Lord within them"—had become "so reprobate in all their ways" that a special "message" of Divine Grace was necessary, as the Hebrew prophets had foretold. "Nothing but the real resurrection of a real man, who had been really dead, could have wrought a thorough conviction."[22] Not Jesus himself but only his miraculous "appointment" was divine; he had no "pre-existence" as the Son of God or (as in the Arian view) the Logos; his was simply the nature of man in its "fullness," raised "above measure" and "filled with the goodness of God." "Never," wrote this Socinian—and the words were to find a clear echo in his son's prose—"was there any other son of man so totally disinterested."[23] And so pleased was the Father with the blameless life and teachings of Jesus that he raised him from the dead as a hope—and a warning—to humanity forever. Christ the Redeemer is not to be worshipped as himself the Saviour; it is the New Testament only, the exemplary life and doctrine "sealed" by the Resurrection, that is man's salvation. God's will is that "all should be saved," but the Justice of Heaven can be expected to show no mercy to those who scorn both faith and virtue. Indeed, this "rational" Presbyterian is still Puritan enough to intimate that only steadfast faith in the Resurrection will thoroughly regenerate virtue and save it from lapsing into the ways of "error." His Christ of Love thus becomes, at the Last Judgment, the stern Judge of the Unregenerate: we are to know that "we also shall be raised, and shortly appear before his awful tribunal, to give an account of the deeds that we have done in the body, when the wicked shall be punished with everlasting destruction, but all the truly penitent and reformed, crowned with everlasting salvation."[24]

The discord here between the benevolist ethos of the doctrine and the traditional Christian eschatology of evil is obvious; and Mr. Hazlitt sought to bridge, or conceal, the gap with the only logic and language that he knew. Along with nearly all parsons in his time, he does not hesitate to appeal to motives of "interest": the Bible "enforces" virtue by "the most glorious promises," and we must "live up to the terms of the blessed Gospel" if we would "infallibly secure" our "immortal interests." Here is the same theological utilitarianism that we meet in Priestley, who defined religion as "the principle whereby men are influenced by the dread of evil, or the hope of reward," or in Paley, who similarly saw in Revelation a delivery of Divine Evidence to convince a sceptical, self-loving mankind that not to believe and obey is to risk the soul's eternal fortunes.[25] Indeed, only a mankind imagined as constantly weighing the happiness of another life against their interests in this world could be expected to credit a Revelation whose efficacy is presumed to inhere, not in the miracle of sacraments, but in a miraculously attested demonstration of the fate of virtue. Yet this same self-interested mankind was also being asked to imitate the "disinterestedness" of Jesus and to pursue, regardless of personal motives, the divine "perfection" of benevolence. No bright and rebellious son of Dissent could fail for long to detect this moral ambiguity; and when Hazlitt perceives it he performs his first act of criticism and discovers his own liberating "truth" of "natural disinterestedness."

Yet in exposing this ambiguity Hazlitt was profiting from something more positive than the honest confusions in his father's teaching. For the minister left his pupil in no doubt as to how important "disinterestedness" was and how it was to be practised, both in the life of thought and the life of action. Calvinism had never been a religion of unalloyed rationalism; and the minister was clearly echoing Calvin's *Institutes* when he wrote that the meaning of Scripture could not be understood by "argument" alone but only through the "harmonious testimony" of spirit communing with Spirit. To look for "system" in the Scriptures is, the minister warns, to indulge some willful "prepossession" of our own; and to correct all "self-willed" passion, whether in matters of faith or in life, is precisely the purpose of Scripture, whose ultimate aim is "not to so much enlighten the understanding as to reform the heart."[26] The "unity" we must find is "the spirit of the whole," and in searching out this "sense" we are not to disregard other manifestations of the "power" of truth— the "sublimity of language," "the energy of the sentiments." The Gospel shows us "the unstudied eloquence of the heart," and we need only "endeavour, whilst we read, to forget all other knowledge, and we shall feel with joy, from that peace of God which they administer to our hearts, that we are in the good way. . . ."[27]

Naïve and sentimental this may be as Christian discipline, but it was admirable teaching for a future man of letters; and we have no trouble discerning here, however dimly, the germ of Hazlitt's critical method—his responsiveness to the "moving power" (5.46), the "character," the "soul and body" of a work of art or literature (8.217). Indeed, we might well ask, without in the least impugning the elder Hazlitt's piety, whether it was not literary-affective "truth" that he had most often in mind when he came to describe "the candle of the Lord"; and it remained for the son to recognize that there was no necessary connection between this "disinterested" love of Scripture and the religious "message" that the minister and his co-religionists found there. For if the "truth" of God is finally knowable only by the "heart" and by "experience"—by what Hazlitt-*fils* would call "imagination"—why should this truth be sought originally, or principally, in the Book of the divine Author? If virtue is the "principal point" at which God aims, then a progression from divine tutelage to man's free reliance on the powers of his own mind and heart would seem to be both just and inevitable. Might not, then, philosophy and literature, if inspired by the "light" of our nature, become the future testament of Liberty—as the Gospel had once superseded the Old Law, and as "rational religion" had supplanted Calvinism? And was not faith in the human works of "divine" reason infinitely less susceptible than Scripture to the perversions of worldy "authority"—precisely such perversions as the minister and his family had suffered from, even in republican America?

It is unlikely that Mr. Hazlitt was ever openly confronted by these questions from his pupil, but he might have found their logic, being implicit in his own, unanswerable. "Infidelity," he once wrote, "is the source of all those destroying vices which take place among us"; and the final irony in the career of this devoted preacher was to have provided his chosen heir with the reasoning that would lead him to at least a provisional infidelity. All "young men" who "love truth," the minister had written in a sermon (and he did not withdraw the personal irony when he published his sermons in 1808), "will readily renounce their former sentiments if they discover them to be opposite to truth. They will not be swayed by the prejudices of education, by any opinions of their fathers . . ."[28]

෴

Hazlitt's entry at Hackney College, in the autumn of 1793, coincided with the upsurge of civil violence in France that would culminate in the Reign of Terror. For young and strong-hearted sympathizers with the embattled republic across the Channel, the rapid decline of prophetic dream into painful nightmare augured no ultimate failure for the Revolution but the stormy Apocalyptic birth of new and more durable hopes for human Liberty. From his humble vantage point on the northern outskirts of London, Hazlitt looked on glumly enough at what seemed, at first, a discouraging turn of events: the war alliance against France of the hereditary monarchies, joined in early 1793 by perfidious England, hitherto the cradle and bastion of freedom in Europe; the growing discord in Paris between Girondist and Jacobin; and then, in 1794, the bloodiness of the Terror and the not dissimilar, if less brutal, policy of repression pursued by Pitt's government at home.[29] Faith, however, in the coming of the Millennial dawn was kept alive and even intensified amid these adversities by a writer who seemed to his admirers "form'd to illume a sunless world forlorn," as the young Coleridge wrote in a sonnet of grateful tribute to William Godwin. *An Enquiry concerning Political Justice* arrived (in January 1793) to assure enthusiasts that their dream of universal freedom and happiness need not be, after all, the vision of a perfected system of law and government. The course of events, even as Godwin wrote, convinced him that not monarchical or aristocratic government but government as such was the source of all evils in society. A "true republicanism" was not faith in a republican constitution but in a future system of equality, in which "truth" would become its own power, where laws and institutions would no longer be needed to enforce the dictates of reason, and where every form of "monopoly"—even private property and marriage—would disappear and all society consist in the "unrestrained and voluntary action" of perfectly free and rational individuals.[30]

"No work in our time," wrote Hazlitt, looking back, "gave such a blow to the philosophic mind of the country . . . Tom Paine was considered for the time as a Tom Fool to him; Paley an old woman; Edmund Burke a flashy sophist" (11.17). Godwin left far behind other Utopian radicals of the time—Fawcett and Holcroft, for instance—in his insistence that the end could be made the means, that the principles destined to rule the Utopian future might govern thought and conduct here and now. Godwin demanded nothing less than an act of revolution in the individual's own mind—an act whereby he broke irrevocably from all "prejudice," from all inherited feelings, all "antecedents" of the past in his own experience, and began leading the truly "independent" life of reason. It was this appeal to the self which lent magic to Godwin's abstract style and made amends to young enthusiasts for all the coldness of his stoicism. The rationalism of English Dissent—and Godwin had once, as Hazlitt later noted, been a Dissenting minister—here shed its Whiggish moderation and returned at one bound to its seventeenth-century heritage of uncompromising "principle." Hazlitt was quick to recognize the secularized echo of Fox and Calamy: "The disciple of the *New School*," he wrote later, ". . . is to be always the hero of duty . . . his feeling of what is right is to be at all times wrought up to a pitch of enthusiastic self-devotion; he must become the unshrinking martyr and confessor of the public good." And when Hazlitt describes the author of *Political Justice* as one who "absolves man from the gross and narrow ties of sense, custom, authority, private and local attachment, in order that he may devote himself to the boundless pursuit of universal benevolence" (11.18–19), he is perhaps paying indirect tribute to the absolution that he himself found in this "confessor" from the authority of "natural piety" and his own most pressing "attachment." For here was doctrine that not only promised to rescue him from paternally appointed destiny but one that enabled him to rededicate himself freely to his father's princples—and with an act of personal commitment to "truth" that had all the intensity of a ministerial taking of vows.

Even in his Hackney years Hazlitt was perhaps never the perfect Godwinite, for he "always found something wanting in Mr. Godwin's *Enquiry* . . ." (19.304); but we will, I think, essentially misunderstand Hazlitt's break from Unitarianism and his "discovery" of "natural disinterestedness" unless we restore his first "metaphysical" ventures to the Godwinian setting and to the context in general of the early seventeen-nineties. Hazlitt in a later essay was vividly to recall the strangely cataclysmic atmosphere of the time, with its paradoxical mixture of visionary prophecy and heedless iconoclasm: "In that head-long career of lofty enthusiasm . . . the thought of death crossing it, smote doubly cold upon the mind; there was a stifling sense of oppression and confinement, an impatience of our present knowledge, a desire to grasp the whole of our existence in one strong embrace, to sound the mystery of life and death, and in order to put an end to the agony of doubt and dread, to burst through our prisonhouse, and confront the king of Terrors in his grisly palace!" (17.197). This passage tells us more, I suspect, about Hazlitt's state of mind as a child of Revolutionary "reason" than would any statement of his philosophic education at the time. We glimpse here what Belsham, his Divinity tutor at Hackney, lamented as "the mania of the French Revolution"; and to this "ferment," and "the general spirit of insubordination" among the students, Belsham attributed both their tendency to "infidelity" and the dissolution of the college itself in 1796.[31] Certainly it is this spirit, as confirmed by Godwin's cult of "independence," that destroyed forever in Hazlitt's thought the solemn piety of his childhood; that obliterated from his sensibility what he later called nostalgically "the mild and persuasive tone of the Gospels" (11.20); that prevented him from acquiring in his two years at Hackney the discipline of systematic learning; and that made his criticism ever after "impatient" with the authority of knowledge and formal structures. But the effects of this *Sturm und Drang* phase were not merely temperamental. Hope that leaped so high soon burnt itself out, but the numious sense of a hitherto unsuspected unity in reality now awaiting discovery—the faith that "the whole of our existence" might now in some mode prove accessible to the mind of the questing self—would never be wholly lost or forgotten. All scholarship today which portrays Romantic doctrines of imagination as elaborations of tendencies already established in eighteenth-century thought simply has not reckoned with this "enthusiasm" of the nineties, when, as Hazlitt's testimony suggests, life and death became mysteries to be reconceived and explored afresh.

"Imagination," wrote Hazlitt of this period, "was unable to keep pace with the gigantic strides of reason, and the strongest faith fell short of the supposed reality" (3.155). Clearly it was only a matter of time before "imagination," to keep from falling so short, would develop new modes of vision and claim new titles of power that would re-unite philosophical possibilities with the concrete perspectives of personal memory.

To elicit and authenticate this new potential in man's conscious-ness meant nothing less, as Hazlitt soon came to recognize, than redefinition of the nature of self, of human individuality—not merely the enlargement and renovation, as Godwin had assumed, of individual reason and conscience. Godwin was an eloquent advocate of an indefinite human capacity for "distinterestedness"; indeed, his thoroughgoing attack on self-love, as Ben Ross Schneider has ob-served, was—or was viewed as—a bold novelty in English moral phi-losophy, or at least in the ethical philosophy of Locke and Paley that dominated the two Universities.[32] But Godwin's conception of "dis-interestedness" was still more prescriptive than descriptive: its status as a "principle" remained that of an ideal to direct and modify man's will to happiness rather than a truth inhering in the given nature of that will. And when Hazlitt at Hackney was moved to read in God-win's philosophical sources, he was struck by the wholly insecure tenure of human benevolence in "the modern philosophy." The doc-trine of "enlightened self-interest" which had hitherto passed muster as the official creed of Revolutionary liberalism now seemed an ironic travesty, in imagination at least, of the motives that led a Chrolotte Corday or a Condorcet to martyrdom on the guillotine. "Suppose," Hazlitt now asked himself, ". . . that it were in my power to save twenty other persons by voluntarily consenting to suf-fer for them: why should I not do a generous thing, and never trou-ble myself about what might be the consequences to myself the Lord knows when?" (1.46–47). To this question Hazlitt found only three systematic answers in his philosophical reading, none of which could satisfy his own "generous" hopes. He found himself confronted by these three theories: that man was 1) constantly and necessarily self-interested, capable of benevolent actions but not of disinterested mo-tives (Hobbes, Helvetius, Baron d'Holbach); 2) originally self-inter-

24

ested, but capable of "refining" self-gratification into benevolent motives (Locke, Tucker, Paley); 3) neither originally selfish or
benevolent, but determined to either or both states by empirical "associations" of pleasure and pain (Hartley, Hume, Priestley).[33] Godwin seems to have wavered indecisively between the latter two positions; but since both of these views attributed the power of
"disinterestedness" not to "nature" but to habit and association, it
was doubtful, as Hazlitt would remark, whether a theory of benevolence that conceded its possibly "selfish origin" would ever encourage "much true generosity, or disinterested simplicity of character"
(1.6).

In only one thinker honored by the Revolution did Hazlitt find
some approach to the possibility of a "natural disinterestedness."
Hazlitt was later to write that in adolescence he "formed" himself on
the "model" of Rousseau's *Émile* (12.224), and certainly no work and
no thinker appears more often, or more prominently, in the notes to
his first exposition of his "discovery," in *An Essay on the Principles of
Human Action* (1805). Indeed, there is scarcely one of his objections
to "the material, or modern philosophy" that is not anticipated by
Rousseau's contempt in *Émile* for *"la philosophie moderne."* That neither thought nor feeling can be resolved into physically determined
sense impressions; that conscience is actuated by sentiment rather
than by reason; that sympathy (*pitié*) is as necessary for thought and
action as self-love; that only by "imagination" does a man "go out of"
himself into the feelings of others—these suggestions from Rousseau, far more than any ideas drawn from an English source, gave
Hazlitt faith in his "discovery" and remained to the end in its argu-
mentation.[34] Perhaps, too, in Rousseau's mounting reputation as a
religious prophet in Robespierre's Paris (in 1794 the philosopher's
remains were brought to the capital for burial in the Pantheon) lies
the clue to Hazlitt's fervent admiration. For in *la profession de foi du
vicaire Savoyard* lay a struggle of conscience not unlike his own: here
he learned of another young man constrained by his parents into the
priesthood, and one similarly unwilling to commit his mind to the
Christian Revelation while still cherishing Christian sentiments. Yet
there was one important difference; and perhaps Hazlitt's sense of
this difference helped to convince him that he could rest content

with nothing less than the postulate of a "natural," as distinct from an acquired, disinterestedness. Rousseau's Vicar, after all, remained a Vicar, a man who never doubted that his faith (that is, his Deism) and his moral conscience were inseparable: "Without faith there is no such thing as true virtue."[35] Precisely this conclusion Hazlitt needed to deny, or at least avoid, if he was to free his mind from his father's insistence on the essential identity of religious faith and the life of reason. Since Hazlitt's conscience could repudiate the Unitarian ministry only on grounds of rational disbelief in his father's "truth"—on grounds other than the mere want of will to serve—and since loss of faith in his father's creed had to be demonstrably motivated by no lapse of his own virtue, his need to find a "natural" virtue independent of faith coincided with his need as a Godwinian individualist to establish disinterestedness on a basis no longer reducible to "refined self-interest."

It is therefore no accident that the moment of his "discovery" should come as he is reading—sometime in 1794 or 1795, in Baron d'Holbach's *Système de la Nature*—"a speech put into the mouth of a supposed atheist at the Last Judgment." Holbach's *athée vertueux*, waking from the sleep of death, learns to his infinite astonishment that the Heaven of Christian fantasy is true after all. Before the Throne of God he rises, still the indomitable *philosophe,* to plead the virtue, if no longer the necessity, of a life on earth without religious faith. In revering only Reason and Nature, and in acting in accordance with their principles, has he not been obedient to the laws of the Author of his being—and perhaps even more faithful than those believers who have worshipped Him superstitiously and fearfully?[36] At least one of the Baron's readers, however, might have supplied the answer of Divine Reason to this rationalist's defiance; for Hazlitt needed only to remember his 1790 letter from Liverpool. Is not a man compelled by nature (so Hazlitt restates, in recalling this moment, what is recognizably his father's argument) to be "sensible" of his interests, and does he not always "bitterly regret the folly and insensibility" of his actions? And was it not precisely to "enforce" fallible human faith with a "thorough conviction" that God had delivered through Jesus and his Resurrection ("a real man . . . really

dead") assurance of the Truth of Heaven? As Hazlitt now paraphrases the lesson he had learned at Wem (and which he had been
paraphrasing in the letter from Liverpool): "I ought as a rational
agent to be determined now by what I shall then wish I had done
when I shall feel the consequences of my actions most deeply and
sensibly"; or in other words, the soul, being always the "same" and
therefore interested in itself, must make faith in its immortal identity
the end and aim of virtue. Yet side by side with this conception of individuality as metaphysically given and constant, another, and a
more distinctly Unitarian, idea of personal identity arises in Hazlitt's
mind as he broods dubiously over Holbach's scene. This is the idea,
derived from Locke and further developed by Hartley and Priestley,
that personal identity is not innate but depends on the progressive
continuity of consciousness in time—an idea that supported Unitarian confidence in education and moral perfectibility. But this idea
proves to be much less compatible with the traditional Puritan vision
of personal immortality, as Hazlitt now, to his great joy, discovers.
For it is when he tries to extend the Lockean idea of identity beyond
a temporal context that the "discovery" comes.[37] He is just about to
let pass unchallenged the supposition that the consciousness of personal identity will "be renewed in me after death," when the *non
sequitur* strikes him; and the liberating moment of recognition would
mean so much to him that in his *Essay* he reenacts it precisely for his
readers. "But stop!" he writes—for would renewal of one's consciousness in eternity necessarily mean that the same *self* is resuming
its consciousness? Would it not be more accurate to say, not that the
same self, but that the same consciousness of "past feelings"—
perhaps now the act or attribute of pure spirit—is being renewed?
And is it not then meaningless to speak of an original and necessary
self-interest? For perhaps the only consciousness that the self can
ever have of its own being, and therefore its only necessary interest,
is not prospective but wholly retrospective. How, then, could a man
of irreligious benevolence be held responsible for an *a priori* interest
in his own happiness (as distinct from the happiness of others) when
his very consciousness of his identity can arise only from a continuity
of sensation with the past—a continuity which may change, or ap-

pear differently, in the future? Whatever that future turns out to be, rationality does not consist in shaping our lives in the present by what we can only *imagine* to be our personal happiness in some future state. Being always the "same" individual—that is, not someone else—is therefore not to be confused with our sense of continued identity, our conscious sameness with ourselves, which is the product of time and memory. "I saw plainly," Hazlitt concludes, "that the consciousness of my own feelings which is made the foundation of my continued interest in them could not extend to what had never been, and might never be, that my identity with myself must be confined to the connection between my past and present being" (1.47–48).

Now it might be said that, up to this point, Hazlitt's "discovery" has exposed only a semantic ambiguity in the word "interest." An "interest" conceived as a prospective advantage or happiness cannot be said to be a motive of the same kind as an "interest" felt in one's immediate or past feelings. Such a fallacy may strike us today as simply a matter of verbal indiscipline; but that fallacy of language had passed for so long undetected because it concealed a pivotal ambiguity in Puritan theology. Its detection meant for Hazlitt nothing less than spiritual liberation—at least for the time being—from his priggish self-consciousness and, more fundamentally, from those Calvinist fears of damnation that we have seen haunting his childhood. To discover that self-consciousness does not imply an innate, metaphysically given, immutable interest of the soul in its difference from other selves was clearly to cut the ground from under his father's utilitarian rationale for faith, with its ultimately grim assumption that only men interested in the immortal welfare of their individuality could be persuaded to restrain or sacrifice their selfish pleasures in this world. Whether the "doubts" that found confirmation in Hazlitt's "discovery" extended beyond this "natural theology" to the doctrine of the Last Judgment itself, we can only conjecture; this question will be postponed to a later chapter, when we have fitter occasion to examine his views on religion. All that he needed, or wished, to demonstrate now was that moral virtue and faith in a Christian Heaven were not necessary consequences of each other or of man's natural love of happiness, as his father had assumed. Religious belief, far from being something that only the unhappy or the less virtuous deny, could exist only *as* a faith, not as a necessary consequence of natural laws: "It can only affect me as an imaginary idea, or an idea of truth" (1.48).

Yet so do all prospective "interests" of the will. And in that corollary lay the positive and hopeful meaning of "disinterestedness" which enabled Hazlitt to reaffirm his loyalty to his past and to restate the Unitarian ethic in terms of Godwinian freedom. The same uncertainty of "interest" that surrounds an afterlife extends to all interests in the future—and indeed, what, apart from mere sensations and memories, are *not* "future objects"? "Objects of rational or voluntary pursuit," or whatever is brought into being by thought or desire, cannot be said to exist as do objects of sense, and must therefore differ radically, as "feeling" in consciousness and as motives to action, from an "impression" which the body senses or the memory records. An object of sense or memory becomes an object of will or action only insofar as it becomes an "idea," and this idea will retain its relationship in "feeling" to sense images in only one way—through "the imagination, by means of which alone I can anticipate future objects or be interested in them" (1.1–3). There is no foundation, then, for both the vulgar and the philosophical prejudice that only "personal motives" are "real" or "natural" while our sympathy with others is purely "voluntary," an interest derived from habit and education. On the contrary, the same faculty of imagination which enables the self to will or act "must carry me out of myself into the feelings of others by one and the same process by which I am thrown forward into my future being" (1.1–3, 9–10). Every man will, to be sure, project his past interests and continuing "associations" into the future with "a greater warmth of present imagination" than he can possibly bestow upon a sympathy with feelings that have sensitive existence only in another's mind. But this "habitual propensity" (1.49) to self-interest does not belie but finally confirms our "natural disinterestedness." However "narrow" our image or idea of self may become (1.14), this interest must have originated, and can be sustained in time, only through essentially the same projective identification with an imagined object by which men remain or become actively benevolent: "I could not love myself, if I were not capable of loving others" (1.2).

※⋮※

Armed with his vindicating truth, Hazlitt left Hackney (having resigned his subsidy as a ministerial student, the only basis on which he could have remained at the college—if indeed an independent Godwinite would have wished to remain at all) and returned to Wem in 1795, determined to serve the Revolution by perfecting his idea and delivering it to the world as rapidly as possible. Yet nearly ten years would pass before the "discovery" reached articulation as a completed essay, and so long a delay is not readily explained. Some uneasiness of unconscious guilt is likely to have followed the prodigal son's return; and though pleasantly surprised to meet with "no reproaches or unkindness" from his parents (Moyne, p. 107), he seems to have found it all the harder now to transfer to philosophy the gifts of discourse withheld from the Unitarian pulpit. He preferred to believe that he wanted only "language" for his thoughts, and that until the saving inspirations of 1798–99—the meeting with Coleridge and the scarcely less important stimulus of his discovery of painting—he was floundering in a "gulph of abstraction" where words and images refused to come, or came at a rate so painfully slow that he could later say that he "was eight years in writing eight pages" (17.114; 9.30).

Clearly more than "language" was wanting. Hazlitt's frustration prefigures a conflict that would be with him always, long after he had given ample proof of his gift for writing a free-flowing, vivid, persuasive prose. In the eighteen-twenties he would speak of his familiar essays as "the thoughts of a metaphysician expressed by a painter" (17.311); and perhaps taking her cue from this remark, Virginia Woolf has described Hazlitt's writing as a perpetual alternation, or quarrel, between "the thinker" and "the artist" in his mind.[38] A relationship of conflict between these two identities is precisely what the essayist himself does not confess; and once we recognize this shadow of concealment, we may learn to question also the adequacy of his terms. For to speak of the abstract "thinker" and the pictorial "artist" is—if we are speaking psychologically—to describe effects, not causes. And to reach the motivation behind these opposed identities we need to reflect on two suggestive remarks that the essayist would make about his essential difference of character from his father: one, that the elder Hazlitt, though a believer in "reason" and immersed in theology, was "not a metaphysician" (17.245); and the other, that "he would rather I should have written a sermon than painted like Rembrandt or like Raphael!" (8.12). When rebellion by rational emulation failed—when commitment to non-theological, "metaphysical" reason failed to release the voice of the imprisoned self—Hazlitt turned passionately in the next decade (at least after 1802, if not before) to his second dream of fame (without, we should note, abandoning the first): his dream of becoming a painter. Here again he was to meet bitter frustration, but this pursuit was less a mistaking of his true, his literary gifts than a necessary prelude to their release. In the painter's world of mutely expressive images, of freedom from polemical "abstraction," he could leave behind him the eighteenth-century voices of his adolescence—and this he had to do if he was ever to repossess his father's tradition and reclaim his own voice. He himself hints at the deeper quest for power in his love of art: "Till I began to paint, or till I became acquainted with the author of *The Ancient Mariner,* I could neither write nor speak" (17.312).

Yet if the painter is clearly in flight from an abstract rationalism, this is not an "artist" repudiating the "thinker" in himself; on the contrary, Hazlitt would always associate his love of painting with his admiration of Coleridge because both were rooted in his growing commitment to another kind of mind-power than Reason—to the idea of Genius and all its attendant values. For the quarrel of painter and philosopher, I propose the more fundamental opposition that we have seen shaping the consciousness of Hazlitt's most formative years—of the Boy and the Prig of Reason (or, since the latter term may seem, if left unqualified, too narrow and invidious, the militant-censorious Preacher of Principles).[39] There is no harm in dividing a man against himself in this way so long as we remember that we are invoking the logic of myth rather than allegory: we are dividing this mind only to rediscover the dynamic of its unity—a unity that exists

31

at a more fundamental level of being than our common-sense images of the self can adequately reveal. The abiding tension between Boy and Prig cannot be described in terms of ideas but only as alternating directions of intellectual attitude: the one defers to Reason, the other pays homage to Genius; the one looks for truth in abstraction and analysis, the other in diversely concrete perception; yet each of these modes of understanding is engaged in the defense of the same conscious values. The difference remains antagonism only in the physiological, the "unconscious" sense: one attitude strives to honor and emulate the father, or to displace his authority by usurping his role as wisdom-figure, while the other seeks to define the self against that authority—an effort which, in conscious terms, becomes simply indifference to reverential memory ("I do not know whether there is much natural piety in my constitution," Hazlitt would confess in a letter written very late in his life[40]). The tension of the conflict becomes, in a word, dialectical—not in the classical sense of moving toward a polarization of logical contraries, but in the biological sense of a rhythmic interdependence between functions of energy and an equally necessary restoration of equilibrium. Each attitude is thus the inseparable reactivity to the other's activity: the affirmation of part against whole or of whole against part. This is why Hazlitt in his youth was never properly a philosopher or a' painter but a writer from the start; for writing was the one act on which Boy and Prig could wholeheartedly collaborate on the conscious level, while at the same time maintaining the necessary dynamic of their unconscious opposition in doing so. And if a young man destined to display manifest literary genius suffered a severe case of writer's block for nearly eight years after 1794, and indeed was not to arrive at his distinctive range of style for another ten years—until 1813, when Hazlitt commits himself to a career in the London press—this arrest of power might have come about not only because the abstraction-loving Prig still controlled his sense of language (as late as 1807, Hazlitt could still believe that his genius was naturally "costive" [1.179]), but because this much time was needed for a recasting of the necessary dialectic in consciously acceptable terms. Writing for Hazlitt had to be both a ritual of loyalty to his past and, in some shape or degree, always a fresh "discovery," an "original" act of expressive independence from his past. And nothing could resolve in consciousness these conflicting motives but the dialectic of a new myth of human freedom—or, rather, a myth that would reincarnate the ancestral Puritan faith in "Liberty," yet do so with a radically new vision of the role of mind in man's "progress" toward that end.

Hazlitt was to identify his myth of the modern struggle for Liberty as (or always in terms very close to these) "the war between power and reason" (11.37). These were the terms that his ritual loyalty compelled him to use, and we need only dwell for a moment on some latent meanings that are jostling each other in the words "power" and "reason" to appreciate the impasse in his youthful consciousness and to understand why he was so long in resolving it. For the internal "war" in the young Hazlitt's mind was the struggle to free his own "power" from paternal "reason," while outwardly the struggle for human freedom had to be conceived by this Dissenter as just the reverse: in society the cause of mind or "reason" had to become not less but more "disinterested," had to overcome or transcend the passional will of the self to "power" in the world. In the next three chapters we shall gradually come to understand why Hazlitt's thought in his youth could not master his conflict in this, its original form: for its resolution required the entire climatic change of Romanticism, whereby "imagination" gradually assumes those functions of purposive unification of experience which the Enlightenment had ascribed to "reason," both in the individual and in society. Firmly empiricist in his inclinations, Hazlitt shies away from—indeed, will be found warning against—the visionary tendencies of Romantic imagination; he stresses instead the affinities of imaginative genius with "common sense" (8.31 ff.); and it is this fidelity to the standards of experiential "sense," not merely a Dissenter's constancy or a thinker's pride, which informs his lifelong appeals to "reason." Nevertheless his faith in the mind's powers remains as tacitly mythopoetic as any other credo in Romanticism; and to be convinced that the mentality of myth is operating beneath the mask of his "plain" prose (17.312), we need only observe how closely Hazlitt's critical themes reflect, even as he transforms almost beyond recognition, the leading ideas in his father's scheme of divinely ordained "progress." For Scripture, Hazlitt is to substitute literature and art; for the Protestant Reformation, the invention in the same era of printing, which made both a public literature and a free society possible (13.46); for Providence, "nature" (or, in historical contexts, progressive "public opinion" as molded by greater understanding of nature); for the Light or Spirit, sympathetic imagination; for Grace, creative genius; for Christ and his Saints, all men of genius who "give light and law to the world" (12.365); for Immortality, "fame"; for Heaven, the "empyrean" or "ideal" world of the most sublime art and poetry.[41]

The parallel breaks down only in the son's silence or ambivalence about the ultimate termination of modern "progress"—of which we shall find him giving both optimistic and grimly pessimistic accounts. All that is constant in Hazlitt's vision of the struggle is the certainty, the inescapable finality of the struggle itself. Whenever his ritual of loyalty becomes obsessive rhetoric, he wills to see his age as the decisive modern foreground of the ancient Biblical landscape of Light and Darkness, whence the antagonists of the Apocalypse have emerged again to meet in Armageddon—but now at last clearly and unmistakably as "the slave" and "the free" (7.9). Yet the battle was never decisively joined, even on the fields of Waterloo; and we shall find that as the years passed, as youth gave way to middle age, Hazlitt came to recognize that the prophetic struggle between Liberty and "Legitimacy" could not define his own relationship, even his moral relationship, to the world. The "progress" of Liberty that was really being made possible by the myth was the progress of his own quest for expressive freedom of power; and with this key to its logic, we are able to trace hidden resolution in apparent confusion, even a personal victory beneath pronouncements of political disaster. Hazlitt's grief over Waterloo was genuine, was indeed almost suicidal;[42] yet it is no accident that only after this event, which he more than once lamented as the death of modern freedom (see 15.269)—does he accomplish his best and most distinctive work, both as critic and writer. Only when he at last despairs of "Rational Liberty," when he begins to relegate his mythic hopes for the future to the personal past—only then does he feel free, in the familiar essays of his last decade, the eighteen-twenties, to reveal frankly to the world what the real commitment of his critical intelligence to "truth" is and had always been. And it is then, too, that we shall find him developing his own vision of democracy and of the modern future—one that his father would have been scarcely able to comprehend. The tendency of all myths of Apocalypse to lapse into some hateful siege of contraries—in this case, of Truth and Error, Light and Darkness, Liberty and Authority—does not finally claim Hazlitt as a victim, whatever the legend and his own rhetoric would have us believe. For since his inward struggle was for power over "reason," that quest could be attained only by at last acknowledging in literary and intellectual form ("familiar" in style yet still indirect) its latent motive—as the quest of a passional self, not merely of a mind, for "power."

The importance of understanding the hidden genesis of Hazlitt's boyish "zest" from his actual boyhood lies in recognizing that only this abiding affinity with the instincts of his rebellious adolescence gives him his expressive delight in power, or (in his own idiom) his "disinterested" sympathy with it—for power *as* power, not merely as the means (or the obstacle) to certain moral or political ends. For it is the Perennial Boy in Hazlitt who feels and thinks with "gusto"—who (to borrow a phrase from Wordsworth) has "daring sympathies with power" (*Prelude* 10.457), whether in art or politics, and whether for good or evil. In this sense Hazlitt did remain "immature": he never outgrew his love for the things all boys love, or are traditionally said to love. He loved strength and prowess, action, combat and spectacle—a prize fight or a "fives" match scarcely less than an Elizabethan tragedy or a mural by Michelangelo. He loved the parry and thrust of impassioned debate; both the fascination of mystery and the stubborn resistance of fact (kept distinct in feeling, as most boys will have them); friendship and camaraderie (as a fraternity of presumed equals, not a clubbing together of attitudes); frankness of response, honest courage, high and firm resolve. And let it be admitted also that, scarcely less than heroic forms of energy, he loved their counterparts in mockery and "mischief" (a favorite word), even to the point of malice when this strain of feeling could be honestly licensed by his hatred of "affectation." Compounded of all these loves was a delight in Liberty which had finally less to do with Puritan virtue than with a boy's animal passion for the freedom of

35

his bodily energies, and which continued unabated physically in the man—in his tireless joy in walking, and in the demands of a sexual appetite that he learned to subject to the needs and responsibilities of his life in society but could never happily sublimate.[43]

It will not do, though, to praise the charm or the energies of the Boy at the expense of the child of Dissent, just as, when we look at portraits of Hazlitt, it is impossible to separate the paradoxical effects of "character" manifest in the face before us—the keenly peering or brightly glancing eyes, the shock of unruly hair above the shyly lowered forehead, the lean and sallow cheeks, the quick and vehement lips, the strongly set, sharply pointed jaw. And just as his prose style needed the interpenetration of both attitudes, so his critical judgment also is compounded, in equal measure, of the boyish enthusiast and the ever-watchful Prig, taught to revere only "a general proposition" (4.102) and mistrustful of all power but "principle." It is the Prig-Dissenter who continually reminds his other self that what he is admiring, whatever else it may be, *is* power—is not to be mistaken for value itself, or is only one kind of value—and is therefore subject to the delusions and abuses of all will to power in the world. If, without the continual defiance of the Boy, the Prig would have been lost in ritual self-deceptions and might have become—indeed, often does become—a retailer of conventional eighteenth-century prejudices, we may also surmise that the Boy without his countervailing censor would have become—alas, too often is—a sentimentalist and an infatuated idolater of "greatness" (for example, Napoleon's, Shakespeare's). True, the Prig had always the most to learn (or unlearn) from experience, but it is our lasting indebtedness to the argumentative Dissenter in Hazlitt that he *does* gradually learn from his hidden otherness—that almost from the start he begins altering his ideas, even the idea of his own "disinterestedness."

Chapter Two

The Metaphysician: Mind and Nature

"MY FIRST Acquaintance with Poets" is a justly famous essay, and there is no need to retell here its unforgettable episodes. We remember Hazlitt waking before dawn and trudging the ten comfortless miles of a muddy winter road to hear Coleridge preach; or the visit of Coleridge to Wem, where the most magical of talkers performs volubly before the astonished old minister and his tongue-tied, brow-hanging son, "for those two hours" struck dumb with admiration (17.109); or the walk back with Coleridge down the Shrewsbury road, now made glorious in its prospects by the poet's invitation to visit him at Nether Stowey; or the meeting there with Wordsworth and the first reading of the *Lyrical Ballads* in manuscript; or then the walking tour with Coleridge through Somersetshire—through the fresh springtime of the year 1798, the *annus mirabilis* that gave to the English-speaking world a new school of poetry and ultimately a new sensibility in literature. Yet the greatness of the essay consists in more than vivid autobiography made doubly memorable by history; for it succeeds, and precisely because it aims only at reminiscence, in recapturing an archetypal experience of the self—the discovery of one's true identity, the passage from adolescence to manhood, the awakening of a mind from timorous innocence to its own expressive life.

It is fidelity to this theme which makes the essay a work of art—and Hazlitt's essay keeps this faith as only the familiar essay can, in a way that is pure and unborrowed from other genres, achieving its unity not by design but through motifs of imagery that are at once symbolic and descriptive, arising inevitably from the immediate circumstances. The change, for instance, from winter to spring, as Hazlitt's journey through the fateful year proceeds, belongs to the very substance of the vision of nature that would rescue him from his "gulph of abstraction"—from the wintry rationalism of the culture dying with the old Dissenter back at Wem. And always linking the nature-imagery of regeneration with the charismatic role of Coleridge—and with the hope, too, of a reconciliation in spirit with his father's faith—is the vocabulary of religious conversion, which is employed half-playfully but nonetheless emphatically. Before Hazlitt sets out for Nether Stowey he visits the vale of Llangollen, in order to "initiate" himself in "the mysteries of natural scenery." Thus fittingly "baptized in the waters of Helicon," he arrives at Alfoxden to hear Wordsworth "chaunt" his verse with "prophetic tones," and he himself reads the new poetry in manuscript "with the faith of a novice"—by now a fully confirmed neophyte of Coleridge's "imaginative creed" (17.114–15).

The fact that Hazlitt never spells out what the new "creed" was may tell us more than we think. It suggests that his conversion was less to a body of doctrine than to a faith—to a confidence in imagination that was still more sure of itself in poetry than in the prose of discourse. Hazlitt was enraptured not so much by what Coleridge actually said as by his way of conceiving and expressing his thoughts; for in the very expression of one thought, he seemed to be conceiving another. "His thoughts did not seem to come with labour and effort; but as if borne on the gusts of genius, and as if the wings of his imagination lifted him from off his feet." Coleridge was "the only man I ever knew who answered to the idea of a man of genius" (5.167).

The "idea," we should note, preceded the living example in Hazlitt's mind—and perhaps, indeed, the idea helped to shape this poet's behavior just as it helped to condition a young idolater's response. Like other eighteenth-century notions, the concept of genius had been undergoing painful rebirth in the fires of the Revolutionary decade; and only if we recall the later vicissitudes of that decade can we understand the magnitude of promise this idea had acquired among some otherwise disillusioned disciples of William Godwin. By 1795 the Apocalyptic mood of the previous two years had bred a severe reaction, and even the most resolute believers in the future Millennium of Liberty began to succumb to the prevailing melancholy. The course of events after 1795—the stagnation of the Revolution under the Directory, the continuance of the war (with French armies now showing signs of becoming aggressors), and the triumph of Pitt's repression—soon cast doubts on the central premise that had hitherto sustained Revolutionary doctrine, that reason either was or could become (in George H. Mead's paraphrase) "the form of the will."[1] And to judge from some anecdotes that Hazlitt would cite in *The Spirit of the Age,* the lives of Godwin's own disciples provided further evidence to confirm the mounting revulsion from "French principles." Two young lovers decided to set up housekeeping together, secure in the faith that "a refined and permanent individual attachment" had no need of marriage, but "vows of eternal constancy" proved strangely fragile "without church security." Another Godwinite lent a friend a hundred pounds for his "immediate and pressing use," but when the lender applied for it again on the same plea, the friend appealed to the disinterested dictates of reason—and retained it "for his own especial, which is tantamount to the public good." Such "heroes on paper," pledged to acknowledge only the light of reason in their own breasts, could offer no surety to their fellows that they might not become "vagabonds in practice." It was, Hazlitt thought, this suspicion among the Godwinian aspirants themselves, directed first against one another and then against the author of their flawed title deeds to virtue, which "broke up the system, and left no good odour behind it" (11.21).

Fortified by his own theory of "disinterestedness," Hazlitt, unlike many of the disenchanted, found in these examples of human frailty no auguries of doom for the Revolution but simply further proof of the inadequacy of Godwin's stoicism. "If we are not allowed to love our neighbour better than a stranger, that is, if habit and sympathy are to make no part of our affections, the consequence will be, not that we shall love a stranger more, but that we shall love our neighbour less and care about nobody but ourselves. These partial and personal attachments are 'the scale by which we ascend' to sentiments of general philanthropy . . ." (16.406). Yet to give Godwinian benevolence an emotionalized redefinition proved far less simple than these words, written two decades later, suggest. Godwin himself, in the second and third editions of *Political Justice,* proceeded to assign greater motivational roles to "feeling" and "the heart"; but Hazlitt was right in remarking that these qualifications—as Godwin had made them, introducing them piecemeal into his text[2]—succeeded only in obscuring the central issues (16.406). For how was the Revolutionary self to cultivate human sympathies yet maintain also the independence of thought and action—the loyalty to the future, the resistance to sympathy with traditional society—that a commitment to ideal values required?

That this dilemma haunted the young Hazlitt's mind is suggested by the depth of his attraction to the new vogue of "Gothic" and *Sturm und Drang* literature. In Goethe's Werther, in the plays of Schiller and Kotzebue, in Rousseau's *Confessions,* and in the Gothic and "Jacobin" novels of the time Hazlitt found relief from his philosophical researches and sentimental balm for what he called (in a letter of 1796: Howe, p. 44) his "wounded spirit." But he was also, as the latter phrase suggests, drawn to this literature for its dramatization of the widening rift between the world of Revolutionary sentiment and the world of fact and action. As he would later observe, the new literature, while it looked to Germany for its models, breathed at every turn the spirit of the Revolution in France: "We see the natural always pitted against the social man." Actions and sentiments in these stories were seldom really "natural," and vice and virtue seemed often "reversed" (bandits here were moralists), but this fault had its warrant in the anomalies of contemporary society, which presented an equivalent disparity between appearance and reality, institutions and ideas, manners and feelings. Not surprisingly, the victory of "nature" in the virtuous or remorseful hearts of these characters was seldom consistently translated from the world of dialogue to the world of action, or at least seldom produced actions (witness Werther's suicide) that inspired much hope of removing the causes of their various distresses in society; indeed, the tendency in this literature was "to make of life itself a long-drawn endless sigh" (6.360–63). Perhaps this impasse between feeling and action went for so long without serious challenge because, for one reason, it flattered the "wounded spirit" of literary Revolutionists at the time—most of whom, like the boy at Wem, now found themselves exiled from the London arena of politics to the solitudes of rural England, where their dream of the future was forced to recede continually inward, finding its prophetic necessity only in their own proud aspirations. But beneath the pieties of "sensibility" in the new literature lay another element which appealed, not to self-pity, but to a radical's defiant pride; and it is this less conscious tendency which accounts for the strength of Hazlitt's fascination.

Scholars of Gothic drama have noted that, toward the end of this decade, the villain begins to exhibit certain heroic proclivities (a greater physical attractiveness, a more sincere, even a chivalric, responsiveness to love and conscience), while the hero gradually ceases to be simply a "man of feeling" and borrows some of his adversary's rebellious intellect. What perhaps has not been sufficiently remarked in this change is the parallel it affords to contemporary changes in the concept of "genius." Just as the benevolent hero and the coldly rational, egomaniacal villain begin to merge into a single rebel-hero who affirms against society the rights, not of reason or virtue, but of the passional self as such, so the essence of "genius" is being conceived in *Sturm und Drang* literature no longer as a capacity for intellectual inventiveness or reverential expression of "the sublime" but as an expressive power of amoral "energy" that Goethe would call "the daimonic"—an impulse not only distinct from faith and conscience but often in conscious and defiant opposition to them.[3] Hazlitt recognizes this further dimension of meaning in the new German vogue when he speaks of its creators as the first modern "Titans"— enthusiasts whom he sees, however, as rebels "not against heaven but against earth," impelled to their extravagant love of the marvellous by the need to protest the "dead weight" of a social system that had "stifled the breath of liberty, of truth and genius" (6.362). And nothing more emphatically shows the continuity of Hazlitt's admiration of this literature with Godwinian individualism than the fact that he finds essentially the same type of hero-sinner—the genius fallen or *manqué*—in the dramas of Holcroft and the novels of Godwin himself. Godwin's Falkland in *Caleb Williams,* a murderer willing to murder again to conceal his crime, seemed to Hazlitt, not (as he was intended to be) the deluded victim of the false pride of "honour," but an enthusiast martyred by his passion for an ideal of "fame," for "immortal renown" and for "the good opinion" of his peers. Hazlitt would identify only one figure in this gallery—Godwin's St. Leon—as a type of Promethean genius, but he nonetheless refused to regard their various deviations from morality as the sins of a ruthless egotism. That he was learning to discern in such characters a mode of disinterestedness distinct from "benevolence" is shown by his description of all Godwin's heroes, not as victims of society or perverters of nature, but as men of intellectual passion who "move in an orbit of their own, urged on by restless thought or morbid sentiment" (6.130–31; 18.307).

Such figures, then, incarnated for Hazlitt both his dilemma and new hope for its resolution. They represented not only the corruption of the will through intellectual pride, but the promise of its homeopathic cure through the power of individual genius to lead the modern reader back by way of his own latent processes of imagination toward a regeneration of "natural disinterestedness." The transition of the Gothic villain-hero into the "metaphysical rebel" of Romantic poetic drama thus parallels also the continuous transition of Godwinian individualism from a program of rational benevolence, conceived as potentially viable for *all* selves (that is, all rational men), into a faith in the chosen individual—the "original genius" capable of speaking both *to* the self in its self-consciousness and *for* its transcendent sympathies with humanity and "truth."

That this sympathetic transcendence might actually be accomplished, sincerely and with "natural" spontaneity, without violence to the freedom of the self, without "abstraction" or self-congratulation on one's own virtue—this was the prophetic light that Hazlitt saw breaking in the pulpit at Shrewsbury from the moment Coleridge began to speak. There where his father had stood before

the world—and where he himself had found it impossible to stand—
Coleridge appeared, and with a voice that spoke directly to a guilt-
haunted adolescent heart struggling to believe in its lonely instincts.
The impression of a "strange wildness," of a primitive prophet, a St.
John "crying in the wilderness," was confirmed as Coleridge gave
out his text—"And he went up into the mountain to pray, HIMSELF,
ALONE"—his sonorous voice uttering the last two words so distinctly
and resonantly that it seemed "as if the sounds had echoed from the
bottom of the human heart, and as if that prayer might have floated
in solemn silence through the universe." And when Coleridge, "like
an eagle dallying with the wind," launched into his sermon "upon
peace and war," Hazlitt felt reverberations of literary power such as
had never stirred his imagination before in all the chapels of his
childhood. Revolutionary "enthusiasm," *Sturm und Drang* passion,
Godwinian solitude, and a poet's fancy here at last were joined happily, in the living unity of an eloquent voice, with the resolute principles of Presbyterian Dissent. All the discords that we have traced in
Hazlitt's education were now suddenly, if only for a brief interlude,
to vanish: "Poetry and Philosophy had met together. Truth and Genius had embraced, under the eye and with the sanction of Religion"
(17.108).

Deliverance from solitude through sympathetic powers of communion that inhere and ripen in solitude itself—this awakening, this
recognition of the paradox that the way to freedom lies in, or
through, the bondage of existential feeling was Hazlitt's lasting indebtedness to the poets of *Lyrical Ballads*. "Coleridge," he wrote
later, "was the only person from whom I ever learnt anything"
(5.167), but Hazlitt includes Wordsworth when he elsewhere explains what he learned in 1798: "I believe I may date my insight into
the mysteries of poetry from the commencement of my acquaintance
with the authors of the *Lyrical Ballads*" (12.226). What he was dis-
covering now was the organic relationship of language and thought
to feeling and consciousness. He was learning that "imagination" is
more than a power of disinterested idealization; it is another name
for the poetic nature of the mind itself; and poetry is rich in "mysteries" because it dwells in all the lights and shadows of consciousness; it is "the very stuff of which our lives are made" (5.2). And if

Coleridge gave the most vividly incarnate proof of how brilliantly and instantaneously poetic feeling could be raised to the power of genius, it was Wordsworth who revealed to the young "novice " the roots of this power in the humbler sympathies of imagination with "nature." When Hazlitt paraphrases Coleridge as saying of Wordsworth that "his genius was not a spirit that descended to him through the air; it sprung out of the ground like a flower, or unfolded itself from a green spray, on which the gold-finch sang" (17.117), the statement may also be read as reflecting his own sense of a mutually enhancing contrast in the respective genius of the two poets. The poet of the *Tintern Abbey* Ode differed from other nature poets in celebrating "pastoral scenes" not so much because they were pastoral as because such scenes were "connected with a thousand feelings, a link in the chain of thought, a fibre of his own heart." Nature for this poet had become "a kind of *home;* and he may be said to take a personal interest in the universe" (11.89). How close this description of Wordsworthian imagination was to Hazlitt's response to landscape nature thereafter, and to what he saw as potentially every man's "love of the country," is clear from his later essay on that subject: "It is because natural objects have been associated with the sports of our childhood . . . with our feelings in solitude, when the mind takes the strongest hold of things . . . because they have surrounded us in almost all situations, in joy and in sorrow, in pleasure and in pain; because they have been one chief source and nourishment of our feelings, and a part of our being, that we love them as we do ourselves" (4.18).

Now this valuation of "nature" may seem merely to amplify familiar eighteenth-century doctrines: here, now thoroughly demechanized, is Hartley's psychology of "association," and here again is Rousseau's distinction between *amour de soi* and *amour propre,* between "natural" and worldly self-love. Yet there is nonetheless a fundamental difference in attitude: self-consciousness, in its simplest expression as joy in self, no longer feels the need to vindicate its rights to feeling by citing the "rational" or "benevolent" effects of such exercise, though such thoughts may, and most often do, remain as conscious notes of pleasure. Paradoxically, the phase of Godwinian alienation that the poets and Hazlitt had endured may have been

the necessary precondition of this rediscovery of "nature." The breakthough of the new vision came when, sometime in the previous year, the poets began to conceive of their withdrawal from society not as the solitary meditation of a "wounded spirit" seeking "tranquillity" (which, we should remember, had always been a Godwinian virtue)[4] but as the return of the self to the origins of its will in the elementary sympathies of consciousness—a self compelled by the very defeat of that will in its own world to rediscover, by contrast, a sympathy with the opposing otherness of nature. Such a return to nature ceased to be a Rousseauist retreat to innocence, from which no way back to the modern world was possible or even desirable, but a state of restorative communion for the will—a state in which, as the *Tintern Abbey* lines describe it, "we are laid asleep / In body, and become a living soul." "Nature" in this invocation yields the intuition of her harmonies only when imagination humbles itself to the elemental solitude of being that the self shares with all living and organic things. And this vision may be said to have become a "creed" when the poets became convinced that "the primal sympathy," as Wordsworth would call it, is not merely the source of a healing self-communion but of the "moral being" that sustains all human intercourse. Just as poetic style in the *Ballads* had broken from the canons of poetic decorum, so now for the first time the concept of humanity had become distinct in poetry from the concept of society, from the "artificial" world of taste and manners; the new "school," as Hazlitt put it later, "was founded on a principle of sheer humanity, on pure nature void of art" (5.162). The one clearly pointed message of "The Rime of the Ancient Mariner" is that a sympathy with nature is the ground and medium of man's moral sympathy with man; and Wordsworth's ballad-vignettes teach the similar lesson that what strengthens the mind in suffering is some survival in "thought" of the radical pleasure inhering in the "organic sensibility" of the self—"the grand elementary principle of pleasure," which is "the native and naked dignity of man."[5]

Confident that here was all the inspiration he needed, a young philosopher of "disinterestedness" returned to Wem eager to resume his essay, but again his thoughts refused to flow—and again came hot tears of frustration. This time, however, the stoppage was the result of more than his own conflicts. How was Wordsworthian "joy" to be differentiated from simple "pleasure"—and how do both differ from the "pleasure" that Lockean empiricism tended to equate with egoism and hedonism? This inquiry would lead Hazlitt into depths of epistemology that perhaps he had never anticipated entering. "Pleasure" could not, he would learn, be defined without considering the many-sided intricacies of perception and cognition. And the process whereby "ideas" are formed—is this also the process whereby ideas become "motives" in the will? But if so, if mind is thus firmly wedded to nature and experience, in what sense (if any) is the will of the self "free"?

Now all this is philosophy rather than the kind of thought normally associated with literary genius, and it takes something of an effort to remind ourselves, in the literary ambience and intimately personal mood generated by Hazlitt's essay, how much philosophy forms the substance of the conversations there recorded between Hazlitt and Coleridge, and even of those with Wordsworth. Hazlitt's inspiration, we should remember, is that "Poetry and Philosophy had met together," that "Truth and Genius had embraced." The two dissonant sides of his character, the Prig and the Boy, were for the first time sharing the same consciousness, thrilling to the same admirations, speaking—or learning to speak—with one voice. "That my understanding . . . did not remain dumb and brutish, or at length found a language to express itself, I owe to Coleridge" (17.107). Poetry was the new dimension of his awareness, the new "language" of truth in his mind, but the truth of "nature" itself was not for him a vision to be possessed in creation but one to be articulated in philosophical "understanding." "Coleridge in truth met me half-way on the ground of philosophy, or I should not have been won over to his imaginative creed" (17.115). When he wrote these words, twenty-five years after the event—years of progressive disenchantment—Hazlitt needed no reminder of the uneasy tension that lurked in this convergence of minds from different quarters of the intellectual world; and it is significant that his essay ends with a glimpse of its principal characters departing in prophetically opposed directions: ". . . I on my return home, and he [Coleridge] for Germany" (17.122). But what the essayist of 1823 still failed to recognize was that his "half-way" accommodation with the poets was even at the time more willed illusion than fact—and not only because of temperamental and other personal differences, which would soon take political form, but because this meeting of minds had taken place on philosophical "ground" that soon proved unstable, not firmly one with the ground of "nature" after all.

Since he would always need emotionally the sense of unity of power, of integrated intellectual will, that the encounter with Coleridge gave him, Hazlitt could neither forgive Coleridge in future years for departing from this ideal image of his "genius," nor bring himself to confess, except by indirect inference, that the union of impassioned hope and strong conviction which he had known then, and would always long for again, could not be maintained intellectually. The lifelong and irresolvable tension between the Prig and the Boy in Hazlitt, between the rationalist and the passionalist, corresponds, I believe, to an irreconcileable tension in Romanticism itself between intellectualism and vitalism—or, to adopt terminology closer to doctrinal issues in Romantic speculation, between Transcendentalism and a resurgent, neo-empiricist, organic naturalism. Surely among the greater ironies of Hazlitt's career is the fact that for nearly fifteen years after 1798 he should labor to articulate and defend an optimistic naturalism—an "intellectual" naturalism, but a naturalism nonetheless—that the poets of the *Ballads* themselves, after their enunciation of it in the 1800 Preface, would almost at once begin to relinquish. Hazlitt would never learn to accept the "apostasy" of the poets from the "creed" of 1798 as something more than personal or political, as philosophically inevitable, just as they could never understand or forgive the polemical hostility of their once adulatory "novice." Hazlitt, too, was at last, in his 1818 *Lectures,* to dissociate himself from the creed of 1798 as an adequate philosophy of "genius"; and we shall begin to learn in this chapter why that termination follows by logical necessity from certain contradictions in the faith of 1798 that Hazlitt's philosophical analysis would expose without being able to resolve.

Yet there is still much to justify Hazlitt's veneration of that year as one of prophetic "truth" in his life ("the figures that compose that date are to me like the dreaded name of Demogorgon": 17.106); for

47

what would always endure from his "acquaintance" with the poets was a faith in "pleasure" and other values as inhering in consciousness itself, and this faith would remain long after its attendant optimism had faded. It is therefore fitting that Hazlitt should finally have made his peace with so decisive an episode in his past through the memorial of a great essay that rises above the ironies of time. And what Hazlitt, in his transcendence of bitterness, sensed by instinct, we can now appreciate from our vantage point in history: we are now able to see that the moment of greatest inspirational unity in his life was also the last moment in the age when it was possible for the various currents of the Revolutionary spirit in England—the literary, philosophical, political, and religious—to meet in genial harmony, flowing together, through the spring-green hills of Somerset, in one poignantly brief and brilliant stream.

※※※

After so long in the making, *An Essay on the Principles of Human Action* was of no great proportions when it appeared in 1805. In the *Complete Works* today it extends to less than fifty pages—a length which suggests that something less than justice had been done to so formidable a subject. Honestly confessing that his ambitiously titled treatise had failed to provide "a general account of the nature of the will," Hazlitt added to the volume, as partial compensation, *Some Remarks on the Systems of Hartley and Helvetius;* but this amendment marked, he knew, only a beginning. It would be necessary "to dig down a little deeper into the foundations of human thoughts and actions than I have hitherto done"; but, for the present, he had unavoidably "laid aside all thoughts of this kind," having "neither time nor strength for such an undertaking" (1.20). At a later point in the *Remarks* he again refers to a "plan" begun but set aside—but this time he prophetically intimates doubt that he "should ever finish" a systematic exposition of his ideas (1.85 n.).

Hazlitt's "plan" went the way of many other grand *opus* projected in the Romantic age. And not only the project but the philosopher himself was soon to disappear from view, translated into the journalist and lecturer of the next decade. Hazlitt liked to suggest that his early ambition was abandoned because even a philosopher had to make a living—and had not the sovereign British public shown its distaste for such "a dry, tough, metaphysical *choke-pear*" as the *Essay* (11.102)? Perhaps the mild contempt or, more often, indifferent silence that greeted Hazlitt's book in the reviews may be more accurately attributed to the shift in the winds of taste and doctrine between the decade of the Revolution and the decade of the Regency;[6] and this change has its counterpart, as we shall see, in certain changes of attitude in Hazlitt himself. But I am inclined, whatever the pressures of personality and circumstance, to trace the abortiveness of his philosophical career to the philosophy itself. And I think it possible to hold this view without impugning the value of the enterprise or in the least disparaging his manifest gifts as a thinker.

We may well ask ourselves whether we would not have inherited a far different image of Hazlitt's mind today if his philosophical writing, even without the "plan," had met with a better fortune—if, for example, his projected history of English philosophy had attracted sufficient subscribers in 1809; or if the *Prospectus* of that history had not vanished from sight for a century; if the *Essay* had been reprinted in his years of fame; or if the *Lectures on English Philosophy,* delivered in London in 1812, had been published in his lifetime; or if the manuscripts of four of these ten lectures had not been left to molder and disappear in a landlord's cellar.[7] Only this circumstantial obliteration made possible the legend that Hazlitt "failed" in his philosophical efforts—"failed," that is, not only in the ultimate sense of failure to produce a coherent system but also in the practical sense, as implying the failure to produce intellectually reputable works of (or on) philosophy.[8] Keats, as we now know, read the *Essay* and made Hazlitt his philosophical mentor, and Reynolds, Haydon, Bewick, and Talfourd were other young men of the time who either took their cue from Hazlitt's ideas or dissented with profound admiration for (in Talfourd's phrase) a "master in the art of thinking." Coleridge, in a letter of 1803, highly praised Hazlitt's originality, and in 1817 at last got around to some public admiration of the *Essay* (which in private he tried more than once to claim as his own brainchild). Lamb (or so De Quincey tells us) thought Hazlitt the intellectual equal of Coleridge (Hazlitt would not have agreed), and Leigh

Hunt wrote after Hazlitt's death that "he was in point of under-standing, essentially a great man—a master mind." We may also recall here a generally forgotten remark of De Quincey's in the first edition of the *Confessions,* before he had learned, as he would in 1845, to adopt his opinion of Hazlitt to the early Victorian climate. In this footnote of 1822 Hazlitt is not, perhaps for fear of offending the politically orthodox, mentioned by name, but from collateral remarks it is clear that De Quincey means no other when he refers to a thinker, possessing "a superb intellect in its *analytic* functions," who, surpassed only by Coleridge and Ricardo, deserves to be known as one of the age's three philosophical luminaries.[9]

This praise may be nearly as extreme in its way as the abuse that met Hazlitt's name elsewhere, but De Quincey's emphasis on anal-ysis—especially if qualified to mean phenomenological analysis—still affords, I believe, our best clue to a just appraisal of Hazlitt's capac-ity to deal with abstruse questions. He was not, as he fancied, a born philosopher whom an unlistening world had exiled to literature; but he was, like many others of the same literary species—Pascal, Mon-taigne, Santayana—an able critic of philosophies and philosophers, and especially of their reductive tendencies. Even in its "analytic functions," of course, his mind has undeniable limitations, which are discernible even, as we shall see in a moment, in his first and most disciplined essay. Always the critic, Hazlitt needed to have another man's ideas in front of him before his own analytical powers could function effectively; and the debit side of this fidelity to the critical object appears in his inability to structure an argument of his own without distraction: "I have," he acknowledged, "no head for ar-rangement" (8.47). But his most grievous limitation is his ignorance of most ancient and nearly all medieval thought—of, indeed, almost all philosophy beyond British empiricism and its French successors (with the one great exception of Kant, and he knew Kant mainly through Coleridge and through Willich's bad translation).[10]

But before we make much of these shortcomings, we must be clear about the applicability of our standards. "Metaphysics" in Haz-litt's England (until the full impact of German idealism was felt) did not refer primarily to cosmological or ontological problems—or it did so only when the term was used pejoratively, as connoting misty, if not wholly fictional, regions beyond the proper sphere of human reason. By a "metaphysician" Southey understood a "psychologist,"[11] and although his sense of the latter term was not ours, this identification suggests the extent to which speculative thought in England had retreated to the domain of "moral philosophy." Hazlitt does occasionally, as we shall see, make cosmological excursions, but in general he respects the line of demarcation from "natural philosophy"; and nothing shows more emphatically than this restriction to ethics and epistemology the bondage of his speculation to his "rational" compulsions as a Dissenter. This conservatism also explains why it will be advisable to deal in this chapter with his metaphysical writing between 1798 and 1812 as one continuous body of work, as if it were all published simultaneously; for although much is happening to Hazlitt in these years (as we shall see in the subsequent chapter), this experience seems not to have reacted observably upon his speculative thought, except in the unconscious sense of gradually deepening his awareness of an ineluctable "contradiction" in man's nature— the thematic emergence of which in some of the 1812 *Lectures* effectively writes finis, if my conjecture is sound, to his "metaphysical" ambition.

What Hazlitt had begun to learn from his baptism in poetic imagination is most apparent in the attention he gives in the *Essay,* and even more so in his speculative writing thereafter, to the problem of "pleasure"—a problem that did not figure prominently in the logic of his 1794 "discovery." Against his original thesis—that ideas, not sensations, determine all voluntary actions—it was still possible to argue that our ideas, precisely because they are free of existing objects, are "indifferent" in themselves and can be actuated as motives only by the mind's habitual sense of pleasure, which, if it implies no necessary self-interest, would seem equally to imply no necessary sympathy with others. (This is the argument of *psychological,* as distinct from *egoistic,* hedonism).[12] Hazlitt is now prepared to challenge this logic by insisting on a necessary distinction between a pleasant sensation and the "feeling" or judgment in the mind that something is pleasurable. The latter can only be an "abstraction"

51

drawn from many variable instances of the former; and failure to recognize this simple distinction had led, he thought, to the error of "the modern philosophy" in assuming that all pleasure is one in the mind and that the difference between pleasures is merely in degree of "satisfaction." "I cannot," Hazlitt observes (and we may incidentally note here the new and more potent "language" that his reasoning had acquired since 1798), "persuade myself that our sensations differ only as to more, or less; or that the pleasure derived from seeing a fine picture, or hearing a fine piece of music, that the gratification derived from doing a good action and that which accompanies the swallowing of an oyster are in reality and at bottom the same pleasure." Objects and situations are not mere "husks" that the mind throws away as "indifferent" in its ideas of them; the "essential quality" of an experience does not "evaporate in passing through the imagination," even though the effect of this quality may not be proportionate to the conscious distinctness of the idea, just "as objects may excite very distinct ideas which have little or nothing to do with feeling." Thus the only continuity possible in the mind between necessarily various pleasures, as between past pleasures and our "ideal" images of future pleasure, is an idea of "good"; and it is this idea which must determine our valuations of pleasure as motives to action (1.13–14n., 23).

Because he insists that "good" is inseparable from pleasure, Hazlitt does not pause in the *Essay* to make an explicit distinction between the general idea of "good" and the general idea of "pleasure." But elsewhere he leaves us in no doubt: "Pleasure is that which is so in itself: good is that which approves itself as such on reflection, or the idea of which is a source of satisfaction" (11.9). And again: "Good or evil is properly that which gives the mind pleasure or pain on reflection, that is, which excites rational approbation or disapprobation" (2.260). Yet Hazlitt also takes pains to guard against the inference that he is defining "good" as an axiomatic intuition, or deriving it from some innate and distinct moral faculty, or limiting its origin to the powers of mind alone, as distinct from nature:

> The actual desire of good is not inherent in the mind of man, because it requires to be brought out by certain accessory objects or ideas, but the disposition itself, or property of the mind

which makes him liable to be so affected by certain objects is inherent in him and a part of his nature. . . . The love of my own particular good must precede that of the particular good of others . . . but I love my own particular good as consisting in the first conception I have of some one desirable object for the same reason, for which I afterwards love any other known good, whether my own, or another's, whether conceived of as consisting in one or more things, that is, because it possesses that essential property common to all good, without which it would cease to be good at all, and which has a general tendency to excite certain given affections in my mind.

And Hazlitt then cautions that this "general tendency," as it becomes an idea "intermediate" between varieties of value, must differ from other ideas of the reason in remaining "indefinite"; for it can never be wholly detached from individual associations and will retain motivational power "no longer than while it implies a sentiment, or real feeling representative of good, and only in proportion to the degree of force and depth which this feeling has" (1.13).

The "good," then, belongs neither to the perceiving mind nor to the object valued but to the relationship of "nature" that subsists between them. And it is worth stressing that "nature" here *is* this relationship, not a complex of qualities or forces existing antecedently to the mind's responses. No passage in the *Essay* seems to me more clearly reminiscent of the *Lyrical Ballads* and their famous Preface; and perhaps we have here, indeed, the one prose statement of the period that attempts to spell out analytically the meaning of "the soul of . . . moral being" that Wordsworth and Coleridge discovered in nature. As we shall understand better in a moment, Hazlitt sees the perception of value as inseparable from the being of consciousness itself; an object is not first perceived and then certain of its qualities abstracted as "good"; on the contrary, it is *perceived* as simply "good" (that is, as pleasurable or inseparably associated with pleasure), and is then consciously *approved* as morally good (not as merely pleasurable) to the degree that it "accords with" and sustains an organic wholeness of activity (a "fullness of satisfaction") in the mind beyond the moment of perception (12.352–54; 20.356). It strikes me as curious, inexpert though I am on the subject, that the Romantic sense of organic value in "nature" has met with such neglect among students of ethical theory; for I doubt that Hazlitt's intellectualist naturalism, as it might be called, can be convicted of what G. E. Moore has called "the naturalistic fallacy"—that is, the fallacy of reducing the "good" to "properties" of things, feelings, or other ideas. Notwithstanding Hazlitt's emotive-empiricist emphasis, "nature" here clearly approximates to Bishop Butler's sense of a "nature" whose predeterminations come to power only as ends formed in and by the "reflection" of the mind.[13] "Moral obligation," Hazlitt wrote in 1809, ". . . expresses the hold or power (be it stronger or weaker) which certain given motives have over the mind. . . . It has its foundation in the moral and rational nature of man, or in that principle—call it reason, conscience, moral sense, what you will— which, without any reference to our own interests, passions, and pursuits, approves of certain actions and sentiments as right and condemns others as wrong. To act right is to act in conformity with this standard" (2.118).

Now I grant that this statement is far from adequate philosophically; for its vague language leaves undifferentiated, and even seems to identify, *standards of* morality and *motives to* morality.[14] Hazlitt overlooks this issue because he is interested less in discriminating the nature of ethical right and wrong than in clarifying the entire life of man's value-consciousness: he does not wish to dissociate aesthetic value, for instance, from ethical "good"; the affective continuity of all human values is precisely his point. And in this insistence Hazlitt should at least be credited with helping to expose the fallacy that had hitherto clouded the problem of standards and motives in ethical speculation. Not only "the modern philosophy" (that is, mechanism, materialism, and sensationist empiricism) but most traditional moralities had assumed that only through an educative process of some kind, whether rational or associational, could the will of the self be assimilated to the moral community of civilization. Kant, apparently ignorant of Butler, never suspected that sense-derived pleasure might be "disinterested"; and Butler himself felt constrained to distinguish a "cool" self-love conformable with conscience from the original "partiality" of the self for its pleasures.[15] Nor was Hazlitt unaware of this broader challenge of his to tradition: his theory, he knew, went "to the direct subversion of one of the most

THE METAPHYSICIAN: MIND AND NATURE

deeply-rooted feelings of the human mind"—namely, that of an "essential difference" between the feelings of self-consciousness and the responses of the same consciousness to feeling in others (1.9–10).

In opposing this assumption Hazlitt most clearly departs from his closest anti-egoist predecessors in British empiricism—Hartley, Hume, and Adam Smith—all of whom had made benevolent "sympathy" dependent upon the past associations of experience: only through the force of association could the will of the self be expected to overcome its natural tendency to turn away from pain and suffering. An episode that occurred during Hazlitt's walk with Coleridge along the sands of Bristol Channel illustrates the difference nicely: a fisherman had been telling them of the efforts of himself and his fellows to save a boy that had drowned the day before, and when Coleridge asked why he and the others had done so "at the risk of their own lives," the fisherman could only answer: "Sir, we have a *nature* towards one another." Coleridge thought this expression a "fine illustration" of Hazlitt's theory of disinterestedness (17.121), but earlier benevolists might have found the fisherman's answer not entirely adequate; for while acknowledging the role of "nature," they would probably have insisted that the fisherman's own "associations" were primarily responsible for the action, if not for the feelings of sympathy. As Hazlitt paraphrases Smith's account of the process of a benevolent action in overcoming feelings of aversion, "the old idea of physical pain must be called up whenever I see any other person in the like danger, and the associated action along with it, just as much as if I were exposed to the same danger myself" (1.80).[16] Hazlitt not only denies that this is a necessary inference but argues that it fails to describe the mind's response even when one's own life is in danger. A child, it is true, fears fire only from some past experience of fire, but when the child encounters another situation of danger from fire, it is not the recollected past event (or events) that he dreads but what his imagination dreaded in the first instance—not the specific circumstance of pain (a particular impression which could exist only *after* the event and which in itself remains distinct from every other event) but the general feeling of pain and fearfulness which enables the mind to relate the new danger to other fears and to actions that remove pain or fear of pain. The essential "object" of consciousness in either experience is not the "painted flame" on the child's senses but an "idea" which instantaneously unites like feelings with unlike, or novel, circumstances, thus "anticipating a new impression" instead of "dreaming of the old one." The child's mind, in both instances, *creates the object* of its fear; only his imagination is able to associate impressions that have never been associated. "It is," Hazlitt observes, "of the very nature of the imagination to change the order in which things have been impressed on the senses, and to connect the same properties with different objects, and different properties with the same objects; to combine our original impressions in all possible forms, and to modify these impressions themselves to a very great degree." And Hazlitt insists that there is no problem in identifying, by the same name of "imagination," this faculty of a man's "disinterested" sympathy with others as "the immediate spring and guide of action" even in seemingly instinctive acts of self-preservation. "But for this faculty of multiplying, varying, extending, combining, and comparing his original passive impressions he must be utterly blind to the future and indifferent to it, insensible to everything beyond the present moment, altogether incapable of hope, or fear, or exertion of any kind . . ." (1.18–27).

Hazlitt failed to appreciate the full import of this analysis; he seems never to have recognized that the truly "metaphysical" novelty of his "discovery" lay not in its implications for moral theory but in transforming the meaning of "sympathy" from the function of a benevolent "faculty" into a primary activity of *consciousness* itself, which is here made nearly synonymous with "imagination." As Max Scheler observes in his monumental study of the problem of sympathy, all "genetic theories" of sympathetic feeling—theories which derive it from something anterior to itself, that is, from mental associations, or a "social sense," or an animal herd instinct—implicitly proceed from (or leave unquestioned) the assumption that only the feelings of self as individual body or mind can be "given" in experience, while "what is given in the case of others is merely the appearance of the body." [17] Hazlitt has broken through this dichotomy; for although he still assumes that the *datum* of sympathy is an "appearance" to an individual mind, the response of imagination to this "impression" is to an ideal or "feeling" of value, and is not the response of a bodily self of inward sensation to an alien "other," to a purely visible body. But what, then, is "self," if it is not a primally given entity in consciousness?

Hazlitt recognizes from the start a fundamental ambiguity in the word "self": he is aware—and indeed, his whole argument for disinterestedness rests upon this distinction—that "self" refers at once to both the physically existent, numerically distinct individual and the idea or image which the individual has of his uniqueness. Yet Hazlitt recognizes also a third, and the crucially mediating, factor in this relationship: namely, the "general notion of self"—the cognitive idea or sense that a man forms of "conscious individuality" in other human beings besides himself. All living individualities, all "organized beings" in nature are, Hazlitt says, necessarily "aggregates of dissimilar things": here is the first of his many adaptations of the *organic* principle learned (or so I suspect) from the poets (although he is to avoid, as a neologism, this adjectival form of the word). But unlike our ideas of other such "aggregates," our perception of human individuality cannot be defined by the principles of analogy, identity, and contradiction that commonly govern our knowledge. A man at any given time may be or seem more like others than like his own past being; his individuality cannot be understood as being "the same with itself in as far as he is positively different from everyone else." Neither is the mere experience "of continued consciousness" in ourselves enough to explain why we should so readily endow other beings—or our own—with a privileged "sameness" of being distinct from all other continuities in our minds. Indeed, the problem is not so much one of understanding the difference of other minds from ours as of understanding why certain feelings and impressions should be thought to be peculiarly one's "own"—that is, not only not another's, but actually or potentially different from their counterparts in other minds. It is, in fact, only the practical need for this distinction that can explain its nature: "The distinction [of self from others] becomes marked and intelligible in proportion as the objects or impressions *are intrinsically the same* [my italics]." I do not, that is, have an instinctive consciousness of my impressions as my own and then regulate my ideas of other human beings by their degree of conformity with this knowledge; on the contrary, only by a sympathetic awareness of otherness, of equivalently the "same" impressions in other beings, do I acquire my self-consciousness—the feeling, in short, of my *otherness among others,* the knowledge, through imagination, that my impressions are my own only insofar as their impressions prove to be their own, that is, incommunicable with mine, and in that very inaccessibility like my own feelings of personal being. "It is," Hazlitt concludes, "by comparing the knowledge that I have of my own impressions, ideas, feelings, powers, etc., with my knowledge of the same or similar impressions, ideas, etc. in others, and with the still more imperfect conception that I form of what passes in their minds when this is supposed to be essentially different from what passes in my own, that I acquire the general notion of self" (1.32–38).

With this analysis we have, I think, arrived at the best, most original and least perishable part of Hazlitt's theory of "disinterestedness"; and in later chapters we shall find this principle of psychological dialectic—his sense of self as always in some mode or degree *intersubjective,* as existing and acting only in tension with real or imagined otherness—looming ever larger in his literary and social criticism. Yet again, as so often happens in his speculation, he fails to pursue the implications of his insight: he fails here to see that he has established, not the "natural benevolence" of the will, but simply the "disinterestedness" of imagination; and indeed this sympathy of imagination is revealed now as functioning not so much through a continuity of "ideas" as through a given organic consciousness of self-cum-otherness. Again it is the minister's son—always finally in charge of Hazlitt's philosophical "conclusions"—who interrupts at this point in the argument to insist upon the selflessness of the mind and reduce self-consciousness once more to an "idea." The result is perhaps the weakest link in Hazlitt's reasoning—his explanation of how the will becomes selfish or habitually egocentric: "We build up . . . an imaginary self, and a proportionable interest in it; we clothe it with the associations of the past and present, we disguise it in the drapery of language, we add to it the strength of passion and the warmth of affection, till we at length come to class our whole existence under one head . . . but all this only proves the force of imagination and habit to build up such a structure on a merely partial foundation. . . . On the same foundation are built up nearly as high natural affection, friendship, the love of country, of religion" (20.179; cf. 1.41–42).

As the style here suggests, this passage is not from the *Essay* but from a later work, although the reasoning remains unaltered; and I have chosen this passage because its excessive reliance on imagery seems to me symptomatic of the shakiness of the argument. Are we really to believe that the conscious ego, while it may originate as our "most distinct" idealization of value, continues "on the same foundation" as all other ideas and that it remains simply the most intimate "object" of imagination—one to which we merely "add" passion through the inertia of "habit," without modification of the imagination itself? That the author of the *Essay* never squarely asked himself these questions is manifest in his never wholly convincing efforts to refute the most telling argument of the opposition—the "uneasiness" theory which the more intelligent exponents of "the modern philosophy" had advanced to explain benevolent actions. According to this theory—which was given currency by Locke, who borrowed it from Hobbes—desire alone is not enough to account for action; the immediate impulse which prompts the will to alter its present condition is always the wish to remove some "uneasiness" of emotion. Insofar as Locke and his successors identified this "uneasiness" as aversion to pain, Hazlitt was right in replying that the disturbance must emanate not from the appetites of the self as such but from the mind; the will feels uneasy until it acts to bring its "idea" of desire into accord with circumstances (1.44–46). But Hazlitt overlooks the fact that the argument of his adversaries basically rests on another postulate. Lockean "uneasiness" echoes the premise of Spinoza (and, in our time, of Freud) that the ego, like everything else that exists in time, strives to conserve its functional condition as a body, and thus tries to assimilate all novelty to its perseverance in existence.[18] Hazlitt too readily assumed that since there is no "permanent" continuity of conscious identity, the only connection between future-oriented volition and past consciousness must be an "idea," limited in its reference only by past awareness of value. He forgot that if actions of the will must conform to an "idea" of imagination, both idea and action must also conform (not merely be limited) to what might be called the organic economy of individuality, which in volition cannot be conceived as anxiously standing by—like Hazlitt's hypothetical child in its first encounter with fire—until imagination has signalled a course of action. Hazlitt failed to consider that "feeling" in volition must mean not simply what is sensed or remembered or imagined but the functional equilibrium of these and other component elements. And the need to maintain this equilibrium in time is likely to alter the shape and tendency of ideas, and to become a resistance in the self to ideas and experiences which have threatened this equilibrium in the past. The love of one's own "particular good" may thus be not merely a version of general good but may involve a rejection of other "particular good": ideas, without ceasing to be "ideal," may be turned against other ideas, our sympathies with value used to form antipathies to other value. And if "uneasiness" in this sense can alter volition, then the self would seem to have more than a retrospective interest in the continuity of its identity. To argue that the will is not originally self-interested is not therefore to infer that the self is "naturally interested in the welfare of others in the same way, and from the same direct motives" as those by which it is interested in itself. Perhaps we may amend Hazlitt's theory to conclude that a sympathy with organic *otherness,* while it makes benevolence constantly possible, implies in itself no "natural benevolence," no impulse toward the good of *others* as such. If our motives are not determined *by* or *for* the self, they may still be determined *to* the self—to the self, not as an ego, but as an existence.

Without confessing his error, Hazlitt is to be found saying almost precisely this—although, significantly, he is never to repeat the amendment—when he resumes his argument for "disinterestedness" in the 1812 *Lectures.* "If it should be said, that after all *we are as selfish as we can be,* and that the modifications and restrictions of the principle of self-love are only a necessary consequence of the nature of a thinking being, I answer, that this is the very point I wish to establish . . ." (2.231; my italics). Surely this major concession, in which the will of self-love becomes the compelling force in motivation and "thinking" becomes merely its qualification, was not Hazlitt's "point" in the *Essay.* To do him justice, however, we should recognize that his theory never pretended to describe either the actual or potential prevalence of benevolent over selfish impulses in the world; he was concerned only to demonstrate man's inherent ("natural") capacity for unselfishness, and by eliminating egoism and hedonism as necessary premises, to "give free play to the social affections" (9.51). The concession italicized above really amounts to tacit recognition that he had failed even to enlarge in theory man's capacity for benevolence; and philosophy has in this respect been right to refuse his claims to have made a historically original "discovery." Butler and Hume were content to argue that self-love and benevolence are consistent and correlative;[19] and Hazlitt's attempt to go further—to reduce both motives to the same mode of "sympathy"—would seem to have necessarily failed. Yet to reduce the limits of Hazlitt's achievement in ethical theory is only to recognize where, like most Romantic achievements in speculation, his true originality as a thinker lay—in rediscovering the primacy of imagination.[20] And what this primacy came to mean for Hazlitt, compelling him gradually to alter his sense of the relationship of "ideas" to will—and especially of his own ideas to his own will—is for us the greatest interest remaining in his speculative work after 1805.

※※

The *Lectures on English Philosophy*,[21] delivered in London before a modest audience at the Russell Institution in the autumn of 1812, are best described as the attempt of a believer in "truth" as "experience"—an *experientialist*, if I may borrow Roy Park's term (p. 38)—to rescue his faith from traditional empiricism. Reductively, but perhaps forgivably so in the light of his own premises, Hazlitt conceives of the tradition of thought descending from Hobbes through Locke, Berkeley, and Hume to the French sensationists (Helvétius, Condillac, Holbach, et al.) as forming one "modern system" of materialism, whether latent or overt—one in which "all thought is to be resolved into *sensation,* all morality into the *love of pleasure,* and all action into *mechanical* impulse" (2.113–14). What he means by this "system" of "materialism," it turns out, is less a body of conscious doctrine than an unchallenged set of assumptions, to be found even in a metaphysical immaterialist like Berkeley—an uncritical faith in the "simple perception" of particulars, whether or not the particularity of the "object" is assumed to have material existence (2.128). In the first three *Lectures* Hazlitt sets out to demonstrate that this and most other "modern" fallacies had developed from a wrong turn taken at the very beginning of the English philosophical revolution—"from a wrong interpretation of the word *experience,* confining it [as, Hazlitt makes clear, the father of this tradition, Bacon himself, had not confined it] to a knowledge of things without us; whereas it in fact includes all knowledge relating to objects either within or out of the mind, of which we have any direct and positive evidence" (2.124).

In even the greatest of the empiricist philosophers—and in Hazlitt's opinion these were Hobbes, Berkeley, Hume, and Hartley[22]—he finds the same failure: an unwillingness to analyze and define unequivocally such terms as "perception," "simple idea," "image," and "impression," around which all their arguments revolved. Despite their extensive revision of Locke, later empiricists had still accepted without serious question the principle, first introduced by Hobbes, of "simple perception"—the supposition, in Locke's words, that the senses, "being conversant about particular sensible objects, do convey into the mind several distinct perceptions of things." Berkeley and Hume, intent on doing away with the Lockean distinction between "primary qualities" (mass, figure, volume, et al., those presumed to exist in matter itself) and "secondary qualities" (color, heat, etc., which are known to exist, as perceived, only in the mind), had not really challenged Locke's more fundamental premise but had, in fact, magnified the principle of simple perception into a denial of his theory of knowledge. They had argued that *all* seemingly abstract ideas (triangles, for instance) are particular images that become generally representative: "An idea," wrote Berkeley, "which considered in itself is particular, becomes general, by being made to represent or stand for all other particulars of the same sort."[23] But Berkeley, Hazlitt observes, never bothered to explain how the mind arrives at this primal idea—of "the same sort" (2.184). And since Berkeley's critique won strong endorsement from Hume, the assumption of the original particularity of all ideas, with the corollary that ideas are made "general" in the mind only through processes of "association," had become so firmly entrenched that Hazlitt was now compelled to go to great lengths of patience, begging his audience to consider the paradox that all particular images might yet prove to be, in the purely literal sense of the word, "abstract" ideas.

Here Hazlitt's practical knowledge of painting came to his assistance, just as Coleridge's knowledge of the classics led him back to the genesis of the word "idea" in Greek: both men returned to the elementary facts of human optics. Every "modern philosopher" since Hobbes had, as Hazlitt put it, "supposed with the vulgar that it was only necessary to open the eyes in order to see. . . . Ask a logician, or any common man, and he will no doubt tell you that a face is a face, a nose is a nose, a tree is a tree, and that he can see what it is as well as another. Ask a painter and he will tell you otherwise" (2.207). The particular impression itself could never produce the perception of its distinctness from, or resemblance to, other things: to perceive even a pebble or a brass stud in a chair requires an "idea"—an act of cognition and recognition—not merely a receptivity to sensations. If consciousness is finite, if it cannot be proved that there is no remainder in our awareness of even the simplest object—"for there is no one object which does not consist of a number of parts and relations," the entire "comprehension" of which is impossible—then this limitation itself implies that perception is necessarily an act of "abstraction" (2.151 ff., 209–15). "There is," Hazlitt says flatly, "no such thing as a single object in nature" (20.443). No object, that is, exists singly in or to our senses, for what we know as such an object is an abstraction from the "multitude" or "dimness" of our sensations as we confront the still indeterminate object in its "aggregate" complexity of parts or its "bundle of relations" with its context. Locke's "simple ideas" thus prove, on inspection, to be simple only in the sense of being our most elementary "general ideas," not derived *from* a series of particular perceptions, but necessary for the perception of objects *as* particular objects. Extension, figure, mass, number, motion, even such qualities as coldness and whiteness—all involve relations and comparison: "The knowledge upon which our ideas rest is general, and the only difference between abstract and particular, is that of being more or less general, of leaving out more or fewer circumstances, and more or fewer objects, perceived either at once or in succession, and forming either a particular whole, aggregate, or a class of things" (2.209).

Of the validity of this analysis as criticism there should be little doubt today. Hazlitt has here put his finger on the two Lockean fallacies that Whitehead has taught us to recognize: the fallacy, first, of "misplaced concreteness," of imputing "simple location" to objects of sense perception; and, no less importantly, the error of identifying "logical simplicity" with "priority in the process constituting the experient occasion."[24] Yet the detection of Locke's errors brought problems of its own for someone unprepared to forsake the native tradition entirely. For how does the mind come by the ability to form "general ideas"—at once to intuit and compare relational wholes in experience? It might seem that Hazlitt has here passed beyond empiricism and has begun to discover in "the reasoning imagination" (9.58) a pure intuition of universals. He has, indeed, abandoned traditional empiricism in showing that imagination cannot be simply reproductive: imagination is able to reproduce the images of the past only because it is productive of "ideas" in all moments of perception. As early as 1798, Hazlitt, on the sands of Bristol Channel, had demonstrated to Coleridge something that (by Hazlitt's account) the latter did not then "know": "that likeness is not a case of the association of ideas" (17.121); that no chain of events of feeling can account for the first conscious linking of discrete sense impressions, or of new with old continuities of association. In his writing after 1805, however, Hazlitt prefers not to identify, as the poets of *Lyrical Ballads* always would, the "abstracting and modifying power" of the mind as "imagination"; he prefers to confine this term to those ideas and associations which have no proper cognitive reference beyond the mind, and to describe acts of perception by invoking less specialized terms—"the understanding" or "the conscious, comprehensive principle" (20.29). And the reason for this shift in nomenclature inheres in his own theory as well as in his fidelity to eighteenth-century language. For Hazlitt does not, as Coleridge does, assign a constant primacy in perception to abstraction (ideas of perceived wholes) as distinct from generalization (ideas of classes to which perceptual wholes belong); he would not have agreed with Coleridge that the former function can be operative without the latter.[25] Despite the fact that in 1807 (before he knew much about Kant) he had indicated an allegiance to "the *transcendental* creed" (1.130), the title of power which he finds for "abstract and general ideas" in the mind is

64

by no means transcendental, as is clear from the 1809 *Prospectus:* "The power of abstraction is a necessary consequence of the limitation of the comprehending power of the mind." And when, a moment before in the same work, Hazlitt writes that "the understanding or intellectual power of the mind is entirely distinct from simple perception or sensation" (2.116–17), he does not mean, as he explains elsewhere, that cognitive acts can ever be "independent" of sensation. "It is quite enough to shew," he later writes in reproof of Kant, "not that there are certain notions *a priori* or independent of sensation, but certain faculties independent of the senses or sensible objects" (20.18 n.). If, as Wellek insists, this statement grossly distorts Kant's meaning,[26] it nevertheless shows us emphatically the difference between Kant's idea of sensation as a mere "manifold" and Hazlitt's vision of an "aggregate" of impressions; the latter for Hazlitt is not merely a "mass" but a "general feeling" which enforces "comprehension" because of certain qualities or tendencies given or latent in the sensations themselves as they converge in the moment of cognition. The perception of "likeness," like that of value, comes not only from the mind but from its active relationship with natural objects, to whose powers of "life" or inanimate "motion" the mind's own activity responds in "sympathy."

Now it might be thought that this appeal to a sympathy of the mind's "vital spirit" with a spirit of "life and motion" in nature (1.23; 18.161) is a begging of the question which assumes the very point in dispute. Hazlitt owns to the charge of a certain "mysticism" in his thought, but the "unaccountable" mystery (1.70; 2.212) that he finds in consciousness is at least one that defies analysis only after his analysis has confirmed it as irreducible in the process of experience. Even the favorably disposed Coleridge could complain during his avid reading of Kant: "I apply the categoric forms of a tree. But first, how do I come by this tree?"[27] That simple question seems to me to express perfectly what Hazlitt means when he confesses that he is "unable to comprehend" the "nature of consciousness" (1.61); for there is no explaining such a feeling as *treeness,* the feeling of "characteristic" being, of the *organic* presence which the various senses, as they meet in "the vital spirit" of the conscious self, communicate to thought. On this issue Hazlitt and Coleridge are, and remain, one: they both insist on life-intuition as the principle of all knowledge; Coleridge's "primary imagination" corresponds to "the conscious principle" which Hazlitt sees as "the common sense" of the bodily senses (2.222; cf. *BL,* 1.202).

The two thinkers adapt very differently, however, the organic principle to the problem of man's knowledge of "nature" in general; and more than any other of their philosophical disagreements, it is this difference which anticipates their future divergence as critics. Hazlitt does not let the dualism of body and mind develop into a contradistinction of opposed tendencies; for him the mind has organic intuitions not merely because its activity is distinct from the bodily senses but because it always acts *as* the mind of an individual body. Abraham Tucker, whose *Light of Nature Pursued* (1768–78) Hazlitt edited and abridged in 1807, had argued that the judgment of cognition in our variable associations is possible because "different impressions" are "all referred by implication to the same simple individual"; and this suggestion, characteristically left undeveloped by Tucker, is extended by Hazlitt from conceptual "judgment" to perception itself. Our impressions become both perceptual wholes and "general ideas" not simply because certain sensations are like or unlike others but because we sense in certain aggregates of sensation a mode or degree of "connection" among them which is like or unlike—or at once like and unlike—the active wholeness, the continuous "action and reaction," of our conscious individuality. Here Hazlitt is applying to perception in general a principle of sympathetic consciousness which he sees as most active in the mind's way of responding to individuality in other human beings and in all "organized beings"—that is, the perception of "such a connection between a number of things as determines the mind to consider them as one whole" (1.34). But he differs from Coleridge in that he does not regard the perception of inorganic objects as definable by the negative contrast of their formal or "fixed" unity as objects with the mind's apperception of its own subjectively organic activity. True, Hazlitt can sound very like Coleridge in describing the process of all perception: impressions are "comprehended" only by being "communicated . . . to one diffusive and yet self-centered intellect, one undivided active spirit, co-extended with the object, and yet ever present to itself" (20.29). Everything in this statement may be said to have an echo in Coleridge except for one crucial phrase, "co-extended with the object." Hazlitt does not clearly explain what he means by "co-extended," but presumably he is referring to Tucker's premise that the mind is "extended" throughout the body yet, unlike the body, is "without parts."[28] "The mind, as it were," Hazlitt would remark in a late essay, "acts over the whole body, and animates it equally" (9.199); all consciousness has therefore a given "elastic" sympathy (20.52) with states of physical motion and extension in nature insofar as such states have manifest correlatives in the life of the human body. In this response to objects more than perception of analogy is involved; for the mind does not sympathize merely with likeness to its own activity but with the power of "action" as such, whether mental or physical; its most frequent experience of "order and connection" among objects is, after all, its own practical experience as a creature acting and suffering in a physical world, of "acting conjointly" with things and "of being acted on by them." And how little Hazlitt is disposed to view this empirical "order" as the mere inertia of physical appearances, essentially opposed to the activity of thought perceiving it, is shown by this remark: "The closest connection between my ideas is formed by that relation of things among themselves, which is most necessary to be attended to in making use of them, the common concurrence of many things to some given end: for example, my idea of [a] walking stick is defined by the simplicity of the action necessary to wield it for that particular purpose" (1.34–35).

With these observations Hazlitt anticipates the pragmatist strain in post-Kantian philosophy, and, in that last sentence especially, shows himself to be a distant forerunner of James and Dewey. And perhaps this approach to a functional relativism suggests why Hazlitt never cared to pursue his analysis into a systematic theory of knowledge. Notwithstanding his professions of allegiance to an "intellectual philosophy" (1.127), Hazlitt's organicism proves, on inspection, to be one of consciousness in its activation by the self rather than of mind as a pure activity of perceiving and thinking "spirit." He seems to have assumed that, to secure the basis of universality, it would be enough to disentangle the empiricist confusion of "innate knowledge of principles," which the mind, as Locke rightly saw, cannot possibly have, with "innate principles of knowledge," without which there would be no "human understanding" for Locke to have written his *Essay* about (2.165–66). Hazlitt, however, seems never to have been able to decide just how these "innate principles" should be defined. At one point he speaks of them—most consistently with his own analysis—as "customary affections of the mind" (2.212), at another he describes them in the classical way as "forms of thinking" (2.165), at other times he mocks "Platonic forms" as "the forms of *nothing*" (20.18n.), and sometimes he seems to be simply washing his hands of the problem: "I do not say that there is any purely abstract or un-comprehended idea as of form without content . . . as the school-men contended (I leave that point untouched and on one side)" (20.446). But the fact is that Hazlitt does not leave this point unex-amined; for he seems to me to be clearly deriving the rational forms of knowledge, not from the act of perception as it issues in concep-tualized abstraction, but from the act of conceptualized perceiving as it becomes the determinate event of object-perception. All of Haz-litt's specific analyses of perception betray a fundamental fidelity to the Lockean belief—although this was one loyalty he would not have wished to admit, having only cold and grudging respect for Locke— that a qualitative judgment of identity and contradiction between sense impressions is the only native logic that the mind knows (20.228). And the change in Hazlitt's opinion of Kant further con-firms his bias against *a priori* forms: for even when he is lauding the Kantian axiom that "the mind alone is formative" (2.153), he is no less strenuously engaged in challenging the inference which Berke-ley had argued against Locke—that "an idea can be like nothing but an idea, a perception like nothing but a perception." This phenome-nalism (the basis of Hume's scepticism and, through Hume's influ-ence, of Kant's epistemology) is grounded, Hazlitt argues, on the fallacy—which William James would later call "intellect-ualism"[29]—that "what is different cannot be the same" (2.181), that entities contradistinguished in the mind are mutually exclusive in re-ality. Berkeley's dictum, Hazlitt insists, amounts only to the truism that matter does not think; and to infer therefrom that what we call "matter" has no substantial existence, or is entirely discontinuous with mind, or that our ideas of the world bear no resemblance to "degrees and kinds of power" in external objects, would be as fallacious as to assume that the uncolored print of a painting cannot possibly represent the original (2.182–86). All that the sceptic may honestly conclude about the relation of consciousness to the universe is that things "cannot exist in nature *after the same manner* that they exist in the human mind" (1.71; my italics).

※※※

In identifying himself as an advocate of "the intellectual philosophy," Hazlitt was using a term that—as students of Shelley have learned[30]—covered a broad range of philosophical positions, some of them mutually incompatible: for example, Cartesian rationalism, Platonic or Kantian idealism, Berkeleyan immaterialism, Humean scepticism, indeed almost everything but a materialist empiricism and the Scottish "common sense" doctrine of unmediated perception. But the common denominator in this diversity, and that which justified the imprecise usage, was a practical faith that the human will is motivated, not by materially determined causes and effects, but by "ideas"; or, as Hazlitt put it, that "the will cannot act without ideas, nor otherwise than as it is directed by them" (1.132). This statement suggests what he had always wanted his discovery of "disinterestedness" to mean as a philosophical anthropology: that there is no disparity but an essential continuity between the "ideas" of man's knowledge of nature and the "ideals" of human value; that the cognitive functions of the mind are ultimately one with its moral and aesthetically expressive functions; that sympathy with organic nature is the ground and sustaining medium of benevolence in society; and that therefore a sympathetic love for the "good" of all humanity inheres potentially in the will and imagination of every self.

Hazlitt wished to believe that these conclusions followed firmly from his analysis of the mind, but the "ideas" governing this optimism really derive from his father's myth of reality—from the myth, namely, that all "truth" is one. If "truth" is intelligible and credible because it forms, or proceeds from, a unity, then all error similarly tends to be one. This would seem to have been Hazlitt's assumption when he argues in 1807 that there are only two "sorts" of philosophy—the "intellectual" and the "material"—and that the materialist perversion of thought has reduced nearly all of "the modern philosophy" to a system that virtually denies the reality and value of thought itself (1.127). The caustic rhetoric, the simplistic dualism of this indictment alike suggest its origin in Hazlitt's ritual loyalty to parental Reason, not in the logic of his own, or most distinctive, analysis of the will—not at least of that analysis as we find it in his 1812 lecture, "On Liberty and Necessity." For there we find him belatedly recognizing an element in his thought which we have seen, in another form, both inspiring and troubling his theory of knowledge—an element which, if we look ahead to its later development in such thinkers as Nietzsche and Bergson, we may roughly characterize as *vitalism*.[31] Man's will may never be able to act "without ideas," but Hazlitt in this lecture is no longer to be found saying that the will is or becomes free through the power of "ideas" alone. On the contrary, he begins now to suggest—although still only dimly at this point, for the minister's son continues to resist the inference—that consciousness itself is largely determined by a complex and paradoxical force of passion and silently working instinct, shaping the will from a "nature" deep within the organic body-mind, or "constitution," of the biologically given self.

Hazlitt was aware that any effort in his time to reconcile the claims of freedom and determinism could not afford to ignore Hume's challenge to traditional notions of causality. Paraphrasing Hume's argument that the seemingly evident inseparability of "causes" and "effects" is simply a "constant conjunction" of associated events, Hazlitt agrees that "in the mere mechanical series of sensible appearances, there is nothing to suggest . . . the indissoluble connection of one event with another, any more than in the flies of a summer" (2.260).[32] But Hazlitt refuses to follow the Kantians in concluding that Hume's critique, by relocating the source of the idea of causality in the mind, had thereby reestablished the freedom of the will as its own self-activating cause, essentially independent of the processes of nature: "He [Kant] sets out with urging the indispensable necessity of answering Hume's argument on the origin of our idea of cause and effect; and because he can find no answer to this argument in the experimental philosophy, he affirms, that this

THE METAPHYSICIAN: MIND AND NATURE

idea *must* be 'a self-evident truth, contained in the first forms or categories of the understanding'; that is, the thing must be as he would have it, whether it is so or not" (16.124). Hazlitt contends that we derive "the idea of cause" neither from sense-perception nor from rational abstraction but from our own self-activity (and this is what Kant was really saying, too, according to some interpretations): "We do not get this idea from the outward changes which take place in matter, but from the exertion of it in ourselves. Whoever has stretched out his hand to an object must have had the feeling of power" (2.119). And Hazlitt goes on to insist that unless the will's self-conscious "power" is conceived as an "original" idea cognate with "the sense of pleasure or pain," and therefore as distinct from yet continuous with correlative "power" in nature, we cannot "avoid being driven into an absolute scepticism with regard to cause and effect" (2.260).

Yet Hazlitt is much less persuasive when he argues that by preserving the principle of "necessity," that is, of regularity and "law," in the moral world no less than in the physical world, he is also preserving an effective freedom of moral choice for the individual. He was certainly right to protest the false opposition of a spiritual freedom to a mechanical determinism—a dilemma which resulted, he thought, from the gradual "sliding" of the term "necessity" from its "original, philosophical meaning" as "the regular succession of cause and effect" into its popular and "practical" sense as a synonym for irresistible force or inescapable circumstance. Here Hazlitt follows an American thinker he greatly admired, Jonathan Edwards, in arguing that the "chain" of antecedents and consequents in human actions bears no resemblance to "gates of brass and bars of iron."[33] To believe that every determination of the will is a "necessary consequence of preceding causes" is, indeed, to believe in "the certainty of the event"—that it could not have been otherwise, given the same antecedents. But this "certainty" should not be confused with a "fixed fate" operative from the beginning of the process, or with a force that is "irrefragable" and "foreign to the will itself." To say that the outcome of human action depends upon its antecedents is only to say that it "depends upon the exercise of choice" as among its causes; it follows from "the concurrence of certain powers of an agent in the production of that event." Thus to believe in "moral necessity" is not to leave the mind "the sport of external impulses" but merely to acknowledge the empirically manifest truth that the will cannot act "without regard to motives"; for "motives do not act upon it simply or absolutely but according to the dictates of the understanding or the bias of the will." Nor is the principle of moral responsibility being called in doubt by this view of "necessity." "To the idea of moral responsibility, it is not necessary that the agent should be the sole or absolutely first cause of the evil. . . . An agent is the author of any evil, when without him, that is, without something peculiar and essential to his disposition and character, it would not exist" (2.266–70).

Most advocates of free will would not, I think, agree with Hazlitt's confident assertion that this argument preserves "liberty of choice" as well as "liberty of action." Hobbes, Spinoza, and Locke— from all of whom Hazlitt claims to be borrowing—had each argued in their various ways that the freedom to act as one wills to act is not the same as, and does not imply, the freedom to choose one course of action rather than another.[34] But by "freedom of choice" Hazlitt means, it turns out, no more than "the exercise of choice" (2.258)—something very close to what Hobbes had described as "deliberation," the power of the will to become conscious of its own given motives, to discover what it really wants to do and to decide whether or how one's desires can be realized in given circumstances. The will is "free," Hazlitt writes in the *Prospectus,* "in as far as it is not the slave of external impressions, physical impulses, or blind senseless motives. It is free, as the body is free, when it is not subject to a power out of itself . . ." (2.118). Hazlitt, in short, is not grounding moral responsibility on a subjective freedom of the mind to shape its own ends, but is rather reestablishing the principle of Liberty—both moral and political—on the responsibility of the will to know its own "necessity" and accept itself for what it is. Whether this bondage of the will to the self can be credited as in any sense a title to "freedom" must depend on whether the maintenance of individuality can be conceived as itself an end inherent in man's being—a determination of nature rather than of variable circumstance. The issue is that raised by the last dogma in the decalogue Hazlitt imputes to "the modern philosophy": "That there is no such thing as *genius,* or a difference in the natural capacities or dispositions of men, the mind . . . becoming whatever it is from circumstances" (20.76). Hazlitt does not exclude temporal circumstance from playing a part in the formation of character, but he believes the main determinant of the will to be the force of "constitutional bias," or, more accurately, the internal adjustment, mediated by imagination, of the self to its given organic "character"—of mind to body and of body to mind (see 12.230 ff.) Thus he does not deny that the "original character" of the self as a body belongs equally to the order of "physical necessity"; and he recognizes that to prove his paradox that freedom is grounded in "necessity" he must find a way of arguing that bodies, too, as bodies, are "free" in nature's order—that "liberty in the most extended and abstract sense is applicable to material as well as voluntary agents" (2.256).

In predicating an analogue to freedom in the physical world Hazlitt was perhaps influenced more than he knew by new scientific doctrines—possibly first learned from Priestley at Hackney College—which had begun to challenge the dominion of Newtonian mechanics by conceiving of nature's energies, no longer as "matter in motion," but as powers acting through monad-like "centers" of force (as in crystals, for example, or in the newly discovered genera of microorganisms).[35] "Every thing," Hazlitt wrote in a late essay, "has a center of its own round which it moves" (17.264)—a remark which clearly suggests that the "absolute impulse" he ascribes to physical things (1.73) is not to be confused with a mechanical inertia. He had been too deeply schooled in Newton, however, to abandon the language of the Newtonian laws of motion (for example, "action and reaction"); nor did he need to abandon this idiom, for the "free agency" he wishes to find in physical things is not a self-originating spontaneity but an "active" freedom in all bodies to move consistently with their own impulses and properties. In both material and animate nature, "anything is so far active as it modifies and reacts upon the original impulse; it is passive in as far as it neither adds to, nor takes from that original impulse, but merely has a power of receiving and continuing it." Even physical action is seldom wholly mechanical—is seldom the inertia of billiard balls propelling each other—but depends upon "cooperation." All effects in nature are modified by the "inherent qualities" of the things acting or being acted upon, and "what the difference of form is to the stone, the difference of disposition is to the mind." The mind in its individual body is no less subject than purely physical bodies to external pressures, but, having its own distinctive inertia, it actively contributes "the positive determinate tendency or the additional impulse to the production of any effect." The human will cannot pretend to "self-motion"; like any other cause in nature, its power produces distinctive effects only "in consistency with other things" (2.268–70).

As an attempt to adumbrate the "principle" of all causation in nature, "the general law to which all things are by their nature subject" (2.266), this has the clear limitations of its abstraction, and a logical positivist today might find semantically naïve this conjuring with "active" and "passive." But in an age when our philosophers of science are prepared to credit electrons with something like free will, we may at least grant that Hazlitt has accomplished his main purpose—which was less to establish transcendent moral powers for the will than to make credible a dynamic, non-mechanical continuity of "power" between man and the cosmos. And whatever pitfalls may lurk in this attempt to reconcile the claims of freedom and universal order, the objections to be brought against it should be recognized as the classical objections which have always met its more systematic prototype in philosophy—Spinoza's vision of nature as a system of parallel modalities of thought and extended substance. While Hazlitt seems to have rejected Spinoza's pantheism as "spectral" (11.33), he has nothing but praise for that philosopher's "exact and beautiful demonstration" of "philosophical necessity"; and he expresses this praise by quoting (or misquoting) the most famous lines of Wordsworth's *Tintern Abbey* Ode, whose vision of "a motion and a spirit" interfused in nature was itself an inspiration to Hazlitt, and for which, indeed, he is trying in this lecture to provide a philosophical gloss (2.268, 20.60). Another influence confirming essentially the same world-view came from Tucker, who speculated that just as the mind may be conceived as extended through the body, so a "mundane soul," endowed with creative power but not itself the Creator, might be conceived as pervading the universe, all objects and lives in nature having their being in and through this energizing spirit, just as all ideas of natural objects exist in and through the individual mind. And that Hazlitt consciously envisions the ultimate unity of nature in terms not unlike these precedents is clear from a recently discovered letter of his to the *Monthly Magazine,* 27 (1809), 19. There he suggests that "thought is a primary, distinct, essential quality of some substance"—of "some ultimate principle or substance" which remains "entirely unknown and undefined," and in which the properties of matter may also be "supposed to inhere." [36]

What Hazlitt continually fails to ask, however, is whether this vision of cosmic nature does not call into question his earlier vision of human nature—and specifically his former descriptions of the body-mind relationship in "imagination." For where now are we to locate "the unity of consciousness" (1.130)? Are we to find that unity in "the momentum of the will" (1.81), as Hazlitt calls it, which seeks to express the needs of "original character" (12.236), the given passional "bias" of the individual body-mind and its ongoing organic processes? Or does that unity inhere in the "idea"-forming power of generic mind, of consciousness itself, which alone can "comprehend" sensations and unify successive moments of experience? There is no doubt how Hazlitt in earlier years would have answered our question: "To perceive relations . . . belongs only to one mind, or spirit, the mind that is in man, which is the centre in which all his thoughts meet, and the master-spring by which all his actions are governed. . . . The mind of man alone is relative to other things . . ; it does not therefore represent the truth by being sensible of one thing but many things (for nature, its object, is manifold) . . ." (1.73). But now compare a later statement, where ideas, although still said to "govern" the will, are no longer sovereign: "The will selects the impressions by which it chooses to be governed, with great dexterity and perseverance" (12.236). Here is emphatic recognition of the "unconscious" factor in motivation—of an expressive, conative function of consciousness which cannot be defined by its cognitive activity. And it is this vision of the force of inward "passion," of the imperious "genius," or "original character," of the self in all creative and expressive acts, which is increasingly to govern Hazlitt's own sense of the power of "mind" in the years after 1812.

75

Although his Unitarian conscience would keep him from confessing the inconsistency in these two versions of the will, Hazlitt does try to accommodate the latent contradiction—to resolve as "natural" the conflicting tendencies of body and mind. He first reveals his growing awareness that man is not only a "compound" (20.349) but a "contradictory" being in this comment in a political essay (on Burke) in 1807, which also stands as his first explicit challenge to one of his father's mythic assumptions: "It is said, I know, that the truth is *one;* but to this I cannot subscribe, for it appears to me that truth is *many.* There are as many truths as there are things and causes of action and contradictory principles at work in society" (7.308). Hazlitt, however, still seems able to contemplate this pluralistic diversity of conflict with equanimity because—or so it would appear from these words—he can still believe that the essential conflict in man is not a struggle of mind with itself but of the "bias" of one mind with that of others. And the lecturer of 1812, still evidently sharing this belief, could therefore readily mistake freedom of action for freedom of choice: mind is still seen as transforming the "impulses" of individual body into generic "ideas"; change or enlarge the fund of ideas, improve the "understanding," provide new "motives" for "bias," and the will of the self is progressively liberated from its original confines. In thus trying vainly to make "motives" continuous in the will with "ideas"—to apply the same logic, the same "principles" to the world of thought and the world of action—Hazlitt's "intellectual philosophy" came to grief. In his theory of perception he had succeeded in resolving, more or less cogently, the Enlightenment dualism of mind and matter, but in his concern to establish at the same time a potential for moral transcendence in the self, he had restored—had even widened—that dualism in the life of the individual will, with the result that he was now in danger of losing precisely those insights into the organically sympathetic nature of consciousness that had been his inspiration, at least since 1798. At all crucial points Hazlitt's analysis of consciousness supports the inference, notwithstanding his own interpretation, that the difference between body and mind is *not,* or cannot be equated with, the difference between organic individuality and generic transcendence. We have seen throughout his analysis that mind is generic *because* it is individual, that is, organically indivisible from sense experience, and conversely, that experience becomes individuated because that is the generic function of consciousness: its function is not to rule over passion, to "govern" the ego or "direct" its will, but to mediate between the various processes of organic becoming, of "necessity." And if that is the nature and function of mind, is it not possible, then, that the process of the will's becoming is not merely one of "action and reaction" but itself one, necessarily, of conflict and "contradiction"? No longer are the antagonists in man essentially ethical adversaries, "reason" and "passion," two powers opposed because different in kind; rather, these opposites must now be seen as two reciprocally dynamic modes of the same vital unity in the self. The process of their relation now becomes a dialectic of powers—of the power of thought in necessary reaction from or against its conscious origins in the limited sense experience of a finite self, and of the will of self in its given "character" reacting against the mind's necessary "abstraction" from its being as a self—the conflict, in short, of an imagination inescapably at war with, even while it continues to express, its passional will. "Man is an intellectual animal," Hazlitt would write in an aphorism of 1823, "and therefore *an everlasting contradiction to himself*. His senses centre in himself, his ideas reach to the end of the universe; so that he is torn in pieces between the two, without a possibility of its ever being otherwise" (9.192; my italics).

But I am getting too far ahead of my story in citing this specimen of his later attitudes, for the pessimism haunting these words is only rarely foreshadowed in the 1812 *Lectures*. Nevertheless some apprehension of this insuperable "contradiction" is, I suspect, responsible—even though it seems not to have occurred in one decisive episode—for Hazlitt's surrender of his philosophical ambitions. The believer in "the intellectual philosophy" does not, of course, disappear, but we shall find him steadily shifting the ground of his faith to accord with his increasing recognition of the "contradiction" in man as dynamic. It is really no paradox to suggest that only Hazlitt's resistance to this recognition made the recognition possible; and the resistance therefore continues, or periodically returns, though it is to change its literary form: the ritual voice of the Dissenter's "abstraction" readily modulates from philosophical polemic into the rhetoric of the partisan journalist (and indeed, as we shall soon see, this transition was already in progress several years before, with the appearance of Hazlitt as political pamphleteer). We must therefore learn to distinguish, although we can never entirely separate, Hazlitt's personal pessimism from his rhetorical invectives against "modern" degeneration, especially when the latter despair becomes a lament for the decline of "reason" and the general loss of faith in the unanimity of "truth." Such complaints betray the accents of the Unitarian moralist who identifies the cause of Liberty with conscious "principle," with "benevolence," and seldom do such accents speak for the vitalist in Hazlitt, who loves and values intensity of "passion," and who would learn at last to find a new kind of hope for man in the dialectic of the will's conflicts. The chastened "metaphysician" of the Revolution, committed to the vision of his *Essay,* could only stand on the shore of this darker "nature" and exclaim: "Spirit of contradiction! When wilt thou cease to rule over sublunary affairs, as the moon governs the tides? Not till the unexpected stroke of a comet throws up a new breed of men and animals from the bowels of the earth; nor then neither, since it is included in the very idea of all life, power, and motion" (19.303).

Chapter Three

Imagination and the Worlds of Power

HAZLITT closed the last of his lectures on philosophy with an Oriental fable, which he thought summed up admirably the pleasures and pains of a life of contemplation. In a forest in ancient Hindustan there once lived a monkey, whose soul had formerly occupied a human body. He had been a Brahmin, "skillful . . . in all abstruse learning," and in order to continue his studies in solitude, retired to a cave on the banks of the Jumna, where, with the passing of time, having "wandered too far from the abode of the social virtues," he neglected his ablutions and declined to "a condition below humanity." Even in his monkeyhood, retaining all his love of abstruse research, he continued to dwell apart from his fellows—and "sojourned in this wood from youth to age, regardless of everything, save *cocoanuts and metaphysics!*" "I too," Hazlitt concluded, "should be very well contented to pass my life like this monkey, did I but know how to provide myself with a substitute for cocoanuts" (20.51–52; Wardle, p. 129).

Perhaps no one else in the scanty audience that evening shared Henry Crabb Robinson's awareness of how painfully apposite the fable was as an allegory of the lecturer's own life. Hazlitt's wilderness had been the solitude of Salisbury Plain; his cave, the cottage at Winterslow where he had been living, "a willing exile," since his marriage in 1808; and his "condition below humanity" the poverty, obscurity, and alienation that he increasingly felt to be his lot in the world. In late 1807 Lamb and Joseph Hume contrived the grim jest of drawing up for Hazlitt, then living in brooding seclusion in London, his obituary; and Hazlitt's marriage in the following year, which moved Lamb to uncontrollable laughter at the wedding, is perhaps best explained as a belated attempt to return to "the abode of the social virtues." He had hoped then to enjoy a rustic domestic life, alternately painting and pursuing his philosophical studies; but this way of life proved as unrewarding to the spirit as it was materially unsuccessful[1] (and what his defeats and frustrations were we shall be considering more specifically a few pages hence). "The worst is," he confessed to his audience by way of comment on his fable, "that much thought on difficult subjects tends, after a certain time, to destroy the natural gaiety and dancing of the spirits; it deadens the elastic force of the mind, weighs upon the heart, and makes us insensible to the common enjoyments and pursuits of life" (20.52).

Here again we may recognize the Boy speaking, not the Prig who so obviously takes the Brahmin's part in the fable—not the Hazlitt who pretended to be content with "cocoanuts and metaphysics." A demand of the soul had lured Hazlitt forth from his speculative solitudes; and his animal need for a livelihood provided the excuse of necessity for this second—and most decisive—act of self-liberation from a life of "cold and dry abstraction" (19.15). In more ways than one, the man who in September of 1812 became Parliamentary reporter for the *Morning Chronicle,* and who then brought his wife and child up to town from Winterslow, was no longer the "metaphysician" we have been observing—no longer the Godwin-inspired "independent intellect" who two decades before had quitted a corrupt Babylon to work out his "metaphysical discovery" in the seclusion of Wem. His love of ideas had not changed; he still relished an abstract argument as much as ever, but the inspiration that once sustained him in his solitude—the surge of hope and confidence in his lonely labors that he had felt at the news of the young Buonaparte's victories in Italy (1.46), or the promise of universal Liberty that as late as 1805 he could still see shining in the evening star above a poor man's cottage, after the victory at Austerlitz (8.13)—these impulses no longer came to him through vernal woods from the distances of an imagined future. The England where his thought had awakened—the nation which through the contending voices of Pitt, Burke, Fox, Paine, and Godwin had championed or anathemized the glowing abstractions of the Revolution—had given way now to the world of the Regency, to a society ruled by the most unphilosophical of politicians and dominated in its sensibility by the most unspeculative of literary celebrities: this was now the England of Liverpool, Castlereagh and Canning, of Scott, Byron, and Cobbett, of Beau Brummell and *Lalla Rookh* and Peacock's *Nightmare Abbey*. A faithful Dissenter would prefer not to admit as much, but Hazlitt was not unresponsive to the dandyish *éclat* of Regency London—not insofar, at least, as that fashion helped to call forth a greater freedom and vividness of expression in his prose, and thus to convince a fledgling journalist that his genius was perhaps not really so "costive" as he had assumed (1.179). "I resolved to turn over a new leaf," he wrote, looking back at the surprise of his first literary successes, "—to take the public at its word, to muster all the tropes and figures I could lay hands on, and, though I am a plain man, never to appear abroad but in an embroidered dress" (17.312).

Regency London had its political compensations, too; for although the most characteristic philosophies of the nineties had perished, the movement for Parliamentary reform was again very much alive—and seemed indeed to be flourishing in the new anti-metaphysical atmosphere, with its emphasis on highly visible, sensuous or "sensible," materially "useful" values. It is therefore no accident that Hazlitt, when he came up to town to look for a house, should choose to reside in the borough of Westminster, or that the house he rented there should be owned by Jeremy Bentham—though the house also had the sentimental attraction of having once belonged to a greater advocate of Liberty, John Milton. James Mill, Hazlitt's predecessor as Bentham's tenant, had not long ago converted his master from a belief in benevolent monarchism to a democratic radicalism; and Bentham's conversion was symptomatic of a general return of

Maidstone Museum and Art Gallery

4. HAZLITT AT ABOUT AGE 35, NEAR THE START OF HIS CAREER AS A
LITERARY JOURNALIST. MINIATURE BY JOHN HAZLITT.

liberal minds to practical reform activity.[2] Renewed hopes for reform had been steadily mounting in Westminster since 1807, when,
thanks to Cobbett's *Political Register* and Francis Place's talent for organization, the radicals succeeded in winning both of the borough's
seats in Parliament. Encouraged by public dissatisfaction with the
war, many Westminster radicals began to hope for a revival in the
House of Commons of something like the old Foxite opposition, a
reform party that might reclaim the Whig tradition in Parliament
from the reactionary spell of Burke. And by 1810 the reformers had

found an influential, if always moderate, voice among the London Whigs in James Perry, Hazlitt's editor on the *Chronicle*, who supported motions for electoral reform in Parliament and who joined in 1812 with old Major Cartwright in founding the first of the Hampden Clubs, which were soon to carry the Westminster message to nearly every city in the kingdom.[3]

Of this movement for reform in its brief years of resurgent hope in the Regency decade—before it was all but crushed in 1819, in the wake of the "Peterloo" massacre and the repressive Six Acts—Hazlitt's was to be the leading literary voice, rivalled only by Cobbett's for tireless vigor and militancy. It is against the background of this movement and its rapid disintegration that we should read *Political Essays* (1819) and, indeed, all of Hazlitt's journalism in the Regency years; for unless this context is kept in view we will continue to confuse the ideas and polemical attitudes of his mature politics with the idealism of the early nineties. One change, of course, has always been recognized—his conversion, and abiding allegiance, unlike most contemporary republicans, to the cause of Napoleon Buonaparte—but even this change has been slighted as aberrant "passion," misunderstood in its larger significance. Hazlitt is the historian's classic example of the English Jacobin turned Buonapartist; and we tend to assume that such a transition necessarily implies a forsaking of principle, or of clear-headed thinking, for infatuated hero worship: is not Buonapartism, after all, the original Chauvinism? Actually what this inference betrays is the venerable Anglo-American habit of assuming that Buonapartism was necessarily a cult of strong-man rule, a sentimentalized "Caesarism" which, by definition, precludes an inherent intellectual dimension, that is, a theoretic commitment to a vision of society, or of political reality, which transcends contemporary circumstance. The fact is that when we examine Hazlitt's "idolatry" in the context of English liberal attitudes in the early years of this decade, we soon discover that Napoleon's regime was often seen and judged, even by lukewarm onlookers, as perhaps the only "enlightened" alternative to the hoary anachronisms that opposed his power. And even the Emperor's campaigns of conquest in the Near East, Spain, the Tyrol, and Russia appeared, however ruthless in specific instances, to be advancing the cause of modern civilization and the rule of cosmopolitan law against the darkest strongholds of superstition and despotic "barbarism." Leigh Hunt was no idolater, and at best ambivalent in his infrequent admirations of Buonaparte, but even he, writing in 1812, believed that the Emperor's most potent "weapon" was his "cultivation of the human intellect."[4]

We get our proper bearings on the question of Hazlitt's altered political attitudes if we look back for a moment to a crucial experience of his in the year 1802—a pivotal year for him as well as for the Lake Poets. The truce established by the Treaty of Amiens in February of that year promised an end to a long and unpopular war; and in the autumn Hazlitt confidently set out, along with many other curious Englishmen, to visit the new France, where he hoped to learn the art of painting in Napoleon's Louvre. In contrast to the impressions of another visitor, Wordsworth, Hazlitt reported a happy and prosperous nation: the First Consul looked to him properly Roman and god-like, and the Revolution, though no longer republican, seemed to be proving its case against a supposedly indispensable *ancien régime*.[5] In the Louvre Hazlitt found the fullest confirmation of his faith, and there for the first time he held almost palpable communion with its essence: "Where the triumphs of human liberty had been, there were the triumphs of human genius" (18.302). We may gauge the impact of Hazlitt's first days in the Louvre if we try to imagine what a lowly young Dissenter must have felt as he found himself walking freely through opulent halls which not long ago had been the exclusive sanctuary of kings and nobles, and which now displayed (at a time, we should note, when museums and public collections of art were still unknown in England) what is still being remembered as one of the greatest collections of paintings (trophies from the French campaigns) ever assembled under one roof:

> You walked for a quarter of a mile through works of fine art; the very floors echoed the sounds of immortality. . . . school called unto school; one great name answered to another. . . . It was the crowning and consecration of art; there was a dream and a glory, like the coming of the Millennium. These works, instead of being taken from their respective countries, were given to the world, and to the mind and heart of man from

whence they sprung. . . . Art, no longer a bondswoman, was seated on a throne, and her sons were kings. The spirit of man walked erect, and found its true level in the triumph of real over factitious claims. Whoever felt the sense of beauty or the yearning after excellence haunt his breast, was amply avenged on the injustice of fortune, and might boldly answer those who asked what there was but birth and title in the world that was not base and sordid—'Look around! These are my inheritance; this is the class to which I belong!' He who had the hope, nay, but the earnest wish to achieve any thing like the immortal works before him, rose in imagination and in the scale of true desert above principalities and powers. . . . Those master-pieces were the true handwriting on the wall, which told the great and mighty of the earth that their empire was passed away—that empire of arrogance and frivolity which assumed all superiority to itself, and scoffed at every thing that could give a title to it. (13.212)

The experience, like the encounter with Coleridge, was a kind of epiphany: it was the moment when a critic's philosophical faith in genius gained the intensity of a personal religion—the Religion of the Louvre, as I shall be calling it, which henceforth is to govern Hazlitt's sense of the meaning and function of all the arts, and is not to be seriously questioned and modified until the last years of his life. Revisiting Paris twenty years later, Hazlitt was to identify his Louvre memories with all his youthful dreams "of fabled truth and good," but the experience really inaugurates, or brings to consciousness, a change in his commitment to "Liberty," a departure from his father's myth that perhaps was prefigured in the "creed" of 1798 but left uncertain at the time in the ambiguities of poetry. The change is now accomplished from a predominantly ethical vision of free men actuated by "benevolence," or by a universal "sympathy," to a vision of men made free by the inspiration of "excellence"—not the excellence of art merely, or of transcendent genius, but of all achievement that springs from the radical powers of an individual and that demands admiration for the passional energies of the self as such, for the human "microcosm" (12.54). As Hazlitt later said of the Louvre, it was "a means to civilize the world" (18.102), but the beauty and truth of genius here revealed was a means to that end only because it was also an end in itself, as the analytical "truth" of his philosophical reasoning could never be. The experience fired his ambition to be a painter; and the ultimate metamorphosis of both metaphysician and painter into Hazlitt the critical essayist may be traced to this dedication in the Louvre to a new, a purely *expressive* dimension of "disinterestedness"—to what Hazlitt would later call the sympathy of "gusto" (4.77 ff.), a power of concrete vision which could reach to the heights or depths of human experience and communicate that universality from self to self without squinting at the consequences for "virtue." And answering to the liberation of his own sense of "truth" from his inherited pieties—something that the charisma of Coleridge could not accomplish for Hazlitt—was a new loyalty born of the Paris experience, although he needed to believe that it was one with his old fidelity to Liberty. A former Godwinite radical here became a sworn Buonapartist (and so, by the way, did Godwin himself at much the same time), and all of Napoleon's crimes of ambition would seem to Hazlitt mere sound and fury in the light of the Emperor's destiny as Defender of the Faith of the Louvre—as the one monarch of the time who himself could wear, and command respect for, the Iron Crown of Genius, the true majesty of humanity.[6]

Nietzsche in *Beyond Good and Evil* was to speak of "the transition of Europe from Rousseau to Napoleon," and speculated that the ascendancy of Buonaparte moved Goethe to reconstruct *Faust* and to reconceive "the whole problem of 'man.' " A not dissimilar transition is observable in Hazlitt during the Napoleonic years;[7] and increasingly after 1805, there is clear evidence in his prose of a decisive turnabout in his attitudes. Napoleon's very successes made necessary some confession of the disparity from earlier expectations: by 1807 Hazlitt could speak critically of Buonaparte's "ambition" and his "scheme of universal empire" (1.165); and although he still regarded this empire as preferable to any visible alternative in Europe, it was now clearly impossible to go on pretending that "LIBERTY, LOVE, GENIUS, VIRTUE" were necessary correlatives of one another, as he had confidently imagined in 1798 (8.186). "Perhaps if the truth were known," he wrote in his *Reply* to Malthus (1807), "I am as little sanguine in my expectations of any great improvement to be made in the condition of human life . . . as Mr. Malthus himself can be"

(1.214). And by 1809 or 1810, when he completed his *Life of Thomas Holcroft* (unpublished till 1816), he was ready to bid a last farewell to the Millennarian dream of the nineties:

> Kind feelings and generous actions there always have been, and there always will be . . . but the hope that such feelings and such actions might become universal, rose and set with the French Revolution. That light seems to have been extinguished forever in this respect. The French Revolution was the only match that ever took place between philosophy and experience; and waking from the trance of theory to the sense of reality, we hear the words *truth, reason, virtue, liberty,* with the same indifference or contempt that the cynic who has married a jilt or a termagant listens to the rhapsodies of lovers. (3.156)

Hazlitt would never again appear so coolly reconciled as he is here to the defeat of his first hopes. But even in the militancy of the Waterloo years, when he preferred to suggest that the Revolution had not perished of its own inadequacies but had been foully murdered in its cradle by the kings of Europe and their minions, he was still careful to warn enthusiasts that the Revolutionary vision of man was irrevocably dead. "We cannot weave over again the airy, unsubstantial dream which reason and experience have dispelled" (4.119). This warning is specifically addressed to Wordsworth, to the author of *The Excursion* (1814); for Hazlitt thought he could still detect a "hint" in that poem that "the triumph of humanity and liberty" might one day be "complete." So "fond" a hope, he insists, is not only visionary but delusory, untrue to nature:

> It is a consummation which cannot happen till the nature of things is changed, till the many become as united as the *one,* till romantic generosity shall be as common as gross selfishness, till reason shall have acquired the obstinate blindness of prejudice, till the love of power and of change shall no longer goad man on to restless action, till passion and will, hope and fear, love and hatred, and the objects proper to excite them, that is, alternate good and evil, shall no longer sway the bosoms and businesses of men. All things move, not in progress, but in a ceaseless round; our strength lies in our weakness; our virtues are built on our vices; our faculties are as limited as our being; nor can we lift man above his nature more than above the earth he treads. (4.119)

87

It is impossible, I think, to overrate the importance of this statement for an understanding of Hazlitt's criticism, both political and literary, in the Regency years. First of all, it shows us undeniably that the basis of his politics is no longer, even in imagination, Utopian. He is not merely lowering his expectations but renouncing the vision of "perfectibility" as a viable ideal; indeed, we shall find him impugning that ideal as a blinding hindrance to the one political end that remains feasible—the practical emancipation of society from oppressive, and specifically from feudal, institutions. Secondly, the theme of "contradiction" we have seen emerging in Hazlitt's philosophy—the idea of a conflict between two modes of the organic principle in man's nature, between the mind of the individual in its "ideal" world of abstract knowledge or reflective consciousness, and the mind of the same self, or body-mind, as it expresses its "original character" in action, or in passional reaction of the will upon the mind's sympathies—here for the first time this conflict is shown to have unavoidable consequences for politics. Hazlitt hereafter insists, against both Wordsworth and Coleridge—and in contrast to his own emphasis in the previous decade—that "the intellectual and the moral faculties of man are different" (19.15), are not to be identified as one. No longer is the will to be defined by its "ideal" objects, or by a sympathetic consciousness of objects assumed to be continuous, through pleasurable associations, with those ideals, but by its conative character—by its expression, through imagination, of an inward necessity of "passion," which all objects in experience serve mainly to "excite" (20.46). And if we ask what remains of Hazlitt's myth of modern history after this transformation of premises, we shall be forced to recognize that he is repudiating here much more than his father's optimism; he is really disavowing the myth, embraced by nearly all liberal thinkers after Locke and Rousseau, that man is "naturally good"—that human evils are not inherent in man's nature but are wholly the products of experience, of alterable circumstances, prejudices and institutions. Man's will, as Hazlitt is henceforth to describe it, is subject to conflict not only with the world and with other wills but with the "mixed" motives of his own passional being; and this subjection of human personality to the "innate perversity" (12.136) of its passions is, as he expressly says elsewhere, the "original sin" of every man (12.233, 348).[8]

More specifically, by a force of "original sin" Hazlitt means "the love of power"—"a love of power in the mind independent of the love of good" (12.348)—and this idea of a primal power-urge in man proves to be a more central and positive principle in Hazlitt's mature criticism than the brief allusion to it in the above passage suggests. Here is the psychological motive, the novel element in his sense of self, that was born in, or from, his Louvre experience, though the germ of this idea might have been growing in his thought for several years before that episode. Say what we will of Hazlitt's infatuation with Buonaparte, it is, I suspect, to his struggle to reconcile that "idolatry" (his own word for it: 7.10) with his earlier faith in the beneficence of genius that we owe the true originality of his critical attitude toward the problems of society and culture. His faith in Napoleonic "power," however misplaced, coinciding as it did with his own quest for expressive power, gradually forced him to think out afresh the relationship of feeling to imagination, to question the simplicity of his inherited notion of evil, to take a more complex view of "mind" as it "governs" will—and at last to develop a psychology of "power" which would make of this principle of motivation not merely a limiting factor in human possibilities, but itself a new and more credible basis in theory for the modern democratic state.

❦

"Power," wrote Coleridge in 1800, "is the sole object of philosophic attention in man, as in inanimate nature."[9] A novel fascination with "power" was inevitable in an age not only of war and political revolution, but of new class mobilities, of the scientific discovery of unsuspected electrical energies in nature, of the meteoric rise and fall of men and nations, and (in England especially) of rapid industrial and commercial expansion. In such a world all modes of energy came to seem continuous, either in fact or in significance, at least when contrasted with the fixed forms of authority and feudal privilege which seemed opposed to them all. Anyone brought up in the idiom of Biblical prophecy now had little trouble thinking mythically about the continuity of "power": under the one "idea of power" Hazlitt included, not only the idea of cause, but "all that relates to force, energy, weakness, effort, ease, difficulty, impossibility" (2.260). But perhaps it was Wordsworth who gave this word its

greatest breadth and resonance of meaning. In his poems, and especially in *The Prelude,* the political overtones of the word mingle
strangely with scientific, religious, and literary (or, more specifically,
neo-Longinian) associations—as when he speaks of "the great ends
of Liberty and Power," or when he recalls the resurgence of hope
that followed the fall of Robespierre: "To Nature, Power had re-
verted" (*Prelude* xi.32; xii.139). And none of these dimensions of
meaning seem absent from his dictum in 1815 that the mission of the
poet is "to call forth and communicate *power.*" [10] Clearly there is an indefinite suggestion here that all naturally given "power" exists in potential harmony, and that this harmony of energies, as it comes to
consciousness of itself through the mind and will of man, might
someday supplant all coercive, artificially constituted authority as the
ultimate unity of Power destined to govern the world. With one
myth or another of Apocalypse floating in their heads, it is not surprising that the English Romantic theorists uniformly failed to provide lucid explanations of why "power" should tend to form one
"idea" (or one polarity of ideas) in the mind. Hazlitt backed out of
the difficulty by saying that there could be no "formal definition" of
the idea (2.119), and the best that De Quincey could do was to
suggest, in a brief parenthesis, that the continuity of all genuine
"power" in the mind is "deep sympathy with truth." [11]

While "power" in this poetic-rhetorical usage was acquiring nu-
minous or sublime connotations, "the love of power" (Juvenal's *libido
potestatis*) survived as a commonplace phrase of mainly pejorative intention, still colored by its Hobbesian associations of tyrannical will
and jealous-aggressive *amour propre.* Before the rise of Napoleon,
there seemed to be no need in liberal circles to interpret "love of
power" as anything but a familiar derivative of self-interest or the
pleasures of self-love; [12] and the more virulent forms of the pursuit
of power could thus still be regarded as the perverse work of social
"prejudice," deflecting the energies of the will from its "natural" objects of good or happiness. Until 1805 Hazlitt seems not to have
found it necessary to distinguish "power" in any essential way from
motives of good or "truth," and only in what seems a late footnote to
his first book does he recognize the distinction as significant: "The
love of happiness even in the most general sense does not account

for the passions of men. The love of truth and the love of power are, I think, distinct principles of action and mix with, and modify, all our pursuits" (1.85 n.).

These words are prophetic of Hazlitt's future emphasis; but the footnote yields no intimation that these various motives to action naturally tend to conflict as they "mix with" each other. One of the missing lectures of 1812, however (as adapted to a newspaper essay of 1815), deals with just such a conflict in the mind. "The two most predominant principles in the mind," he now writes, "besides sensibility and self-interest, are imagination and self-will, or (in general) the love of strong excitement, both in thought and action." Here is the first indication I can discover in Hazlitt's prose of the term "imagination" being used in a sense other than that which implies a sympathy with "truth" or with organic values of good or pleasure. Once in the *Essay*, it is true, Hazlitt had spoken of "an irritable imagination"; but this irritability was described then as a condition of "uneasiness" brought on by the desires of the bodily "appetites," not as a state of passion induced by a love of power in the will. Hazlitt, moreover, had wished the reader of the *Essay* "to be apprized that I do not use the word *imagination* as contradistinguished from or opposed to reason" (1.45–46). But now, and henceforth in his criticism, it is precisely to motives of feeling distinct from, or averse to, reason—to irrational and sub-rational, not merely to pre-rational feelings—that "imagination" refers, unless context otherwise qualifies his use of the term. And that this change had not come about without some readjustment of his psychological premises is clear from the start of this same essay of 1815, where Hazlitt pauses to make an adverse criticism of Rousseau (hitherto never a philosophical antagonist): "We are seldom masters either of our thoughts or of our actions. We are the creatures of imagination, passion and self-will. Rousseau, in his *Emilius*, proposed to educate a perfectly reasonable man, who was to have passions and affections like other men, but with an absolute control over them. He was to love and be wise. This is a contradiction in terms. Even in the common transactions and daily intercourse of life, we are governed by whim, caprice, prejudice or accident" (20.43–44).

The repudiation of *Émile*, the model of his adolescence, suggests that his new awareness of the conflicts of "passion" came not only from changes in the public world but from vicissitudes of his own "self-will." In Hazlitt's passage from youth to maturity we can distin-. guish no one emotional crisis: nothing like Lamb's resolute confrontation of insanity, or Coleridge's opium-melancholy in a loveless house. With Hazlitt there is only a steady series of rebuffs and frustrations—of small hope-inspiring victories followed by larger defeats, each effort of his will to escape oblivion only plunging him deeper into obscurity and self-doubt. The young painter who returned with sanguine resolve from Paris, convinced that he must surely have learned some of the secrets of the Old Masters, was soon flinging his brush away in despair (though he was often, with much the same results, to pick it up again). In 1807 his *Reply* to Malthus, which he hoped would demolish forever that philosopher's population theory, met with no better reception than his *Essay* two years before, and in 1809 he could complain to Godwin of having "had three books . . . suppressed" (Baker, p. 171)—presumably the *Essay,* the *Reply,* and his projected history of English philosophy. The "Sabine subsistence from the booksellers," which, as Coleridge in 1803 described Hazlitt's life plan, was to sustain him "in nursing up his genius" for its true fruition now seemed, as the years passed, to have become itself his destiny. The analytical editor of Tucker's philosophy graduated from that study to become the editor of an anthology of Parliamentary speeches and the compiler of an English grammar. Nor did Hazlitt's personal life bring compensation or consolation. The well-known escapade in the Lakes which brought to a violent close his visit to the poets in 1803—when, after spanking a girl who scorned his advances, he narrowly escaped an avenging village mob—had its ludicrous aspects that did not elude Lamb, but it must surely have confirmed Hazlitt in the conviction of his incurable lovelessness. This suspicion might have been endured without undue pain if a metaphysician of "sympathy" had not also been led to suspect that he was thought scarcely more amiable in other company. "Hazlitt, how easily raised," complained Coleridge, not without cause, "to rage and hatred self-projected!" Other observers managed to discover in Hazlitt's countenance something not unlike the "expression of kindness" which Coleridge claimed never to find there, but the complaint does help us to understand the ambivalent motives which drove the lonely Hazlitt, after a period of brooding seclusion relieved by occasional "wenching," into his ill-fated marriage in 1808. And as each year thereafter brought further proof of the folly of his dreams of happiness, a worshipper of Genius would have counted all the more heavily on his lingering hopes for "fame"—for an undisputed recognition of intellectual achievement, clear alike to himself and to the world. But when at last a measure of fame did come to him in the years after 1814, the sense of his tormented impotence as a creative will never wholly left him. Even in the full tide of his celebrity as a writer and critic, he complained bitterly to the young painter William Bewick, "I can literally do *nothing*" (Landseer, 1.136).[13]

The effect on Hazlitt's thought of this lesson of his self-experience was twofold: while it reawakened his Calvinist awareness of an evil bondage in human passion and robbed him of his faith in the moral regeneration of the world, it also brought him the conviction that "the love of power" is inseparable from the will to live. It is significant that his first purely literary work, a series of essays appearing mainly in the *Examiner* (1813–16) and collected in *The Round Table* (1817), should open with "On the Love of Life," an essay designed to cure the reader of the "vulgar error" of supposing that we love life for its "enjoyments." We are, on the contrary, "attached" to life because "without life there can be no action—no objects of pursuit—no restless desires—no tormenting passions"; and "the vehemence of our passions is irritated, not less by disappointment than by the prospect of success." Only the greatest extremity of suffering can break the will of the self to be and to act: "Passion, imagination, self-will, the sense of power, the very consciousness of our existence, bind us to life, and hold us fast in its chains, as by a magic spell, in spite of every other consideration" (4.1–3). This version of "disinterestedness," however, while it still echoed the *Lyrical Ballads* theme of "indestructible" impulses in human nature,[14] was no longer one with Hazlitt's original affirmation of "nature": he was now prepared to acknowledge that the conflict between good and evil is rooted in the nature of the will itself, not merely in the conflict of an instinctive love of "happiness" with the evils of the social world. The belief in "perfectibility" encouraged by "the modern philosophy," a doctrine which Hazlitt through most of his youth had clung to while attacking its other dogmas, had now to be abandoned along with all other fond illusions fostered by the pleasure-pain psychology of Lockean liberalism. "The substitution," he wrote in 1817, "of right for might, even in theory, is among the refinements and abuses of modern philosophy."

Where Hazlitt found this illusion most potently exposed, "without equivocation or disguise" (4.288), was in Shakespeare; and it was, I suspect, largely under the tutelage of Shakespeare that Hazlitt sometime after 1805 completes his psychology of the self, learning from England's greatest master of the passions what might be called the principles of unconscious "reaction" in the mind, as distinct from morally self-conscious *Principles of Human Action*. And with this change from a philosophical ideal to a dramatic model of "truth," Hazlitt's conception of genius and imagination gradually ceased to draw inspiration from the precedents of Wordsworth and Coleridge. No less than the poets, Hazlitt had learned to distinguish the visionary perspectives of youth from political reality; and far more clearly than they he had learned to say farewell to the vision of "joy" as definitive of nature's "power" in, or over, man. It is thus by no means mere happenstance that Hazlitt, when he comes to insist most strongly on the irreducibility of "the love of power," should be moved to recollect a dispute with Coleridge. The poet had asked him whether he had ever known "a child of a naturally wicked disposition," and Hazlitt returned this answer, which made Coleridge laugh incredulously:

Yes . . . there was one in the house with me that cried from morning to night, *for spite*. . . . The author of the 'Rime of the Ancient Mariner' (who sees farther into such things than most people) could not understand why I should ever bring a charge of *wickedness* against an infant before it could even speak, merely for squalling and straining its lungs a little. If the child had been in pain or in fear, I should have said nothing, but it cried only to vent its passion and alarm the house, and I saw in its frantic screams and gestures that great baby, the world, tumbling about in its swaddling clothes, and tormenting itself and others for the last six thousand years! The plea of ignorance, of folly, of grossness, or selfishness makes nothing either way: it is the downright love of pain and mischief for the interest it excites, and the scope it gives to an abandoned will, that is the root of all evil, and the original sin of human nature. There is a love of power in the mind independent of the love of good, and this love of power, when it comes to be opposed to the spirit of good, and is leagued with the spirit of evil to commit it with greediness, is wickedness. (12.347–48)

Coleridge, of all people, should not have missed the point beneath Hazlitt's paradox; for the problem is one dramatized in all the "magical poems" of Coleridge, and perhaps most dramatically in the Ancient Mariner's *acte gratuite,* his shooting of the albatross. We can all understand, of course, that we love our own energies and the act of their expression, and often to the disregard of everything else; but it is among the greatest of enigmas that this impulse should not only prove stronger than the love of good but should so often become the urge to deny or deliberately destroy the good, as when the Mariner knowingly aims his crossbow at the bird of good omen. The problem was no matter of abstract speculation for the opium-driven, guilt-haunted Coleridge, who dearly earned his title as the first English discoverer (though Blake had really been there before him) of the unconscious mind—of thought, that is, that moves in images, obeys another logic than reason, and comes to the surface of consciousness only in dreams. Hazlitt undoubtedly profited from Coleridge's exploration of dreams; but again it is the difference from Coleridge—or at least from the poet's later theory[15]—which best defines his own view of "power" in imagination. If Coleridge is the English precursor of Jung, Hazlitt clearly anticipates the Freudian analysis of dreams, as this passage sufficiently attests:

We are not hypocrites in our sleep. The curb is taken off from our passions, and our imagination wanders at will. When awake, we check these rising thoughts, and fancy we have them not. In dreams, when we are off our guard, they return securely and unbidden. We may make this use of our sleeping metamorphosis, that we may repress any feelings of this sort that we disapprove in their incipient state, and detect, ere it be too late, an unwarrantable antipathy or fatal passion. Infants cannot disguise their thoughts from others; and in sleep we reveal the secret to ourselves. (12.23)

If we allow for some vestigial rationalism, here is a remarkable anticipation of the Freudian concepts of repression and regression, notwithstanding Hazlitt's unawareness here of a similarly repressive censorship, a subtler "disguise," in the dream process itself. Elsewhere Hazlitt seems even to have caught a glimpse of the blind, anarchic Freudian *Id:* he speaks of "the *ferae naturae* principle that is within us" (20.323), and of "that silent operation of the mind which preys internally upon itself, and works the decay of its powers the more fatally, because we dare not give it open and avowed scope" (12.353). Dimly prefigured in these words is the psychoanalytical premise that all desire which is felt to contradict "the reality principle," or which, repressed by the censorious superego, is unable to find sufficient release through sublimation, will not be content with expression in dream images but will vent itself in symptomatic acts of aggression against others and may finally be turned against the ego itself.[16] And Hazlitt's account of how this comes about—of how emotion becomes compulsive—again proves to have more than a few echoes in Freud's theory of neurosis. Just as Hazlitt came to recognize that pleasure and sympathy with objects of "good" could not explain all motives of imagination, so Freud was forced to modify his early theory of dreams as "wish-fulfillment" when he came to analyze certain traumatic dreams (of soldiers suffering from shell shock), in which the dreamer kept returning to the moment of shock, instead of escaping from or remitting the pain. What Freud knew as the problem of "repetition compulsion" is being similarly described—and explained—in Hazlitt's analysis of the experience of a young girl who, locked up in a room with a corpse and unable to escape, at last flung herself in desperation upon it. Hazlitt comments: "The progress of the passion does not seem to have been that of diminishing or removing the terror. . . . but of carrying this terror to its height from an intense and irresistible impulse, overcoming every other feeling." Similarly, other and more common instances of "the power of fascination" (20.45–47)—the self-inflicted tortures of melancholy, the flirting with danger, the primitive worship of bloody idols, the abject trust in charms and curses, the criminal's twisted pride in the confession of guilt—these, too, cannot be reduced to motives of "inclination" or to the wish to dispel "uneasiness." Such phenomena can only be explained as actions of a mind "possessed" by "some object of a disturbed imagination" and from which it "cannot well escape" except by in some way "grasping the phantom" of its anxiety (9.190)—by identifying the irresistible power of the obsessive object with the power of the mind's own activity, whether by a desperate and willful act of passion, or by some "extravagant" intensification of the object in the mind through associative processes of imagination. However imprecisely phrased, this is essentially the logic of neurotic emotion as Freud describes it. Whether in dreams or life, all compulsive anxieties are, in Freud's analysis, efforts of the mind to "bind" some tension, however painfully or mistakenly—are "attempts at restoring control of the stimuli by developing apprehension, the pretermission of which caused the traumatic neurosis."[17]

No more than Freud does Hazlitt wish to confine such behavior to pathological cases; unconscious "fascination" with power is not for him a peculiar "madness" but is present to some degree in all passion and all imagination. "The soul," he writes in 1824, "by reason of its weakness, is an aggregating and exclusive principle; it clings obstinately to some things, and violently rejects others" (11.8–9). And in some remarks that perhaps were taken from the 1812 *Lectures,* Hazlitt more fully explains this paradoxical genesis of the power-impulse from the "weakness" of the self. Both "muscular and voluntary power" are, he observes, originally perceived and felt as one power—as when, for example, a child first extends a hand to an object (2.260), or discovers the infinite thrills of lung power. Presumably it is when (and here I am explicating the process by inference from Hazlitt's scattered observations) this sense of power, which at first is simple delight in energy, outruns in imagination or desire the means of power as limited by the given capacities of the self, by "original character," that the love of power is born from the sense of weakness, emerging only then as distinct in motivation from pleasure or "good." "Men and all animals," Hazlitt was later to write, agreeing with an observation of the painter James Barry, "are malicious and cruel in proportion as they are impotent" (18.126)—or, as he might have added, to the degree that they *feel* themselves to be wanting in power. And to the degree that the individual continues to

97

feel frustration of his powers, self-love becomes one with "self-will," alienated from others by "the spirit of contradiction" and increasingly tempted to revert, as does love of power in the animal world, to "the *ferae naturae* principle that is within us and always craving its prey to hunt down" (20.323).

How far have we come, with that last remark, from the youthful discoverer of "natural benevolence"! Yet Hazlitt's rejection of the myth of "natural goodness"—of the belief that man is naturally free of evil—is still not to be confused with "original sin" as it is traditionally understood.[18] For in predicating a tendency in compulsive passion to identify with evil, he still insists that the "love" of the power-impulse is for the power in evil, not for the evil itself, which the mind continues to know only by contrast with values of good. We do not, he insists (5.7), "like what we loathe" (and here, we may note, is the difference from the idea, so fashionable today, of a primal sadism or "blood-lust" in man): that is, we do not love our hatreds as we love our happiness, nor does imagination cease to have a sense of evil *as* evil even when the will learns to fear or hate its own weakness more. "Power" and "good," pleasure and truth retain their distinctness as motives; their involution in each other is, in Freudian language, "economic," a "displacement" of energies, and the mind never willingly accepts this disorientation, which is disturbing precisely because it is resisted by the mind's unconscious memory of its original condition. Hazlitt is therefore not contradicting himself when he describes as "the love of power" both the strength of a "masterless passion" and the conscious strength whereby the will subdues a weakness: in both cases some "strong excitement" of feeling is being identified, whether through imagination or overt action, with a power of active intensification in the mind itself as it struggles to bring its unconscious and conscious impressions into functional accord, which is the precondition of all voluntary pursuit of the good. Even when imagination seems to be yielding helplessly to an object of fear or hatred, the mind is still actively exercising its sense of power—of the only power that may remain to it, intensification of the passion itself. And whether this "sympathy with power" will pass into a conscious strength of will or remain a "torment" of weakness will depend on the degree to which the passion succeeds in realizing, either in thought or action or in both together, "conscious power" over itself. Hazlitt may thus be said to be supporting the great Freudian paradox that, in Lionel Trilling's words, "we are all ill in the service of health": neurosis is "the form of the mind's dynamics,"[19] and the process by which the self becomes obsessed or inhibited is always potentially the same as the process by which the ills of the psyche may be cured or creatively transcended. Hazlitt similarly believes that all passion contains the potential of a homeopathic cure in this movement toward intensity—a tendency to restore the mind to "nature" by lashing awake its vital energies in a dramatic confrontation of its disturbance:

> Not that we like what we loathe; but we like to indulge our hatred and scorn of it; to dwell upon it, to exasperate our idea of it by every refinement of ingenuity and extravagance of illustration; to make it a bugbear to ourselves, to point it out to others in all the splendour of deformity . . . to arm our will against it, to know the worst we have to contend with, and to contend with it to the utmost. . . . We do not wish the thing to be so; but we wish it to appear such as it is. For knowledge is conscious power; and the mind is no longer . . . the dupe, though it may be the victim, of vice or folly (5.7).[20]

Hazlitt is talking here, however, mainly of the appeal of tragic drama and "impassioned" poetry, and he does not stint from recognizing that the same "logic of passion" (4.259) which gives imagination in the world of art its power of knowledge over evil also enables man's love of power to sustain and magnify itself as evil in the world. The seed of his future pessimism—and, as we shall learn, of its correction, too—lies in his belief that the love of power is inseparably bound to the sense of weakness, which in turn is ineluctably rooted in the "original character" of the individual. Hazlitt recognizes that external circumstances wield a "prodigious influence" over behavior; and personal conduct, therefore, as distinct from internal feeling, is alterable. But the greatest "force of nature" in man remains the "stamina," the "unconscious bias" of the self: "The mind contrives to lay hold of those circumstances and motives which suit its own bias and confirm its natural disposition, whatever it may be, gentle or rough, vulgar or refined, spirited or cowardly, open-hearted or cunning" (12.230–44).

Yet this version of "original sin," as an inborn fatality of personal character, is still not to be interpreted as a covert surrender to egoism, whether of the old Hobbesian kind or of that variety which still lay over the nineteenth-century horizon. For to admit that all acts of the will, even benevolent acts, are in some degree acts of the love of power is still not to sanction the pursuit of power itself as the intrinsic end or object of the will. Hazlitt's psychology of "self-will" remains in this respect essentially distinct from, though historically akin to, Nietzsche's or Adler's doctrine of "the will to power."[21] Hazlitt, indeed, may sound like their unwilling precursor in his embittered moods (and here, incidentally, is further evidence of his ambivalence toward Buonaparte): "This paltry *self*, looking upon itself as of more importance than all the rest of the world. . . . cannot bear a rival or a superior; despises and tramples on inferiors, and would crush and annihilate all pretensions but its own. . . . The worm puts on the monarch, or the god, in thought and in secret; and it is only when it can do so in fact, and in public, and be the tyrant or idol of its fellows, that it is at ease or satisfied with itself" (16.332–33). But this impulse to superiority is never for Hazlitt an "instinct" of aggressiveness toward another's power; his version of "the *ferae naturae* principle" implies no radical alienation of the self from otherness. He would have agreed heartily with Freud's mockery of Adler's theory: the latter's notion of a child's being originally suspicious or fearful of people—in Freud's paraphrase, "comparing their strength with his weakness, and recognizing in them a danger to his existence"[22]—was not very far removed from the simplistic vision of the ego that Hazlitt had attacked. Like Freud, Hazlitt saw sympathy and power (libido and ego) as dialectically interdependent; and for Hazlitt the lasting consequence of this truth is that the will to power is never intrinsically *against* others but merely *toward* and *over* them. And the wish to have power over others is really the wish to have power over their thoughts and feelings—over their imaginations. For only by this power of "significance" can the strength of even the most egocentric will be brought home to itself: "No man is truly himself, but in the idea which others entertain of him. The mind, as well as the eye, sees not itself, but by reflection from some other thing" (12.117, and see 9.193).

꽃

Once we are aware of Hazlitt's psychology of "power," we may be less puzzled by the paradoxical fact that the erstwhile advocate of "disinterested" imagination is the very same writer who, at the end of the Regency decade, can speak of "that innate love of inequality and injustice, which is the favourite principle of the imagination" (8.115).

The intrusion of political language into Hazlitt's speculation has always been a cue (or excuse) for scholars not to take such passages seriously;[23] and since many of his disparagements in this decade of "poetry" and "imagination" are written at the same time that he is praising the powers of poetry in his literary criticism, it is tempting to regard these aspersions simply as blasts of rhetoric aimed at, or provoked by, the political "apostasy" of the Lake Poets. Yet Hazlitt never recants the ideas expressed in his attacks on his former mentors, although he would, in *The Spirit of the Age* (1825), apologize to Wordsworth for certain excesses and personal misrepresentations (11.94). "No man has lashed political apostasy with more severity," wrote William Hone, the radical bookseller who published *Political Essays* (1819), in a pamphlet puff for his book;[24] and that violent "lashing," which from the start became Hazlitt's *cachet* as a partisan journalist, has remained ever since as the stigma of notoriety attending his political criticism. Today his "vendetta" (as it is commonly called) against the poets is most often approached in a literary-biographical context, and in that perspective the accuser's vindictive aggression is likely to seem no less, if not more, reprehensible than the poets' sins of inconstancy to an abstract political principle. But if we restore the charge of "apostasy" to its original context in the columns of the *Examiner,* we learn soon enough that what seems violence done by partisan journalism to the cause of poetry is really motivated by a greater concern for the cause of literature itself, and especially by concern for the independence of genius from all "power" but that of its own conscience.

From the time of its founding in 1808, the Sunday weekly edited by John and Leigh Hunt had prided itself on its critical freedom from all ties of "party." And it is this character which explains why in early 1814 Hazlitt is to be found transferring his talents to the *Examiner*—as he had, somewhat earlier, to another liberal journal, John Scott's *Champion*—from the *Morning Chronicle*, whose devotion to the cause of reform was always less reliable than its solicitude for Whig interests in Parliament. The *Examiner*'s editors vigorously defended the eighteenth-century English tradition—whose heroes included, as Leigh Hunt remarked, Whigs and Tories alike—of the necessary independence of literature from both aristocratic and "court" (Crown or ministerial) patronage. And on this basis the Hunts launched in 1813 their attack on Robert Southey's appointment as Poet Laureate—an attack that had really begun some months before his nomination was known, with a ridiculing of the anachronistic office itself: the Laureateship, by reducing a poet to "panegyrist," serves only to "make genius contemptible."[25] The issue of principle had thus been securely established well before Hazlitt enters the fray; and he makes that entry at a time when his motives cannot be reduced to the vengeful passion of a defeated Buonapartist (Napoleon's Empire being at that time, although seriously threatened, still firmly intact). For it now appears that Hazlitt strikes his first blow as early as April of 1813, and not in prose but in verse—in four doggerel quatrains (two of which will suffice to quote here), published first in the *Chronicle* and then in the *Examiner,* on Wordsworth's recently announced appointment as Stamp-Distributor for the County of Westmorland:

> When Favour's golden hook is baited,
> How swiftly patriot zeal relaxes;
> In *silent* state see WORDSWORTH seated,
> Commissioner of Stamps and Taxes.
>
> Wordsworth, most artless among Bards,
> Who talk'd of MILTON and of Freedom,
> Scorn'd service purchased by rewards,
> And pitied those who chanced to need 'em.

Now the charge of "apostasy" implied here, we should note, is not that Wordsworth has "changed" his political convictions, or betrayed the French Revolution, or embraced Tory beliefs and prejudices—although that eventuality will be suggested in the next quatrain[26]—but simply that the poet has surrendered the independence by which he formerly held and expressed his convictions; his allegiance as a poet can no longer be given purely and freely to "nature" and "humanity." This for the *Examiner* writers was, and remained, the principal issue in the entire controversy—although the issue of literary independence, that is, the freedom of literary (or, more broadly, intellectual) power from political power, would soon lose its distinct visibility amid the welter of other issues precipitated by the climactic episodes of the war against Napoleon and the restoration of the Bourbon monarchy. Then the temperature of all political debate rises sharply, and Hazlitt's attitudes become more expressly partisan. But even at this time he brings the poets to the bar, not of his own convictions merely, but of principles that they themselves had professed prior to 1814. The nationalistic insurgence against Buonaparte, sparked by the Spanish revolt of 1809, which gave birth briefly to a liberal constitutional monarchy in Spain, had tempted many Englishmen, as Hazlitt said, to imagine "that the hatred of the oppressor was the same thing as the hatred of oppression." Leigh Hunt was himself a convert to the hope, after Napoleon's first downfall (during the Emperor's short-lived exile to the island of Elba), for a new era of peace and freedom; and Hazlitt was perhaps thinking of Hunt's chagrin when he spoke of "romantic admirers of patriot kings" who, after news came of what was actually happening at the Congress of Vienna, "hang their heads and live in hopes of better times" (7.82). And how would Wordsworth, Coleridge, and Southey respond to this reversal of expectations?

The poets who had stood aghast at Napoleon's invasions said nothing as the sovereigns of the Quadruple Alliance renewed the Slave Trade and parcelled out Norway, Germany, Poland, and Italy among themselves, in blind disregard of the spirit of national self-determination which had brought them to the conference table. The author of "The Female Vagrant," the same Wordsworth who had warned Napoleonic France that "by the soul / Only, the Nations shall be great and free," and the same moralist who hailed "Duty" as "stern daughter of the voice of God," now not only failed to protest the massacres of the White Terror at Nîmes (in July 1815) as he gave thanks for the victory at Waterloo, but felt constrained, in his "Ode: 1815," to assure God that "Carnage is Thy Daughter!" The Coleridge who denounced the crimes of "the Corsican upstart" could now—despite a parenthetical lament on the state of affairs in Spain, where Ferdinand, the restored Bourbon king, was reviving the Inquisition—announce that "Providence has disciplined all Europe into sobriety" and that the Bible confirms the *jus divinum* of monarchical government.[27] In 1809 Southey had proudly devoted his talents to the cause of Spanish Liberty, but the Poet Laureate refrained from dedicating a single ode to his former allies, those same Spanish patriots who, as Hazlitt reminded him, were now being "hanged, banished, imprisoned, sent to the galleys, assassinated, tortured" (7.95). Instead, Southey found occasion in 1816 to praise himself, in his *Lay of the Laureate,* for having

> raised the high thanksgiving strain
> Of victory in a rightful cause achieved:
> For which I long had looked and not in vain,
> As one who with firm faith and undeceived,
> In history and the heart of man could find
> Sure presage of deliverance for mankind.
> (Proem, St. 11)[28]

It was this boast of long-suffering and triumphant virtue for the "deliverance of mankind"—a theme heard no less strongly in Wordsworth and, more faintly, in Coleridge—that Hazlitt could not stomach and that called forth his increasingly savage exposure of "apostasy." His virulence, we should note, makes its appearance only in the later months of 1816, when the poets had been given ample opportunity to reconsider their attitudes. From men who had exhibited so sensitive a conscience during the war years, surely some agonized cry at the pain of balancing the claims of moral justice against patriotic loyalties might reasonably have been expected. But instead to proclaim, with all the authority of the humane voice of poetry, that Justice was now returning to the world, that the spirit of Christ was again triumphant, that God had looked upon the "social order" of Europe and had found it good—this is surely not an anomaly to be explained or excused, either then or now, as visionary idealism. Whatever our politics or the degree of our affection for these men, it was, and is, surely the function of criticism to expose and brand in no uncertain terms *le trahison des clercs*—the intellectual sanctioning as just or good of a regime or state of affairs that prevails in society only because it has the power to silence or suborn the mind. That the poets should have represented manifest political evil not only as circumstantially necessary, which was Hazlitt's defense of Buonaparte (see 7.10–12), but as heroic and religious deliverance from evil—this is the stain upon their careers that no amount of time will wash away; and although we may, and should, forgive them this lapse in the light of their services to literature, we should also respect Hazlitt's courage in reminding them, and us, that this is indeed an "apostasy" from principles, a dereliction of literary conscience, and, while forgivable, is not to be forgotten.

Apologists for the poets may at this point reply that Wordsworth, Coleridge, and Southey gave their loyalties not to the status quo but to the existing order only as it represented the continuity of national traditions, which they hoped to revitalize morally. So much, of course, is true; but when we shift the controversy onto this higher ground, we find that we must deal with another of Hazlitt's satiric thrusts. There is one passage rich in savage, but also comic, gusto, where the poets are likened to three gallants who are lured by an "old bawd masked," claiming to be in great distress, into a "bad house." There her three escorts, noble sentiments unimpaired to the end, even after the grim and naked truth is revealed, "put a grave face upon the matter, make it a point of conscience, a match for life—*for better or worse*, stick to their filthy bargain, go to bed, and by lying quiet and keeping close, would fain persuade the people out of doors that all is well, while they are fumbling at the regeneration of mankind out of an old rotten carcase" (19.204–05). The metaphor may be grossly indecorous (although it can claim some Biblical sanction), but Hazlitt's development of it perfectly sums up the themes in his attack: the prostitution of poetic vision to vanity or hypocritical venality, the suppression of guilt in an impotent clinging to youthful idealism, the fear both of institutional authority and popular reprisal. And if we are still inclined to remember, and sympathize with, the sufferings of the lonely Coleridge at Highgate, and to contrast invidiously the lofty, dispassionate theorizing of the *Lay Sermons* (1816) with the "malice" and "scurrility" of Hazlitt's attack, we should remember also that the rules of the political game were not the same for both writers. Behind Coleridge lay all the panoply of Government power, with its *ex officio* informations, its laws against "seditious libel," its packed juries, its jails and gallows and ships to Botany Bay—all the "fetters," to use Coleridge's euphemism, that popular unrest "necessitates"[29]—while behind Hazlitt lay only the traditional English regard for freedom of speech, a sentiment still without political (as distinct from civil) rights under existing law; that is, there was freedom from censorship before publication, but not from Government prosecution afterwards. To advocate a republican government for England, to question the sovereignty of Crown or Constitution, to accuse the King's ministers or even the House of Commons of irresponsibility—all this was indictable as "sedition"; and even the demonstrable truth of specific published statements was considered inadmissible evidence for the defense when the charge was libel of the Government.[30] Under these conditions such anti-Government journals as the *Examiner* had no recourse but to direct their attack upon literary and other public apologists for Government; and since doctrine could not be equally and openly matched with counter-doctrine, it is little wonder that the attacks became "personal."

Hazlitt does not neglect, however, whenever feasible within these stringent limits, to carry his attack to the level of doctrine, although in *Political Essays* it is seldom the poets' own doctrines that he chooses to honor with protracted argument. Long before this time Hazlitt had grappled with a theory of society—that of Edmund Burke—which anticipated and helped to shape the poets' ideas of a historically organic nationalism. Since at least 1796, Hazlitt had admired the author of the *Reflections* as not only "the most accomplished rhetorician the world ever saw" (19.271) but also as "a profound commentator on that apocalyptic chapter of human nature [that is, the French Revolution] . . . arranging and analyzing the principles that alternately pervaded the vast chaotic mass, and extracting the elements of order and the cement of social life from the decomposition of all society" (7.320). And what was Burke's vision of the "principles" of social "order"? Since Hazlitt deserves recognition as the first English liberal to credit Burke with wisdom (or the first to do so and remain a liberal), it is worth quoting his understanding of the *Reflections* at some length:

> Burke was so far right in saying that it is no objection to an institution, that it is founded in *prejudice*, but the contrary, if the prejudice is natural and right. . . . Thus he contended that the prejudice in favor of nobility was natural and proper, and fit to be encouraged . . . because such an institution has a tendency to enlarge and raise the mind, to keep alive the memory of past greatness, to connect the different ages of the world together, to carry back the imagination over a long tract of time, and feed it with the contemplation of remote events. . . . He also conceived that by transferring the respect from the person to the thing, and thus rendering it steady and permanent, the mind would be habitually formed to sentiments of deference, attachment, and fealty . . . that it would be led to fix its view on what was elevated and lofty, and be weaned from that low and narrow jealousy which never willingly or heartily admits of any superiority in others. . . . Nobility did not therefore exist to the prejudice of the other orders of the state, but by and for them. The inequality of the different orders of society did not destroy the unity and harmony of the whole. The health and well-being of the moral world was to be promoted by the same means as the beauty of the natural world; by contrast, by change, by light and shade, by variety of parts, by order and proportion . . . (7.306–07)

Hazlitt later regretted "the fit of extravagant candour" in which he had written this account of the *Reflections;* but even in 1807 he was careful to add that Burke's arguments are not "conclusive"; they are "profound and true" only "as far as they go"—only as the vision of a principle, not as its proper or inevitable application. Yet to hold these reservations was not to deny Burke's demonstration of positive advantages which are "necessarily inherent" in a "mixed form of government" and perhaps "compatible in the same degree with no other" (7.301 n., 307).

This concession to the virtue of "mixed government" is important; for it is the first of several indications that Hazlitt, whom we never hesitate to label a "radical" or "republican" or "democrat," had become by 1807, if not long before, a "constitutional Whig" in his practical politics. There is really nothing to surprise us in this alteration, for it marks a retreat to familiar ground—the return of a disciple of Paine and Godwin to the Hanoverian loyalties of the Presbyterian tradition.[31] And for a Buonapartist who approved, although not without qualms, the establishment of the Empire in 1804, it would really have been hypocrisy to go on believing that the "king of a free people" is a contradiction in terms. Fully as much as the poets, Hazlitt had learned, as he would write in *The Life of Napoleon,* that monarchy "seems vastly adapted to the constitution and weaknesses of human nature." In its very flattery of human weaknesses, monarchy performs a function: a king provides a "royal self" for the love of power among his subjects, and since this compensatory image of unconscious desire appeals to all members of society and transcends envy, it "baffles" civil discord and fosters a mutual accommodation of interests, interposing a barrier in the will itself "to the tormenting strife and restless importunity of the passions in individuals" (14.235–37, 19.256). Hazlitt was by no means willing to grant that monarchy and hereditary aristocracy are therefore inevitable; but he was prepared to accept them historically as institutions whose latent tyranny might be held in check, and which could not happily be eradicated until modern opinion—or, more precisely, the modern imagination of power—had developed other customs, institutions, and sentiments capable of performing nearly as well those functions of "order" and "deference" that Burke had justly defended.

In his politics, then, as in his general theory of the mind, Hazlitt had learned respect for continuity with the past; and this reconciliation with national traditions was manifest in his prose well before his journalistic celebrity in the Regency years. His first political pamphlet, published at his own expense, *Free Thoughts on Public Affairs* (1806), was written in support of "the Old Opposition" (that is, those who stood with Fox in Parliament against Pitt's war policy), and it marks the beginning of Hazlitt's constant effort thereafter to take the force of English prejudice away from Tory "Legitimacy" and realign radical sentiment with the traditions of liberal Hanoverian Whiggism. The Whig gospel of "the balance of the constitution" emerges as the major theme in his notes to a historical anthology of

Parliamentary speeches, *The Eloquence of the British Senate* (1807), where the heroic age of English Liberty is, significantly, not the Puritan Commonwealth but the period from the 1688 Revolution through the first two Hanoverian kings, when "old English character" was never more itself and when even many Jacobites understood and honored the principles of Liberty. And Hazlitt makes it clear that the source of the later degeneration was not the power of the Crown as such, nor even the headstrong George III, but that king's ministers, who, having mastered the arts of corruption first introduced by Horace Walpole, had succeeded by the second Pitt's time in transforming a once eloquent House of Commons into a petty assemblage of factions—each contending for the spoils of patronage and debating their selfish interests with "bastard sophistry" (1.148).

Obviously the note of radical dissidence was not being lost in Hazlitt's appeal to "Old England" (7.7). Although a strong believer in national character and national "genius," he had nothing but scorn for the new mysticism which, in reaction against French rationalism or Napoleonic domination, revered the principle of nationhood as an absolute "spirit" or "soul" of a people, and which retained respect for ideals of universal freedom and justice only as these were embodied in traditional *Volksrecht*. Hazlitt granted that patriotic feeling in the city-states of Greece and Rome or in the clans of Scotland might once have been a "pure flame," solely "the offspring of physical and local attachment"; but in the "great states" of the modern world, where men were no longer "mortised" to the state, patriotism could only be an "idea" or a "sentiment," the "creature of reason and reflection." To pretend that we are "bound" to our country by more than "moral and rational ties," or that principles of "abstract justice" are "a violation of natural affection" (4.67–68), was to misunderstand the true continuity of English imagination that Burke had revealed. No less important than continuity with the past for the life of imagination was continuity with "the *ideal* principle" (17.350), which—to recall Hazlitt's argument in the *Essay*—operates in the will as a "projection" of good, an anticipation of the future. And if national feeling should lose this tendency "to enlarge and raise the mind" and to "nourish the hopes" of English-

109

men as individual beings, it would soon lose also its true kinship with the past (7.307; see also 13.127–33).

After Waterloo, however, Hazlitt increasingly came to distrust the adequacy of this honorific account of the function of imagination in politics. In July 1816, in the course of an essay on Shakespeare's *Coriolanus,* Hazlitt unexpectedly launches a digression which makes unmistakable his break with the mentorship of Burke in politics as of Wordsworth and Coleridge in poetics. This passage stands as the first recorded statement of a theory of imagination which will henceforth be recognized in this study as his mature theory, in contradistinction to the theory outlined in the *Essay.* And here also is our first clear indication that Hazlitt was finding it difficult if not impossible to go on thinking of the poets simply as "apostates" to the "creed" he had shared with them in 1798. For if they were still chargeable with betraying the disinterested independence of literary genius, they had done so at least by yielding to their own instincts as poets:

> The cause of the people is indeed but little calculated as a subject for poetry. . . . The language of poetry naturally falls in with the language of power. The imagination is an exaggerating and exclusive faculty: it takes from one thing to add to another: it accumulates circumstances together to give the greatest possible effect to a favourite object. The understanding is a dividing and measuring faculty: it judges of things not according to their immediate impression on the mind, but according to their relations to one another. The one is a monopolising faculty, which seeks the greatest quantity of present excitement by inequality and disproportion; the other is a distributive faculty, which seeks the greatest quantity of ultimate good, by justice and proportion. The one is an aristocratical, the other a republican faculty. The principle of poetry is a very anti-levelling principle. It aims at effect, it exists by contrast. It admits of no medium. . . . It has its altars and its victims, sacrifices, human sacrifices. . . . 'Carnage is its daughter.' Poetry is right-royal. It puts the individual for the species, the one above the infinite many, might before right. (4.214–15)

Students of Hazlitt's thought have strangely neglected this passage, yet the idea it introduces is perhaps the most original, and surely the most heretical, idea in the entire range of his criticism. Indeed, there is good reason to approach this idea with gingerly caution; for not only does the main thrust of its argument run counter to Hazlitt's own earlier doctrine, as to most Romantic faith in imagination, but it seems even to challenge one of the sacred articles of humanist faith since the Renaissance—belief in the beneficence of poetry, in the essential virtue of the Muse herself. Poets had been accused before, as Hazlitt knew, of being "Tories by nature" (19.255),[32] and there was ample precedent, both classical and Puritan, for scorning the dangerous "shadows" of "fancy"; but, to my knowledge, no critic or philosopher had ever before asserted that a contradiction in tendency naturally exists between poetic imagination, however susceptible to madness and error, and the values of a humane morality, of "justice" and "right." Gifford's reviewer in the *Quarterly,* quick to sense the affront to his literary education, queried his author with pert and confident irony: "Do we read with more pleasure of the ravages of a beast of prey, than of the shepherd's pipe upon the mountain?" "No," was Hazlitt's reply in his *Letter to William Gifford* (1819), "but we do read with pleasure of the ravages of a beast of prey, and we do so on the principle I have stated, namely, from the sense of power abstracted from the sense of good; and it is the same principle that makes us read with admiration and reconciles us in fact to the triumphant progress of the conquerors and mighty hunters of mankind, who come to stop the shepherd's pipe upon the mountains and sweep away his listening flock" (9.37).

Not kings only, we should note, but "conquerors and mighty hunters of mankind." The point bears examination, for it suggests that Hazlitt was aiming his rebuke not only at the ways of poets merely but at power-adulation in all men—not excluding his own "admiration" of Napoleon Buonaparte. Buonaparte himself always valued "imagination" as a factor in public policy ("Imagination," he once said, "rules the world": qu. 15.302); and Hazlitt in the *Life* was to suggest that the Consul turned Emperor, becoming too consciously the heir of Caesar and Charlemagne, vainly trying to "dazzle" and overawe the courts of Europe (14.84, 98 ff.), had helped to bring about his own downfall (and in a way not unlike the fall of Coriolanus)—by losing sympathy with the true basis of his power in popular feeling and in the revolt of modern opinion from feudal institutions. Indeed, all political will is in some measure tempted, by its very nature, to revert from the modesty of reason to the ancient

> logic of the imagination and the passions; which seek to ag-
> grandize whatever excites admiration and to heap contempt on
> misery, to raise power into tyranny, and to make tyranny abso-
> lute; to thrust down that which is low still lower, and to make
> wretches desperate: to exalt magistrates into kings, kings into
> gods; to degrade subjects to the rank of slaves, and slaves to the
> condition of brutes. The history of mankind is a romance, a
> mask, a tragedy, constructed upon the principles of *poetical jus-
> tice* . . . (4.216)

Hazlitt is not, however—as Lionel Trilling assumes, and as this mocking rhetoric may suggest—limiting the meaning of "power" as an object of imagination to "the strong and proud and feral."[33] The late Professor Trilling, alone among the influential critics of our time in acknowledging the originality and importance of this passage in the *Coriolanus* essay as a theoretic statement, strangely failed to recognize that Hazlitt means by love of "power" not merely attraction to manifestly forceful power but, as we have seen, the impulse to "conscious power"—the transformation by the mind of given or irresistible objects of power into objects of its own passional desire for power. Hazlitt is therefore not denying that there is frequently, in life as in poetry, an "ideal" dimension in the intensification of power by imagination, partaking to this extent of modifying associa-tion with "truth" and "good"; and in all his diatribes against the Lake Poets, he does not charge them with losing or repudiating their youthful benevolence, however often they may have suppressed that "enthusiasm" or mixed it with private and more regrettable motives. Nevertheless, since the quest of imagination is finally for more "con-scious power," its idealizations can never be pure, never wholly free of the "logic" that binds it to other images of power in the world; for the common denominator of all power in the mind is, by Hazlitt's theory, the compensatory strength it offers to some hidden "weak-ness" of the self; indeed, it is this need, if not perhaps only this need, which explains why the power-impulse should so often seek expression in imagination rather than in the life of action. Nothing else, Hazlitt insists, will explain the disregard of man's fascination with power not only for common justice but for simple self-interest: "Things strike the imagination from privation, contrast and suffering, which are proportionably intolerable in reality" (13.51).

This one paradoxical law of the imagination defines for Hazlitt the true consistency in all tergiversations of the poets' minds since he first knew them—from their first sympathy with the most wretched of human beings in *Lyrical Ballads* to their later, and more traditionally poetic, reconciliation with the exalted oppressors of that humanity, having themselves suffered the aggravations of human weakness—their proud hopes humbled and their resolution impaired or divided by neglect, obloquy, and persecution. Men, to the degree that the desire for power is frustrated in their own lives, tend to identify with the source of the power that has dominion over them; the bondslave, Hazlitt remarks, only "hugs his chains the closer," the longer and more severe his bondage (7.148–49); and the poets, "creatures of sympathy," were no exception to this simple paradox of human frailty (11.37). Even the last hope for human progress that remained in the poets' vision, the ideal of a renascent national Church, might, Hazlitt argues, be sufficiently accounted for—questions of religious belief aside—by the same law of "privation" and "contrast" in imagination. For was it not the very remoteness from their own lives, the exotic incongruity with modern conditions, in short, its contemporary impossibility, which made their vision of a religiously united England loom, like all other nostalgias for the medieval past, with such idealized intensity in their minds (7.228 ff., 11.65)? Hazlitt reminds Coleridge, by 1816 a defender of the Bible as *The Statesman's Manual*, that "under the true Jewish theocracy, the priests and prophets cashiered kings"—and would "our lay-preacher . . . take this office upon himself as a part of the *Jus Divinum?*" (7.121).

꿨

Although its reputation does it less than justice, *Political Essays* is an angry book, and it therefore tends to be impatient with political theory—even with well-intentioned liberal theory, like Robert Owen's proto-socialist scheme for a "new" society (7.97 ff.). As Hazlitt begins by saying in the *Preface,* and he repeats the theme relentlessly thereafter: the "love of liberty" consists neither in sentimental prejudice nor in subscription to a doctrine but in "a hatred of tyranny and a contempt for its tools" (7.7, 151). The selections from his journalism written between 1813 and 1816 reinforce this simple emphasis, and the focus is therefore as much on foreign as on domestic affairs; but in the later essays of 1816 we notice a change. Starting with the late summer and autumn of that year, as the post-war crisis rapidly worsens and the population theories of Malthus and his converts among the economists begin to invade and divide the liberal camp, Hazlitt increasingly turns his attention to matters of social doctrine; and the essays in the latter half of the volume, while still rich in satiric invective, again reflect their author's love of analysis and argument. So long as Hazlitt could continue to think of the enemy of Liberty as anti-Napoleonic Legitimism, the "mock-doctrine" of "divine right" (7.150–51), satire was weapon enough to expose the passivity, irrationality, and servile piety—in short, the sheer absurdity implied in the pretended submission of John Bull to neo-feudalism. But when a new, an economic "Legitimacy" reared its head and threatened to capture the reform movement itself, Hazlitt recognized that this unprecedented antagonist had to be met on its own grounds of theoretic reason, for it threatened to change the very meaning of "rights" in society. Indeed, it is regrettable that Hazlitt could not—without risking almost certain prosecution—have strengthened this challenge by including in the volume an essay which stands as his fullest and ablest defense of political democracy, "A Project for a New Theory of Civil and Criminal Legislation."

Some of the arguments in this long pamphlet essay (which remained unpublished until after his death) may go back to very early youth—back even to "the first time I ever attempted to think," to his fourteenth year (19.302), as Hazlitt at the start, rather unwisely, informs his readers—but most of the reasoning unmistakably belongs, like the style, to his maturity. And especially the arguments here for the validity of "natural rights" proceed directly from his mature psychology of "power." He defines a "natural right" as that "which has the sanction of the will as such"—that is, not that "which is good or useful in itself" but only whatever "is thought so by the individual"; for as soon as a right is taken to mean that which *is* right and good, it ceases to mean a right at all and becomes a modification of will by something beyond itself, not an original prerogative of individual power. This is essentially the reasoning of Hobbes, that "fine sturdy old fellow," as Hazlitt elsewhere calls him (20.164), whose *Leviathan* he seems not to have read until after 1805, and whose political reasoning he learned to respect even while rejecting his materialism. Having, like Hobbes, postulated the power-motive as primal in man, Hazlitt does not flinch from confessing that a real or potential aggression informs or attends, in some shape or degree, every encounter of wills in society. But Hobbes had assumed that this aggressiveness necessarily implies antipathy or indifference to the will of others,[34] and it is just this inference that our discoverer of "natural disinterestedness" is now enabled to deny. Here we must remember that for Hazlitt there is no self-consciousness except by being conscious of self in others: the antipathy of aggression depends upon a prior act of imagination, however limited or "unconscious" this may be. Just as the physical clash of wills gives rise in the most primitive society to "natural justice," with its simple logic of revenge (19.225 ff.), so the encounter of strange wills fosters in all society a primitive sense of equality, for only this sense enables the encounter to become or remain "civil." The self recognizes, through imagination, its counterpart: organic power responds to organic power, and thus an "adjustment of force against force" takes place—a mutual sense of "reaction," whose general effect in society is the tacit recognition of "inherent rights, balancing and neutralising one another." The system of laws made necessary by the inevitable conflict of these rights need not, therefore, invalidate or diminish, or banish to a "state of nature," the principle of equality:

> The only thing that limits them [the natural rights of individuals] is the solidity of another right, no better than my own, and, like stones in a building . . . each remains not the less firmly riveted to its place, though it cannot encroach upon that next to it. . . . Equality, instead of being destroyed by society, results from and is improved by it; for in politics, as in physics, the action and reaction are the same: the right of resistance on their part implies the right of self-defense on mine . . . One body impinges against and impedes another in its fall, but it could not do this, but for the principle of gravity. (19.302–07)

Slenderly developed though it may be, Hazlitt's conception of a principle of self-balancing order inhering in the nature of freedom itself, in the reactive consciousness of "rights," marks an appreciable advance over the benign piety or implausible abstraction that had hitherto vitiated most "natural rights" theory.[35] True, "society" here is still being mistaken for an assemblage of individuals; but it may also be true that Hazlitt is describing a principle of "civil" order no less indispensable to the state than the positive, historical order of traditional culture—that is, the "order" that Burke had defended. Society, whatever else it may be, is always human intercourse; modern society, at least, has always to renew itself from the meeting of strangers; and Hazlitt may be right in insisting, with his metaphor of mutually secure "stones in a building," that the "principle of equality" is in some form necessary to insure the stability of the positive order, which he sees as impaired precisely to the degree that it ignores or violates this principle. But from the natural democracy of civil intercourse one may only infer the necessity of equal civil rights under the law—not, as Hazlitt would have us believe, the logical necessity also for equal political rights in determining what the laws should be. Simply by balancing right against right, how does a society of equals build, or maintain when built, the governing structure of the state, the order of law as distinct from both custom and the freely determined relations of individuals?

Here is the stumbling block of all classical liberal theory—the paradox of deriving the authority of government from individual will—and Hazlitt's theory promises no more cogent a solution to this enigma than his predecessors. He does not, however, try to make the problem easier by denying or ignoring the coercive nature of political authority: there is, he says (again following Hobbes), "nothing liberal" in the essential business of law—"the crime, the officer, the prison, the judge and the gallows" (2.146). Reappearing here is a Godwinite-Dissenter's distrust of institutional authority, but Hazlitt recognizes now its basis in the social nature of "right" itself, as the "aggregate" defense of all rights against aggressive will: "Government is not necessarily founded on common consent, but on the right which society has to defend itself against all aggression." Authority, moreover, is not dangerous insofar as it is authoritative but only insofar as it pretends to "moral" sanction and thus usurps the function of will itself—pretends, that is, to control opinions or actions which do not manifestly injure or imperil the freedom of others. Hazlitt grants that there are many cases in law where it is by no means clear, that is, rationally demonstrable, just what constitutes "aggression"; and in such cases legal authority, as the "emanation" of "the general voice," supersedes the "strict political right" of the individual to decide for himself what the proper limits of his freedom are. This "general voice," though, must be truly general, and to help insure that it is, democratic suffrage finds its just warrant. It is the best means of recurring "to the general voice for settling the boundaries of right and wrong, and even more for preventing the government, under pretense of the general peace and safety, from subjecting the whole liberties, rights and resources of the community to its own advantage" (19.310–20).

Hazlitt acknowledges that all government, to the extent that it endures, may be said to rest implicitly upon the "aggregate will" of the people, but only in modern times has *vox populi* become aware of its difference from law and inherited prejudice, conscious of its distinctive power as "public opinion." "Liberty," he remarks, looking askance at the primitivists among English reformers, "is but a modern invention, the growth of books and printing" (11.141). Here again we may recognize his Presbyterian myth of the Reformation, with "books" succeeding the Good Book as the agency of Light dispelling barbarous darkness. Yet in his modification of the myth Hazlitt is not covertly returning to the rationalism of his father's tradition. On the contrary, he now postulates a function for literature in its own right, one whereby the sympathy of imagination for good or for power beyond the will is turned against its own "exclusive" instincts for power. The very act of reading, he argues, forms "standards" of thought and conduct in the self, less by rational inference than by unconscious identification with an expressive movement in language which is like (in feeling or in meaning) one's own self-consciousness, yet sufficiently unlike it to enable the mind to escape the confines of personal experience. Self-love and self-will are now suspended or "abstracted," "right" gradually freed from "might," imagination reallied with reason. And what sustains this freedom of conscience is the reader's awareness that other men are forming the same or similar standards. When he returns to his life in society, the reader may forget or ignore the ideas, whether true or false, found on the printed page, but he cannot escape the consciousness (which may of course be purely imaginary) that modes of taste and opinion he has shared in that reading are being invoked by others in their responses to his speech and actions, just as he finds himself judging others by them (17.325–29). Thus the sense of what men could be or should be, as distinct from what they are, is no longer a purely abstract ideal but becomes an operative reality—a "collective sense" pervading all classes in society. The potential now exists for a universal community of "humanity," although only to the degree that this "consolidation" of manners and opinion really does represent a sense of timeless humanity transcending the prejudices of the existing society. "Public opinion," in its essential principle, is not to be mistaken for vulgar, contemporary, or majority opinion; for it "expresses not only the collective sense of the whole people, but of all ages and nations, of all those minds that have devoted themselves to the love of truth and the good of mankind . . . who have thought, spoken, written, acted and suffered in the name and on the behalf of our common nature" (7.269).

The process just described is what Hazlitt most often calls the modern "abstraction" of mind from self, and I have chosen to stress its beneficent tendencies—its approximation (especially in those last words above) to what Matthew Arnold, with far less democratic intentions, would call "culture"—in order to counter the emphasis in some recent scholarship on Hazlitt's awareness of the dangers of this same "abstraction" for creative imagination. On perhaps no other issue do the Prig and the Boy in Hazlitt have more divided attitudes, but they share nonetheless the belief that modern man is free of the ancient servitudes of body and mind only to the degree that he is, or is becoming, a "public creature" (18.304). Indeed, Hazlitt would not learn until the next decade to question and revise one of the optimistic assumptions on which his confidence in literate opinion rests—the assumption, namely that society, as it becomes increasingly "public," is moving in only *one* direction of change, toward a "levelling" of class distinctions, toward a "uniformity" of thought, manners, and sentiment (4.12). He had ceased to believe that the minds of men were becoming "disinterested," but he still wished to believe that as men became literate and more homogeneous in behavior, to that extent they were also less exclusively selfish. By 1816, however, there was already one formidable movement in English opinion which gave the lie to this generous inference, and which could no longer be dismissed—although this was Hazlitt's tactic—as a monstrous aberration. He now found himself confronting a "public" conspiracy of selfishness, one armed with all the modern sanctions of learning and "science": the rapid ascendancy in middle-class opinion of Malthusian economics, with its unmistakable message that class divisions in society are necessary, politically inescapable, and perhaps even morally just. The test of Hazlitt's conscience as a political critic lies, as it must for every nineteenth-century liberal, in the degree of his willingness to recognize the irony that England's Protestant worship of Liberty, its faith that freedom means nothing if not the absence of restraint, might itself be breeding a new tyranny in the world—a new absolutism founded on the sanctity of property rights.

If Hazlitt was reluctant to acknowledge this rift developing in the doctrine of "natural rights," it was in part because he thought it demonstrable that no fundamental conflict need exist in society between the claims of individual Liberty and those of democratic Equality. This is not the place to review his life-long polemic against Malthus,[36] but we must pause long enough to understand its importance for his political—and even his literary—criticism, and to understand also why his 1807 *Reply* to Malthus has been winning an ever greater admiration from historians of the controversy. Hazlitt has the distinction of being the first thinker of his time to isolate and define the central fallacy lurking in the major premise of the *Essay on Population*—the premise that population growth necessarily tends to outstrip the production of food. Hazlitt challenges this gloomy prophecy by arguing that the very "decency and comfort" which foster an *increase* of population act also to prevent that population's *excess*. For along with augmented economic means, with what we have learned to call better "standards of living," come a greater will and capacity to insure a continuance of the comforts enjoyed, not only through a more intelligent control of sexual passion but also

119

through steadily improved agriculture and a broader distribution of the food supply. He thus led the way, as Harold A. Boner observes, to the conclusion of much later theorists that "socially remediable factors," not inexorable laws of nature or the imprudence of the poor, are responsible for overpopulation.[37]

But Hazlitt was not simply engaged in lifting a burden of guilt and hopelessness from the poor, and thus in vindicating the charity and the wisdom of the Elizabethan Poor Law; he was also intent on shifting most of the blame from the poor to their employers, whose spokesmen among the economists had extrapolated from the Malthusian "discoveries" the famous "wage-fund" concept, which gave a new logic of inviolability to property rights. In the "Project" as in the *Reply,* Hazlitt opposes this doctrine with a theory of economic value as "productive labor." Anticipating Ruskin and Morris, Hazlitt insists that the toil of the laborer is as necessary to the value of land (or industrial property) as the investment of the proprietor; and the "real funds" for labor can thus mean only "the actual produce of the soil [or the shop]," to which the "industry" of all concerned, not merely the proprietor or investor, has contributed. Property rights may therefore be judged inviolable only as they coincide with the natural right of every self to resist aggression; and on the very same principle the state has not merely the right but the obligation to prevent encroachment of one man's right to property over another's right to life and to labor for support of life. Yet Hazlitt was careful not to extend this "police" function into a state wardship that would jeopardize the principle of economic liberty itself. The employer's freedom of contract implies also, on the part of the laboring class, "the right to *strike*" (1.313; Hazlitt, by the way, seems to have been the first to use that term in theoretic discourse, just as he was perhaps the first to recognize the term's validity as a principle). He saw the "right of combination" as the most potent and reliable weapon of the poor, and since he had "labored this point hard" in the *Reply,* he was glad to see it winning some public acceptance, however slow and grudging, as the years passed (19.306).[38]

Yet more than a generation had still to pass before John Stuart Mill and other liberal thinkers began to develop more systematically these and other arguments advanced in the *Reply.* And that so long a time would elapse before the liberal tradition learned to challenge the new "science" suggests the tyrannous depth of the spell that Malthusian doctrine had begun to cast over middle-class opinion. It was useless for Hazlitt to go on taxing his adversaries with duplicity about the "moral" element in social processes, when the simple fact was that for the Malthusians the word "moral" no longer connoted what it meant for him. By the principle of "moral restraint" upon sexuality the Malthusians, while they still spoke reverently of "human happiness," really meant not only a "check" upon improvident marriages, but upon all feeling and conduct that would honor pleasure ("indolence") or suffering ("misery") above "prudence" and "industry." Privileged status was conferred upon men of property— men of "independence"—not by institutions but by Nature itself, whose processes of life and death enforced this law of virtue by preserving an order of inequality that rewarded the pious and prudent while it humbled and punished, through the "negative checks" of "vice and misery," the rebelliously improvident. It was this grim mystique, combining first with Evangelical morality and, later in the century, with Darwinian theories of social evolution, that gave a binding force of fear and militant pride—not to mention unconscious guilt—to the Victorian *embourgeoisement* of "progress." So often described as a reaction from the "excesses" of Romanticism, "Victorianism" (if we mean by that term a shift in ethos and a new attitude toward society, as distinct from a configuration in literature itself) is already taking visible shape in the Regency years; and English Romanticism, by the time of its second generation of writers, might more accurately be described as a reaction, not from eighteenth-century mechanism, but from this new moralizing of "necessity." To a man, the Romanticists despised Malthus and his theory— on this issue Hazlitt and Southey were comrades in arms. And how estranged their minds were from the new center of gravity in English opinion is suggested by the fact that by 1817 both the *Edinburgh* and the *Quarterly Reviews*—the one secular and "liberal," the other piously Tory, but alike in catering to an upper-middle-class readership—had been firmly won over to the Malthusian position.[39]

It is impossible to understand (or forgive?) Hazlitt's tireless invocation of "sympathy," of "passion," of organic "nature" in his literary and art criticism unless we are aware of this countervailing view of reality in his time—of a Nature which authorized not a delight in universal "humanity" but a universally repressive order of class consciousness. "The French Revolution," Hazlitt would write in the next decade, "has . . . left no two ideas in the public mind but those of high and low"—that is, "the jealousy of gentility, the horror of being thought vulgar" (18.400). It is this ironic awareness which accounts for the new note of sardonic anger that enters Hazlitt's political writing in 1817, as he watched the reform movement divide and splinter along class lines. When government fears intensified after the two bad harvests of 1816 and 1817, leading to suspension of habeas corpus in the winter of 1817, this crisis, instead of prompting reformers to close ranks, generated only more dissension. In Parliament the Whigs refused to countenance the reform program of Sir Francis Burdett (whom Hazlitt and the *Examiner,* not uncritically, supported); Burdett and his following were soon alienated by the demagogic appeals of Cobbett and "Orator" Henry Hunt; Cobbett, in his turn, before he himself quit the field in 1817 (fleeing to America for fear of arrest), lost no opportunity to snipe at Burdett for lukewarmness in the cause; while more and more alienated from all these groups were the new "philosophical" radicals, scornful of all reformers who refused to see the new light of Bentham, James Mill, Malthus, and Ricardo.[40] The fact that nearly all of these leaders were being at the same time abused by their common enemies in the ministerial press went for nothing; for "in proportion as they were scouted by the rest of the world, they grew more captious, irritable, and jealous of each other's pretensions" (12.375). So Hazlitt wrote seven years later, but in 1818 he was not so ready to resign his flickering hopes for a rallying of the old Westminster *esprit de corps.* To help restore it Hazlitt and John Hunt, in January of that year, launched a new weekly, *The Yellow Dwarf,* with this urgent motto blazoned on its masthead: "Unite, and be free!"

"The Politics of the Day," the leader articles of the new journal (evidently written by John Hunt but presumably expressing the opinions of his coadjutor as well), warned against dogmatic extremism, pleaded with reformers not to lose the good will of moderates who feared for the security of their property, and proposed, as the only viable alternative, a reform of suffrage that would prove remarkably prophetic of the Reform Bill of 1832.[41] Nothing shows more conclusively than this neglected episode in Hazlitt's journalistic career his antipathy, even in these truculent years, to revolution by force, and his continued commitment to gradual reform—progressive approximation toward a democratic republic through the liberalization of opinion and the steady enlargement of "representative government." "Timely reforms are the best preventives of violent revolutions" (7.280). These words appear in the course of what is perhaps (if we except the Preface) his finest political essay, and surely his most eloquent contribution to *The Yellow Dwarf*. "What is the People?" is an essay designed to save the unifying concept of popular sovereignty from both demagogic debasement and the contempt or neglect of the ideologically sophisticated. Hazlitt's title-question becomes, in the first sentence, a blow in the reader's face: "And who are you that ask that question? One of the people. And yet you would be something! Then you would not have the People nothing." This appeal to middle-class pride in self describes the rhetorical punch of the essay throughout; and it is mainly with this strategy that Hazlitt seeks to counter the tendency in these years to think of "the people" no longer as the God-inspired antagonist of thrones, but as synonymous with "the lower orders"—with, in short, the Malthusian *misérables*. Hazlitt gives short shrift to the notion that not the common people of England but only their "betters" have the capacity to "remedy" their "grievances." "The people is the hand, heart and head of the whole community," and just as reason in a man becomes his will only insofar as it represents feeling, so "popular feeling" rightly demands direct expression in the government of the body politic; for otherwise the state will scarcely know its own ills, much less have the will to remedy them in action; it must have "the same interest in providing for them, as an individual has with respect to his own welfare." And Hazlitt proceeds to transform this analogy with self into a maxim for the state, one that also stands as his ultimate definition of democracy: "Can any one doubt that such *a state of society in which the greatest knowledge of its interests was thus combined with the greatest sympathy with its wants, would realize the idea of a perfect Commonwealth?*" (7.266–68; my italics).

The maxim I have italicized is worth rescuing from the journal-istic dustbin; it gains with rereading, and may someday find an hon-ored place among the great statements of nineteenth-century politi-cal thought. Unlike such rubrics as "the greatest happiness of the greatest number," Hazlitt's formulation of the democratic ideal af-fords an internal safeguard against the vices of collectivism—against both "the tyranny of the majority" and the usurpation of power by authoritarian ideologues. Although he does not single them out for attack in this essay, his axiom seems expressly aimed at the Bentha-mites, who were attempting to adapt Malthusian and other "science" to democratic purposes through a program of legislative reform based on "knowledge" of "interests" alone. Their prescription of "useful knowledge" not only had no need of passional "sympathy" but was actually designed to eliminate the dependence of morality on "sentiment," and thus to free "interests" from all motives but those of manifest "utility."

Perhaps even more than the defection of the poets and the as-cendancy of Malthusianism, the rise to dominance of this new breed of Westminster radical tempted Hazlitt to despair for the cause of English reform in his lifetime. And certainly the rise of Utilitar-ianism helped to convince him of the primal importance of literary culture in sustaining the "humanity" of modern opinion; for without it, as the "sour" manners of the Benthamites made clear, the "use-ful" tended, despite their theoretic disclaimers, to degenerate into an antipathy to whatever commonly gives pleasure—into a preference, not merely a tolerance, of "the disagreeable" (20.256–59). And how destructive these allies could be to his own values was vividly brought home to Hazlitt in 1819, when, thanks to an experimental scheme that his landlord had projected, he was faced with the prospect of losing his lease on the old house in York Street and of losing the view from its windows that he loved—of the tranquil beauty of the garden, shaded by stately trees, where Milton once had walked. "To show how little the refinements of taste or fancy enter into our au-thor's system, he [Bentham] proposed at one time to cut down these beautiful trees, to convert the garden where he had breathed the air of Truth and Heaven for near half a century into a paltry *Chres-tomathic School,* and to make Milton's house (the cradle of *Paradise*

124

Lost) a thoroughfare, like a three-stalled stable, for the idle rabble of Westminster to pass backwards and forwards to it with their cloven hoofs" (11.6).

No thoroughgoing democrat, certainly no "populist," wrote these words; and indeed Hazlitt stands apart from nearly all reformers in his time in his refusal to endorse the idea of popular education as indispensable to social progress. Though he believed in greater public literacy, the appeal to education as a grand panacea for England's social ills seemed to him a pious way of avoiding political realities: would, for instance, the manufacturing districts really be any better for having "the *farina* of knowledge sprinkled over them?" (1.184). The one "mode of education" that wins his firm praise is precisely that abhorred by the Cobbettites and the Benthamites as idly, perversely aristocratic—"classical education." Hazlitt was not himself, of course, the beneficiary of an education that could be called "classical" (although he had a more intimate acquaintance with the classics of ancient literature than is generally assumed), but he thought that he knew enough of its character to identify—he would later do the same for its faults—its essential virtue. "It teaches us to believe that there is something really great and excellent in the world, surviving all the shocks of accident and fluctuations of opinion"; and by fixing men's "thoughts on the remote and permanent, instead of narrow and fleeting objects" (4.4–5), it provides the only sure antidote to "the spirit of trade" and its effects on the mind. In drawing this opposition Hazlitt was not simply condemning "the commercial spirit" as the latest version of human selfishness in society; he sees it, rather, as an unprecedented danger, a new form of power-consciousness which finance capitalism (or what he calls the mentality of "the Exchange") fosters to the virtual exclusion of other ideas and judgments of human power, whether for good or evil. "As they [manufacturers, shippers, and other investors in the trade of the expanding British Empire] believe money to be the only substantial good, they are also persuaded that it is the only instrument of power." This foreshortening of the consciousness of power and value not only conduces to an acquiescence in "present power and upstart authority" (1.115–17), but deprives men of the true means to pleasure or satisfying power in their own lives. And in this impover-

ishment of feeling, not in any new necessities of society, Hazlitt locates the source of the idea of property as an "exclusive" right:
"Having little of the spirit of enjoyment in ourselves [as English-
men], we seek to derive a stupid or sullen satisfaction from the
privations and disappointment of others. Everything resolves itself
into an idea of *property*, that is, of something that our neighbours
dare not touch, and that we have not the heart to enjoy" (20.287).
Sympathy with the power of others as giving pleasure to ourselves,
or an interest in our own pleasures and passions as expressive of values found in all human power—this sympathy with "excellence" only
the great humanity of the past can teach. "By conversing with the
mighty dead, we imbibe sentiment with knowledge; we become
strongly attached to those who can no longer either hurt or serve us.
. . . We feel the presence of that power which gives immortality to
human thoughts and actions, and catch the flame of enthusiasm
from all nations and ages" (4.5).

Democratic ends, therefore, cannot entirely dispense with aristocratic means, and our former Buonapartist is not afraid to say so.
Although in an essay of the next decade he amuses himself with a
parody of the concept (8.205 ff.), Hazlitt really did believe in an "aristocracy of letters," and he believed, or wished to believe, that this
nobility of intellectual "fame" might not only supplant the "aristocracy of rank" (12.365–66) but continue to perform, and perhaps as
well or better, those functions of inculcating "deference" and
"fealty" to time-transcendent ideals that Burke had attributed solely
to the influence of hereditary privilege. And although this nobility of
genius could pretend to no prescriptive rules of membership, it is by
no means a misnomer for Hazlitt to describe its qualities as "classical," in contradistinction to "modern"; for he was unwilling to divorce the moral function of literature, in creating and enlarging
"sympathy," from the principle of permanence, or his faith in timeless excellence from the principle of authority, of a universal "scale"
of values (20.386). For Hazlitt had seen too much of the frailty of literary genius to believe that "the weak sides of human intellect,"
those which induced its "conversion" to the support of "arbitrary
power," could be cured or sufficiently held in check by the growing
public influence of literature itself, or merely by directing public

126

taste to a greater interest in the values of the past. There have always been, he writes in 1817, four principal weaknesses impeding the progress of Liberty: "the grossness of the imagination, which is seduced by outward appearances . . . ; the subtlety of the understanding itself, which palliates by flimsy sophistry the most flagrant abuses; interest and advancement in the world; and lastly, the feuds and jealousies of literary men among one another." "Literary men," he remarks with characteristic hyperbole (although within a year the writers of *Blackwood's* would, to his own sorrow, prove his words almost literally true), "exist not by the preservation, but the destruction of their species; they are governed not by the spirit of unanimity, but of contradiction" (7.145–46). To counteract this perpetual discord at the very heart of literary culture, as well as to balance the "love of inequality and injustice" in popular or "gross" imagination, society needs "general standards of taste"—a beneficent inequality of truly higher and truly lower values, a "scale of opinion" (4.5) to guide individual judgment and foster consensus of feeling. "What we need is a more Catholic spirit in literature; an Act of Uniformity in matters of taste and opinion. Till we have this, we shall be deficient in decency and zeal; and can never expect that 'long pull, strong pull, and pull all together,' which has been so earnestly called for, and which can alone ensure the triumph and permanence of any public object. What is the good of each person's having his own sulky or fanciful opinion in such matters, as he has his own pipe or pot of porter and newspaper, if there is no point of union, no common creed?" (20.284–85).

This was written in 1829, and although much would change in his attitudes by that time, Hazlitt's sense of the modern function of the arts would not change—the function, namely, of saving modern society from its diversities of will through a new and enlarged communion of imaginative experience. Strangely enough by Arnoldean lights, it is the stubborn Dissenter among his contemporaries who aspires to, and most consistently practices, a "catholic faith" (19.29) in his responses to literature and art—this critic so often labelled an "impressionist," so often described as doing, feeling, and judging as he jolly well pleases. And how hard, in fact, it was for Hazlitt to come by this vision, and how difficult he knew it to be for all Englishmen, is echoed in the quiet irony of his hyperbolic language: another "Act of Uniformity" for John Bull, indeed! Yet this is no abstractly willed recognition of necessity; for his vision owes its inspiration to that moment of revelation in 1802 which, as I have tried to suggest, lies at the heart of both his political and his aesthetic criticism. Here is the logical culmination of that "Religion of the Louvre," as I like to call it, which reshaped the young Hazlitt's sense of the meaning and promise, the "glory," of modern Liberty. It is mainly because of the abiding intensity of that memory that he would never admit his demand for "standards" in a culture of freedom to be essentially ironic or implausible: transcendence, he insists, can be achieved, and universal values communicated, precisely because excellence in art, and our sympathy with it, is always individual. Just as he would always be given to illustrating his ideas of creative genius from the art of painting, so it is always to the "shrine" of the Louvre that his mind returns to renew and rekindle his lonely, embattled faith in the democratic beneficence of genius. And that faith, although severely tried by his later disappointments, was perhaps never more resolute than when, not long after Waterloo, many of the greatest treasures of Napoleon's Louvre were "dispersed" forever, returned to their "legitimate" owners. Convinced that he had witnessed "a means to civilize the world" (18.102), Hazlitt was more than ever determined to recreate that vision in criticism.

Chapter Four

A New Aesthetic for Old Masters

IN *The Spirit of the Age* Hazlitt pauses to remark that "the study of the fine arts . . . came into fashion about forty years ago [the early seventeen-eighties], and was then first considered as a polite accomplishment" (11.166). Historians today would wish to assign a much earlier date to the vogue of painting, but we should note that Hazlitt is describing a new "direction of the public taste," not a fashion among the aristocracy and gentry. Art had become for the first time a broadly "public" interest, and the consequence was that the English middle class, hitherto almost exclusively literary in its habits (witness Doctor Johnson, who, as Boswell said, "had no taste for painting"), was learning to debate more and more aesthetic matters in the language of the visual arts. As recent studies have shown, "pictorialism" (the drawing of critical analogies between painting and poetry) was not something that dies under the rising musical tides of Romanticism but something that Romantic vision reanimates and, in its criticism, redefines. "Perspective," "relief," "light and shade," "colouring," "keeping," "gusto"—the frequency of this vocabulary in Hazlitt's criticism suggests that painting and literature, if no longer aesthetic twins, were still "sister arts," and in some respects more firmly and intimately linked than ever before by their complementary differences as expressions of imagination.[1]

To say that a taste for the fine arts was becoming "public" is to say that it had become inseparable from political consciousness. English patriotic pride, made jealous by the example of Napoleonic France and its extensive patronage of the arts, had helped to inspire the founding in 1805 of the British Institution, which held exhibitions rivalling in popularity those of the Royal Academy. The crowds that flocked to these and to the Academy exhibitions were, to judge from Hazlitt's description, from all ranks of the middle class, including clerks, milliners, and even schoolboys eager to improve—or perhaps only to prove—their taste (18.47). Elsewhere in London the print-sellers' shops did a thriving trade in watercolors and in all manner of engravings, and even more symptomatic of the new vogue was the growing number of young men who wished to be artists, designers, and illustrators. If many of these tyros were young men bent on making their fortunes, others, like Haydon and Wilkie, cherished heroic dreams of glory—dreams made confident by a faith in the dawning glory of British art. In a nation learning to respect its painters and to feel pride in all native genius, British art seemed to these aspirants already making rapid strides toward the great destiny prophesied by Sir Joshua Reynolds—the emergence of an "English school" which would equal or surpass its predecessors on the Continent.[2]

One would think that a critic who once called painting his "favourite art" (12.338), and especially a critic with so strong a commitment to the cause of "public opinion," would have sought to encourage and guide the upsurge of hopes around him for a great national art. Hazlitt had the good fortune to ride the crest of this fashion to his first celebrity as a critic, but in doing so he refused to flatter the ambitious pretensions of contemporary painters and their supporters in the press—Robert Hunt, for instance, the *Examiner*'s art critic (Leigh's younger brother), who never failed to greet the huge canvases of Benjamin West as England's answer to Raphael and Domenichino.[3] Such abuse or dereliction of the critical office by a political ally helps us to understand Hazlitt's resolve from the start to expose the ego-seducing blandishments of the mystique of "modern progress," here being mistakenly translated from one sphere of advancing "civilisation" to another. "The diffusion of taste," he warns in one of his earliest criticisms, "is not . . . the same thing as the improvement of taste . . . [and] it is only the former of these objects that is promoted by public institutions and other artificial means." To assume that art needs only "encouragement" to flourish, and to set about providing that stimulus by systematic means, would not lead to an increase in the number of genuine artists but only in "the number of candidates for fame and pretenders to criticism . . . while the quantity of genius and feeling remains the same as before." Yet not quite the same either, for "the man of original genius is often lost among the crowd of competitors . . . and . . . the voice of the few whom nature intended for judges is apt to be drowned in the noisy and forward suffrages of shallow smatterers in taste." And as proof or augury of the effects that English art could expect from "public" support, Hazlitt offers this appraisal of the annual Academy exhibition, where the paintings displayed and their admirers bear an ominously close resemblance to each other:

> Can there be a greater confirmation of these remarks than to look at that assemblage of select critics, who every year visit the exhibition at Somerset House . . . ? Is it at all wonderful that for such a succession of connoisseurs, such a collection of works of art should be provided; where the eye in vain seeks relief from the glitter of the frames in the glare of the pictures; where vermilion cheeks make vermilion lips look pale; where the merciless splendour of the painter's palette puts nature out of countenance; and where the unmeaning grimace of fashion and folly is almost the only variety in the wide dazzling waste of colour. Indeed, the great error of British art has hitherto been a desire to produce popular effect by the cheapest and most obvious means. . . . to lose all the delicacy and variety of nature in one undistinguished bloom of florid health, and all precision, truth and refinement of character in the same harmless mould of smiling, self-complacent insipidity. (18.45–46)

Really to appreciate this scene, we must reconstruct, in more precise visual terms, the "dazzling waste of colour" to which Hazlitt alludes. Prints of the time show us the Great Room at the Exhibition hung with hundreds of paintings (in some years well over a thousand entries were displayed), their frames massed together in a vast mosaic from floor to skylight, with scarcely an inch of the walls *and* the ceiling left unoccupied. Here indeed was "merciless splendour," and each contribution had to be strikingly splendid if it was not to be lost in the surrounding "glare." In this atmosphere the more ambitious painters were quick to learn what had to be done to win recognition, and some of them went so far on "varnishing days" as to alter their colors when they saw the "lights" of their neighboring competitors. Constable is only the best-known instance of a genuine artist forced under these circumstances to compromise his vision—to brighten and pleasantly "finish" his pictures according to the prescribed fashion.[4] As Hazlitt formulates the unacknowledged secret of success at an Academy exhibition: "To please generally, the painter must exaggerate what is generally pleasing, obvious to all capacities and void of offence before God and man . . . that which strikes the greatest number of persons with the least effort of thought" (18.107).

The scene at Somerset House is never far from his mind when he despairs of modern, and especially British, art. Against this background, his long war against the Academy reveals its true nature: this institution seems to him pernicious less beacuse it is Royal than because it is, in its more lasting effects on taste, "common" and "popular." Hazlitt's age saw the beginnings of the modern liberal doctrine, now enshrined in the Committees and Foundations of our own day, that state or "public" patronage of the arts is the natural successor to aristocratic and religious patronage—the doctrine, in his ironic paraphrase, that "we can inspire corporate bodies with taste, and carve out the directions to fame . . . on the front of public buildings" (18.38). The political partisan who in these same years was stigmatizing "imagination" as the enemy of democracy did not hesitate to balance the account: "The principle of universal suffrage, however applicable to matters of government, which concern the common feelings and common interests of society, is by no means applicable to matters of taste, which can only be decided upon by the most refined understandings." "The highest efforts of genius, in every walk of art, can never be properly understood by mankind in general: there are numberless beauties and truths which lie far beyond their comprehension." Thus "the public taste is . . . necessarily vitiated, in proportion as it is public; it is lowered with every infusion it receives of common opinion." Contrary to the legend of his wayward "impressionism," Hazlitt is adamant and unequivocal on the need for an authoritative criticism to protect and perpetuate the proper evaluation of excellence: "The reputation ultimately, and often slowly, affixed to works of genius is stamped upon them by authority, not by popular consent or the common sense of the world. . . . . . . Is Milton more popular now than when the *Paradise Lost* was first published? Or does he not rather owe his reputation to the judgment of a few persons in every successive period, accumulating in his favour, and overpowering by its weight the public indifference?" (18.46–48).

"Taste," therefore, is not, as many liberal optimists in the previous century believed, a given responsiveness to beauty and sublimity, present to some degree by "nature" in every mind, which criticism merely "exercises" and elucidates in reasonable terms. Hazlitt, too, insists that taste is "natural," but this "highest degree of sensibility" is natural only in the "few whom nature intended for judges," and even their innate capacity has still to be "cultivated" (18.46–47), informed by an intimate knowledge of genius; in that sense, "taste" is better described as "an emanation from genius" (16.215). The true critic's "authority" is never a self-arrogation of intellectual power but must continually prove its warrant by discriminating, communicating, and, not least, defending against hostile pretenders the sovereign powers of genius. And that Hazlitt was in no danger of valuing critical sensibility for its own sake, that is, independently of its objects and functions, is suggested by a use that he finds, after all, for "public buildings." "The only possible way to improve the taste for art in a country, is by a collection of standing works of established reputation, and which are capable by the sanctity of their name of overawing the petulance of public opinion" (18.101). Here is an early plea for England's own Louvre, for a National Gallery—a proposal not to be realized until 1824, and then with ridiculously modest beginnings.

When we remind ourselves that the exhibitions at the British Institution were virtually unprecedented—that before 1815 there had never been a public exhibition in England of the European Masters[5] (except for auction-room showings and private galleries, like that at Dulwich, made available to the public by their owners)—we begin to understand the inevitable paradox of Hazlitt's art criticism: that it is at once, and for the same reasons, conservative ("classical," in his own parlance: 20.386) and revolutionary. His acquaintance with original works of Italian Renaissance painting was, despite the fact that he would not visit Italy until late in his life, perhaps unrivalled in the early Regency years—until, at war's end, the Continent was again open to English travellers. Even then Hazlitt still brought to his criticism the rare authority of someone who had seen the undispersed glories of the *Musée Napoleon;* and he also had managed in his youth to beg, bribe, or cajole his way into most of the country-house galleries in England that could boast of Renaissance or seventeenth-century originals. Few painters in the Regency decade could claim anything like this firsthand knowledge, their studies of the Masters being limited to a set of uncolored and graphically fallible prints. In this situation it is little wonder that in his essays and reviews of art Hazlitt should constantly aim at giving his readers the illusion of *seeing* the picture he describes—of feeling what he sees and of seeing what (and simultaneously *as*) he evaluates; and his excursions into theory are similarly engaged in removing conceptual blinders from his readers' sense-consciousness.[6] Indeed, all of his descriptive appreciations of art may be said to recapitulate and enlarge upon those moments in his youth when—as at the auction-room showing in London, sometime in the winter of 1798–99, of the Duke of Orleans collection, when he beheld for the first time works of Renaissance painting in their original glory—"a mist passed away from my sight: the scales fell off. A new sense came upon me, a new heaven and a new earth stood before me" (8.14).

Yet Hazlitt did not share Haydon's confidence that once the Academy and its authority were overthrown, and its influence replaced by a better acquaintance with authentic models, English taste and creativity would be free to find their true level of excellence, however modest that achievement might prove to be.[7] The enthusiastic awareness, so strong in Haydon, Keats, and other artists and writers in this decade, of a mutually inspiring interplay among the arts of poetry, drama, painting, and sculpture, and which reflects the growing Romantic sense everywhere of the necessary interdependence of the arts, was tempered, in Hazlitt's case, by the understanding that the counterpart to the "modern" continuity of the arts was the inevitable socialization of taste—the subjection of aesthetic sensibility to the motives and interests of men in society (16.216–20). What is troubling Hazlitt as he contemplates the scene at Somerset House is not only the vapid "glare" and insipidity but his sense of an insidious cultural poison spreading through all art and imagination in his time from the increasingly "public" alliance of aristocratic and middle-class prejudices. Here again he is intent on exposing that peculiar compound of affected vanity, opulent intimidation, and moralized deference to wealth and privilege which became, in other walks of the same society, the mentality of "Legitimacy." And lest we underestimate the potent mixture of glib banality and hidden bigotry that Hazlitt had to contend with at the outset of his career in the London press, it might be well to recall here some of the opinions that he cites in an essay of 1815 as typical of the "commonplace critic" at the time, the "pedant of polite conversation":

He will give you to understand that Shakspeare was a great but irregular genius. . . . He considers Dr. Johnson as a great critic and moralist. . . . He thinks Pope's translation of the Iliad an improvement on the original. . . . He thinks there is a great deal of grossness in the old comedies; and that there has been a great improvement in the morals of the higher classes since the reign of Charles II. He thinks the reign of Queen Anne the golden period of our literature, but that, upon the whole, we have no English writer equal to Voltaire. . . . He thinks Jeremy Bentham a greater man than Aristotle. He can see no reason why artists of the present day should not paint as well as Raphael or Titian. . . . He thinks it difficult to prove the existence of any such thing as original genius, or to fix a general standard for taste. In religion his opinions are liberal. He considers all enthusiasm as a degree of madness, particularly to be guarded against by young minds; and believes that truth lies in the middle, between the extremes of right and wrong. He thinks that the object of poetry is to please; and that astronomy is a very pleasing and useful study. Though he has an aversion to all new ideas, he likes all new plans and matters-of-fact: the new Schools for All, the Penitentiary, the new Bedlam, the new Steam-Boats, the Gas-Lights, the new Patent Blacking; everything of that sort but the Bible Society. (4.138–39)

Obviously there was only one real consistency in this tissue of platitudes: "The common-place critic carries about with him the sentiments of people of a certain respectability in life, as the dancing-master does their air, or their valets their clothes" (4.40). Hazlitt is depicting here, perhaps for the first time in literature, and in all its bland impenetrability, that nominal elevation but real vulgarization of art which was destined to become the most pernicious form of nineteenth-century Philistinism. Far from being (as he has actually been accused of being) an early abettor of the reduction of taste to middle-class self-satisfaction,[8] Hazlitt is the first English critic to identify and oppose the phenomenon—without confusing it, as Coleridge generally did, with political liberalism and with the very idea of "a reading public." Indeed, it is because Hazlitt could still believe in a "reading public"[9] that he thought it possible to obviate or transcend the vulgarization that would continue to result from a "public taste" left wholly and irredeemably "public." He had not lost his *Lyrical Ballads* faith in a "pleasure" inhering in consciousness itself, and this faith may be said to constitute his one firm bond with the middle-class sensibility of his time—this and a corollary faith in a "common sense" distinct from common prejudice, a collective wisdom, as it were, of the organic life senses ("the just result of the sum total of . . . unconscious impressions in the ordinary occurrences of life, as they are treasured up in the memory, and called out by the occasion": 8.32). This conviction, and not simply the demands of the journalistic marketplace, accounts for the "familiar," the consciously pleasurable style that Hazlitt from the start begins to cultivate in his art criticism. Yet this appeal to instinctive pleasure is not, as the passage above makes abundantly clear, to be confused with conventional assumptions that art should "please"—should satisfy preconceived expectations, or should serve, if not existing institutions, values pre-existing in society. For Hazlitt brings to art another faith that was not widely shared: he holds, as we shall see, what aestheticians today would recognize as a "truth" or "language" theory of art.

And this insistence of his upon new pleasures and new revelations of reality insures that his readers will not for long go on assuming that they already know what "truth to nature" is in a work of art.

What this faith means in practice is that "genius" and "taste," although ideally forming a continuity, also tend to form, when Hazlitt's descriptions of art pass into judgment, a duality—distinct if inseparable frames of reference. For genius is always original, while taste implies, in some sense, as the above passage reminds us, a "general standard." We would therefore be well advised to let this duality dictate the sequence of problems in our presentation of Hazlitt's aesthetic theory and its correlation with his practical criticism. We shall be exploring, first, his account of genius, of the *creative process,* of art as it is brought into being—a process which he most often prefers to illustrate from the methods and problems of painting, rather than from the literary arts—and then his account of the judgment of "taste," of *aesthetic experience,* when creative meets critical imagination and the work of genius is experienced and valued *as* art, in its generic "truth"—in its implicit relation to antecedent works and to other arts, no less than in its individual power.

꠸꠸꠸

Hazlitt was not content merely to challenge contemporary pretensions in art; he also bade his readers consider the possibility that "the decay of art . . . [is] the necessary consequence of its progress" (18.46). At the time this was not nearly so bold a paradox as it may seem to us, for the premise of a necessary tendency to decadence found ready confirmation in the prevailing assumptions of art history, which had yet to challenge the precedent established by Giorgio Vasari in his *Lives of the Painters.* The Vasari pattern is clearly visible in Hazlitt's version of the "fate" of Italian painting: "After its long and painful struggles in the time of the earlier artists, Cimabue, Ghirlandaio, Masaccio, and others, it burst out with a light almost too dazzling to behold, in the works of Titian, Michael Angelo, Raphael and Correggio; which was reflected, with diminished lustre, in the productions of their immediate disciples; lingered for a while with the school of the Caraccis, and expired with Guido Reni" (18.39).[10] It is the same pattern of rise, decline, and fall which Hazlitt has in mind when—and he is thinking also of English literary history—he generalizes that "those arts which depend on individual genius and incommunicable power, have always leaped at once from infancy to manhood, from the first rude dawn of invention to their meridian height and dazzling lustre, and have in general declined ever after" (18.6).

More and more thinkers in the latter half of the eighteenth century came to believe in the necessary degeneration of the arts; for until the influence of Reynolds' *Discourses* and the optimism motivated by cultural nationalism, the dominant opinion was to regard the growth of science, rational morality, and the modern "refinement" of taste as tendencies steadily estranging the artist from the inspiration and undistracted observation of "nature."[11] Hazlitt brings to this argument a new and firmer logic based on his own distinctions between imagination and rational knowledge. There can be, he insists—and this famous article of Romantic doctrine seems enduringly valid—no progressive perfection in the arts as there is in the sciences; for "science depends on the discursive or *extensive,* art on the intuitive and *intensive* power of the mind." "We judge of science by the number of effects produced—of art by the energy which produces them." And Hazlitt then proceeds, long before De Quincey's celebrated essay, to draw the famous line of distinction: "The one is knowledge—the other power."[12] "Increase of knowledge" in science "does not depend upon increasing the force of the mind, but on directing the same force to different things," while the excellence of art is always the product of genius, of "original force" in the mind, a power which cannot be dissociated from the objects it creates or represents, and cannot, therefore, be increased, although it may be diminished, "by rule and method." So far Hazlitt's logic is consistent and wholly credible; but he fails to see that although art does not progress qualitatively, it may yet acquire new dimensions and new means of power; and many such developments (some waiting just over the horizon: new possibilities for color in painting, for orchestration in music) may be traced directly to discoveries in scientific (or science-inspired) knowledge. His argument therefore ends in what must seem to us a glaring *non sequitur:* the arts, he reasons,

Maidstone Museum and Art Gallery

5. HAZLITT'S REMBRANDT-LIKE PORTRAIT OF HIS FATHER AT WEM (SEE PAGE 141). SELECTED FOR ROYAL ACADEMY EXHIBITION, 1802.

139

National Portrait Gallery

6. HAZLITT'S TITIAN-LIKE PORTRAIT OF CHARLES LAMB, DRESSED AS A
VENETIAN SENATOR (1804). (SEE PAGE 141).

140

do not and cannot progress; ergo, they decline and decay (18.5–10; 4.160–64).

There are signs that Hazlitt had not always believed in the inevitability of modern decadence. After his Louvre inspiration, he had returned to England with the confident determination to "engraft Italian art on English nature" (17.139). And his earlier efforts in the years after his return (especially a Rembrandt-like portrait of his father, and of Lamb in Titianesque pose and costume: see Figs. 5, 6) do show proof of a definite if rather tentative and slender talent. He never details for us his deficiencies as a painter—a reticence which perhaps is a measure of the pain they cost him—but many faults which he describes as typically English no doubt reflect his own frustrations as a portrait painter: the English incapacity, for example, to master "the organic expression of passion," a failing which he traces mainly to Protestantism and northern "self-seclusion" (18.11, 17.139). And certainly he is describing his own inhibiting self-consciousness of "taste" when he speaks of the modern student of art who "finds it easier to copy pictures than to paint them, and easier to *see* than to copy them," who "takes infinite pains to gain admission to all the great collections," and "from having his imagination habitually raised to an overstrained standard of refinement . . . becomes impatient and dissatisfied with his own attempts" (18.41–42).

But there were other, more purely technical reasons why his attempts to imitate Titian and Rembrandt were foredoomed to failure—reasons which he himself could not have suspected, and which reveal how modern and English he inevitably was in his sense of himself as "irreclaimably of the old school in painting" (8.14–15). William Bewick's records of conversation with his friend show us how little Hazlitt understood the difference between his own direct painting and the indirect techniques of the Masters, whose surfaces were built up slowly from a number of layers of underpainting, some of them left to dry for months at a time before work on the picture was resumed. The "rich glow" of Titian's flesh, which Hazlitt so much admired, was the effect of light penetrating a number of layers of varying thickness, opacity, and hue, all conditioned by the ground tones beneath; the result was not a matter of Titian's eye, hand, and "feeling" uniting in one supreme moment of power, one

141

continuous act of organic "genius." Practical knowledge of the craft traditions of Italy and Flanders had, rather mysteriously, disappeared in England, or had been corrupted beyond recognition, by the latter half of the eighteenth century—perhaps, in part, because of the cult of "genius," with its demand that all effects emanate immediately from the painter's "execution." The consequence was that when the "direct" painter turned reverently to imitate the Masters, he soon found that he was left, after his paints dried, with "dead" colors and lumpy textures. And if, like Hazlitt, he was most often trying for a deep golden-brown richness of tone, he could only approximate that effect by using—as Reynolds had used—more and more asphaltum (a highly unstable bituminous tar) as a pigment, followed by more and more glazes of an equally unstable varnish, "megilp." The result was that Hazlitt lived to watch many of his efforts to recapture timeless truths of nature crack, darken, and begin receding into almost entire invisibility (8.9 n.).[13]

The change in painting methods is worth noting, for it helps to clarify the context of the emerging debate over the meanings of "truth" and "nature" in art. Many of the Academy painters whose glaring colors Hazlitt mocked in his reviews were conscientiously trying to escape the tyranny of aging varnish and to introduce new tonalities keyed to the necessities of direct painting. Turner was the best-known and most influential of "the white painters," as they were called, who had followed the lead of the English watercolorists in painting up from a lighter ground and in using brighter colors— colors not only more stable but admirably suited to certain "aerial" effects in landscape. Turner, Hazlitt granted, was "the ablest landscape painter now living," but his pictures are "too much abstractions of aerial perspective, and *representations not so properly of the objects of nature as of the medium through which they are seen.* They are the triumph of the knowledge of the artist, and of the power of the pencil [that is, a fine brush] over the barrenness of the subject" (4.76 n.; my italics). And after an exhibition of contemporaries at the British Institution in 1815, where Turner's ascendant influence was unmistakable, Hazlitt's remarks on Turner sharply reduce the qualifying praise and concentrate on the issue of principle: "We wish to enter our protest against this principle of separating *the imitation* from *the thing imitated*" (18.95). Much more prophetically than Ruskin, Hazlitt saw where Turner's interest in the effects of light and air was heading—namely, toward an exclusive emphasis on "visual properties," toward a severance of color and purely pictorial values from other values in nature. The first premonitory sounds of the distant war over Impressionism may be heard in Hazlitt's scorn for Turner's "quackery": he charges him with "painting trees blue and yellow, to produce the effect of green at a distance" (18.110).[14]

There is surely intolerance in these remarks, but it is the positive prejudice of a humanist, alarmed at the tendency of his time to think of visual "truth" and love of "nature," by analogy with the new vogue of primitive and atmospheric landscape, as something separable in its interest from human forms, isolated from the life of thought and moral action. Hazlitt once went so far as to speculate that landscape painting is "the obvious resource of misanthropy" (16.289). As his own habits of color handling suggest, Hazlitt was steeped in the prejudices of the studio tradition to which his brother and most of his painter friends belonged—the tradition of Reynolds, for whom landscape painting was inevitably a minor genre, something associated with small-minded Dutchmen, and not to be encouraged if English art was ever to conform to Italianate standards of "the Grand Style."

Fundamental doubts about the worth of landscape as itself a fitting subject, not as background for a scene in "history-painting" (that is, paintings of great actions or events, whether really historical or taken from literature and legend) would always remain with Hazlitt, and perhaps this scepticism explains why he so seldom recalls his own efforts in this genre. Yet he did make more than a few such attempts, and not without a certain success, if we may believe Margaret Hazlitt, who recalls her brother sketching and painting for long hours in the woods and fields near Winterslow (Moyne, p. 109). Hazlitt himself tells us of trying to capture the tone of a certain field with its "green, dewy moisture" (10.63), and it is a similar quality that he highly praised in Constable—a "green, fresh and healthy look of living nature"—when he saw that painter's *Hay Wain* exhibited in the Paris Salon of 1824 (10.126–27).[15] That "living" quality was precisely what Hazlitt had looked for and failed to find in Turner, and he complained of not finding it either in the earlier English landscapists—in Gainsborough and Wilson, for example, where there was often beauty of coloring and richness of sentiment but little or no concrete "character," no "new interest unborrowed from the eye" (18.25–27, 36; note the significant adaptation of Wordsworth's phrase from lines 82–83 of the "Tintern Abbey" Ode, *Po W* 2.261). What was missing might be found prodigiously in Titian, and "both in the colouring and forms"; in *Actaeon Hunting*, for example, the branches of the trees seem "rustling" in the wind, "the sky [is] of the colour of stone" and everything shares "a brown, mellow, autumnal look": imagination is prepared to "hear the twanging of bows resound through the tangled mazes of the wood." Here "the impression made on one sense excites by affinity those of another," so that the eye "acquires a taste or appetite for what it sees"—acquires what Hazlitt likes to call "gusto."

Gusto, as applied to art, was one of those loose conversational words, brought back from Italy and France by connoisseurs, which Hazlitt sought to infuse with a philosophical consistency of meaning. When we first begin to read this *Round Table* essay "On Gusto," which opens with the statement that "Gusto in art is power or passion defining any object," it might seem that he has in mind only the intensification of particular objects in nature: "There is," he explains, "hardly any object entirely devoid of expression, without some character of power belonging to it, some precise association with pleasure or pain: and it is in giving this truth of character from the truth of feeling, whether in the highest or the lowest degree, but always in the highest degree of which the subject is capable, that gusto consists." But then we read on to learn that the gusto of a master like Titian consists not only in vivid rendering of a given kind of particularity (for example, the *"morbidezza* of his flesh-colour") but also in the power, as in the instance of the landscape cited above, "to give . . . an appropriate character to the objects of his pencil, where every circumstance adds to the effect of the scene" (4.77–79). The "object" here that the artist's passion defines would seem to be the entire aesthetic object—the work of art in its imaginative unity. Indeed, Hazlitt is redefining "gusto" in order to demonstrate to his contemporaries that the connection between particulars, whether in nature or art, and the aesthetic object as a whole is not necessarily one of "general" form or "idea" but a unity of "character," of a "power" distinct from the already known pleasures of beauty, the power of an originally expressive *intensity;* and that without this further mode of unity in imagination, visual form itself must lose significant "truth," that is, meaningful relationship to other forms.

Put another way, Hazlitt's "gusto" may be said to be an attempt to provide a mediating and reconciling principle between two contending sets of values in the art of his time, the "ideal" and the "picturesque." Apart from its function in portrait, the valuation of particularity was mainly associated with "picturesque" art; and it was generally assumed that the more intensely particularized such painting became, the less conformable with "ideal" or "high art" it must be.[16] Hazlitt recognizes the real difference in mode represented by the two terms: Claude Lorraine's landscapes, for example, are "ideal" rather than picturesque, for "they lay an equal stress on all visible impressions." "His eye wanted imagination"; nature here has been "released from its subjection to the elements," seen without gusto, as if "the eye had rarefied and refined away the other senses"; his trees, for instance, "are perfectly beautiful, but quite immoveable." In contrast, Rubens' landscapes are filled with the gusto characteristic of picturesqueness; his fauns and satyrs epitomize that quality, for they "catch the atention by some striking peculiarity," by an "excess of form," or by some circumstance of "situation" which enforces an arresting sense of "discrimination and contrast." Thus the difference from "ideal" history painting—from, for example, Raphael's "Cartoons" depicting Biblical scenes, or Poussin's paintings on mythological subjects—lies in the fact that picturesque scenes are less contemplative and "internal" in interest, more empirically expressive and "momentary," more subject to nature and time as context, to change and "accident" (8.317–20; 18.107). Yet this antithesis does not mean, as Reynolds assumed, that the "ideal" painter is necessarily less detailed in his finishing (Claude, for example, gives, in purely visual terms, exquisite detail), or has necessarily less gusto for the intricacies of individual nature (and Hazlitt bids his readers look again at the careful articulation of passion in the faces and gestures of Raphael's Madonnas and Prophets: 18:80). Hazlitt, too, often speaks of "picturesque effect" as implying a difference between art and nature (that is, as applied to values of "sight" peculiar to the pictorial medium: 8.140; 18.107), but never as implying that such effect requires dilution of detail. Indeed, the English illusion that such negation is required is entirely the consequence of the fact that picturesque "gusto" is "not in the national character" (18.107). "Impressions do not work upon us till they act in masses," he remarks in explaining why the same traits of associational imagination which make England's poetry so varied and richly animated have made its painting relatively flat and lifeless (6.191). And the great irony in the reputation of the *Discourses* was that the nation's most honored authority on art, far from offering, as Reynolds had pretended, a "classical" corrective to provincial prejudices, had instead provided the wherewithal "to encourage our constitutional indolence and impatience by positive rules, . . . to incorporate our vicious habits into a system" (18.63).

Reynolds was, however, in another respect thoroughly "classical"—in his veneration of sculpture. "Michael Angelo," Hazlitt remarked, "took his ideas of painting from sculpture, and Sir Joshua from Michael Angelo" (18.83 n.). Since Hazlitt has been accused of failing to recognize in Reynolds a thinker after his own heart, another "Romantic" mind engaged in defending "imagination" if not "genius," it might be well to note how radically they differ, as this comment suggests, on the nature of "grandeur" in art. And the same comment also suggests how radically Hazlitt's sense of "ideal" painting differs from that of another famous attacker of Reynolds, William Blake, who shared with his hated Academic adversary a fundamentally sculptural sense of form.[17] When Blake defends "particulars" against Reynolds he is thinking of hard and exact lines, of "precision" in drawing, and not at all of the empirically organic detail of "nature" to be found in the walks of art that Hazlitt held dear, for all of which Blake recorded his scorn: portrait, oil painting, Titian and the Venetian-Flemish tradition, with its emphasis on color. For Reynolds, as for Blake, the "ideal" element in art *is* always a form, that is, a figure to be defined not by its substance or texture but by its outline, mass, position, relief, attitude; and just as each figure in a painting is to be conceived as a "lesser whole," so the whole in its entirety consists in the grouping, balancing, and configuration of the parts in a "general design"; hence Reynolds continually speaks of grandeur in Michelangelo as "grandeur of outline." Without denying that there is "abstract grandeur of form" in Michelangelo, Hazlitt insists that this sublimity continually departs from the criterion of a "middle" or "central form" of beauty, conceived by Reynolds as beauty purified of all "minute" and "accidental" particulars—that pure "abstraction" of the universal form of a species which Reynolds held to be the "standard" of all "ideal" excellence in its representation. On the contrary, Hazlitt answers, Michelangelo's figures and their attitudes typically verge on "extremes," through a heightening of characteristic detail whose "freedom and boldness" of line Hazlitt dares to call *"picturesqueness* of form" (18.54 n., 114; on this point, of course, Blake would agree, though not, we may surmise, with Hazlitt's name for it). The principle of this grandeur cannot be identified with uniformity or the harmonies of formal beauty: its principle is "power"; Michelangelo's forms "every where obtrude the sense of power upon the eye"—and not merely "muscular strength" but the energy and confidence in repose of great will; his gusto is always for "conscious power and capacity" (4.78). Yet expressive power through form alone is also the limitation of Michelangelo's genius, as of any style or conception of painting modelled upon sculpture (see 18.114). Hazlitt illustrates the contrast from the more "dramatic" unity of interest in the works of Raphael, Reynolds' other great exemplar of "the Grand Style."[18] Among Raphael's Cartoons, in *The Sacrifice at Lystra* various images of innocence—piping children, terrified animals—relieve and give poignant significance to the "grave countenances," the "thoughtful heads" of the priests; while, very differently, in *The Miraculous Draught of Fishes* some storks on the shore "are not the least elevated or animated part of the picture," as "they exult and clap their wings and seem lifted up with some unusual cause of joy" (10.47–48). From these examples it is at once clear why Hazlitt refuses to admit a potential conflict between "ideal" unity and natural particulars: "there is . . . in this process nothing of softening down, of compromising qualities, of finding out a *mean proportion* between different forms and characters; the sole object is to *intensify* each as much as possible." For only through this intensification of parts does each part emerge distinctly enough to be capable of "reaction . . . upon the rest," and thus produce in imagination that organic consistency of "nature" which is also the "truth" of the work of art to itself, or what Hazlitt calls *"keeping* in the whole and in every part" (18.146, 158–59).

But is the intensity of the "ideal" attainable by, as Hazlitt also insists, in adamant italics, *"the immediate imitation of nature"* (18.111)? He takes great pains to convince his readers that there is nothing inimical to intellect or the refinement of "taste" in the mimetic principle— nothing "gross" in even the most humbly meticulous imitation of natural objects. Reynolds' theory still labored under the old empiricist illusion, which Hazlitt's epistemology had scouted, that all perception begins with particular images and that consequently art attains to "ideal" universality only to the degree that it ascends by an "abstraction" of form from given sense impressions, which will otherwise remain subject to "singular" and "local" experience. As Elisabeth Schneider has pointed out, it is because Hazlitt conceives of the mind as habitually perceiving an object through "a confused mass" of impressions, conditioned and mediated by the stereotyped abstractions of our "general ideas," that a scrupulous particularity in art becomes necessary: "Art shows us nature," he says, "divested of the medium of our prejudices" (4.72–75). Because a natural object has but one name in discourse does not mean that it is always "one thing" in art; the true artist demonstrates quite the contrary; not a mere "deception," not a "repetition of the same idea" moves the mind of the beholder to recollect and imagine the corresponding object(s) in nature, but the impact of what are actually "new ideas"—an awareness of "new properties, and endless shades of difference" (4.72–75).[19] And if the most literal still life implies the presence of ideas, then there is no problem in conceiving of "ideal" art as continuous with mimetic: to achieve ideality is still to imitate nature, but to represent only "what is fine in nature." "The Ideal is only the selecting a particular form which expresses most completely the idea of a given character or quality, as of beauty, strength, activity, voluptuousness, etc., and which preserves that character with the greatest consistency throughout." And only an "immediate imitation," a watchful attention to nature's living "inflections," will insure that this expression of "extremes," this "carrying any idea as far as it will go," does not go too far (18.158–59).

Now it is easy, deceptively easy, to reduce this argument to caricature. Here is Stanley Chase's comment: "You have formed an ideal of grace or grossness, Hazlitt argues, but you are impotent to put it on canvas till you are lucky enough to meet with some individual who precisely answers to your mental image." That unfair "precisely" really turns the ridicule back upon Hazlitt's accuser—for Hazlitt was, after all, aware that his beloved Masters painted satyrs and angels. Chase entirely misinterprets Hazlitt's conclusion when he reads him to mean that "literally nothing which cannot be found in nature is to be allowed to the imagination."[20] Turn that statement around and we really do arrive at Hazlitt's meaning: there is literally nothing in nature which cannot excite "ideal" imagination and make it stronger and finer than it would otherwise be. As Hazlitt himself states the difference in one of his latest definitions of ideality in art: "The *ideal* may be regarded as a certain predominant quality or character, carried to the utmost pitch that our acquaintance with visible models, and our conception of the imaginary object, will allow. It is extending our impressions farther, raising them higher than usual, from the *actual* to the *possible*" (16.357).

That "possible," of course, still leaves the practical problem unresolved, as a question of method: is the painter to imitate what is "fine in nature" as it is fine *in* nature, or is he to trust his vision of the "ideal" possibility in determining how finely he should imitate the natural model before him? This is a problem that would haunt Victorian art, and perhaps it is our sense of the blizzard of graphic detail about to descend on English canvases which prompts us to suspect a fatal flaw in Hazlitt's doctrine. One scholar has speculated that he would have approved the "detailed realism" of the Pre-Raphaelite program,[21] and more than a few statements in Hazlitt seem to support this view: "The utmost grandeur of outline, and the broadest masses of light and shade, are perfectly compatible with the greatest minuteness and delicacy of detail, as may be seen in nature" (18.71). I doubt, though, that he would have been happy with the reliance of many Pre-Raphaelites on still-life techniques; he expressly warns against the danger of confusing "subtlety" of detail with "minuteness"; and he would certainly have objected to their neo-medievalist repudiation of High Renaissance "grandeur." The notion that Hazlitt prizes concrete particularity for its own sake may be largely due to the fact that the bulk of the evidence he cites against Reynolds comes from the naturalistic detail of the Elgin Marbles (the celebrated fragments from the Parthenon brought to England by Lord Elgin in 1806 and purchased by the Government, after much dispute, in 1816). But whenever he turns to make his point from painting, his "picturesque" loyalty reasserts itself, and we learn that the particulars of nature he values most are those that can be shaped in imagination to pictorial wholeness, directed and intensified "to one end" (8.38–39; 18.163). "The objects of fine art are not the objects of sight but as these last are the objects of taste and imagination, that is, as they appeal to the sense of beauty, of pleasure and of power in the human breast, and are explained by that finer sense, and revealed in their inner structure to the eye in return" (8.82). Regrettably, the close of that sentence again darkens the issue, by suggesting that the naturally organic and the aesthetically organic are never at odds in imagination; and precisely this equation of values in one universal "truth" was to prove Hazlitt's principal legacy of confusion to Ruskin and the Pre-Raphaelites.[22] Nevertheless his own priorities emerge clearly enough: it is the "gusto" of genius, the human counterpart to the energies of organic generation in nature, which taste. must learn to discern and respect, whatever mimetic liberties genius may take. Hogarth, for instance, is forgiven his relative indifference to natural detail; it was in keeping with the character of both his genius and his subjects to execute his effects "by a few decisive and rapid touches of his pencil, careless in appearance, but infallible in their results" (8.145).

This priority of "genius" tends to be forgotten in the efforts of Hazlitt's commentators to resolve the seeming discrepancy of imagination and mimesis in his theory by invoking the principle of "selection," conceived as a distinct act or phase of mind in the creative process.[23] We should remember that his idea of genius, as an emanation of "original character" in the individual, implies some given predetermination of the subject-object relationship in the artist's consciousness; and Hazlitt therefore refuses to offer a programmatic formulation for the interaction of "ideal" vision in art and the organically real in nature. Not all genius has an equal gift for "ideal" creation, and Hazlitt is careful to ground this power, when it does appear, in the same disposition to take a distinctive "view" of its "object" that all genius exhibits, even in something so modest and mundane as portrait. "The ideal," he expressly says, "is not confined to creation, but takes place in imitation, where a thing is subjected to one view, as all the parts of a face to the same expression" (20.390). That "view," that slant of "gusto" or feeling for "expression," is the given impulse with which the creative process begins; it is what the man of genius imitates because it is what he essentially *sees* in nature as being *there* to imitate; Wordsworth, for example, is said to be like Rembrandt in creating "out of himself, by the medium through which he sees and by which he clothes the barrenest subject." And in "ideal" creation it is the same angle or "bias" of vision, some "intense sympathy" with nature (8.44, 49) which determines what the artist will add or omit (cf. 20.304), and even what he invents, by associative analogy with the same feeling. A selective bias that remains "unconscious," that is, not self-conscious of what it does (and Hazlitt insists that "imagination always works unconsciously; at least in creation it is so": 4.24) will be an instinctive selection *of* objects from nature, but not an intellectually purposive, thought-directed selection *from* the sense data of perception. There is, to be sure, as in all deliberate activity, a "pre-conceived idea" in the artist's mind as he works (18.78), but the "imaginary object" of his vision does not imply an object altered by thought from its appearance as felt or seen in life; rather it is being created in order to be seen and felt more perfectly as an object of passionally organic consciousness, that is, disentangled from what other men have seen, or from what all men are conditioned by their societal prejudices to see or feel. "Genius in ordinary," Hazlitt comments, "is exclusive and self-willed, quaint and peculiar. It does some one thing by virtue of doing nothing else: it excels in some one pursuit by being blind to all excellence but its own" (8.41–42).

When, therefore, we look beyond painting and reflect upon Hazlitt's general definition of genius in *Table-Talk*—"*Genius is some strong quality in the mind, answering to and bringing out some new and striking quality in nature*"—we must be wary not to let "intellectual" connotations of "mind" take precedence over its psychologically functional meaning. Nothing seems to me more important for an understanding of Hazlitt's aesthetic than to be clear about this fundamental premise—to recognize that he locates creative power in the organic "mind" of the self in its passional being, not in intuitions of cosmic harmony, not in some transcendence of passion by powers of understanding or imagination, not in original "intellect" as such. To make the point epigrammatically, for Hazlitt the concept of genius defines the concept of imagination in art, not *vice versa*. "Genius is the power which *equalises* or identifies the imagination with the reality or with nature" (12.334; my italics). Here is a neglected statement which indicates, if we note the order of priority among its terms, Hazlitt's relative freedom from the common Romantic habit of idealizing "imagination" itself, or of honoring with the accolade of "genius" only manifestly imaginative originality.

This perhaps is the greatest debt of Hazlitt's theory to painting, and to portrait in particular: poetry's sister art forced him to differentiate between genius and imagination. The latter term he defines as "more properly [that is, as distinguished from genius, from originality in creation], the power of carrying on a given feeling into other situations." The highest degree of the latter power is Shakespeare's distinctive excellence; but far from regarding such universality and disinterestedness of sympathy as the theoretic norm or ideal model for artistic creativity, Hazlitt sees it rather as the exception which proves the rule: it was "the striking peculiarity" of Shakespeare's mind to be "generic," to have "no one peculiar bias." Hazlitt does not wish to minimize the role of intellection, but its proper exercise consists less in refinement or abstraction than in "carrying on" the suggestions of feeling, by analogy, toward the greater "comprehension" of experience (18.76; 12.290); Gainsborough, for instance, "wanted the vigour of intellect which perceives the beauty of truth" (4.36). The powers of conceptual thought cannot, however, take the lead in "new and unknown combinations"—then the mind "must act by sympathy," and "there can be no sympathy where there is no passion, no original interest." Hazlitt grants that "the personal interest" may sometimes "oppress and circumscribe the imaginative faculty" (as in the case of Rousseau), but generally "the strength and consistency of the imagination will be in proportion to the strength and depth of feeling; and it is rarely that a man even of lofty genius [the author of *Paradise Lost* is cited as the classic example] will be able to do more than carry on his own feelings and character, or some prominent and ruling passion, into fictitious and uncommon situations" (8.42).

Clearly the power of even the most transcendent genius has no privileged purity of motive, no exclusive prerogatives of intellect: its "ideal" creations are governed by the same intensive "logic of passion" that rules the will to power in all imagination. When the imagination of genius idealizes nature, it is still seeking to "pamper" and "aggrandize" what it admires as a self—to intensify, as all passion does, some "favourite object"—and the only essential difference from common humanity in this process is that the love of power in genius expresses itself as sympathy with objects of organic value in nature. Rembrandt's *chiaroscuro,* Titian's gusto for the color and texture of flesh, Rubens' sense of dynamic "motion" in the body, Pope's satirical instinct for the petty, Wordsworth's feeling for the role of natural objects in the continuity of personal identity—these themes and qualities are the unmistakable signatures of genius because they are, or were when they appeared, "both true and new." "The value of any work of art . . . depends chiefly on the quantity of originality contained in it"; and its novelty is recognized as "true" because the "prism" of an individual mind has, by being faithful to its own perceptions, "untwisted" for the first time "various rays of truth"—a part of the spectrum of the mind's light of feeling hitherto unacknowledged or invisible, although a part of all men's seeing (20.296–302).

※※

There is no better specimen of Hazlitt's sensibility as a critic of art, and no more reliable test of the consistency of his theory with practice, than his description of Titian's *Diana and Actaeon,* in *Sketches of the Principal Picture Galleries of England* (1824). Hazlitt begins, predictably, with praise of Titian's coloring; but what is less than typical is the highly intricate description that follows, which strangely mixes enthusiasm and precise analysis, with the result that more than one scholar coming upon the passage has been led to locate Hazlitt's purpose in the highly colored rhetoric rather than in his tracing of the chromatic interplay of tones in the picture. Are we really here "well on the way," as M. H. Abrams believes, "to critical impressionism"? "The figures seem grouped for the effect of colour," Hazlitt begins by saying, and he then proceeds to document this premise. "Look at that indignant, queen-like figure of Diana . . . and see the snowy, ermine-like skin; the pale clear shadows of the delicately formed back; then the brown colour of the slender trees behind to set off the shaded flesh; and last, the dark figure of the Ethiopian girl behind, completing the gradation. . . ." And so the description proceeds through several more such sentences. These, to be sure, are "impressions" communicating pleasure, but they respond to and reflect not Hazlitt's own "feeling-tones," but Titian's color tones and their demonstrable relations within the painting itself. To characterize a few brief and conventional apostrophes of praise ("a woof like that of Iris," "like a divine piece of music") as "verbal equivalents" of feeling which "translate" impressions into new "sense-modalities" in a "prose-poem"[24] is not only to misrepresent some traditional rhetoric but to mistake also the conviction which informs Hazlitt's enthusiasm—his belief in the inviolable integrity of great painting ("That picture is of little comparative value which can be completely *translated* into another language . . .": 18.11)—and thus to misrepresent also his commitment to what he calls, at the start of this critique, "the severity and discipline of art" (10.32–33).

Still less, though, at the other extreme, does his praise of the picture bear out the view that Hazlitt estimates a work of art mainly for its qualities of realism, for truths of objective "character," whether in man or nature. "To express a heightened and perceptive grasp of objective reality": this, says Walter Jackson Bate, is for Hazlitt "the end and aim" of art (*Criticism,* p. 287); but what "objective reality" is there to grasp in *Diana and Actaeon?* Its harmonies of color may all have their counterparts in nature, but the aesthetic "object" in this case has passed far beyond definition by cognitive model-objects in reality. Again Hazlitt has his eye on particulars, but he admires them now as notes in a pictorial design, not as notations of nature: "The most striking contrasts are struck out, and then a third object, a piece of drapery, an uplifted arm, a bow and arrows, a straggling weed, is introduced to make an intermediate tint, or carry on the harmony." And Hazlitt returns to this theme in his summing-up: "Everywhere tone, not form, predominates—there is not a distinct line in the picture—but a gusto, a rich taste of colour is left upon the eye as if it were the palate, and the diapason of picturesque harmony is full to overflowing. 'Oh Titian and Nature! which of you copied the other?' " (10.32–33).

Which, indeed? For in Hazlitt's view of the aesthetic experience (as distinct from the act of creation), the more intense our sense of the quality of "living" nature, the more intense also will be our consciousness of art. Meaning and value which are largely "unconscious" in the passional urgency of creation, and which can only be realized by an unselfconscious sympathy with organic nature, now flower into conscious life in the responsive imagination of the fully sympathetic observer, as he responds to the work of art not only as mimetic representation but *as* art, as an object with its own object status. Thus Hazlitt's rhetoric has another function to perform than the mere recording of personal exuberance: it serves to call attention, by its allusions to myth and poetry, to the *symbolic* intensification of reality in art, and beyond this awareness, to the symbolic magnitude of the aesthetic object in its unity—the "ideal" equivalence of the work, in its integrity as art, to all other experiences of intense "harmony" in imagination.

Art, then, has a significance not to be defined by the creative process alone. As completed in the experience of the created object, art proves to be neither mimetic nor emotive in its meaning but *symbolic:* individual feeling and universal truths of perception meet in the unity of the aesthetic object as symbol, whose concreteness coincides with an objective representation of existing nature only insofar as it is also an "ideal" objectification of value. Now the word "symbol" itself is rare in Hazlitt's writings on art, but what is not rare is the equivalent term "language": "Nature is also a language. Objects, like words, have a meaning; and the true artist is the interpreter of this language. . . . The more ethereal, evanescent, more refined and sublime part of art is the seeing nature through the medium of sentiment and passion, as each object is a symbol of the affections and a link in the chain of our endless being" (8.82–83). We recall Hazlitt saying in "On Gusto" that almost everything has "some character of power belonging to it, some precise association with pleasure and pain"; everything, in short, has symbolic potential in the mind, since all "particular" perceptions are "more or less general." But only the concrete yet "comprehensive" power of art can rediscover the sensory counterparts of ideas, can restore man's abstractions to the true connections of experiential meaning, and so enable the "web of thought and feeling" (8.83), that is, the human nervous system in its conscious life, to glimpse its own depth and range of power. Like nearly all Romantic theorists, Hazlitt is intent on shifting the sense of symbolic meaning in the arts from—in Gérard's terms—an "extrinsic" to an "intrinsic" reference, from the isolated, emblematic image to its continuity in imagination with other things;[25] and this emphasis helps to explain his reliance on the word "language." The language of common speech and discourse is "a thing altogether arbitrary and conventional"; and precisely because it is, the translation of experiential meaning into aesthetic symbolism is necessary. For much the same reasons, Hazlitt has little respect for "allegorical" themes in art, for any attempt to abstract meaning from its nexus in the passional affinity of the senses in imagination. And this condition means also that no one art can claim to be the purest or most perfect translation of nature's "language"; for each has its own medium of intensive communication which limits and modifies, even as it enhances and illumines, the mind's original language of affective sympathy. Thus music is "the language of pleasure" (5.296); sculpture is "the logic of form" (10.168); and poetry, "the language of passion," is the most comprehensive because least limited by the senses—"the universal language which the heart holds with nature and itself" (5.1). Painting, too, far from being a transparent medium, has its own "artificial language," one of "hieroglyphics" (18.138). Painting presents not the "naked" object in nature, which only science can do, but the "clothed"—divested of commonplace "prejudice," yes, but not of what Hazlitt calls "the veil of truth," the mediating "web" of perception and feeling. And "the veil of truth," he remarks, looking askance at worshippers of science, "must be drawn aside before we can distinctly see the face" (20.301). It is this lifting of the veil, so that we see and feel its beauty or power yet sense more clearly also the truth beneath—a reality whose power lies in the world forever beyond art—that is the symbolic moment of art.[26]

The relation of aesthetic value judgments to extra-aesthetic "truth" thus becomes an acute problem for Hazlitt, and not only because of his fealty to mimetic "nature" but because he is intent, as Reynolds was also, on defending the concept of a "general standard of taste," a "comparative scale" of excellence (20.386). Hazlitt has no trouble describing the lower levels of this scale: at the bottom he places literal, or minimally symbolic, imitation, and, considerably above that, art whose symbolic meaning lies in "truth of character," or of manners, but with little appeal (for example, Van Dyck's portraits, Wilkie's genre painting) to "ideal" values or imaginative passion. He recognizes, though, that since all higher value in art consists in originality, its relative excellence cannot be measured by any "absolute" or precisely formulated standard; there can only be general principles of approximation to the "highest" degree of genius, to that intensive yet comprehensive assimilation of diverse truth and value which constitutes creative greatness (20.386–89). Following eighteenth-century precedent, he distinguishes two principal modes of such excellence: "The highest art is . . . that which conveys the strongest sense of pleasure or power, of the sublime or beautiful" (18.154). Note, however, his "or," which proves to be no casual conjunction; for beauty and grandeur, though continuous in nature, tend to divide, as symbolic motives of feeling, in the mind. "If I see beauty, I do not want to change it for power; if I am struck with power, I am no longer in love with beauty" (20.304).

This remark suggests that pleasure and power are to remain motives as distinct, though just as inseparable, in Hazlitt's aesthetic as in his psychology of the will. Beauty for Hazlitt is the delight of man's sentient consciousness in its own as in all organic life and being: it is "the soft and pleasurable" in sensation, the "graceful" in movement; and although its perception depends upon an act of our imaginations, it is no less "inherent in the object." All beauty derives from the "original harmony of forms" (with analogues in the "gradations" of sound and color, in "measured intervals" of rhythm); it is, in his fullest definition, "the principle of affinity between different forms, and their gradual conversion into each other" (4.68–72; 18.164–65). Thus Hazlitt does not hesitate to say that beauty in the arts is symbolic of *"universal harmony"* (18.83–84). Yet he also makes it clear—and here he is challenging a premise dear to both classicism and Romantic Idealism—that the Beautiful in art, or the principle of aesthetic harmony, is not the same as aesthetic unity, even when they perfectly coincide, as in *Diana and Actaeon*. "There is also a principle of contrast, of discrimination and identity, which is equally essential in the system of the universe and in the structure of our ideas of both art and nature" (8.137). This is not organic pleasure but the energy of organic power, the stamina of all individuality in nature, variously manifest in art as the "picturesque" (where the interest remains individual, or becomes symbolic only by natural association); as, on the next higher level, the "historical," or "nature in action" (where the interest shifts from form to action, and individual character becomes symbolic of all kindred intensities of human will and passion); and lastly, as the "grand" or "sublime," which arises from "an excess of power, so as to startle and overawe the mind," and between whose "extremes" of power the gradations of beauty serve to mediate.[27] Whether manifest in a natural landscape or a scene in art, sublimity makes itself known as a "principle of connection between different parts," a mode of "aggregate" unity which remains entirely distinct from, although it always interacts with, the purely pleasurable unity of the Beautiful. While the latter "harmonizes," the former "aggrandizes our impressions of things" (18.161, 164–66).

The "highest" degree of artistic excellence, then, is what Hazlitt calls, following Reynolds, "the grand style"—an art whose beauty and sublimity unites, without confusing or compromising, qualities of pleasure and power which tend to remain in our other experience discordant or exclusive. This is art which presents not a "different" but a "second nature"—"nature such as we have never seen, but have often wished to see" (8.169–70). Raphael's "great style" is said therefore to be superior to Hogarth's "familiar style" because the former presents a "mightier world," a "universe of thought and sentiment" where "things [are] like not what we know and feel in ourselves, in this 'ignorant present time,' but like what they must be in

themselves, or in our noblest idea of them" (6.146). But how are we
to understand the reality of this higher "world" in the mind: is its
transcendence due primarily to aesthetic "truth," to the distinctive
powers of imagination as expressed in art, or to the attractive power
in imagination of extra-aesthetic values, of moral and spiritual
ideals? Hazlitt goes so far as to flirt with a widespread belief among
visionary religionists of the age, most explicitly stated by Blake and
by Haydon in his *Lectures,* that the mission of imagination in the plastic arts is to reveal the glory of the Creation before the Fall.[28] Poussin's heroic landscapes show us "the first integrity of things," "the
world in its first naked glory" (8.169). I do not think that Hazlitt in
such passages is simply bowing to the pieties of his time; rather,
when he says that this higher world "exists only in conception and in
power" (6.146), he would seem to be engaged in finding a way to
reconstitute admiration for religious art in a culture becoming increasingly sceptical and secular. At a deeper level, of course, we may
recognize here the shadow of his own religious prejudices: the Unitarian son, the prig-rationalist who must square all experience of
"truth" with the moral and "metaphysical" ideals of his conscience,
has returned to seize control of the argument—as the modulation
into rolling rhetoric invariably suggests. It is this Hazlitt who informs
his readers that the only difference in value between greater and
lesser works of genius resides not in the "imitation" but in "the thing
imitated"—in the degree of "grandeur" in the "subject" (20.389;
4.75). But the painter in Hazlitt knows better; he knows, and makes
clear in his practical criticism of Raphael, that the transcendent "interest" of the "ideal," if it begins with a given "idea" or sentiment,
can be achieved or communicated only *through* the work of art in its
unity: "The characters and forms must be such as to correspond
with and sustain that interest, and give external grace and dignity to
it" (6.147). And if it is always some "original interest" in the mind of
genius which creates this "ideal" transcendence, should there not be,
in the observer, a similarly organic mode of sympathy which answers
to this intensity, however indispensable the mediation of conscious
"ideas"? May there not be, in short, a sympathy in our imaginations
not with the "ideal" as such but with the idealizing "gusto" in its passional individuality—and therefore less with symbols in their "intel-

lectual" reference than with the symbolic act or movement, the "web" of expression in the work of art itself?

Hazlitt would learn to answer this question in the affirmative, but not until he makes his second pilgrimage to the Louvre on his European tour of 1824–25. It was no longer the same Louvre; many of the glories of the *Musée Napoleon* had long since departed—but a number of old friends were still there, among them Titian's portraits. Pictures with a "heroic look," he now remarks, "tire" the mind (for "you cannot be always straining your enthusiasm"), but in Titian's portraits "there is that exact resemblance of individual nature which is always new and always interesting, *because* you cannot carry away a mental abstraction of it" [my italics]. It is worth quoting at some length Hazlitt's description of a work of art which perfectly epitomizes his belief that painting has its own plastic language of meaning, one that communicates symbolic truth only through the intricate unity of the work itself:

> Thus in his [Titian's] celebrated portrait of Hippolito de Medici, there is a keen, sharpened expression that strikes you, like a blow from the spear that he holds in his hand. The look goes through you. . . . The whole face and each separate feature is cast in the same acute or wedge-like form. The forehead is high and narrow, the eye-brows raised and coming to a point in the middle, the nose straight and peaked, the mouth contracted and drawn up at the corners, the chin acute, and the two sides of the face slanting to a point. The number of acute angles which the lines of the face form are, in fact, a net entangling the attention and subduing the will. . . . It is a face which you would beware of rousing into anger or hostility, as you would beware of setting in motion some complicated and dangerous machinery. The possessor of it, you may be sure, is no trifler. Such, indeed, was the character of the man. This is to paint true portrait and true history. (12.286)

Hazlitt has often been described as a critic concerned almost exclusively with individual psychology, with problems of "character" in art and literature; but we need only look closely at this critique of the painter he most admired to learn that he is concerned with "characteristic" meaning in a far subtler sense—as *a relation of self to self,* of the beholder's self-consciousness to the self being portrayed, and of both to the self of the artist. Portrait remains for Hazlitt the prototypical model for all expression in art, not only because of the discipline of disinterested "imitation" that portrait enforces upon the painter, but because of the distinctive "truth" that it communicates, through the organic sympathy of mind and eye with another mind and eye, in a form at once mimetic and symbolic.[29] Bate is to this extent right in saying that art for Hazlitt is not definable as "self-expression" (*Criticism,* p. 285), for it is not "subjective" in a purely, or primarily, personal sense; but art is, for this very reason (as I shall be arguing more fully in subsequent chapters), *intersubjective.* The sympathy of the reader's or beholder's imagination, unlike the creator's, is not given to the cognizable "object" as such, but only to objects and their multiple associations as they are unified in significant "gusto," through the expressive movement of the passional self of genius, culminating, and cohering, in an organic presence which is not a merely formal unity of parts but the sense-perceptible equivalent of the perceiver's own self-consciousness of organic being. The "solitary grandeur" of Michelangelo's figures (18.116); the "self-possession" in Raphael's faces and the want of it in Hogarth's, contorted with "selfish passion" (10.45); the Greek statues which "in their faultless excellence . . . appear sufficient to themselves," so that they "seem to have no sympathy with us, and not to want our admiration" (5.11)—in these and innumerable other, less obvious instances Hazlitt is suggesting that every work of art, insofar as it is "original," communicates the organic presence of a self—and does so precisely because vitally "disinterested" communication is all but impossible in life, where all selves are imprisoned in the unique doom of their diversities.

This way of responding to art suggests why, and in what sense, each of Hazlitt's criticisms tends to become a "character"; and this also is why every work of art, in whatever medium, tends to assume in his response to it the feel and shape of a painting—of something with a manifest entirety of presence yet instinct with, as he says of Shakespeare, "moving power," an inward dynamic of intensive "movement." When Hazlitt speaks, as he tirelessly does, of "genius" in his specific descriptions, he is not thinking of personality as a source or will that exists beyond the work of art, but as an informing "soul"

active, though transcendent, within the novel "body"; and it is this
"genius of the performance" which is the true "subject" of his praise.
"A genuine criticism should, as I take it, reflect the colours, the light
and shade, the soul and body of a work": it should try to define
"what the essence of the work is, what passion has been touched, or
how skilfully, what tone and movement the author's mind imparts to
his subject or receives from it . . . the feelings of pleasure and pain
to be derived from the genius of the performance, or the manner in
which it appeals to the imagination" (8.217).

Whenever the supremacy of "the Grand Style" is in question,
Hazlitt, faithful corrector of Reynolds, "irreclaimably of the old
school," is reluctant to acknowledge this incipient shift in his standard of greatness in art from the expression of "the ideal" to an
ideal of expression itself. But to be convinced that the shift is there
we need only compare some of his judgments of art in *Notes of a
Journey through France and Italy* (1826) with those in his article on
"Fine Arts" (1817) for the *Encyclopedia Britannica* (an influential essay
which endured in the *Encyclopedia* until 1842, through the seventh
edition), where Hazlitt still names Raphael, Michelangelo, Leonardo,
and Correggio as the Masters "who have carried historical expression to the highest ideal perfection" (18.116). In Florence the same
critic dares (anticipating Heinrich Wölfflin's opinion[30]) to find Michelangelo's *David* ugly; at the Vatican, the *Last Judgment* in the Sis-
tine Chapel appals him with its baroque "extravagance"; and at As-
sisi and Bologna he feels more admiration for the Giottos and
Ghirlandaios than for the "affected" Correggios he had just seen at
Parma (10.203–20, 241). The moment of most strongly expressed
defiance comes when Hazlitt reaches Venice and stands at last before
Titian's *Murder of St. Peter Martyr,* a painting (fated to be destroyed
by fire in 1867) that he had seen and loved in the Louvre twenty
years before. Now he finds that it surpasses his expectations: he is
convinced that it is "most probably, as a picture . . . the finest in the
world." These figures "stand out with noble grandeur of effect
against the sky; Raphael would have buried them under the horizon,
or stuck them against the landscape, without relief or motion. So
much less knowledge had he of the picturesque!" Hazlitt was troubled by the heresy of this preference: "My taste may be wrong; nay,

even ridiculous—yet such it is" (10.272–3). And just how prophetic his heresy would be of future generations is epitomized by his response, at the Paris Salon of 1824, to the originality of Delacroix, whose controversial *Dante et Vergil* Hazlitt praises for its independence from the tyranny of sculpture, undisturbed by its bold juxtaposition of reds and blues, which challenged the conventional color harmonies of the Grand Style: he does not hesitate to judge this work "truly picturesque in the composition and the effect. . . . The forms project, the colours are thrown into masses" (10.137).

Here, then, well before Ruskin and Baudelaire, is recognition and clear authentication of the expressiveness of pictorial form and color in their own right, although Hazlitt was never to be quite so bold a rebel from classicism as to suggest that such elements should be, or could be made, expressive apart from the representational function of faces and figures. It is only in literature that he permits purely expressive values of creative "gusto" to emerge in conscious distinction from both "ideal" and mimetic truth. This no doubt reflects a Romanticist's prejudicial view that the visual arts are physically specialized and therefore more limited, in content or cultural function, than literature; but this subordination should not be confused with "poetic" tyranny in another sense—with the subjection of pictorial expression to literary antecedents or to verbally translatable meanings. When Hazlitt praises painting and sculpture for their "ideal" qualities, he has in mind not only the beauty or sublimity of the forms represented, but the purity and intensity of the same forms as art; for him, these are the most *intensive* of the arts, because in them the aesthetic object "is given entire without any change of circumstances, and where, though the impression is momentary, it lasts for ever." Hazlitt expressly warns against confusing this "ideal" integrity with the essentially "dramatic" intensity of literature; "for description in words (to produce any vivid impression) requires a translation of the object into some other form, which is the language of metaphor and imagination; as narrative can only interest by a succession of events and a conflict of hopes and fears" (20.304–05).

For too long the myth of Hazlitt's "critical impressionism" has encouraged us to think that a confused displacement of literary and pictorial contexts is continually going on in the process of his "enthusiasm" for art; and it would be foolish to deny that this does sometimes occur, given his penchant, especially in his last decade, for personal reminiscence. Yet it is worth remarking that those who have recorded most dissatisfaction today with his criticism of art have been literary scholars, not those who seek out and attend as closely to Claudes, Titians, and Poussins as he did, and who (among them Sir Herbert Read and Sir Kenneth Clark) can still find insight in his praise. There may be, by any standards, "more warmth than light" in Hazlitt's appreciations, but the preponderance of one of these qualities matters less—or mattered less to him—than the mutual activation of both, the secret of which we seem to have lost. Perhaps because he had no fear of sinning against the Light of Art, he became, as Morton Dauwen Zabel sums up his achievement, "indisputably the most original and intelligent critic of pictures that his century can boast before Ruskin." [31]

Chapter Five

Shakespeare and Tragedy: The View from Drury Lane

IN Hazlitt's London *critic* was a term that still called up the image of a man of taste exercising his virtuosity at the theater, where he would sit in judgment on the performance and—as Sheridan's Dangle fancied his responsibility—"decide for the whole town."[1] Hazlitt had passed more than twenty years in the traditional playgoing apprenticeship to his craft before, in the autumn of 1813, he was given the chance to try his hand at a review; and although he owed most of his sudden fame thereafter to his criticism of painting, he owed scarcely less to this earliest of his loves among the arts. Luckily a new production of *The Beggar's Opera* was mounted that fall and Hazlitt's review at once took the town's fancy, with its winning defense of Gay's satire on "the vulgarity of vice" (5.194; 8.292).[2] And later that season, when Hazlitt reviewed the debut performance of a young tragedian up from the country, most London playgoers found themselves warmly agreeing or hotly disagreeing with the *Chronicle*'s new writer on theater. Hazlitt's bold praises tipped the balance in the controversy raging over Edmund Kean; and while the curious crowds kept pouring into Drury Lane, Hazlitt acquired his own celebrity in greenroom circles as the critic who had saved a man of genius from obscurity and, in doing so, helped to save one of the Theatres Royal from bankruptcy. By 1816, when Hazlitt's reviews were adding to the luster of the *Examiner,* another aspiring actor, Macready, could exult that his career, too, had been favorably launched by an "authority . . . almost supreme on subjects of theatrical taste." It is this meteoric reputation which explains why the young critic's talents were so soon and so often solicited by the *Edinburgh Review;* why in 1817 he could publish under his own name *Characters of Shakespear's Plays,*[3] which at once went into a second edition; and why in 1818 he could follow this success with *A View of the English Stage,* which gave the almost unprecedented dignity of a book to a newspaper critic's reviews of theater.[4]

Yet to recall the course of Hazlitt's fame in his own time is to be brought up sharply against the paradox of his reputation today as a critic of drama. The man whom Bernard Shaw admired as not only a "lofty, keen and free-minded" writer but a "first-rate demonstrator" of acting, and whom Eric Bentley has called "the father of dramatic criticism in our language,"[5] is also the critic accused of taking the greatest works of English theater into the closet—of reading Shakespeare's plays as "poetic romances," of forsaking "action" and "dramatic context" in studies of character.[6] The paradox is first found, however, written large in Hazlitt himself. "Poetry and the stage," he confessed, "do not well agree together" (4.247), yet the same critic could also believe that "actors are the best commentators on the poets" (4.256). The lover of Shakespearean imagination who admitted, echoing Lamb, that "we in general do not like to see our author's plays acted" also found himself imagining in his closet "the meaning of a look, the grouping, the *bye-play,* as we might see it on the stage" (5.48).

Hazlitt himself felt no inconsistency in these statements. For somewhere behind both points of view stands the phenomenon of Edmund Kean, and it is our critic's ambivalent fascination with Kean's genius—an admiration that Lamb and Coleridge could never share in the same degree—which spells the difference between Hazlitt's Shakespeare and theirs. Although *Characters of Shakespear's Plays* is warmly dedicated to Lamb, and although Hazlitt quotes with approval his friend's famous essay (written, significantly, before Kean's performances) on the impotence of the stage to realize Shake-speare's imagination, it is not Lamb but Kean whom we find most frequently consulted in the text—over a score of times and often at length.[7] Any of these allusions to Kean never fails to lead on to Hazlitt's distinctive themes: a constant concern with "the force of passion" in Shakespeare (5.46), and an awareness, unparalleled in his time, of tragedy as a genre which poses many-sided, enigmatic problems for its proper understanding. These were the interests which would always call Hazlitt's mind back, however reluctantly, to his apprenticeship in the theater. "I do not wish to speak disre-spectfully of the stage but I think higher still of nature, and next to that, of books" (6.246–47): here was an order of values which per-haps not only his own prejudices but the English stage itself had taught him.

What Hazlitt was escaping in his closet was not "the stage" as such but the Theatre Royal of his time. At Drury Lane or at Covent Garden he found himself entering an atmosphere which—not unlike the "glare" of the Royal Academy Great Room—"oppresses the imagination and entombs it in a mausoleum of massy pride" (18.291). By patent from the Crown, the two Theatres Royal still held a monopoly of all legitimate drama; and they had swollen, through successive rebuildings in ever grander modes of The Grand Style, to rival enormities by having both to compete with the fashion-able Opera and with the smaller "minor" theaters, which had learned to evade illegitimacy by weaving music into their popular "melo-dramas." Burnt to the ground in 1809, Drury Lane had re-opened in 1812, and its investors hoped to pay for its new hugeness (it could seat 3,600) by luring the ordinary Londoner into vistas of wealth and elegance otherwise denied him in life: he was expected to marvel at the concourse of fashion in the vast piazza, the sight of the rich and great in their mahogany boxes, the massive chandeliers overhead, the stunning pink-and-gold décor, the great proscenium arch soaring above the vast cavern of the stage from flanking mar-ble pillars. But the management had not reckoned on the fact that once the effect of the splendid novelties wore off, there might be little enough to see—not to be seen, but to *see*.[8] "As soon take a seat on the top of the Monument"—this was Hazlitt's opinion of the worth of a seat in the upper boxes or the galleries. Far down on a stage nearly a city block away, even Kean at his passionate best seemed "a little fantoccini figure, darting backwards and forwards . . . starting, screaming, and playing a number of fantastic tricks before the audience" (8.277).

It was not easy, then, unless one shared Hazlitt's willingness to fight for a seat in the front of the pit, to have a good view of the English stage; perhaps that irony lurks somewhere in the title he gave his collection of reviews. But if the critic's eye had its afflictions at Drury Lane, his ear fared worse. We may wonder that Hazlitt and Lamb should so readily assume a discord between poetry and "stage-effect"; but one reason may be that few harmonious subtleties of language ever reached their straining ears across the noisy abyss of the two great theaters. The tradition of Elizabethan turbulence had never quite perished (it was still the custom to applaud or hiss after every scene) and now this exuberance mingled with the Restoration tradition of playgoing—for which an event at the theater was an occasion for witty sociability—to produce a medley of noises that might at any moment swell to tumult but scarcely ever subsided to silence. In the manner sanctioned by Doctor Johnson himself, ladies and gentlemen in the dress boxes (those few, that is, who did not prefer the Opera) felt free to chat at their pleasure; in the upper boxes, prostitutes and other ladies of casual virtue carried on transactions with "box-lobby loungers" to the accompaniment of pinch-provoked screams, giggles, and slamming doors; and down among the benches of the pit—where the champions or hecklers of actors lost no opportunity to clap, hoot, and hiss—a fistfight over a seat, or at least a loud quarrel between sitters and standers, might be expected nightly. Overhead, meanwhile, the gallery "gods" grew progressively noisier as they abandoned hope of hearing the performance, and not a few of them took their revenge on all the dim figures below (including those on stage) with bellows and catcalls or, fortunately less often, with apples and oranges.[9]

The audience, however, was almost never offensively large, seldom filling more (so Barnes estimated) then a tenth of the house.[10] The problem of the theater managers was always to fill the cavernous silences and keep the noises happy; and the solutions that

Drury Lane devised toward this end have remained those since brought to technical perfection by what is now more honestly called "the entertainment industry." Laughter, of course, was the surest remedy; for it was still the golden age of English farce, and a long tradition of comedians, culminating in the face-making Munden and the antic Liston, had long since mastered the art of reaching the galleries. And John Bull, made proudly conscious of himself by the French Revolution, never failed to be hushed to tears by his favorite domestic and patriotic sentiments, especially when he could laugh and weep by turns at the scrapes of *The Poor Gentleman* and *The Soldier's Daughter*.[11] But how could this audience, ever ready to hiss, be kept content when duty had to be done to high tragedy? Obviously one solution was to add to tragedy's solemnities a melodramatic dash of the same popular sentiments. This trick the adapters of Germany's romantic "tragedy" were quick to discover: their formula, as Hazlitt said, was "to put ordinary characters in extraordinary situations, and to blend commonplace sentiments with picturesque scenery" (5.366). Perhaps it was the scenery that mattered most to the managers, always hopeful of luring a crowd with spectacle. Hazlitt reports fully-rigged ships on the stage, raging thunderstorms, castles on fire; mere horses and carriages were now a commonplace.[12] Perhaps the acme of Theatre Royal art had already been reached many years ago with the staging of Sheridan's *Pizarro:* in its most spectacular scene the patriotic Peruvian hero, fighting off pursuers with one hand, bore his beloved's infant son over a tree-bridge flung precariously across a chasm; and this moment of terror was made sublime by an actually raging cataract below, with the snowy peaks of the Andes towering against blue sky in the distance. And if, despite his poetry, Shakespeare still proved popular, this was because the Bard had become an endless source of profit and delight for the machinist, the musician, the costumer, and the scene painter. The Bard's verse, as an earlier generation discovered, could always be cut or restyled to liberate the horrors of Macbeth or Richard III, and the comedies could be carried by the songs and the clowning. Now, too, there was a way to make even *Antony and Cleopatra* and *Coriolanus* moderately successful favorites—by getting up an elaborate sea fight, an imperial Roman triumph, a vast mob scene, or simply by having the hero—as John Philip Kemble played him at Covent Garden—eloquently declaim his lines while posing statuesquely before vast scenic perspectives of Egypt or Rome.[13]

Such was the "legitimate" theater Hazlitt was fated to review, and it goes without saying that he was not to review it very seriously. The style he assumes from the outset—with the one great exception of his pieces on Kean and Kemble—takes its cue from Leigh Hunt, who in the previous decade, as Hazlitt said, "first gave the true *pine-apple* flavour to theatrical criticism, making it a pleasant mixture of sharp and sweet" (18.381). This is essentially the style that has persisted ever since among critics of commercial theater, for only this mixture seems to solve the problem of chiding vulgarity without alienating the audience which is keeping the theater (and the critics) alive.[14] And especially in an age of stage-abominating religious pietism, Hazlitt was careful never to lose the theme of pleasure in venting his contempt. Here, for instance, is his damnation of an actress: "Her acting is said to have much playfulness about it; if so, it is *horse-play.*" Nor is the note of pleasantry lost even when he damns a tragedy by the Evangelical Hannah More: "From the very construction of the plot, it is impossible that any good can come of it till all the parties are dead; and when this catastrophe took place, the audience seemed perfectly satisfied" (5.258, 260).

Far from being a bland compromise with Philistinism, as this tactic has since become, Hazlitt's resort to innuendo and his reluctance to project his standards militantly are motivated by his concern for those standards in their larger function as values of community. Hazlitt had always a democratic sense of the theater; he loved it as the one institution of genuinely communal "sympathy" that remained in an England infected by the class-consciousness of "Legitimacy."[15] The interest, less as art than as life, of the theatrical event itself—this at last is all, notwithstanding many philosophical digressions, that Hazlitt thought worthwhile judging in his reviews of the stock drama of his age; for even this rudimentary appeal of theater Hazlitt saw in danger of perishing in his time. Given a theater forced to survive by tricks of "effect," desperately reduced to a condition which, however perverse, could not be corrected until political and literary opinion had changed, Hazlitt knew better than to press his demand for a "national drama" (20.284) by demanding radical reforms in the theater itself. Except in performances of Shakespeare and other established classics, the only art that this reviewer permits himself to take seriously is the art of the actor, not of the enslaved playwright. In a theater which made an intensity of dramatic illusion almost impossible to sustain—and not only because of the noise, but because the chandeliers were always ablaze—and which combined in a single evening the appeals of the circus, the concert hall, the gallery, the museum, and the prizefight ring, the one pleasure that a critic could honestly share with his fellow spectators was a delight in individual virtuosity. "Mr. Kemble's Cato," "Miss O'Neill's Elwina," "Miss Boyle's Rosalind": nearly half the titles in *A View of the English Stage* are in this form, and they testify to what it was that the sophisticated playgoer could still find at the two great theaters to enjoy, to read about in the morning, and to argue about in the day's conversation.[16] Interest in the actor, as distinct from the play, is perhaps always a symptom of dramatic degeneration; and it is no accident that a critic whose excellence, as Bentley observes, is his graphic and analytic description of acting should have begun his reviewing in the decade when, if William Archer is right, English drama sank to the lowest ebb of its long-declining fortunes.[17] But fate at least granted to Hazlitt a truly stellar actor to review—an artist who made the very badness of conditions at Drury Lane a challenge to his resources of passion.

Indeed, it was chiefly for its memorials of Kean's acting that Hazlitt thought it worthwhile publishing his collection of reviews (5.174–75). We are tempted, as we read his praise of "nature" in Kean's portrayals—and especially if we have heard of the aging Kemble's remark when he saw his young rival act, "He is terribly in earnest"—to interpret Kean's revolt from classicism as inaugurating those traditions of naturalism which would gradually come to dominate acting style and which still rule our stage today. But neither Kean nor his critical defender were able, given the conditions of performance, to conceive of acting excellence in any other terms than those of controlled *scenic* impact;[18] and by this standard the relative merit of an actor lay in the degree to which he was willing and able to manipulate the histrionic potential of scenes toward revelation of character, rather than letting demands of scenic effect simplify or distort consistency of character. All acting is, in Hazlitt's view, "studied and artificial" (5.202), and the major theme in his praise of Kean is that this actor does not sacrifice nature to the necessary consciousness of his art—to what Hazlitt calls, in a brilliant phrase, "the actor's obstetric art" (18.362). Alive to shock and travail of circumstance, Kean sought to have his characters "perfectly *articulated* in every part," in contrast to the stately Kemble, who could not "lend dignity to the mean, spirit to the familiar" (5.342–44)—who could not, in a word, be truly Shakespearean.

This judgment suggests the continuity of purpose linking Hazlitt's reviews of theater to his criticism of Shakespeare in general. He soon found it necessary to accompany, or interpolate into, his reviews of Kean extended analyses of the roles that the actor was performing, in order to win recognition for Kean's genius as "capable of doing singular justice" to the Bard's "finest delineations of character" (18.194). Hazlitt's first such effort, from which these words are taken, was a sketch of Richard III (much of it to be incorporated in *Characters*), written in support of Kean's second portrayal from Shakespeare; and similar studies in the months to come make it clear what, in this phase, Hazlitt's larger intention was—not merely to defend Kean's unorthodoxy but to help him "clear away the rubbish" from the tragic stage (4.324). How, for instance, could an audience brought up on the odious, ogre-like Gloucester of Cibber's stage version (which Kean was still forced to act) possibly hope to understand the great closing moments of Kean's performance, when his Richard, his sword taken, stands "with his hands stretched out . . . as if his will could not be disarmed, and the very phantoms of his despair had a withering power"? (18.191–94).

Clearly the public had to be re-educated from the text—and so too, not seldom, did the young actor himself, who, after his disappointing performance as Hamlet, is urged "to give one thorough reading" to Shakespeare (5.406). If Kean's Shylock (his debut performance) had forced our critic to revise his sense of that character—and to confess that he had been swayed more by the memory of previous actors than by the text itself—Hazlitt now returns the favor by bidding Kean consider whether the characters he has since portrayed have not been too simply conceived: either too broadly contrasted or, in their points of resemblance, made insufficiently "distinct" from each other. Kean's ironical Hamlet was too much like his cynical Richard; his Gloucester lacked a buoyant sense of power in his villainy, while his Iago was too much the "careless, cordial, comfortable villain" (5.187–90; 4.14–15). But before the 1815 season was over, Hazlitt was forced to acknowledge— notwithstanding Kean's unprecedented achievement in that season of performing, with equal brilliance, Iago and Othello on alternate nights—that his admonitions to the actor were having, and could have, little effect. After hearing Kean's hollow attempts at melancholy in *Richard II,* Hazlitt was in no doubt that the failure stemmed from an irremediable fault of nature: Kean "wants imagination"; he "is energetic or nothing" (5.223, 271). A master of expression who could play Massinger's Sir Giles Overreach with an authenticity of violence that made women in the audience scream and even his fellow actors flub their lines proved unequal to Shakespearean passion in its extremes of "despair" or in its tender "repose": "He sinks into pathos from the violence of the action, but seldom rises into it from the power of thought and feeling" (5.210).

By this time, though, Hazlitt may already have decided to become an interpreter of Shakespeare in his own right—to complete the folio of his sketches of Shakespearean character, and to publish them as his first book of literary criticism. The result was a collection of thirty-four essays, cut to the same *Spectator*-format length and written in the same stylistic manner as those of *The Round Table,* published in the same year. The unpretentious little book proved to be seminal, as it revived, and gave new dimension to, the "psychological" or "character" criticism of Shakespeare inaugurated in the previous half-century.[19] But the title of the book points away from the theatrical concerns in the reviewer's sketches, and especially from his overriding concern with tragedy. And Hazlitt's Preface, where he endorses the precedent of Schlegel's recently translated *Lectures on the Drama* and attacks Doctor Johnson's theory that Shakespeare's characters represent types ("species") rather than being individuals (4.171–78), has further helped to obscure the original, Kean-inspired impetus of the book as a defense of Shakespeare's supremacy as a tragic dramatist. The tragedies clearly dominate the first half of *Characters* (only three of the book's first fourteen essays deal with non-tragic plays), and the consensus of readers since is that the book rapidly dwindles in quality and interest as it winds to a dutiful close through a series of essays on the comedies (which we shall be considering in a later chapter).

Hazlitt, of course, wants no generic limitation placed on Shakespeare's genius; but we need only recall at random almost any of his general comments on tragedy to recognize the central importance of the genre for his literary theory—and even for his political theory. If the visual arts, and the simpler forms of poetry and music, were for Hazlitt means for augmenting man's resources of pleasure, and if the theater in general is a "teacher of morals" by improving our "sense of humanity" with its "intelligible picture of life" ("a bettered likeness of the world, with the dull part left out": 4.153), it is tragedy which constitutes for him the greatest, because most penetrating and irresistible, "discipline of humanity." "It is the refiner of the species," for it not only "gives us a high and permanent interest" in something "beyond ourselves" but, through its pathos, "subdues and softens the stubbornness of the will" (4.200).

Yet this statement of tragedy's moral power shows us again the conscientious Dissenter speaking, not the Boy in Hazlitt who loves Shakespearean "power" for its own sake. Indeed, perhaps it is the conflict between the two faces of poetic "power" in his mind, and not merely the phenomenon of Kean, which is drawing Hazlitt to his interest in tragedy at this time. He had just endured the despair of Waterloo and Vienna, and we have seen him wondering whether "the history of mankind" was not doomed to be "a mask, a tragedy . . . a noble or royal hunt . . . in which the spectators halloo and encourage the strong to set upon the weak" (4.216); yet in these same years he was also enjoying the first sustained exhilaration, and the first public satisfactions, of his own will to expressive power as a writer. The disparity between these two responses to the passional urgency of "power" in man's will was not yet a sense of their irreconcilability; for Hazlitt still clung defiantly to his Louvre myth of a modern Humanity progressively liberated from feudal evils through the concerted powers of Genius; and, as late as August of 1816, a faithful Buonapartist could even indulge some slender hope for the return of his fallen hero, who might somehow come back from Promethean bondage on the rock of St. Helena " 'like a cloud over the Caspian' " (7.98). Thus his fascination with the "truth" of Shakespeare's mastery of "passion" could still be felt as one with a faith in the transfiguring beneficence of tragedy—not, to be sure, as a transcendent purification and regeneration of the will, but as the humanizing enlargement of passional self-awareness beyond "mere selfishness." The polarity informing his own self-awareness—his love, not unlike Kean's, for poetic-dramatic energies as their own expressive ends, pulling in tension with, and at times against, commitment to his political myth of literary power—could still consciously issue, to adapt Hazlitt's phrase for the tragic catharsis, in "a balance of the affections" (4.200). And perhaps only this delicate balance of countervailing motives, of compassionate sympathies of "good" and organic sympathies of mind with amoral intensities of "power," enables him at this time to write a work of criticism which, as soon as two or three years hence—when the tension within him yields to pessimism, issuing then in a new direction of self-awareness—he might not have been able to complete, or even to conceive. It is significant, I think, that after 1820 Hazlitt never returns (except, incidentally, in one essay) to Shakespearean criticism.[20]

≈

"Shakespeare alone [among the dramatists of his age] seemed to stand over his work. . . . He saw to the end of what he was about, and with the same faculty of lending himself to the impulses of Nature and the impression of the moment, never forgot that he himself had a task to perform, nor the place wich each figure ought to occupy in his general design" (6.215).[21]

Written in 1819, two years after his book on Shakespeare, these words might be thought to sound rather unlike Hazlitt—unlike, that is, the prototypical "character" critic that he is traditionally assumed to be. "Character" critics are not supposed to be interested in the "design" of a play, and Hazlitt has been accused of indulging in the worst habits of the breed: "abstracting" characters from context, and fraternizing familiarly (making "friends for life") with the *dramatis personae.*[22] There is, no doubt, considerable basis in fact for such charges, and I am not about to propose that *Characters* is really a study of dramatic form. But it may nevertheless be true that its author, at least in his essays on "Shakespear's four principal tragedies," *Macbeth, Othello, Lear,* and *Hamlet* (4.186), is engaged in a critical enterprise that his later reputation[23] has tended to obscure and distort. For in these essays, especially when read in conjunction with his speculation elsewhere on the nature of tragedy, Hazlitt's psychological interests may be seen as subsumed in a larger study of the ways of dramatic *imagination*—the supreme "faculty" of Shakespeare's genius, that which shapes the unity of a play even as, and indeed because, it sympathizes with "the impulses of Nature."

When he is describing "nature" in the plays, Hazlitt knows that he is making a statement also about "art" in Shakespeare.[24] "In art," he once remarked (and he was referring specifically to theatrical art), "nature cannot exist without the highest art" (5.299). Here is a paradox that would have puzzled the eighteenth-century critics, who, although they learned to discover "art" in the plays, would never have suggested that Shakespeare is a master of "nature" *because* he is a master of "the highest art." Just as, in Romantic theory, all reality is perceived through forms and modes of imagination, so the organic unities of imagination constitute the necessary condition for the truth of "nature" in Shakespeare's dramatic art: this is why the Romantic critics insist that the poet and the dramatist in Shakespeare are one and indivisible, whereas the eighteenth-century commentator had liked nothing better than to rescue the Bard's wisdom from the excesses and irregularities of his Elizabethan medium. "In the world of his imagination," Hazlitt says of Shakespeare, "everything has a life, a place and being of its own" (5.50)—an individual being, exactly as in nature. But "everything" means precisely that— individual (irreplaceable) words, characters who are individuals, and, not least, equally individual plays. Hazlitt is therefore prepared to deal intensively with the characters as potentially "independent" of each other (5.185); but he is also aware, on the same organic principle, that these creatures owe their being, not to primary "nature," but to the creation of an organic world—to the dramatic unity of relations of which they form a part. When Hazlitt speaks of "nature" in Shakespeare, then, it is (unless context indicates otherwise) to Shakespeare's created world that he is referring—to this "second nature," as he calls it elsewhere (8.169–70).[25]

The essentially "dramatic," Hazlitt once paused to note, is "the essentially individual and concrete." It is clear that the latter adjective connotes for him not mere particularity but coalescence, the mutual involvement and interrelatedness of characters, although the binding force between them may, and usually does, take the form of negative reaction and counteraction. "Within the *circle* of dramatic character and natural passion, each individual is to feel as keenly, as profoundly, as rapidly as possible, but he is not to feel *beyond it*. . . . Each character, on the contrary, must be *a kind of centre of repulsion to the rest;* and it is their hostile interests, brought into collision, that must tug at their heart-strings, and call forth every faculty of thought, of speech, and action" (18.305; italics mine).

This "circle of dramatic character," or "the mutual contrast and combination of the *dramatis personae*" (4.300), to use Hazlitt's more formal language elsewhere—this for him is the first law of dramatic "design" in Shakespeare. There was nothing new, of course, in emphasizing the importance of "contrast" in Shakespeare: his "striking and powerful contrasts," as Hazlitt notes, "could not escape observation." But there was novelty, as we shall see, in suggesting that "contrast" might be not only a principle of antithetical definition but also a principle making for continuity of feeling, at least when seen as working in constant conjunction with another principle beneath the conflicts of the action: "The use he [Shakespeare] makes of the principle of analogy to reconcile the greatest diversities of character and to maintain a continuity of feeling throughout, has not been sufficiently attended to." In *Cymbeline,* for instance, "there is not only the utmost keeping in each separate character; but in the casting of the different parts, and their relation to one another, there is an affinity and a harmony, like what we may observe in the gradations of color in a picture."[26] And what is true of *Cymbeline* in this respect Hazlitt finds true of "most of the author's works" (4.183)—although many of Hazlitt's subsequent essays will reflect also an important difference between the sense of structure shown in this opening study and his sense of "design" in the tragedies.

That difference derives mainly from a distinction that Hazlitt draws toward the end of the present volume (4.225–26; and, more fully, elsewhere) between character in drama and character in the narrative genres—a distinction that becomes fundamental to his conception of the unity of tragedy. It is ironic that the very quality which for Hazlitt differentiates *Cymbeline* from most of the other plays—its "romance" aspect (4.179)—should so often be said to dominate his reading of all the plays; he has been accused of approaching them as "poetic romances" (Bradbrook, p. 50), as works more lyrical and narrative than dramatic. The fact is that Hazlitt, at least where the understanding of "character" is concerned, warns us against precisely this confusion. He sees Chaucer's characters, for instance, as "narrative" in conception, Shakespeare's as "dramatic": "In Chaucer we perceive a fixed essence of character. In Shakespeare there is a continual composition and decomposition of its elements, a fermentation of every particle in the whole mass, by its alternate affinity or antipathy to other principles which are brought in contact with it" (5.51). This is not to say that there is no discernible "essence" in Shakespeare's characters: they have the "predisposing bias" (12.230) of all individuals, and Hazlitt still speaks of this bias in the "general," and somewhat reductive, terms of the previous century (Caliban is "the essence of grossness," Cleopatra's "whole character is the triumph of the voluptuous": 4.239, 229). But Hazlitt departs from this eighteenth-century tradition in believing that a given predisposition of feeling implies no "fixed" identity: personal differs from logical identity in that no uniformity of will or consciousness is necessary to insure that the self remains the "same" entity. What makes a dramatic character consistent, therefore, is a consistent *process* of feeling in response to change, and especially in the character's sympathetic or antipathetic relations with other organic natures like itself; for it is only, we remember, through intersubjective responsiveness to others, as mediated by imagination, that a self is able to become conscious of its own nature, to know and express an "idea" of its feelings.

This is ultimately what Hazlitt means by an "individual" in Shakespeare: it is less our "psychological" idea of a unique structure of personality than an ontological concept, whereby the unity of "passion," of instinctive and sympathetic feeling in the self, is endowed with primal status as being, correlative with the life of all "organized beings" in nature. Indeed, we should not go very far wrong if, taking our hint from the etymology of the word, we said that individuality means for Hazlitt (and perhaps for most of the Romanticists) the organic *indivisibility* of the self and its passions—a generic tendency to an expressive unity of feeling, always different in expression from, yet responsive in that expression (that is, imagination) to the same principle of sentience in others—a "humanity" that actually or potentially exists in all character, however much society and experience may have divided this unity from consciousness of itself through prejudicial "associations" of habit and custom.[27] And Shakespearean tragedy is for Hazlitt the greatest of all dramatic achievements because its "depth" (6.30) and extreme "projection" of passion breaks through the surface diversities of character to reveal, and precisely *through* that diversity, the latent unity of "soul" that makes the whole world kin: "The passion in Shakspeare . . . is not some one habitual feeling or sentiment preying upon itself, growing out of itself, and moulding every thing to itself; it is *passion modified by passion, by all the other feelings to which the individual is liable, and to which others are liable with him.* . . . The human soul is made the sport of fortune, the prey of adversity: it is stretched on the wheel of destiny, in restless ecstasy. The passions are in a state of projection" (5.51; my italics).

This passage helps us to understand why, whenever Hazlitt tries to specify the distinctive "principle or moving power" of Shakespeare's genius, it is not "character" on which he lays most stress but "passion"—"the force of passion, combined with every variety of possible circumstance" (5.46). "Passion" emerges in his essays on the tragedies as an elemental "force" which, while it emanates only from within the characters and can be understood only through a knowledge of them as individuals, becomes more powerful than the several wills and minds through which it moves; it seems to acquire a life and momentum of its own, as Hazlitt expressly suggests when he speaks of the "sea," the "storm," the "tide" of tragic passion in Shakespeare (e.g., 4.202, 5.52). This larger dimension of "passion" is worth emphasizing, for it brings us to the crucial difference between

Hazlitt's criticism and all "psychological" criticism before or since. The "character" critic, at least as defined by current legend, is interested in emotion as inward state of mind, as the motivation of unique and separate individuals, but Hazlitt's interest is in "passion" as the energy of human *conflict*—as the dynamism of "circumstance," a force generated by sympathies and antagonisms, by the motives of individuals as they exist *only* in combination with one another and in response to some extraordinary challenge to the generic resources of "the human soul."

In this sense, of course, dramatic "passion" becomes the very antithesis, as Hazlitt was well aware, of passion in its common and theatrical connotation—in which the word suggests simply the forceful expression of an emotion—not a psychic energy striving to reunify and direct its feelings even as it gives them potent relief. His objection to the acting of both Kean and Kemble is that both had failed to grasp the poetic modulation and intensive continuity of Shakespearean passion: the brilliantly explosive Kean could reveal only "the anarchy of the passions" (18.284), while the stately Kemble reduced all passion to declamations of heroic will or to stoic resignation of will (5.376).[28] Yet Hazlitt also insists that the failure was not theirs primarily, but the fault of the foredoomed marriage between "poetry and the stage." In reading a play, our imaginations are able to "qualify" the impact of any one moment through "the mixed impression of all that has been suggested," but this "ideal" (that is, intellectual) dimension "can have no place upon the stage, which is a picture without perspective; everything there is in the foreground" (4.247).

What "perspective" means here is best explained by this comment on *Antony and Cleopatra:* "The jealous attention which has been paid to the unities both of time and place has taken away the principle of perspective in the drama, and all the interest which objects derive from distance, from contrast, from privation, from change of fortune, from long-cherished passion . . ." (4.231). This idea might seem to lure us again into the regions of "romance"; but once we are clear that Hazlitt's retreat from the contemporary stage was carried out in the name of "poetry"—that is, not for a denial of drama as art but for the sake of greater art—then it becomes clear also that Hazlitt was not really retiring to a "closet"—to a private and non-dramatic seclusion—but to what Donohue aptly calls "the theater of the imagination."[29] The background of "thought" that Hazlitt demands for tragic passion implies no rejection of the theatrical "foreground"; on the contrary, what Eastman calls Hazlitt's "scenic awareness" (pp. 103, 109) suggests that he is continually visualizing "groups" on the "foreground" of a picture-frame stage, and that the "ideal" power of the mind performs its true function only as it illumines the action and the passion observable in that foreground. Thus Hazlitt's "perspective" retains the logic of a pictorial metaphor: it does not connote, as in "psychological" causality or in the plot of a realistic novel, a pattern of forces moving in putatively "real" time out of the past into the present. Rather "perspective" refers to the entire imaginative "world" of the dramatic action as it takes shape in our minds only from that action, and in turn reacts upon and modifies our sense of the consequences of that action: "Years are melted down to moments, and every instant teems with fate" (5.51).

Perhaps no essay in *Characters* so well demonstrates the interworking of these "principles"—of contrast, analogy, intensive passional "movement," perspective—as the first of the essays on the tragedies, that on *Macbeth*. This essay will enable us to see how the elements of design function to project Hazlitt's sense of tragic meaning—a significance in "passion" beyond the mere development of character.

There was good cause for Hazlitt to be concerned with *Macbeth*'s unity; for perhaps none of Shakespeare's tragedies had been more often accused of "Gothic" crudity and barbarism. We may best follow the line of Hazlitt's defense if we remind ourselves that the issue of the play's credibility is by no means dead today; the issue has reappeared in Stoll's celebrated contention that the essential paradox in Macbeth—that so good and noble a man should become a murderer and a butchering tyrant—makes sense only as theater, not as "nature" or "life."[30] As if Hazlitt were making a prophetic rejoinder to Stoll, he insists that "Macbeth in Shakespear no more loses his identity of character in the fluctuations of fortune or the storm of passion than Macbeth in himself would have lost the identity of his person." There is, to be sure, a "contradictory principle" at work throughout the play; but the contradictoriness of its sudden "transitions," whereby "every passion brings in its fellow-contrary," must be seen in the context of a primitive and violent world "at the farthest bounds of nature," where "the action is desperate and the reaction is dreadful."

The storm center of this "unruly chaos" is the imagination of Macbeth himself, who "stands in doubt between the world of reality and the world of fancy" and whose "energy springs from the anxiety and agitation of his mind." Not simple "ambition" but his heroic imagination of himself, intensified by "preternatural solicitings," impels his will to realize the fatal prophecy. It is the dream of "future good" that makes him resolve to overcome his fears of evil; yet the same quality makes him "distrust . . . his own resolution," and as his anxiety mounts to a pitch of tension with his vision of a great destiny, he is moved to murder Duncan with "daring impatience," and with much the same "desperate" misgiving that he shows in recoiling from the act in horror and remorse. Lady Macbeth, with her "obdurate strength of will and masculine firmness," provides the contrast needed to define the struggle in her husband's mind; but her "unshrinking fortitude in crime" must also be seen in its "striking contrast" to the "cold, abstracted, gratuitous, servile malignity of the Witches," whose hardness of heart she can rival only through intensity of passion, through a "swelling exultation" in imagination as she contemplates the "promised greatness." Nor does the consistency in the leading characters vanish as the plot moves toward an ironic reversal of their roles—a reversal in which Macbeth becomes obdurately cruel while his wife succumbs to the madness of guilt. Although still a man of imaginative conscience, Macbeth plunges into the world of action; he "endeavours to escape from reflection on his crimes by repelling their consequences, and banishes remorse for the past by the meditation of future mischief." Lady Macbeth, meanwhile, is driven mad by her sleepless imagination and dies "for want of the same stimulus of action." The passion thus moves inexorably, on the level of action, toward the bloodiest extremes of evil; but its "dreadful" reaction upon itself in Macbeth's, and in the spectator's, imagination—its final movement toward full perspective—is not to reveal the metamorphosis of an ambitious egotist into a tyrant-murderer (as in the case of Richard the Third) but to "call back all our sympathy" for Macbeth as a man, whose "manliness of character" has been doomed by his own "waking dream" of heroic and human fulfillment:

> . . . honour, love, obedience, troops of friends,
> I must not look to have, but in their stead
> Curses, not loud but deep, mouth-honour, breath,
> Which the poor heart would fain deny, and dare not.
> (4.186–94; *Macb.* v.iii.25–28)[31]

Yet Macbeth's fate does not reveal its generic significance as a tragedy of "the human soul" until the perspective opens out in imagination to encompass the full poetic "impression" of the play. With this "ideal" amplitude of meaning the rest of Hazlitt's essay is concerned. Here it helps to recognize the painter's knowledge in his use of the term *design:* the fundamental meaning of the word is *drawing,* and its larger reference to pictorial unity derives from a graphic artist's awareness that the entire "design" must be drawn and composed in a way that is consistent with the drawing and shading of the individual figures. Hazlitt therefore sees the "outline" of Macbeth's character as part of a larger design; his interest in the hero is not in the will of an individual struggling with forces external to his own being but in a figure which functions as the inward center of the entire imaginative world of the play. Macbeth's mind is the microcosm of which the play is the macrocosm.

Hazlitt may be said to be writing a "character" of the play itself (and one that anticipates, even in style, the method of G. Wilson Knight):[32] "It moves upon the verge of an abyss, and is a constant struggle between life and death. . . . It is a huddling together of fierce extremes, a war of opposite natures which of them shall destroy the other. There is nothing but what has a violent end or violent beginnings. The lights and shades are laid on with a determined hand; the transitions from triumph to despair, from the height of terror to the repose of death, are sudden and startling. . . . The whole play is an unruly chaos of strange and forbidden things, where the ground rocks under our feet." And Hazlitt recognizes that this world depends for its very existence on the special way in which language is used by the poet to sustain a movement of passion; he comments on "the abruptness and violent antitheses of the style, the throes and labor which run through the expression" (4.191). Clearly this description passes beyond the eighteenth century's concept of "unity of interest" (although Hazlitt still uses that term: 4.260); for the power of imagination that Hazlitt is describing here is no longer a unifying of affective elements from above and outside the action, but itself a condition and motivating power within character and action. *Macbeth,* as Donohue suggests (pp. 328, 341), is a tragedy *of* and *about* imagination.[33] Or in Hazlitt's own words, "This tragedy is alike distinguished for the lofty imagination it displays, and for the tumultuous vehemence of the action; and the one is made the moving principle of the other" (4.187).

Just how, in general terms, we are to understand this reciprocity Hazlitt neglects to make clear until we reach the long digression on poetic imagination in his essay on *Coriolanus.* Hazlitt had earlier remarked that *Macbeth* is "done upon a stronger and more systematic principle of contrast than any other of Shakespear's plays"; and now we learn how germane to all imagination, and to all action, "contrast" is. We recall Hazlitt saying in this digression, already quoted in the chapter on his politics, that "the principle of poetry . . . exists by contrast"; it "seeks the greatest quantity of present excitement by inequality and disproportion"; its "language . . . naturally falls in with the language of power." And when he adds that poetry "rises above the ordinary standard of sufferings and crimes," we are meant to recognize the relevance of this intensive "logic of the imagination" not only for an understanding of power as *kratos* but for our "admiration" (in the ancient sense of that word) of all passional power in tragedy (4.214–16), not excluding such fearfully fascinating power as that manifested in the Weird Sisters. "Power," so understood to mean any cause or effect of "strong excitement," whether in the world of thought or of action, becomes a central term, as we shall see, in all of Hazlitt's discussions of tragedy: "The sense of power is as strong a principle in the mind as the love of pleasure. Objects of terror and pity exercise the same despotic control over it as those of love or beauty" (5.7). Given Hazlitt's premises about the nature of individuality, it is not hard to see why he should regard the love or the

want of power as an omnipresent motive in tragedy. For if passion is
organically "logical"—that is, if it tries to assimilate all energies toward some "favourite object" (4.180, 214)—then under certain circumstances imagination will tend inevitably—since its object of desire is always an organic wholeness of feeling (or an image of such
wholeness)—to confuse the organic will of the self to power with the
will to organic value, to life-sustaining "good." Conversely, any good
of "conscience" which cannot be assimilated to the prevailing vision
of power will be rejected as weak, pusillanimous—as contemptible
because powerless. This, as Hazlitt sees it, is the tragedy of Macbeth
and his Lady, whose minds are held spellbound by the terrible "contrast" in their imaginations—and from which there is no escape except through the spiral of more and more "desperate" acts of tyrannical power, followed by an ever more dreadful "reaction" of the
mind or will upon itself, driven to despair by its own powers of out-
raged humanity.

⁂

Yet the distinctive "contrast" of Macbeth is for Hazlitt not only its
great excellence but also its limitation as tragedy—as his comparison
with the more intimately "human" tragedy of Othello suggests. In
Macbeth "there is a violent struggle between opposite feelings . . . almost from first to last," but in Othello "the chief interest is excited by
the alternate ascendancy of different passions, by the entire and un-
foreseen change from the fondest love and most unbounded confidence to the tortures of jealousy and the madness of hatred"
(4.201). It would seem, then (if I am right in surmising that Hazlitt
ranks Othello somewhat above Macbeth), that a tragedy becomes more
purely, more humanly tragic to the degree that it moves beyond polarity ("contrast") and generates a *transformation* of feeling—to the
degree, in short, that imagination not merely dramatizes a conflict of
powers but generates an organic power of its own.

"What is the end and aim of all high tragedy? It is to resolve the
sense of pain or suffering into the sense of *power* by the aid of the
imagination . . ." (20.274). This power, however, since it remains
dependent upon imagination, is not to be confused, as in classical
theory, with "heroic" power. Unlike the heroes of ancient tragedy,

endowed with "strength of will" and "firmness of purpose," Shakespeare's protagonists, although always large-hearted and large-souled, are always vulnerably human; for "the object of modern tragedy is to represent the soul utterly subdued as it were, or at least convulsed and overthrown by passion or misfortune" (16.76). Thus "the love of power" that Hazlitt discovers everywhere in the passion of Shakespearean tragedy (even in its females[34]) is not the expression of human greatness or potential greatness of will; it is motivated, on the contrary, by compensation for "weakness"—by the moral or physical "frailty" (5.211) of man's nature, not by some essential immunity or transcendent recovery of the will from evil.[35] Hazlitt grants that in all tragedy the "soul" must in some way "rise superior" to "fortune and circumstances," but in Shakespeare this "grandeur" consists less in superiority of character than in greatness of "conception" (18.196; 20.274, 305)—as indeed had to be the case if Shakespeare was to keep faith with his sense of human nature as "a mingled yarn" of "good and ill together" (*All's Well* iv.iii.83–87, quoted in 4.158).

"Our strength lies in our weakness; our virtues are built on our vices" (4.119): nowhere is the paradox of "power" more evident than in Hazlitt's account of *Othello,* where Shakespeare is expressly praised for "unfolding the strength and the weakness of our nature" (4.201). If this paradox is kept in mind, much that appears glib and conventional in Hazlitt's characterization of Othello as "noble" will appear much less so—will appear, indeed, imbued with an acute sense of tragic irony. Whereas other critics have sifted Othello's words for clues to the enigma of why he succumbs so easily to Iago's insinuations—why he should so readily surrender not only confidence in Desdemona but all faith in his own love—Hazlitt accepts this paradox without much question because he sees it as manifesting a deeper and more constant paradox: the organic consistency of potential contraries in Othello's character. Reproving Macready for suggesting in his acting of the early scenes that Othello is naturally quick-tempered and impulsive, Hazlitt remarks: "He is calm and collected; and the reason why he is carried along with such vehemence by his passions when they are roused is, that he is moved by their collected force" (5.339). Hazlitt does not pause to explain the meaning hidden in the ambiguity of *collected;* but his statement makes perfectly good sense once we are alerted to his sense of the "movement" of tragic passion—the dialectic of power exposing hidden weakness, and of this "frailty" in turn generating unexpected power. What was once the strength of self-possession in Othello—the ability to act, whether in war, in the wooing of Desdemona, or in the very poetry of his speech, with all his passions and their memory-associations in concert as a complex and supple flow of will—this now becomes, under Iago's manipulation, his tragic vulnerability. It is the very integrity of Othello's passion that destroys him; for he is unable to dissociate thought from action, love from hatred and the other emotions of war, his confidence in Desdemona from his trust in Iago's loyalty, his wrath from honor, his pity from regretful and absolute revenge. Thus it is not the force of any one passional tendency, such as most "character" critics have proposed—not jealousy, vanity, self-hatred, or brutal lust—which explains the transformation. Rather, it is the irruption of "love and hatred, tenderness and resentment, jealousy and remorse"—a fusion of all the passions latent in his nature, each alternating in wave-like "ascendancy" yet gathering to a flood tide of "uncontrollable agony"—so that at last "he loses all command of himself, and his rage can only be appeased by blood" (4.201–04).

For Hazlitt, however, the ironic inversion of Othello's lordliness into bestial violence is true only, or mainly, of the third act of the play—and then only of the action, not of the "reaction" in imagination, which gives a new dimension to the strength of Othello's rage. To understand this aspect of the tragic transformation of "power," and to be convinced that Hazlitt sees it not as excluding but as assimilating the tragic irony, we need first to consider his analysis of Iago. Iago as an "artist in evil,"[36] or, in Hazlitt's own famous words, "an amateur of tragedy in real life"—this image of Iago is familiar to all students of Shakespeare criticism, but less, I suspect, from acquaintance with Hazlitt than with A. C. Bradley, who missed (perhaps because he had no use for) the essential point of his predecessor's characterization: that Iago is less a dramatic artist *manqué* than the tragic ironist *par excellence.* The basic impulse of Hazlitt's Iago is again "the love of power," but the form Iago's will to "mischief" takes is not primarily aesthetic or creative but practical and critical.

Soldier that he is, he has a "craving after action of the most difficult and dangerous kind," and he has none of the artist's sympathy with pleasure; his "licentious" bent is always "saturnine," and stems from "a desire of finding out the worst side of every thing, and of proving himself an over-match for appearances" (4.208). Although deceitful, "honest Iago" does see and reveal truth; his "licentious keenness of perception is always sagacious of evil, and snuffs up the tainted scent of its quarry with rancorous delight" (4.16–17). Hazlitt never doubts that Iago's "poison" works in Othello only because it has the fatal power of truth. Alone among nineteenth-century critics, he dares to suggest that Iago is right in his suspicions of Desdemona: there is both purity and grossness, both "timidity and boldness" (4.205) in her impassioned innocence; she falls in love with Othello, not because she see his nobility in his "mind," but because of his unique physical charisma—because he is exotic and black (and therefore a suitor unacceptable to her conventional father), primitive and full-blooded as well as dignified, a thoroughly powerful male (20.401).[37]

Iago, then, is "diabolical," but only in his want of sympathetic affections; in all other respects Hazlitt cannot help admiring his penetrating "indifference" of mind (4.206–08). For it represents to him what might be called the amorality of the tragic intelligence—the knowledge and resentment of passional "weakness" and the impulse, born from that weakness, not only to "know the worst" about human nature but to "contend" with it, however perversely, "to the utmost." So understood, Iago's will to power over weakness proves strangely akin, in principle, to the striving of Othello's mind for "command" over its agony, as well as to our own "admiration" of that evil when we go to witness it on the stage. Iago's will to power is also akin, ultimately, to the poet's delight in creating both the torment and the tormentor:

> Not that we like what we loathe; but we like to indulge our hatred and scorn of it; to dwell upon it, to exasperate our idea of it by every refinement of ingenuity and extravagance of illustration; to make it a bugbear to ourselves, to point it out to others in all the splendour of deformity . . . to arm our will against it, to know the worst we have to contend with, and to contend with it to the utmost. . . .—We do not wish the thing

to be so; but we wish it to appear such as it is. For knowledge is conscious power; and the mind is no longer, in this case, the dupe, though it may be the victim of vice or folly. (5.7–8)

The implications of this passage, when considered in the light of Hazlitt's fundamental paradox—that all human "strength," moral or emotional or intellectual, "lies in our weakness"—are staggering. For Hazlitt seems to be suggesting nothing less than this: that all "power" in Shakespearean tragedy, both the good and the evil, "the power of inflicting torture and of suffering it," finally become one "sense of power" in the tragic transformation, just as they are originally one in the poetic "force of conception" (4.201–02) that created their opposition. "The tragedy of Shakspeare, which is true poetry, stirs our inmost affections; *abstracts evil from itself* by combining it with all the forms of imagination, and with the deepest workings of the heart, and rouses the whole man within us" (5.6; my italics).

Yet what is the nature of this new unity of power—this fully human power that was not manifest in humanity before the tragic experience? Most Romantic theory answers this question by appealing to tragedy's poetic medium. For Coleridge the poetic unification of opposites reflects, and restores, the harmony of human powers that the "imbalance" of faculties in the various characters has destroyed. For Schlegel, tragic suffering awakens an "infinite" power of spirit, "the consciousness of a vocation transcending the limits of this earthly life." And Shelley gives the same assumption a Platonic twist: "The spectator beholds himself . . . stript of all but that ideal perfection and energy which every one feels to be the internal type of all that he loves, admires, and would become."[38] Hazlitt does not expressly deny the possibility of such transcendence, but everything he says about "power" and "passion" in tragedy belies such an inference. Poetry, he insists, is only "the highest eloquence of passion"; its power is "the flame of the passions, communicated to the imagination" (5.3, 7); and even his extremest praise of Shakespeare's "universal" art never suggests that the dramatist's imagination enables protean "sympathy" to transcend earthly nature (4.238, 347). But how, then, if the oneness of power is "passion" acting and reacting upon itself—if even at the end of tragedy "our strength lies in our weakness"—how is the tragic "superiority" of "soul" still conceivable?

189

This is the ultimate difficulty in Hazlitt's theory of tragedy, and he makes this challenge the principal theme in his essay on *King Lear.*

Lear seems to Hazlitt the greatest of the plays because it is the most profoundly impassioned and the most purely tragic (as distinct from epic)—this tragedy of a king who is, or becomes, the least heroic of men, "a poor crazy old man, who has nothing sublime about him but his afflictions" (16.61). Hazlitt does not hesitate to conjecture that in this play Shakespeare "was the most in earnest. He was here fairly caught in the web of his own imagination." And this, Hazlitt thinks, was inevitable, since "the greatest strength of genius is shown in describing the strongest passions," and the passion which forms the " "subject" of *Lear* is the strongest of all—"that which strikes its root deepest into the human heart."

All the major characters are seen as taking their places in the play's design according to whether the sexual-familial "root" of passion in them has been severed or stunted, or twisted into perverse desire, or torn from its native earth, or remains, like Lear's, though fatally tortured, deeply grounded in the being of things. Lear and Cordelia are alienated by the very resemblance, the "simplicity" and "obstinacy," of their faith in filial love. The story of Gloucester, both victim and banisher of a child, forms a "counterpart" to Lear's suffering. Goneril and Regan are contrasted not only with their sister and father but, in the "deliberate hypocrisy" of their infidelity, with the honesty of the cynical Edmund. The wit of the Fool relieves—and reveals—the terrible folly, the "pitiable weakness" of the king. "Lear's real" is further contrasted with "Edgar's assumed madness." And the theme of madness (that is, the disintegration of the natural unity of the passions in imagination) is reinforced and echoed by the desolation of the scenery, a corresponding "wildness" in the poetry and the great "bustle" of the concluding scenes (4.257–60).

But is that ending, however logical, defensible? Can the human soul still be said to "rise superior" to evil when the innocent and wronged (Lear, Cordelia, Gloucester) are indiscriminately crushed along with the guilty? "The concluding events," Hazlitt concedes, "are sad, painfully sad; but their pathos is extreme." That rather startling "but" may be said to sum up the entire logic of Hazlitt's conception of tragedy. Hazlitt quotes with approval Lamb's contempt for Tate's revision of the play, with its happy and "just" ending; but unlike Lamb, Hazlitt does not equate Lear's welcoming of death and his revulsion from "flesh and blood" with purely spiritual power—with a "grandeur" which from the start of the drama belongs to the protagonist's "mind" alone.[39] On the contrary, the "soul" of Hazlitt's Lear, as he says of all truly tragic souls, "gathers strength and grandeur from its despair" (18.196). What torments Lear in the flesh is what sustains and elevates, while it maddens, his imagination: it is the "fixed, immoveable" rootedness of his passion, the "anchor" of his love, digging all the more deeply into his being the more savagely it is "wrenched," that gives the old king his one hold on life, so that his soul towers in its madness "like a tall ship, driven about by the winds, buffeted by the furious waves, but that still rides above the storm."

For Hazlitt all the redeeming energies of greatness in the play arise only from the "depth" of the suffering, from the "extreme" sense of weakness that the action inflicts upon Lear's mind and upon our own; for only the impact of such extremity is capable of eliciting and intensifying all the powers of thought and feeling; "the extremest resources of the imagination are called in to lay open the deepest movements of the heart." Only because of Lear's abysmal anguish and humiliation is his passion reborn from blind pride to a profound honesty of suffering which flows purely from the soul, and which rises to its height of "awful beauty" when he is united with Cordelia only to lose her, moments later, forever (4.258–70). There is, to be sure, no effective "superiority," no consolation or redemption possible in the world of the play's action; Lear's soul is "abandoned of fortune, of nature, of reason . . . with the grounds of all hope and comfort failing under it" (18.332). Yet precisely because all hope is denied in that world, the same power in the spectator's imagination is moved, in the final "reaction," to affirm its own being: "In proportion to the greatness of the evil, is our sense and desire of the opposite good excited." This is still no victory of transcendent "good" over evil; it is rather a "balance" of opposed modes of organic power (4.271–72)—of the "doomed" power of will in action, where "the whole being" is "crushed" (16.76), and the compensatory, "ideal" power of reaction in the mind. For only this balance, this dialectical unity of contraries, which the tragic design reveals in its full perspective, rouses "the whole man" in imagination to intense consciousness of all that it means to be human: "The storm of passion lays bare and shews us the rich depths of the human soul; the sum total of our passions and pursuits, of that which we desire and that which we dread, is brought before us by contrast; the action and reaction are equal; the keenness of immediate suffering only gives us a more intense aspiration after, and a more intimate participation with the antagonist world of good . . ." (5.6).

It remains to be asked whether that last remark does not threaten the integrity of Hazlitt's vision—whether he can consistently speak of "aspiration" to a *"world* of good" [my italics], which would seem to imply an object of value transcendently distinct from tragic evil, after suggesting, only a moment before, that the wholeness of Shakespeare's tragic world of the "soul" lies precisely in its revelation of organically inseparable contraries. If Hazlitt, in his account of catharsis, had been content to forget Aristotelian precedent and to reaffirm his own sense of passional dialectic, he might be remembered today as the one Romantic critic who refuses to deny the enormity of evil and the finality of death and despair in tragedy—a critic who, indeed, continually envisions an extreme magnitude, an inescapable "depth" of suffering as the necessary condition for tragic sublimity.[40] This seems to be what Hazlitt has in mind when he praises Shakespeare as "the only tragic poet in the world in the highest sense"—the one poet "who durst walk within that mighty circle . . . shewing us the dread abyss of woe . . . and laying open all the faculties of the human soul to act, to think, and suffer, in direst extremities" (6.31). Here "the perfection of tragedy" still consists, as Hazlitt says elsewhere, in "the terrible reaction of mental power" upon suffering (18.196): man is the equal in spirit, precisely *because* he is not the equal in the flesh, of the adversary powers in his existence, and he is able to remain thus indomitable because his true and distinctive power consists in appropriating to his own consciousness ("knowledge is conscious power"), consists in transmuting into forms of "ideal" imagination, the very energies that are destroying him. But Hazlitt's humanistic instincts were evidently disturbed by the terrible starkness of this vision, and he therefore felt constrained

to assure his readers that the perspective of the tragic catharsis is finally moral—that tragedy "strengthens the desire of good" (5.6).
This is not quite what he had been saying in the *Lear* essay, where
the powers of good and evil are kept in continuous "balance" (the
"sense" of both is strengthened, not simply "good"), and where the
suffering "soul" itself, its contraries of passion at last made conscious
of their unity in being, constitutes the final "strength" of humanity,
of "the whole man within us."

The unresolved question here is not whether tragedy produces,
in whatever degree of effective force, a reaction in the direction of
"good"—for the testimony of all ages (except perhaps our own) con-
curs that it does—but whether the resulting sense of value must not
necessarily differ from human "good" as it exists prior to, and apart
from, the tragic experience. Hazlitt leaves us in the dark on this
issue; but fortunately there is evidence that he was not confusing
cathartic "good" with common societal morality or with a power of
mind or spirit that transcends man's passional nature. He recalls that
the tragedy which first impressed him with "a deep sense of suffering and a strong desire after good, which has haunted me ever
since" was, significantly, not one of Shakespeare's tragedies, but
Schiller's *Don Carlos* (6.363)—a tragedy whose story, typical of the
time, was one of tyrannical persecution, unjust imprisonment, and
deprivation of love. This is the "sense of suffering" which young
men growing up in the shadow of the French Revolution would
never cease to be "haunted" by: their sympathy was most instinctively given to the sufferings of *will,* to the longings of the self for
love and happiness—to the aspirations, in a word, of "Liberty." And
there was, of course, one play and one famous character in Shakespeare which did seem to suggest that beneath all tragic suffering lay
a longing like their own for the ultimate freedom of the self from
evil: this, I suspect, is the true explanation for the Romantic fascination with *Hamlet.*

In contrast to other tragic heroes, Hamlet's character, Hazlitt
observes, is not "marked by strength of will or even of passion"; but
Hazlitt is reluctant to draw the obvious conclusion—that this protagonist differs from his counterparts in refusing to identify with his
suffering, or only with his personal and private suffering, which he

opposes to the shams and injustices of the world. In his essay on *Hamlet* Hazlitt does, for once, write a standard "character" criticism, one "abstracted" from the play as a whole; and here he does ignore design, for he wants Hamlet's detachment from the other characters to be the very meaning of his tragedy. Hazlitt embraces the myth of an incapacity in Hamlet's character for "deliberate action" because this premise enables him, as it does all the Romanticists, to project onto Hamlet's figure their own ambivalence toward tragedy: that is, their obsession with evil in the world, their longing to escape from knowledge of it in themselves, their pessimistic sense that suffering changes nothing and that the world must go on as it is. Hamlet thus becomes for them more the spectator than the actor of his tragedy: he becomes, indeed, the sceptic who looks ruefully on all tragedy, the spokesman for a sense of personality that refuses to find re- deeming virtue or grace in suffering unless it confirms the "good" of the free self as such. This, indeed, if we look closely enough, is the scarcely hidden theme of Hazlitt's celebrated statement: "It is *we* who are Hamlet . . . whoever has borne about with him the clouded brow of reflection, and thought himself 'too much i' the sun' . . . who has had his hopes blighted and his youth staggered . . . he to whom the universe seems infinite, and himself nothing; whose bit- terness of soul makes him careless of consequences, and who goes to a play as his best resource to shove off, to a second remove, the evils of life by a mock representation of them—this is the true Hamlet" (4.232–34).

It is now a commonplace of criticism that the Romantic affirma- tion of self necessarily induced alienation from tragedy. But Hazlitt's essays on the other three tragedies are a reminder that the Hamlet- melancholy is not so pervasive or so typical as it has been thought to be; moreover, those essays help us to understand why the Romantic failure to create tragedy should coexist with innumerable insights into Shakespeare's tragic power. For the Romantic commitment to the self was less, or less often, a vision that turns away from tragedy than one that tries to look through and beyond tragedy—toward an ideal of being or becoming that gains its only freedom from evil by assimilating the strength of the experience of suffering. Hazlitt could never bring himself to disavow the identification, sealed by all the hopes of his youth, of the sympathetic "good" of "humanity" with the "good" of a will that serves political Liberty; and this understandable reluctance helps to explain why his theory of tragedy is finally incomplete and was doomed to lead a shadowy and fragmentary existence in his pages.

It remained for Keats to rescue the essence of Hazlitt's theory from these prejudicial confusions, and to recognize that his favorite critic's insistence on intense and supra-personal "passion" as the true "power" of tragic imagination was leading toward a new vision of poetic art as free of the doctrinal will (that is, toward a sense of what Keats called "negative capability")—a vision of tragedy as purgatorial rebirth, and of all human suffering as potentially a process of "soul-making." And it is Keats, too, who enables us to glimpse, in the wish that ends his sonnet on *Lear,* what perhaps was always the "desire" at the heart of Hazlitt's praise of Shakespearean passion—the love, which the "character" critic and the advocate of "Rational Liberty" could never happily confess, for the tragic fire as the flame of the soul's freedom:

> . . . when I am consumed in the fire,
> Give me new Phoenix wings to fly at my desire.[41]

Chapter Six

Poetry:
The English Muse

WHEN in the winter of 1818 Hazlitt delivered his *Lectures on the English Poets,* he was still in the happy ascendancy of his fame. Now an established author with a number of books before the public, he hoped to put behind him the life of routine journalism for a career of independent writing and lecturing—ultimately with a view to abandoning all servitude to the public and returning to his work on metaphysics. Already there were ominous glimpses of the doom awaiting this intention—in the past year *The Round Table* had been thoroughly vilified in the Tory *Quarterly*—but the success of his first venture at literary lecturing must have tempted even the unsanguine Hazlitt, as he looked out from his rostrum at consistently large audiences, to believe that his critical reputation might be winning a security beyond partisan cavil. He was immediately requested to repeat the series; and even *Blackwood's,* on the eve of its ferocious attack upon him, could praise the lecturer as "sometimes the very best living critic," and as certainly one (along with Francis Jeffrey) of "the two most eminent speculators on literary topics." [1]

Until recently it was the custom to see the author of the *Lectures* as the common-sense popularizer of ideas of poetry imbibed from

197

Wordsworth and Coleridge; and although this mistake is no longer so simply made, the view persists that Hazlitt, however original in his philosophy of imagination, remained a Wordsworthian in his poetic values and, on theoretic questions, a "rebellious disciple" of Coleridge[2] who repudiated only the more mystical and Germanic aspects of Coleridge's teaching. No matter how finely qualified, this view can only misrepresent the *Lectures,* which reveal their contemporary significance only if we restore them to the emerging quarrel between those two celebrated "schools" of poetry, the "Lake" and the "Cockney." These epithets were, of course, designed not for use but for abuse, and only in a very special, highly qualified sense may we fairly speak of two contending "schools" in contemporary poetics. When Leigh Hunt in 1816 began proclaiming the advent of a "new school" in English poetry, he was certainly not excluding the Lake poets: indeed, as allies in reviving the spirit of "our older and great school of poetry," Hunt cited the names of Wordsworth, Coleridge, Byron, Lamb, Keats, and Shelley, and even the archenemy of the Lake poets, the *Edinburgh Review,* which in its recent admiration of the Elizabethan poets had shown itself to be "still the leader in the new" as it was once "the greatest surviving ornament of the old school [that is, the Augustan]."[3] But Hunt's eclectic optimism flew in the face of contemporary realities—as Wilson and Lockhart, the ambitious young editors of *Blackwood's,* were quick to recognize. In their first number (for October 1817) the new editors of "Maga" began a series of articles under a title, "The Cockney School of Poetry," designed to make satiric capital of Hunt's prophecy. The label "Cockney" proved to have great sticking power, and it owed this pertinacity to Lockhart's recognition of the socially revolutionary fact that a "plebeian" like Hunt, without a university education or other social pedigree, should be dedicating a poem (*The Story of Rimini*) to Lord Byron and giving himself airs of fellowship with Jeffrey, a dig-. nitary of the Scottish Bar. When Hunt's "immoral" theme, his "gloating" in the poem over "adultery and incest," was regretted as "likely to corrupt milliners and apprentice-boys," or when reading his poem was likened to entering "the gilded drawing-room of a little mincing boarding-school mistress"—then the point of the charge could scarcely have been lost upon the reader: here was a poet who was immoral because (unlike Lord Byron) he had presumed to venture beyond the legitimate confines of his social class. And the poet who had hitherto (that is, in Jeffrey's reviews in the *Edinburgh*) incurred the onus of the "low" was now held up as a paragon by contrast. Wordsworth possessed a "patriarchal simplicity of feeling" which Hunt could not possibly admire, for "the two great elements of all dignified poetry, religious feeling and patriotic feeling, have no place in his [Hunt's] mind." These were mild jibes when compared with the gratuitous insults flung in subsequent articles at the "starved apothecary," Keats, and at "pimpled Hazlitt," the latter being an especially "paltry creature," his "raving" prose unfit for "the tables of gentlemen."[4] Many an orthodox reader must have been taken aback at this unprecedented defense of the traditional pieties in the shameless tones of cavalier raillery—in a style which resembled nothing so much, said Hazlitt, as the taunts of tavern brawlers who, for sport, "throw open the windows and abuse the passengers in the street for their want of religion, morals, and decorum" (16.232).

The battle was thus drawn along the lines of post-Waterloo Legitimism; but this fact does not mean that the contention between the two camps is without lasting intellectual significance. *Blackwood's* would never have been able to exploit the connotations of "Lake" and "Cockney" unless these terms really did signify—even as they served conveniently to conceal—two antithetical orientations for poetry, and for Romantic imagination in general. What this divergence is, Hazlitt's *Lectures*, more than any other document of the period, helps us to understand; for it is there that genuine differences in poetic attitude first begin to emerge articulately from the smoke of politics, however much the tone and animus of a partisan rhetoric may still color Hazlitt's style. Hunt, too, had tried continually to transcend politics, but he had done so by pretending that a "new" school of poetry could readily be formed under the banner of fidelity to the poetic values, if not always to the stylistic manner, of the pre-Augustan past. It is this comfortable illusion, variously indulged in both "Lake" and "Cockney" poetics, that Hazlitt proceeds to attack. In his third lecture, "On Shakspeare and Milton," Hazlitt pauses to suggest that the very words "nature" and "art" were coming to mean something very different, as conscious values, from what they had once meant, in the greatest poetry of the past:

> The great fault of a modern school of poetry is, that it is an experiment to reduce poetry to a mere effusion of natural sensibility; or what is worse, to divest it both of imaginary splendour and human passion, to surround the meanest objects with the morbid feelings and devouring egotism of the writers' own minds. Milton and Shakspeare did not so understand poetry. They gave a more liberal interpretation both to nature and art. They did not do all they could to get rid of the one and the other, to fill up the dreary void with the Moods of their own Minds. (5.53)

As that last phrase suggests (with its echo of a heading that Wordsworth gave to a group of poems in his 1815 collection), this is aimed principally at the master of the Lake School, but it deals a glancing blow also at all modish self-indulgence in contemporary poetry, not excluding that of our "Cockney" critic's fellow liberals—Byron, Moore, and Shelley. And more specifically, as a statement of theory, this challenges the critical efforts not only of Hunt but of Coleridge, in *Biographia Literaria* (1817), to identify the Wordsworthian revolution with the revival of the Elizabethan-Renaissance tradition.[5] But therein lies a problem confronting Hazlitt himself as a theorist: what then *is* the role of the self, of original "passion," in the poetic process? The answer would not be fully forthcoming until Hazlitt resumes his attack on the Lake School in his closing lecture, but the logic on which he builds that conclusion is established in his introductory performance, "On Poetry in General."

※

Hazlitt's theory reflects the ambition of all the Romantic critics to achieve a universal definition of poetry. Where we speak of "the artist," Romanticism spoke of "the poet"; and this difference in nomenclature is not lightly to be disregarded. Poets to us are not one breed but essentially plural, being no less different among themselves, or from themselves, than other writers are; and the poems they write have, we assume, the sovereign right to be judged on their own terms as unique works of art, independently of any canons of universality. The idea of "poetry" as something distinct from, and existing antecedently to, poetic texts and their creation seems to us all but inconceivable—as absurd, say, as calling someone a poet who never writes a poem. Yet this is precisely what the Romanticists believed to be possible, and they did not hesitate to say so. When Wordsworth described his brother John as "a *silent* Poet,"[6] he was not paying him a figurative compliment but describing, with solemn literalness, what he felt to be the fundamental continuity in mental processes between himself and his brother. For Wordsworth's belief was that he and his brother and, potentially, all mankind spoke a silent language of self-communion, and of sympathetic communion with others; and that only this "music of humanity" enables imagination to transform common speech, prose, and verse into poetry— into what Hazlitt calls "the universal language which the heart holds with nature and itself" (5.1).

Not the least importance of Hazlitt in Romantic criticism is that he, more than any of his contemporaries, makes us aware that the Romantic concept of universal poetry, or of what Friedrich Schlegel called *Universalpoesie*,[7] is not to be confused with the cognate ideal of poetry as universal prophecy. Roy Park seems to me essentially right when he says that "in the early nineteenth century the credit for the formulation of the philosophical basis of [an] approach to poetry as poetry and not as science, religion or anything else must go to Hazlitt" (p. 6). But Park scarcely mentions the issue I am raising; or insofar as he does, he seems to be saying that for Hazlitt poetry is universal only to the degree that poets abandon conscious ideas of universality, along with all other "abstraction." Earlier, Walter Jackson Bate had insisted that Hazlitt's poetic values are all grounded in "gusto"—in sympathetic (or empathic) identification of imagination with organic individuality, whether in man or nature (*Criticism*, pp. 287–92). And now in Park's book this tendency has surely reached culmination; for here Hazlitt's vision of poetry emerges as something less like other literature than like painting—something essentially concrete, "existential," non-abstract and therefore undefinable—alien to all ideas of universal "truth"; for "generality" of any kind would "subvert the autonomous and self-authenticating nature of poetry" (pp. 27–28, 210).

Hazlitt has thus begun to acquire a new identity in poetic history as one of the fathers of the modern doctrine of "pure poetry"—of a poetry which differs from mere "verse" not by its subject matter or intellectual content but by an expressive "intensity"—a term that Hazlitt first made central to criticism, but that probably owes its persistence today to its adoption by Hazlitt's most prestigious disciple, Keats. I have no wish to call in doubt the lineal descent from Hazlitt of this sensibility or this sense of poetic value, but it is one thing to recognize what Hazlitt is coming to mean as a precedent for the poetics of our time, and quite another to assume that this is necessarily what he himself means when he comes to define poetry. For despite Park's arguments to the contrary, Hazlitt does offer a "general" definition of poetry—and he does it with no hesitancy whatever, indeed with all his proverbial enthusiasm. And as symptomatic of the unfriendly reception his own definition of poetry would be likely to meet with in our time were it better known, George Watson's opinion of it is worth noting—or at least will provide emphatic evidence of how firmly entrenched among us are certain misreadings of Romantic theory.

"The best general notion," Hazlitt writes, "which I can give of poetry is, that it is the natural impression of any object or event, by its vividness exciting an involuntary movement of imagination and passion, and producing, by sympathy, a certain modulation of the voice, or sounds, expressing it" (5.1). Now Watson finds in this statement "hopeless confusion." He asks: "Whose impression (poet's or reader's?); and how does anyone's impression 'produce' modulations?" Watson is assuming that by "poetry" Hazlitt can only mean a poem, and this non-Romantic assumption is compounded with another: that a poem can only be a poetic text, that is, an *object,* an entity existing over against consciousness as would any object of our senses: on one side of this object stands, or stood, the poet, and on the other, the reader—and their "impressions" must therefore be discontinuous, however much or often they coincide. This is a sense of the poetic object that we are all likely to have today; but it was not at all Hazlitt's sense of a poem, which for him was, as he says, a "movement"—a movement of the poet's mind calling forth a correlative movement in the reader's mind. However sceptical we may be of Hazlitt's rhetoric about the universal "heart," let us remind ourselves that there is nothing ridiculous in the premise that a poem is not an autonomous entity but a "movement" that the reader brings into being as well as the poet. At least one thinker in our time, Jean-Paul Sartre, has argued that no literary object can be said to have an existence analogous to that of a physical object, except perhaps to a spinning top, and then only to "a peculiar top that exists only in movement": "to make it come into view a concrete act called reading is necessary," and only a "conjoint effort of author and reader . . . brings upon the scene the concrete and imaginary object which is the work of the mind."[8] But it is not finally an antipathy to the role of the reader in poetry—for critics, after all, are readers—that accounts for Watson's hostility. He goes on to scorn what he calls Hazlitt's "pompous claims for poetry," and he quotes Hazlitt as follows: "Wherever there is a sense of beauty, or power, or harmony, as in a motion of a wave of the sea . . . there is poetry, in its birth . . . Fear is poetry, hope is poetry . . ." And Watson then asks: "Does 'is' mean 'equals' or 'is the subject of'?" The question is intended as a mockery, and Watson does not stay for an answer; instead, turning triumphantly, as it were, to the jury, he throws up his hands in mock despair: "But no use the machinery of siege—there is nothing to be taken. Hazlitt, as usual, is not saying anything, he is simply making a noise to suggest to us that he is, or has been, excited about something" (p. 137).

So blatant an insult seems to me worth quoting only because the questions that Watson raises in his attack prove to be more apposite than he knows for a revaluation of Hazlitt's poetic criticism. First of all, his words suggest how intolerant we are to the concept of "passion" in poetic theory. We may want our poets to be passionately intense, but our theory—like most theory, before or after Hazlitt—is reluctant to assign to passion a crucial function in the creative process—that is, to passion as such, not to the "noble" and "sublime," idealized passions that the Longinian tradition celebrated, which, of course, carry their own antidote within them, their own salvation from the putative blindness and chaos of passion in general. We tend, I suspect, to agree with Coleridge that in poetic composition "the property of passion is not to *create;* but to set in increased activity." Coleridge is assuming—and when we relegate the study of passion in poems and poets to what we call "biographical" criticism, we are making the same assumption—that passion, being motivation, is empirically individual, and that only imagination can be universal (or in Coleridge's terminology, "generic").[9] Hazlitt dares to challenge this supposition, but he does not simply reverse the argument: he argues that, yes, passion *is* always individual, but imagination too, although more generic in its sympathies, is no less subject to individuality; it is only when these two elements interact and merge indistinguishably in one "movement"—when "the flame of the passions [is] communicated to the imagination" (5.3)—that the necessary transcendence of universal poetry becomes attainable.

Here, then, is the paradox that Hazlitt in the *Lectures* sets out to explain and defend—the mystery of how the non-transcendent powers of the self produce poetic transcendence. The question is indeed, as Watson says, "How does anyone's impression 'produce' modulations?" Watson may think that he is reducing Hazlitt's reasoning to absurdity, but actually he has succeeded in restating, and quite succinctly, the inescapable question confronting all Romantic theory—and perhaps all modern theory. For if one begins with the individual personality as the creative agent, then the question for poetic theory is and remains: how do we get poetic music out of the noise—or the silence—of emotional excitement? Wordsworth was the first to raise and attempt an answer to that question, in his 1800 Preface to *Lyrical Ballads;* and although Coleridge brilliantly demolishes Wordsworth's answer in *Biographia Literaria,* he lets the question go begging; *his* only answer to the question of how feeling produces modulations is to invent a built-in modulator, or what he calls "a high spiritual instinct of the human being impelling us to seek unity by harmonious adjustment" (*BL*.2.56). And this is of a piece with Coleridge's general thesis about poetic imagination: as Pater objected, he continually confuses the ideal product with the actual process,[10] so that we end with a tautology: Organic unity organizes organic expression; Poetic wholeness unifies whole poems. This kind of thinking, which escapes circularity only by appeal to supra-rational mysticism, Hazlitt called the "cant in the present day about genius, as everything in poetry" (5.74), and he was determined to abjure and oppose it; true, he too extolled "genius," but always as a gift for original expressiveness, never as a gift for the intellectual or "spiritual" intuition of universals. And this pretentiousness was, he thought, not merely obfuscating theory but threatening to destroy the cause of a "catholic faith" in poetry (19.29), by making imagination not less but more individual, in the negative sense of the word—by making the poetic impulse egocentric, vain, spiritually proud, jealous of other claims to greatness. Among Hazlitt's readers and listeners at the time, only Keats, only the advocate of "negative capability" seems to have understood the connection between Hazlitt's definition of poetry (which will otherwise seem, as it has seemed to many observers, thoroughly Wordsworthian[11]) and his attack on Wordsworth's "egotism"; for perhaps only a poet, and only a young, ambitious, troubled poet—a poet torn between the example of Wordsworth at one extreme and of Shakespeare at the other, could have seen the originality and momentousness of Hazlitt's idea of poetry as opening up new creative possibilities. We can see Keats in his letters gradually coming to understand Hazlitt's ultimate purpose in the *Lectures:* not merely to draw, necessary though it was to do so, the invidious contrast between Elizabethan greatness and the new poetry of self-expression, but to bring again into continuity, to reconcile—by the same theory of poetic "movement" and the same universal standards of "intensity"—Shakespearean "passion" with its modern, more subjective, Wordsworthian counterpart, the "music of humanity."

I believe that Hazlitt's paradox—the idea that only individual passion makes poetry universal—does merit Keats's admiration, does make sense, and good sense, on his own terms, although we must be very clear about those terms. In most contexts Hazlitt's own terminology still proves serviceable, but now it will be necessary to invoke a term that I have so far used sparingly—*intersubjectivity*—in order to eliminate a troublesome ambiguity that has grown up around Hazlitt's words, "sympathy" and "disinterestedness." For "sympathy" has been largely reduced in Bate's account to empathy, and "disinterestedness" is too easily confused, as again it generally is in Bate, with objectivity, selflessness, and anti-subjectivism.[12] To get our proper psychological bearings on this problem, it may help to remind ourselves again that for Hazlitt there is and can be no given self-consciousness, for this is acquired only through the instinctive "sympathy" of the mind of the self with the organic being and vital expressiveness of other selves: only by a sympathetic act of imagination does the mind learn that it *is* a self. We have noted Hazlitt's awareness that this original sympathy is soon suppressed, weakened, narrowed, or twisted into self-love; for although men are not naturally selfish, the very fact that they learn by sympathy that they are necessarily individuals gives them an aggressive "love of power" which, more often than not, perverts the natural bond of sympathy into defensive reaction, or into what Hazlitt calls "exclusive" feelings. It is therefore precisely the function of art, and especially of poetry, to restore, enlarge, and strengthen this original communion of humanity—to transform what was once instinctive communion into the conscious and moral community of civilization. "This," he says, "is the true imagination—to put ourselves in the place of others, and to feel and speak for them" (18.345). And poetry can do this best because imagination in this art is the mind speaking in its most human condition as the voice of a passional self—and transforming as it gives utterance to its passions the very bondage to self which makes for evil and selfishness in the world into a new sympathy with humanity. In the following passage, notice how directly Hazlitt points to the mutual responsiveness of one self to another as, in his own phrase here, "the root of our imagination":

> The interest we take in our own lives, in our successes and disappointments, and the *home* feelings that arise out of these, when well described, are the clearest and truest mirror in which we can see the image of human nature. For in this sense each man is a microcosm . . . Man is (so to speak) an endless and infinitely varied repetition; and if we know what one man feels, we so far know what a thousand feel in the sanctuary of their being . . . As is our perception of this original truth, *the root of our imagination* [my italics], so will the force and richness of the general impression proceeding from it be. The boundary of our sympathy is a circle which enlarges itself according to its propulsion from the centre—the heart. (12.54–55)

Now this passage clarifies several things for us when we place it alongside Hazlitt's definition of poetry. The "root" of imagination is clearly subjective, but the sympathy between these subjectivities does not depend upon consciousness of a countervailing world of objects; here, in short, there is no trace of either the Lockean or the Kantian dualism of subject-mind and object-nature which scholarship has led us to believe is the indispensable frame of reference for an understanding of Romantic poetics. We do find a "mirror" mentioned, but this "truest mirror" is doing what Abrams insists only the Romantic Lamp can do (p. 52); indeed, this light is radiating from a self only as and because it reflects and expresses another self. In poetry the "object" of our sympathies is even less bound than in painting to the given world of nature: "the natural impression of any object," with which poetry begins in Hazlitt's definition, is not to be confused with an impression of a natural object. Hazlitt is himself happiest with poetry whose imagery is drawn from empirical nature; but the object in poetry is always a *passional* object—an "object" in the conative, not the cognitive, sense—an object of "power," of our love of power. No other Romantic critic speaks less honorifically of "power" in poetry; indeed, Hazlitt suggests that this power is no different in essential impulse from feral, destructive, and tyrannical power, from the will to power in the world. We remember the *Coriolanus* essay: "The language of poetry naturally falls in with the language of power. The imagination is an exaggerating and exclusive faculty . . . it accumulates circumstances together to give the greatest possible effect to a favourite object" (4.214). Yet for Hazlitt this is only to say that the pursuit of any imagined "object," in poetry as in life, remains bound to the passional self, even when idealized or directed toward otherness: "the true imagination," we should remember, is "to put *ourselves* in the place of others" (18.345), "to feel for others *as for ourselves*" (12.55; my italics): that last qualifying phrase is often forgotten. Now this might seem to doom poetry to an abyss of subjective passion; but Hazlitt bids us remember that power in poetry can only be what he calls "conscious power," a power of heightened consciousness; and in order for the disturbing passion to gain power for itself or over other passions, it must call in aid all the resources of consciousness. And these "other forms" and "other feelings" (5.3), while in some ways their associations serve to aggravate the force of the original feeling and its "object," also challenge and expand the limits of habitual self-consciousness, so that desire for power soon becomes indistinguishable, in the resulting movement of imagination, from the power of conscious desire and delight in its own intense activity. "The poetical impression," Hazlitt writes, "of any object is that uneasy, exquisite sense of beauty or power that cannot be contained within itself; that is impatient of all limit; that (as flame bends to flame) strives to link itself to some other image of kindred beauty or grandeur; to enshrine itself, as it were, in the highest forms of fancy. . . ." (5.3).[13]

But it is time now to illustrate this movement in concrete terms—for to deny that a poem has an autonomous existence is not to deny the need for objective analysis of its movement; and this, Watson to the contrary (p. 136), Hazlitt does not neglect to provide. One of his favorite passages in Shakespeare was this sequence of lines from *The Winter's Tale*—from Perdita's well-known catalogue of the flowers of spring:

> . . . Daffodils
> That come before the swallow dares, and take
> The winds of March with beauty; violets dim,
> But sweeter than the lids of Juno's eyes,
> Or Cytherea's breath . . .
>
> (IV.iv.118–22)

Hazlitt's account of the movement of these lines begins with a description of the "feeling" as it exists in its antecedent or purely subjective state, before passion and imagination have modified it: "The feeling of the contrast between the roughness and bleakness of the winds of March and the tenderness and beauty of the flowers of spring is already in the reader's mind, if he be an observer of nature . . ." In modifying this feeling, the challenge to the poet, as Hazlitt goes on to say, is to convey "the extreme beauty and power of the impression with all its accompaniments"—that is, to intensify, to resolve into a unity of conscious power this disturbing tension of opposing responses. Yet this unity must be accomplished without in the least diminishing the force of the contrast which is its interest for passion; for poetry, Hazlitt insists, always "exists by contrast"; that is the necessary condition for its continuing impulse to power. Shakespeare therefore resorts to a "fiction"—yet not to a "pure fiction" but "a fanciful structure raised on the groundwork of the strongest and most intimate associations of our ideas." "The poet, to show the utmost extent and conceivable effect of this contrast, *feigns* that the winds themselves are sensible of it and smit with the beauty on which they commit such rude assaults." And Hazlitt proceeds to point out how, in the same spirit, the movement of intensification continues and enlarges in the succeeding lines on the violets, mingling the humblest beauty in nature with allusions to ancient myth and divine power, all united by the vernal theme of awakening sensuous love (20.210–11). And such associations are united also, at a more fundamental level—are kept from having an effect of "levity"—by the "momentum" of the passion, by the constant presence of a self, of a feeling voice that is speaking to us through this imagery, however "fanciful." "It requires the same principle to make us thoroughly like poetry, that makes us like ourselves so well, the feeling of continued identity" (5.151).

That remark suggests to me the only possible transcendence that Hazlitt sees as taking place in poetry. There is no transcendence for the poet—the voice of passion remains, however unified with itself, the voice of passion—but in the *poem* there *is* transcendence; for the very fact that the voice remains the expression of a self enables the self of the reader to sympathize with an aspect of the poem's unity which the poet himself cannot know or enjoy as power—with what Hazlitt calls the "character" of its genius, the uniqueness of its continued identity as a voice; and this sympathy of the reader becomes a transcendent pleasure of its own, a pleasure in genius as congeniality, in the human "truth" of the passion, although the reader may not consciously acknowledge it as such. It is therefore no accident that Hazlitt, as he concludes his definition, should use the word *sympathy* in describing the modulations of sound in poetry; for the organic sympathy which enables one sense, one faculty of consciousness, to harmonize with another in the same individual is also the same sympathy with organic power which solicits and implicates the reader in the movement of the poet's language. It would be too simple to say that for Hazlitt the speaking *voice* in poetry is the individual, self-expressive element, while the "music" of versification, the *ear* in poetry—or the capacity of the voice to listen to itself and react upon itself—is the generic element, the surrogate of humanity; but such a formulation would at least not do violence to his sense of the difference between poetry and prose. In a prose narrative the "interest," he remarks, "is worked up . . . by an infinite number of little things . . . by a repetition of blows, which have no rebound in them." Thus the "sympathy excited" in the reader, unlike that in poetry, "is not a voluntary contribution . . . There is a want of elasticity and motion. . . . The heart does not answer of itself like a chord in music." And this too is the contrast with prose rhetoric, which "tries to persuade the will and convince the reason," whereas "poetry produces its effect by instantaneous sympathy" (5.14–15 and n.). Clearly what makes, in Hazlitt's view, the sympathy instantaneous is the harmonious union of the passion with the versification (or its rare equivalent in the rhythms of prose), which, by appealing to our sense of the vital harmony of our own organic being, enables us to sympathize in poetry—as we cannot do in life—with the love of power and its expression in another self.

There seems to me only one term which is adequate to describe both the passional "sympathy" and the transcendent "disinterestedness" in this conception of imagination. I have chosen the term *intersubjective*, for that seems to me precisely what Hazlitt's sense of the poetic "movement" is: a communication of subjectivities without the necessary mediation of reference to a public object-world (whether conceived as a world of culture or objective "nature"), and without the further mediation of a work of art conceived as having transcendent object-status of its own. Only by way of this premise, it seems to me, can we fairly extrapolate from Hazlitt's definition of "poetry" to poems—a poem being, by this logic, definable as a movement from subjective feeling, through metaphoric or symbolic intensification of passion, to sympathetic transcendence, to the pleasure or "truth" of intersubjective consciousness, which, when attained as conscious power, completes the movement of imagination.[14]

※※※

Once we are clear about the intersubjective principle in his theory, we may be able to find more merit than confusion in another of Hazlitt's critical ideas—his distinction between two "styles" in poetry, the "natural" and the "artificial." T. S. Eliot professed to find nothing but absurdity in this distinction. He singles out for ridicule the statement which opens Hazlitt's fourth lecture: "Dryden and Pope are the great masters of the artificial style of poetry in our language, as the poets of whom I have already treated, Chaucer, Spenser, Shakspeare and Milton, were of the natural . . ." (5.68). Eliot, after pausing to assure us that Hazlitt "had perhaps the most uninteresting mind of all our distinguished critics," discovers that "in one sentence" Hazlitt commits "four crimes against taste": "It is bad enough to lump Chaucer, Spenser, Shakespeare and Milton together under the denomination of 'natural'; it is bad to join Dryden and Pope together; but the last absurdity is the contrast of Milton, our greatest master of the artificial style, with Dryden, whose *style* (vocabulary, syntax, and order of thought) is in a high degree natural." [15]

Justice now demands that Eliot's sentence—almost literally the sentence of death for Hazlitt's reputation in this century (or until very recent years) as a critic of poetry—be submitted to an equally precise scrutiny. It is bad enough, after impugning Hazlitt's use of the term "natural," to adopt the same term without pausing for definition; it is bad not to recognize (or admit) that Hazlitt has been using "style" in a general sense (as in *grand style, baroque style*) not to be confused with individual idiom (although not to be separated from it either); it is bad to confine the meaning of style to "vocabulary, syntax, and order of thought" (and just what, one wonders, would a natural "order of thought" be?); but the last and most fatal sin against rational criticism is to evade (or conceal) the issue Hazlitt has raised—of whether there is not a radical difference in poetic kind between, on the one hand, the art of Dryden and Pope, however obvious their differences, and, on the other, the poetry of their greatest English predecessors, however dissimilar the same four poets may appear when approached for other critical purposes.

To make this rejoinder is not to approve Hazlitt's nomenclature, which is easily exposed today as the language of a judgmental myth of poetic history, not unlike Eliot's own mythic antithesis (and to make way for which, of course, Hazlitt's had to be demolished) between a "sensibility" (Shakespearean-Metaphysical) which is said to unify thought and feeling, and another (post-Miltonic, Romantic), in

POETRY: THE ENGLISH MUSE

which these elements have allegedly undergone "dissociation." [16] Each of these myths may claim its measure of truth, and both may appear equally justified when viewed as performing corrective functions in their respective times, but Hazlitt's seems to me, on balance, considerably less arbitrary, more hospitable to poetry's variety. Hazlitt did not originate the contradistinction between "natural" and "artificial" poetry, or its application to these poets—indeed, the logic of the contrast extends far back into eighteenth-century criticism [17]— and Hazlitt does his best to prevent invidious misunderstandings. Eliot might have been amazed to learn that Hazlitt elsewhere praises Dryden's verse (in the satires) as "the perfection of uncorrupted English style." But the "masterly ease" (9.236–38) of Dryden's idiom does not preclude definition of his work in its general character—in its order of thought, shall we say?—as belonging to the "artificial" style in that it undertakes mainly to "describe artificial life [society as governed by codes, conventions, and fashions] and convey general precepts and abstract ideas." In contrast, Chaucer's poetry belongs to the "first" or "natural" class, for "he describes the common but individual objects of nature, and the strongest and most universal because spontaneous workings of the heart" (9.236–38). Chaucer's style is, in short, "natural" to poetry, is consistently intersubjective, while Dryden's "artificial" style imports into the poetic process the extraneous mediation of general ideas and other associations which do not originate in the expressive sympathies of the passional self and thus remain essentially foreign or indifferent to the "power" of poetic imagination. And that this, and no other, is Hazlitt's criterion—that he means by "nature" nothing fixed or absolute in feeling, imagery, or use of language—should be clear at once if we actually attend to his comparison of the four great English masters:

> In comparing these four writers together, it might be said that Chaucer excels as the poet of manners, or of real life; Spenser, as the poet of romance; Shakspeare as the poet of nature (in the largest use of the term); and Milton, as the poet of morality. Chaucer most frequently describes things as they are; Spenser, as we wish them to be; Shakspeare, as they would be; and Milton as they ought to be. As poets, and as great poets, imagination, that is, *the power of feigning things according to nature* [my

italics], was common to them all: but the principle or moving power, to which this faculty was most subservient in Chaucer was habit, or inveterate prejudice; in Spenser, novelty, and the love of the marvellous; in Shakspeare, it was the force of passion, combined with every variety of possible circumstances; and in Milton, only with the highest. The characteristic of Chaucer is intensity; of Spenser, remoteness; of Milton, elevation; of Shakspeare, every thing. (5.46–47)

Far from "lumping" these poets together, Hazlitt is discriminating their respective powers as definitive excellences in the four major genres they represent: realistic or humorous verse-narrative, pastoral-chivalric romance, tragic (or tragicomic) drama, and the epic, or "heroic" poetry in its noblest grandeur and sublimity. Once the generic dimensions are recognized, it is clear also that Hazlitt is identifying the "principle" of each of these genres with a mode or phase of intersubjectivity—with an elemental aspect of the life of the passional self in its responsiveness to other selves or to the otherness of external nature and the universal conditions of self-consciousness (Spenserian romance, for example, shows us "things . . . as we wish them to be"). And lest we wonder whether the term "style" is not being stretched beyond all coherent sense in this usage, we may remind ourselves of Flaubert's definition of style as *"une manière de voir";* for Hazlitt, too, is thinking of style as an integration of the real through an original consistency of perception, so that the poet's use of his medium ,becomes, in John Middleton Murry's phrase, a "a mode of experience." [18] Hazlitt once defined "style" as "the mode of representing nature" (16.352), and what makes these several styles equally "natural" (Hazlitt does not deny "nature" or "truth" to the "artificial" style, but the great difference is that the latter's universality does not derive from individual expression) is not only their originality but the intrinsic relation to each other—their mutual complementarity. They enhance, define, complete each other; each is implicit in all, and all in each; indeed, that is Hazlitt's point in "comparing" them. Together, they represent the four quadrants of the poetic compass, the principal directions of perspective which, beyond mere song or description, the "imitation of nature" may take in poetry—four ways of integrating passional experience, ways which diverge infinitely in their concrete representations of human nature but return to meet inwardly in the intersubjective self of "sympathy" that stands at the center of all imagination. The poetry of nature "has its centre in the human soul, and makes the circuit of the universe" (5.70).

Hazlitt's method, though, of "character" criticism could not always be happily adapted to this novel vision of "nature." The logic of the method, as Hazlitt came to it through the criticism of Dryden, Pope, and Johnson, required the critic to establish a dominant "principle" or "ruling passion" in a writer's work;[19] and this precedent leads Hazlitt to try to pack complexities of literary character into a single term—Spenser's "remoteness," Chaucer's "intensity"—which escapes vagueness only by seeming reductive. Nevertheless, by the time Hazlitt has done with Chaucer, he has made a convincing case for that poet's "intensity," provided that we are not misled by the word's modernist connotations. He speaks of Chaucer's "downright reality," of his "severe activity of mind," of the absence of metaphorical indulgence in his language, of his "picturesque" yet "dramatic" concentration upon the "tangible character" of things, of details of dress and other "external appearances . . . as symbols of internal sentiment"—the latter "interest" especially being Chaucer's forte (as seen in the Prioress, for example, or the suffering of Arcite in "The Knight's Tale"). "In depth of simple pathos, and intensity of conception, never swerving from his subject, I think no other writer comes near him, not even the Greek tragedians" (5.26–29). Similarly, by "remoteness" in Spenser Hazlitt means nothing so simple as exotic escapism. Rather, Hazlitt intends this term to stand for that poet's tendency to all "visionary" extremes, whatever the purpose, fanciful or intellectual. "He luxuriates equally in scenes of Eastern magnificence or the still solitude of a hermit's cell—in the extremes of sensuality or refinement." Thus Hazlitt minimizes but does not repudiate the allegory in Spenser; for it is Hazlitt's point that moral issues in Faery-land are, like the landscape, beautifully luminous and clear; in this sense, too, Spenser "fulfills the delightful promise of our youth." Beauty may here prevail over Chaucerian "truth," but insofar as such "voluptuous" episodes as the Bower of Bliss are truly erotic in their delight, theirs is no narcotic pleasure, remote from the life of the mind or the will; for "pathos," too, is never far away, even sublime pathos, and there is consequently "no want of passion and of strength" in *The Faerie Queene.* The organic senses, although they join in depicting a purely ideal world, remain united in a gusto of "harmony" whose outward and visible sign of sympathetic grace is the beauty of the verse itself. Perhaps no other critic has described so well the distinctive power of the Spenserian stanza, or at least its potential in the Romantic age (the charm it held, for instance, for the author of *The Eve of St. Agnes*):

> It is a labyrinth of sweet sounds, 'in many a winding bout of linked sweetness long drawn out'—that would cloy by their very sweetness, but that the ear is constantly relieved and enchanted by their continued variety of modulation—dwelling on the pauses of the action, or flowing on in a fuller tide of harmony with the movement of the sentiment. It has not the bold dramatic transitions of Shakespeare's blank verse, nor the high-raised tone of Milton's; but it is the perfection of melting harmony, dissolving the soul in pleasure, or holding it captive in the chains of suspense. (5.34–44)

But Milton's "high-raised tone"—can his style, too, so unlike the manner of his fellow masters, be justly described as "natural"? Hazlitt freely concedes "the quantity of art" in Milton, and although he insists that the poet's "imitation" and sophisticated learning were always matched by the native resources of an impassioned mind ("the fervor of his imagination melts down and renders malleable, as in a furnace, the most contradictory materials"), Hazlitt knows that he cannot rest his case on a mere analogy between a mind's genius for assimilation and "the force of nature." Earlier Romantic solutions to this problem had been content to stress the universality informing the poet's prophetic intention; but Hazlitt directly challenges the legend of Milton, when he wrote *Paradise Lost,* as a blind old man but star-like spirit, his mind raised "above" the senses, encompassing the harmonies of nature through a pure music of intuitive or faith-inspired vision. Coleridge, for example, had argued that Milton's "ideas" are "musical rather than picturesque," and Hazlitt's rebuttal of this thesis provides further evidence of how little he shared his former mentor's theory of imagination, now thoroughly

Transcendentalized. The specific importance of this question is not confined to the period; for Coleridge's insistence on the musicality of Milton's genius has since been turned against the poet's reputation, becoming the proposition (in such later critics as Pound, Eliot, and Leavis) that the elaborate diction and constant Miltonic crescendo stultify and desensitize powers of perception and feeling that poetry ought typically to cultivate.[20] Milton perhaps served Coleridge as chief model for that re-creative "shaping" of "secondary" imagination which "dissolves, diffuses, dissipates" primary sense perceptions into a musical "order" of language (*BL*, 1.62, 202; 2.12 ff.). And it is no less true that for Hazlitt, too, poetic transformation consists in an organic "harmony" of elements normally disparate in consciousness ("It is the perfect coincidence of the image and the words with the feeling . . . that gives an instant 'satisfaction to the thought' ": 5.7). But although he grants that in Milton "the ear . . . predominates over the eye," Hazlitt contends—and proceeds to adduce several convincing examples—that "where the associations of the imagination are not the principal thing, the individual object is given by Milton with equal force and beauty." He bids us remember the figures of Adam, Eve, and Satan, which are "always accompanied, in our imagination, with the grandeur of the naked figure; they convey to us the idea of sculpture." And even when the visual sense seems in abeyance, Hazlitt finds no weakening of Milton's "double" gusto, his relishing of both palpable oject and expressive word (4.79–80). Keats was soon to salute Milton as "Chief of organic numbers!"; and a remark of Hazlitt's in this lecture helps us to understand (as perhaps it suggested) the young poet's tribute: "The sound of his [Milton's] lines is moulded into the expression of the sentiment, almost of the very image." There is no room here to review Hazlitt's illustration of this power from the rhythms of various passages, but to convey his general point it may be enough to recall his praise of two exemplary lines—the comparison of Satan to

> Leviathan, which God of all his works
> Created hugest that swim the ocean stream
> (i.202–02)

—on which he comments: "What a force of imagination is there . . . ! What an idea it conveys of the size of that hugest of created beings, as if it shrunk up the ocean to a stream, and took up the sea in its nostrils as a very little thing!" (5.58–62).

Yet another objection to Miltonic as "natural" style remains to be answered. What is the point of praising *Paradise Lost* as "natural" poetry if the poet's essential concern is with man's relationship to God and eternity—with, in short, the soul's transcendence of nature? "Supernatural poetry" is, Hazlitt insists, "allied to nature, not to art [that is, artificial civilization], because it relates to the impressions made upon the mind by unkown objects and powers," which "baffle and set at nought all human pretence." Satan, it is true, "is an artificial or ideal character: but would any one call this artificial poetry?" (19.82). The figure of Satan, indeed, stands at the center of Hazlitt's, as of all Romantic, thinking about Milton; but Milton's fallen Archangel is not being transformed here into another Romantic Prometheus, a rebel-hero of Nature or Liberty who defies an atavistic Heaven of Fear. The symbolic meaning that Hazlitt finds in Satan is nothing more nor less than "the abstract love of power, of pride, of self-will personified, to which last principle all other good and evil, and even his own are subordinate." Whatever the force of Milton's own "love of rebellion," Satan is necessarily a heroic figure, for his power is essentially the "power of thought," which cannot, by its very nature, be reconciled to "non-entity" and must therefore, though sunk and eclipsed in "the clouded ruins of a god" (5.63–65), remain essentially indestructible, even (presumably) by God himself. Calling in aid our previous chapters, we may reconstruct how Hazlitt's mind has been working in understanding the epic conflict in the poem: the "everlasting contradiction," here seen in its primal form, is again that between the love of power (Satan) and the love of good or happiness (unfallen Adam and Eve). Hazlitt defends the later books of the epic against the charge of a falling-off of "interest" through the absence or infrequency of exciting "action"; and in this defense Hazlitt shows conclusively that he was not surrendering the principle of organic value in consciousness to his mature awareness of organic "power" in the self. It is not merely innocent beauty, the paradisial "freshness," the pristine "grandeur" of the scenes in Eden that Hazlitt values, but the "repose" of the mind and its senses upon nature; for it is this repose, denied to Satan, that Hazlitt sees as the enduring source of the human mind's strength after the Fall, when, in the closing episodes, the epic "interest" shifts from the beauty and love of Edenic life to the pathos of its loss. Indeed, if there is a "heroic" principle that Hazlitt is affirming in his account of Milton it is this transcendent force of natural "pathos," not Satan's defiant will; for Hazlitt makes it clear that Satan is not man; his "unbending" spirit is "ideal," his strength not the fruit of "weakness"; and it is the vain desire for such power, the "impossibility of attaining" it only whetting that desire the more, which is the Satanic legacy of evil to mankind. Milton was therefore right, Hazlitt implies, to withhold such passion, as well as such action, from his relatively unspoiled human protagonists: Adam and Eve depart from Eden with "sorrow" but not with "impious and stubborn repining." In this view of evil, what reconciles fallen Man with his lot—and here Hazlitt departs from his author—is neither faith nor reason nor conscience but the retrospective "sorrow" of all mortal passion, recognition and acceptance by the mind of a natural process in the Fall itself—"the loss of unspeakable happiness and resignation to inevitable fate" (5.63–68).

That Hazlitt sees the theme of universal "fate" in Milton as the culmination of all themes of "nature" in his predecessors, as elevating to its full range and height of intersubjective consciousness the "pathos" inhering in all poetry of "the natural style," emerges in this praise of Milton, which may also stand as Hazlitt's definition of the epic genre: "Milton takes the imaginative part of passion—that which remains after the event, which the mind reposes on when all is over, which looks upon circumstances from the remotest elevation of thought and fancy, and abstracts them from the world of action to that of contemplation" (5.52). However much we may be drawn to Hazlitt's defense of the integrity of *Paradise Lost,* we must recognize that three distinct ideas are being confused in this statement: the concept of epic poetry in general, Milton's own religious imagination (resulting in an epic singularly different from any other ever written), and the concept of the "highest" poetry as that in which moral and aesthetic values become one in "contemplation." We may learn, not from Eliot but from the Keats of the revised *Hyperion,* the gravity of error in the general effort of the time—from which only stylistic delusion and frustration could follow—to establish Milton's style as germane to "heroic" imagination, and as therefore, presumably, the inspirational model for the character and tone, if not the idiom, of all poetry of "elevation," of what Arnold would call "high seriousness."[21] What Raphael and Poussin were to Hazlitt's sense of painting, Milton was to his sense of "grandeur" in poetry, tempting him to conceive of the "higher" poetic intensities as the "ideal" impulse to "enshrine" and "consecrate"; and thus to conceive of the entire edifice of English poetic genius by analogy with a cathedral—in his own phrase, a "temple" of "true Fame" (6.176). Here is the mythic element that finally invalidates Hazlitt's terminology of "natural" and "artificial"; for his insistence upon "nature" rests upon a residual optimism, his belief—not to be challenged seriously in his own mind until the next decade—that there is finally no expressive contradiction between morally ideal values and "ideal" greatness in art. The element of myth appears clearly enough when we consider that Romantic criticism does not merely couple Shakespeare and Milton as the greatest English poets: this age also assumes that Miltonic imagination is implicit in Shakespeare's—that the "sublimity" of the two Masters is finally one—and with this assumption the Romantic critics were able to arm themselves against the starker implications of Shakespearean tragedy.[22] Indeed, it is perhaps chiefly the shade of Milton which leads Hazlitt to believe that the tragic catharsis in Shakespeare at last "strengthens the desire of good" (5.6), and to believe also, against the analytical thrust of his theory, that epic poetry, notwithstanding essential affinities with drama (5.53), tends to move away from the conflicts of passion, of the "everlasting contradiction" in man, toward a "contemplation" that is closer to lyric than to tragedy (4.110).

༔༠༔

Insofar as the *Lectures* can be said to have a unity of structure, it lies in a narrative pattern of descent from a Golden Age, not unlike the "Four Ages" myth about poetry that Peacock was more explicitly to develop.[23] Hazlitt sees English poetry as having "declined, by successive gradations, from the poetry of imagination, in the time of Elizabeth, to the poetry of fancy (to adopt a modern distinction) in the time of Charles I; and again from the poetry of fancy to that of wit, as in the reign of Charles II and Queen Anne." From there "it degenerated into the poetry of mere common places, both in style and thought, in the succeeding reigns," until "it was transformed, by means of the French Revolution, into the poetry of paradox [i.e., of *para-dox* in the original, rhetorical sense, as the controverting of commonplaces]" (5.82).[24]

To understand the logic of this decline we must turn aside for a moment to another of Hazlitt's lecture series, that *On the Dramatic Literature of the Age of Elizabeth,* delivered late in the following year (1819), after the series on comedy. The Elizabethan lectures are perhaps the weakest, on the whole, of the three series—the most desultory and disorganized, without a clear direction of purpose— but Hazlitt's opening "General View" of the Elizabethan age still merits, and rewards, reading as a pioneering example of historical criticism. Hazlitt would have none (except, as we shall see, where comedy itself was concerned) of the "Merry England" myth that was growing up around the Elizabethan revival; he leans almost too far to the contrary extreme, projecting the violence of the Elizabethan tragic stage onto the historical landscape. "Man's life was (as it appears to me) more full of traps and pit-falls; of hair-breadth accidents by flood and field; more way-laid by sudden and startling evils . . . while the imagination, close behind it, caught at and clung to the shape of danger, or 'snatched a wild and fearful joy' from its escape." Even more important for literature than the birth of national pride, the liberating ethos of the Reformation, and the visionary stimulus of new transoceanic discoveries, it was, he believed, this interpenetration of the passions in Elizabethan experience, enabling the eye of imagination to observe in outward life what it felt within, that gave so many of Shakespeare's contemporaries, and especially Marlowe and Webster, their lyrical and dramatic mastery. "The movements of the heart were not hid from them," and the language of the darker passions could still be read "in the workings of the face, the expressions of the tongue, the writings of a troubled conscience" (6.181–91).[25]

Because of this firmly organic basis in experience, Elizabethan poetry was not overwhelmed but invigorated by the new classical learning that then came to England's shores, and especially by the "rich and fascinating stores of the Greek and Roman mythology" (6.186). Here is further indication that Hazlitt's contrast of "nature" with "art" implies no scorn of intellectual sophistication, provided that the ends of passional "truth" are not being lost in the conscious means of "power." Yet this is precisely the irony of fate that he sees overtaking Elizabethan and Caroline poetry, as the art became victimized by its own wealth of resources. He singles out Beaumont and Fletcher as the principal agents of this change in the drama: they were the first "who laid the foundation of the artificial diction and tinselled pomp of the next generation of poets, by aiming at a profusion of ambitious ornaments, and by translating the commonest circumstances into the language of metaphor and passion." Such "indiscriminate display of power" (6.249–50) was rooted in the very vitality and richness of the Elizabethan age—the germ of the vice is seen in Marlowe, for instance (6.209–11)—as imagination became increasingly conscious of its poetic strength. Even Shakespeare could succumb to the vice in such early poems as *Venus and Adonis* and *The Rape of Lucrece,* where "the poet is perpetually singling out the difficulties of the art to make an exhibition of his strength and skill in wrestling with them" (4.358). And the same tendency makes Hazlitt lose all patience with Sydney's *Arcadia,* "one of the greatest monuments of the abuse of intellectual power upon record," where scarcely an image or a sentiment is left unspoiled by the "systematic interpolation of the wit, learning, ingenuity, wisdom and everlasting impertinence of the writer" (6.319–20).

Hardly formed to sympathize with the ideal of the perfect courtier, Hazlitt is betraying some impertinence of his own in these judgments; and nowhere is the prejudice more apparent than in his relegation of the Metaphysical poets to a hostile chapter in *Lectures on the English Comic Writers.* But let us be clear about the nature and extent of Hazlitt's bias against "the false and fanciful style" (6.322), for we should recognize that he is not endorsing Coleridge's postulate that "fancy" and "imagination" are distinct faculties (*BL,* 1.60, 202).[26] Hazlitt does not absolutely condemn the technique of the "conceit" (he could accept and even enjoy it in Petrarch: 16.43–44; 6.301), and he does, in fact, find a good deal to admire in seventeenth-century poetry: he likes (and helped to rediscover) Marvell, is more fascinated by Donne than he cares to admit, and acknowledges great "depth of feeling" in most of these poets. But a true "poetry of the passions" should, as in Shakespeare, show "the same feeling as connected with objects and circumstances more palpable and touching," however various or "remote" these may be; and with this sense of the proper function of metaphor, Hazlitt finds himself continually baffled—and the bafflement, predictably, comes out as resentment. Approving, for once, Doctor Johnson's opinion, Hazlitt remarks that these poets "strain and distort the immediate feeling into some barely possible consequence or recondite analogy, in which it required the utmost stretch of misapplied ingenuity to trace the smallest connection with the original impression." The difficulty was not, I think, that Hazlitt's poetics of intersubjectivity were here being manifestly disproved; it was rather, perhaps, that he found himself in the presence of a poetic culture whose intersubjective modes were not only strange but often contrary to his own—as he himself suggests when he says of these poets, "They seemed to think there was an irreconcileable opposition between genius, as well as grace, and nature" (6.51). By the lights of his own psychology, the creation of learned "riddles" and "labyrinths" in verse could mean only indulgence in esoteric associations which belong exclusively to the conscious will; and such indulgence, being motivated only or mainly by the love of intellectual power, must finally reduce poetry to the values and motives of self-love.

This, indeed, is for Hazlitt the entire logic of the post-Elizabethan decline. The love of power in imagination that once happily found its object in nature had become conscious of itself first as the pursuit of "novelty" and intellectual "excitement" ("fancy"), and had then taken the inevitable further step into self-conscious "wit," finding its power in a will that at last delighted in "thwarting" nature (6.51). Yet the point that Hazlitt wants his audience to grasp is not the moral censure but the historical point: that the power of genius itself, once it produces models for emulation, breeds the conscious love of "art" which soon vitiates responsiveness to nature and, finally, even responsiveness to originality of "fancy." Whereas "men at first produce effect by studying nature, ... afterwards they look at nature only to produce effect" (6.248). Hazlitt thought that by the end of the seventeenth century the writer's sense of power, of "effect," had almost entirely changed from what it was at the start: when Dryden translates Chaucer and Boccaccio, he does so with "a greater knowledge of the taste of his readers and power of pleasing them, than acquaintance with the genius of his authors" (5.82). The "good taste" originally created by genius had by that time supplanted "the power, and even the wish, to do the like" (6.187).

The triumph of the "artificial," then, is a necessary consequence of the triumph of "the natural style." For Hazlitt "artificial" verse rightly becomes the dominant mode of poetry in an age when, as in Augustan England, society—or, more precisely, its ruling class—has succeeded in creating a man-made world of uniform culture distinct from both the necessities of nature and inherited prejudice, and when the sense of personal identity is determined more by norms of "taste" and "refinement" than by the responses of organic character and "inveterate" sentiment. In such a world self-love becomes the ruling principle—itself a conventionalized means of intersubjective sympathy, as well as of satiric antipathy. Now made acutely conscious of itself, self-love in this world becomes potentially a virtue, both for poetry and for society. The poet is now the defender of the equable and the "exquisite" in taste and conduct, and as such, though liable to affectation himself, his own vanity, being more finely equipped, becomes the inevitable instrument to expose and chastise the grosser excesses of self-love in others. And because Pope combines to perfection these functions—because he is the more consciously "artificial" master of the artificial style—Hazlitt judges his poetry to be generally superior to Dryden's, however inferior it may be in range of subject or variety of versification (5.79–80).

In drawing his "character" of Pope, Hazlitt seems to accept the legend of a hunchback's spite and morbid vanity, but what seems like the familiar denigration is to be understood rather as an effort to reconstitute Pope's merits—to have this master remembered as *not* the famous translator of Homer: "It cannot be denied that his chief excellence lay more in diminishing, than in aggrandizing objects; in checking, not in encouraging our enthusiasm . . ." "The Rape of the Lock," for instance, is "the perfection of the mock-heroic," and Hazlitt so much admires this poem that he tends to view in the light of its bejewelled brilliance the entire Popean canon. Pope "judged of beauty by fashion; he sought for truth in the opinions of the world; he judged of the feelings of others by his own." Yet the very contraction of Pope's sensibility gave to his work a "double-refined essence" such as he "alone possessed." Hazlitt's Pope is not finally the petty unmasker of human pettiness but a poet with a vision—a vision almost epic in scope, of the endless permutations of man's instinct for *littleness,* for the "fine" as well as the small and the "mean" in all things: "What discrimination, what wit, what delicacy . . . what pampered refinement of sentiment! It is like looking at the world through a microscope, where every thing assumes a new character and a new consequence, where things are seen in their minutest circumstances and slightest shades of difference; where the little becomes gigantic, the deformed beautiful, and the beautiful deformed" (5.70–79).[27]

With a disdainful glance at the Wordsworthians, Hazlitt concludes: "And shall we cut ourselves off from beauties like these with a theory . . . and go about asking our blind guides, whether Pope was a poet or not?" The question, so put, answers itself, and by the time Hazlitt reaches his closing lecture, "On the Living Poets," he has turned the question around: what right to the honored name of poetry has the "new school" if it is willing to acknowledge no excellence but that which supports its own pretensions? Hazlitt grants that "the poetry of paradox" had come as a welcome change at the end of the previous century, when the poetry of classical "commonplace" had "degenerated into the most trite, insipid, and mechanical of all things, in the hands of the followers of Pope and the old French school of poetry." But the irony he recognizes now—and to which he had been oblivious in 1798—is that the revolt of the poets of *Lyrical Ballads* from aristocratic pride was itself subject to the tyranny of fashion—the fashion most in vogue in the nineties, when "a singularly affected and outrageous simplicity prevailed in dress and manners, in style and sentiment." "All was to be natural and new," in poetry as in society; "all things" were therefore regarded as "by nature equally fit subjects for poetry"; or if there was a "preference to be given," it went to "the meanest and most unpromising," as allowing "the greatest scope for the unbounded stores of thought and fancy in the writer's own mind." The consequence was that these poet-reformers were soon

> surrounded, in company with the Muses, by a mixed rabble of idle apprentices and Botany Bay convicts, female vagrants, gipsies, meek daughters in the family of Christ, of ideot boys and mad mothers, and after them 'owls and night-ravens flew.' . . . . He who was more than man, with them was none. They claimed kindred only with the commonest of the people: peasants, pedlars, and village-barbers were their oracles and bosom friends. Their poetry, in the extreme to which it professedly tended, and was in effect carried, levels all distinctions of nature and society; has 'no figures nor no fantasies,' which the prejudices of superstition or the customs of the world draw in the brains of men . . . : it breaks in pieces the golden images of poetry, and defaces its armorial bearings, to melt them down in the mould of common humanity or of its own upstart self-sufficiency. (5.161–63)

Hazlitt was to give a far juster account of the democratic character of Wordsworth's Muse in *The Spirit of the Age* (where we will find him making ample amends also to several other contemporaries). But to dismiss these comments of 1818 as a mere interlude of partisan satire, an aberration from his abiding devotion to Wordsworth's genius, is to overlook certain developments which helped to alter Hazlitt's attitudes after 1814, when he wrote his balanced but generally favorable review of *The Excursion*. There had been, first, Coleridge's elevation of his friend in *Biographia Literaria* (1.60–62; 2.77) to equality of genius with Milton; Wordsworth's visit to London in December of 1817, when he informed the raptly waiting Keats (who had just read the passage to him) that the Hymn to Pan in *Endymion* was "a very pretty piece of Paganism"; the equally patronizing condescension shown in 1816 to the memory of another poet, in *A Letter to a Friend of Robert Burns* (which received due satiric attention from Hazlitt in the previous lecture); and, not least, the Essay Supplementary to the Preface of 1815, whose ideas Hazlitt might have found repellent even without the veiled attack, as Baker has noted (p. 345), on his abilities as a critic (called forth, presumably, by the insufficiently laudatory review of *The Excursion*).[28] Wordsworth in this essay, appealing to the dictum of Coleridge that every original genius "has had the task of *creating* the taste by which he is enjoyed," proceeded to attribute the unpopularity of his work to the "pride" of readers in their own taste, which the poet of genius must patiently overcome "in establishing that dominion over the spirits of readers by which they are to be humbled and humanized, in order that they may be purified and exalted" (*Pr W,* 3.68, 80–81). Hazlitt was, I suspect, glancing at this assumption of spiritual "dominion" when, in his second lecture, he says of Chaucer, "He does not affect to shew his power over the reader's mind, but the power which his subject has over his own" (5.22). Wordsworth's pious militancy since 1814 seems to have convinced Hazlitt that Jeffrey might, after all, be more right than wrong in chastising the new school as a *"Lake* School" (Hazlitt here makes his first critical use of the term: 5.161), one falsely opposing "nature" to "art"; and that Wordsworth's celebrated "egotism" was no mere trait of character but a compulsive, programmatic power-consciousness which, in pretending to restore "imagination" to poetry, threatened to make a mockery of truly universal standards of poetic imagination. Hazlitt is writing less in jest than in earnest when he concludes his invective by concentrating on the Wordsworthian ego in all its sublime enormity: "A thorough adept in this school of poetry and philanthropy is jealous of all excellence but his own. . . . He tolerates only what he himself creates; he sympathizes only with what can enter into no competition with him, with 'the bare trees and mountains bare, and grass in the green field.' He sees nothing but himself and the universe" (5.163).

Yet we should be careful not to let this invidious contrast with greater "poets of nature" in the past tempt us into the inference that Hazlitt is disavowing, or simply forgetting, his theoretic faith in the continuity of Wordsworth's egocentric genius with all poetic genius—even with Shakespeare's. Indeed, one way of paraphrasing his most constant praise of Wordsworth's originality ("the most original poet now living," as he does not neglect to observe here, before launching his attack) is to say that Wordsworth for Hazlitt remains the discoverer of the intersubjectivity of solitude. As we saw earlier in this study, Hazlitt may have owed to the poetry of *Lyrical Ballads,* almost as much as to his reading of Shakespeare, his own discovery of the intersubjective principle—or at least of his sense that poetic feeling consists in communicating the organic presence of a self. Nevertheless this "primal sympathy," as Wordsworth calls it in the *Intimations* Ode, remains in his own poetry, as Hazlitt continually suggests (19.10 ff.), a response of subjectivity to subjectivity—of the poet finding correlatives to his own being in the primal life of nature or in other solitary beings, and of the reader consciously sharing the poet's self-consciousness. The movement of imagination in Wordsworth does not lead on from this mode of intersubjectivity to other, more universal modes—to those sympathies which do not and cannot flourish in solitude. If we think for a moment of the famous daffodils in Wordsworth's lyric "I Wandered Lonely as a Cloud" and compare them with Perdita's flowers (in the passage that Hazlitt has analyzed), we see clearly enough what he meant in 1814 when he characterized Wordsworth as a poet of "sentiment" rather than of "imagination"—that is, of imagination as "fanciful invention" (19.18–19). For Wordsworth's flowers remain particular memory-images; the experience is intensified but undergoes no metaphoric transfiguration. In fact, if we follow a further suggestion of Hazlitt's (though he himself does not compare the two poems), the Wordsworthian daffodils might even be said to be a good deal *less* natural than the Shakespearean variety in one important respect: they may "dance" in the breeze but they remain, unlike Perdita's, singularly non-erotic in this dalliance with the wind; their appeal to passion is, in a word, strictly vegetarian. As Hazlitt wryly remarks in the preceding lecture, "If the species were continued like trees . . . , Mr. Wordsworth's poetry would be just as good as ever." He was losing none of his respect for Wordsworth's vision of personal identity; but when the same fidelity to solitude became an austere asceticism that encouraged, in the name of transcendence, "a total disunion and divorce of the faculties of the mind from those of the body" (5.131), then Hazlitt did not hesitate to record his dissent from still another form of modern literary "abstraction" (19.15)—an abstraction, in this case, of poetry from the fully vital integrity of its powers in the passional self.

"The evident scope and tendency of Mr. Wordsworth's mind is the reverse of dramatic. It resists all change of character, all variety of scenes, all the bustle, machinery, and pantomime of the stage, or of real life . . ." (19.11). This statement, from his review of *The Excursion*—his first, and in many ways his best, appraisal of Wordsworth—not only suggests that the "Lake"-"Cockney" opposition really does reflect a discord of values in the poetry of the age; it also suggests what the essential difference is, as a matter of general "style," between "natural style" in the past and the new poetry of "nature." The difference emerges as one between an intersubjectivity which, even in its lyrical forms, is essentially *dramatic,* a poetry that "exists by contrast" and delights in it (see 11.66–67), and a poetry that is intersubjective only through the sympathy of imagination with the self-communion of personality—a poetry which, in effect, turns the life of thought and feeling away from the life of action and event (see 12.53–54). Hazlitt's insistence upon "passion" has traditionally been mistaken as a license for a spontaneously emotional lyricism, but it is, demonstrably, nothing of the kind. Shakespeare and Milton were his definitive models from the start; and the logic of his premise of intersubjectivity points directly to epic and tragic poetry as the genres which have the greatest potential for revealing man's passional nature to itself. Long before Arnold, Hazlitt sought to reclaim for poetry some of its lost Aristotelian character as the imitation of "actions" as well as the representation of thoughts and sentiments. And that this was understood at the time as the general thrust of Hazlitt's warning is most evident in the response of Keats and Shelley to his critical challenge. Both poets begin at about this time to abandon the Wordsworthian precedent—to turn away from personal lyricism and the pastoral-philosophical romance toward a poetry of heroic will, mythic vision, and epic dimension, a poetry reuniting, in Hazlitt's words, "imaginary splendour and human passion" (5.53).

Hazlitt's pervasive influence on the changing tastes of his time was probably greater than we think, but there is evidence of only one firm convert to his critical leadership. The impact of the *Lectures* on Keats was instantaneous and overwhelming—compelling him almost at once to reconceive and rededicate his powers. With Hazlitt's distinction still vivid in his mind, Keats records with excitement, in a letter to Reynolds in February of 1818, his defiant revolt from the Wordsworthian standard: "Are we to be bullied into a certain philosophy engendered in the whims of an Egotist. . . . I will have no more of Wordsworth or of Hunt in particular. . . . Why should we be owls, when we can be Eagles?" And some months later, the alienation from his former self-consciousness becomes entire and explicit: he now says that "the wordsworthian or egotistical sublime is a thing per se and stands alone"; he sees it now as wholly distinct from "the poetical character" in general, to which he aspires, for that "has no self—it is every thing and nothing—it has no character—it enjoys light and shade; it lives in gusto, be it foul or fair. . . . What shocks the virtuous philosopher, delights the camelion poet." This not only goes further than Hazlitt had gone, this threatens to contradict his theory; for poetic disinterestedness is not to be mistaken for a transcendent freedom of the poet from his own passions; and the poetry Keats was soon to write would amply confirm that inescapability. Indeed, sporadically through 1818 and with increasing conviction thereafter, Keats came to wonder whether the difference in kind Hazlitt had described really was a final separation—an impassable gulf for a self-expressive lyricist.[29] Hazlitt had insisted that the rift from the past should not be widened, but it remained for Keats to discover that the distance between Wordsworth and Shakespeare was a breach in imagination that might still be healed, in the self and by the self, although not without great pain. And the result of this reunion of the two extremes in Keats's mind was a series of poems which come as close as any in the language to a genuine—to a genuinely dramatic—lyricism of intersubjectivity. The *Ode to a Nightingale* seems to me an almost perfect illustration of Hazlitt's idea of a poem as a "movement" from a state of purely personal consciousness ("My heart aches, and a drowzy numbness pains my sense"), through states of increasing passional intensity and sympathetic enlargement of imagination, toward the speaker's recognition of his intersubjective humanity—a movement that at last leads back, as in Wordsworth, to the "sole self," but a self no longer lonely in its passion, now thoroughly humanized and acquiescing in its generic human bondage. And is not all the controversial ink that has been spilled over Keats's *Grecian Urn*—over the meaning of the Beauty-Truth equation, and especially over the punctuation of the last two lines—is not most, if not all, of this dispute reducible to our unwillingness to recognize that both the Urn and its poem may not be independently existing Art-Objects but expressions of man's intersubjective imagination—which is here communing with itself, and still being true to itself, across the ages? And who is the beautiful Muse-Goddess presiding over these poems—who is Psyche, what is she if not the incarnation of that same intersubjective spirit, the immortal and universal human Divinity born from the mortal dreams of man's subjective self?

"He gave the greatest promise of genius of any poet of his day." This is Hazlitt's retrospective estimate of Keats—in the "Critical List" of poets in his anthology, *Select British Poets* (1824). But Hazlitt cannot be said to have returned, in nearly the same degree, his disciple's admiration. For he adds that Keats "wanted . . . manly strength and fortitude to reject the temptations of singularity in sentiment and expression," though "some of his shorter and later pieces [the Odes, presumably] are . . . as free from faults as they are full of beauties" (9.244–45). Even the critically forearmed Keats, then, could not escape the age's endemic affliction of "paradox." Hazlitt's response to his young friend's work was, I suspect, mainly impaired by his sheer inability to believe that any further greatness in poetry was possible beyond Wordsworth. In the great exponent of the "primal" self, poetry had become conscious of its roots in individuality—and had it not therefore fatally exhausted its resources of power, if not of further "refinement"? "Original genius"—a Collins, a Burns, a Keats— would always appear, but native power alone is not enough "to produce the highest excellence, without a corresponding state of manners, passions, and religious belief" (5.96): here is perhaps the first lament in criticism for the modern poet's crippling "alienation," his want of an "audience." And by the early twenties, moreover, Hazlitt was losing not only his youthful faith in the Muse but much of his critical interest in poetry. He had begun to long for a "conscious power" in literature more in tune with the character of the age—for a "dramatic" power no longer subject to poetry's seductive music, the metrical harmonization of opposites, whose beauty is "truth" for all inward selves but not for the larger world beyond them. It is therefore no accident of chronology that our lecturer should turn next to comic literature; for this interest coincides with the ripening of his own powers in prose, and with his mounting respect for a form of literature that he was the first critic to explore seriously—the novel.

Chapter Seven

The Modern Difference: Comedy and the Novel

"JOYS laugh not! Sorrows weep not!" Blake's proverb was certainly true of the Romantic age, which found tranquillity of spirit in contemplating the still, sad music of humanity and was seldom more solemn or melancholy than when it spoke of Joy. Byron remembered a Methodist preacher shouting in the direction of some profane grins, "No *hopes* for them as *laughs!*"—and this warning of grave spiritual dangers in laughter found an echo in a contemporary of another faith, the young Shelley, whose hopes for mankind similarly moved him to deplore "the withering and perverting spirit of comedy."[1] There was still, of course, plenty of convivial laughter in Regency England, but wit and humor were increasingly constrained, at least when removed from the arena of politics, to be morally circumspect and "amiable." The professional jesters of the age—Lamb, Peacock, Sydney Smith—were masters of the art of keeping their shafts of satire inoffensively light and were ready at a moment's notice to modulate their humor into earnest doctrine or serious sentiment—the one inconsistent exception to this rule being the defiant author of *Don Juan.* Nor did Hazlitt, with his own sacred pieties to defend, escape the prevailing conspiracy against Momus. Leigh Hunt tells the story

233

of being in company with Hazlitt and Lamb one evening when the conversation turned to a line in a poem of Marvell's, describing a tidal flood in the Netherlands, where the fish were said to have come swimming up to Dutch dinner tables "And sat not as a meat, but as a guest." Hazlitt insisted to his friends that this "forced, far-fetched" conceit was not the least bit funny; and he was about to launch "into a very acute discourse to prove that we ought *not to laugh* at such exaggerations, when we were forced to interrupt him by a fit of laughter uncontrollable." [2]

A certain resistance to risibility may be, however, more of an asset than a liability for the critic of comedy. Hazlitt's distrust of wit does breed difficulties for his theory of comedy, but the fact is that he is never consistently better as a descriptive critic, never more at ease with his materials, than in *Lectures on the English Comic Writers* (1819).[3] Whenever Hazlitt pauses in his theory to give vent to his moral suspicion of wit, we may recognize again the voice of his priggish Unitarian conscience; and the same voice may be heard more ambivalently in his protestation that his temperament is, to a fault, "more saturnine than mercurial" (4.316) and that he possesses not "a grain of wit" (20.263). The first statement may be true enough of Hazlitt the man, but the latter is by no means true of the writer, as not a few quotations in this study will attest. Hazlitt had inherited a good deal of his father's "monkish pleasantry" (17.111 n.), and although in the son that humor was more deeply fused with the Hazlitt earnestness, the fusion made for a happy balance of values in his criticism—insuring both a congenial response to, and a deliberate judgment of, the ways of comic genius. Of the intimate nexus between the comic sense of irony and his critical faculties, Hazlitt was keenly aware: the poets of the *Lyrical Ballads,* he once observed, would never say that "I got my liking for the novelists or the comic writers . . . from them. If so, I must have got from them what they never had themselves. . . . In forming an estimate of passages relating to common life and manners, I cannot think I am a plagiarist from any man" (12.226).

Hazlitt knew, moreover, that the paradox of a saturnine man secretly in love with laughter was no anomaly in England. When Hunt described his friend as a man with a strong sense of humor but without "animal spirits enough" to revel in merriment, he was really describing what Hazlitt would have recognized as a familiar variant of the English character. English "mirth," he observes in his essay "Merry England," is "a relaxation from gravity"; a jest is welcomed as "a streak of light" athwart "our natural gloom." Among the French or Italians too lively "a pitch of animal spirits runs away with the imagination" and tempts the mind to "take a jest for granted"; but "the ludicrous takes hold" of an Englishman's mind from the very "hardness and repulsiveness" of his feelings, which are "not easily reconciled" to an equivalent "obtuseness" in the minds or bodies of other Englishmen (17.52–58). Hazlitt might have added to this account that the very word *humor,* in its modern and pleasurable sense as applied to character and expression in comedy, is an English invention. As Stuart M. Tave has shown, a long and gradual revolution in English comic theory had "essentially reversed" the original meaning of "humour" as a willful or knavish aberration to be exposed and mocked out of existence (or into humility) by the critical genius of "wit." Hazlitt's sense of his own credentials for criticism of comedy exhibits this new tolerance for the eccentric; both the lecturer and his audience were prepared to find the greatest pleasure of comedy, not in deft ridicule of fools and rogues, but in those amiable and picturesque "originals" of quirky humanity—a Falstaff, a Don Quixote, an Uncle Toby—who bear witness to the comic genius of Nature herself.[4]

Yet just as there is more acidulous wit in Hazlitt's intelligence than he cares to admit, so more of the Augustan conception of "wit" survives in his theory of the comic than his Romantic predilection for the greater humaneness of "humour" would suggest. Hazlitt formulates three main types of comedy, which he correlates with three phases in the development of English comedy, and also with— though he does not obtrude the connection upon his audience— three "degrees of the laughable" described in the opening lecture, "On Wit and Humour." The first phase, and most elementary type, is "comedy of nature," found at its purest in Shakespeare and his age; this type is succeeded by "comedy of manners" or "artificial comedy," which has its greatest flowering in the Restoration and which Hazlitt is to praise as the "highest" comedy; and this in turn is followed by the "sentimental comedy" of the eighteenth century and of his own time, which for Hazlitt is not properly comedy at all, since it retains only the forms of comic drama without its essence. What differentiates the three phases as types is their way of combining— or, in the latter case, of failing to combine—the "degrees" of laughter: the "merely laughable," the "ludicrous," and the "ridiculous." The first degree, present in all comic incident, is laughter provoked by simple surprise and contrast—by some sudden "disconnection" between expectation and event, an incongruity which in itself may be meaningless, mere "accident." Laughter on this level is therefore not properly comic until it coincides with the second degree, the "ludicrous." Here laughter is sustained by a further incongruity in character or situation, so that the surprising event does not merely startle by its oddity but contradicts our sense of "what is customary or desirable," yet is still not so shocking or offensive as to be noticeably unpleasant. This is the basis for "comedy of nature," whose ruling principle is "humour," or "the describing the ludicrous as it is in itself" (that is, without express or implied comparison with something else). Only incidentally does this mode of comedy attain to the "ridiculous," which is the forte of "artificial comedy." This type is characteristic of a more advanced stage of society, when the laughable arises less from incongruities "of nature and accident" than from something "which is contrary . . . to sense and reason, or is a voluntary departure from what we have a right to expect from those who are conscious of absurdity and propriety in words, looks, and actions." Here the sense of the incongruous finds expression, as in Restoration manners comedy, in satiric "wit," which seeks not merely to present or describe but to mock what is ludicrous by "comparing or contrasting it with something else." As soon as wit succeeds, however, in making vice, vanity, and folly appear ridiculous, a public reaction sets in against the licentious vanities of wit itself; and then the values of moral sentiment overwhelm both wit and humor in "sentimental comedy," which finds more pleasure in the tears of sympathy than in laughter at absurdity. From this sad decline English comedy had not yet recovered—and, Hazlitt feared, would never recover (6.7–8, 15, 35–36, 49–55).

This scheme is impressive, and much of it still makes good

sense; but as a historical formulation it is, of course, much too logical to be descriptively adequate; it is, indeed, in the most fundamental sense, not historical at all, for it assumes that the major phases in the development of comedy are serially predetermined by a "natural" logic inhering in certain causes and consequences. And as a theoretic description of the comic impulse, the logic of this scheme proves to be less consistent with Hazlitt's own psychology than with the rationalism of the previous century. As various commentators have pointed out, Hazlitt's theory has direct eighteenth-century antecedents: the distinctions on which he bases his "degrees" had at least been adumbrated before; his originality lies mainly in the psychological rationale that he provides for these terms and in applying them to correlative periods in literary history.[5] It is perhaps ironic that a theory which leads to the condemnation of eighteenth-century comedy should have originated in the most characteristic assumptions of that century; for the "incongruity" theory of comic laughter, which descends from Aristotle, ultimately depends on the sentiment of rationalism—on belief in a constant, predictable if not intelligible order in the world. No one would deny that "incongruity" is in some sense indispensable to all comic effect, but to make it the motive of all laughter is to reduce comic pleasure to the status of a neural symptom—the transitory accompaniment to an intellectual act which restores to consciousness the cognitive norms of probability (or, if there is moral judgment as well, of "propriety").[6] By this theory, people never really *expect* to laugh; and when they do, they laugh only to rid themselves of the anomalous disturbance. "It is astonishing," Hazlitt once remarked, "how much wit and laughter there is in the world . . . and yet, being excited by what is *out of the way* and singular, it ought to be rare and gravity should be the order of the day" (20.262). To us it may seem more astonishing that a theorist who could entertain this reflection should have lost none of his confidence in the theoretic sufficiency of the incongruity principle.

There are moments in his first lecture when Hazlitt's theorizing seems on the verge of proposing new and sounder premises for comedy, and not the least promising moment comes with his opening statement: "Man is the only animal that laughs and weeps; for he is the only animal that is struck with the difference between what things are, and what they ought to be." The close conjunction here of laughter and tears is further established by some remarks on the behavior of children—observations on their exuberance and "animal spirits," their sheer readiness to laugh, the sudden, sometimes instantaneous transition from laughter to tears and back; on the rhythm of this movement, the "alternate excitement and relaxation of the imagination," which seems itself pleasurable to the child, or not wholly dependent on the discontinuity of appearances which is its exciting cause. Yet these insights, pregnant with new theory, are then abruptly forgotten as Hazlitt proceeds to analyze the "comic" in its contradistinction to the "serious." The latter is defined as "the habitual stress which the mind lays upon the expectation of a given order of events": when this stress or "weight of interest" is increased or "overstrained" by some "violent opposition," the serious mounts into "the pathetic or tragical," but when "abruptly loosened or relaxed," dissolves into the "ludicrous" (6.5–7). As long as we keep our focus on the extremes in this contrast, Hazlitt's reasoning seems convincing enough; but we need only consider the intermediate range between these extremes to recognize that comedy and tragedy do not inhabit emotionally alien spheres but respond to the same polarity, partake of the same life-tension in consciousness. One is not more congruent with the nature of things than the other; they are concerned not with a different "opposition" but, in different ways, with the same human predicament—the disparity between reality and desire, actuality and value, things that "are" and "ought to be." The comic in literature, unlike the "laughable" in life, can only be a mode of awareness, not a state of feeling. Literary genres cannot be made to correspond to distinct psychological states, and only in his theory of comedy does Hazlitt's literary theory fall into this error.

Where his theory most obviously betrays its literary inadequacy is in his account of Shakespeare's comedies—although the same lecture (the second, "On Shakespeare and Ben Jonson") provides, as so often happens in Hazlitt, the means, in its incidental insights, for correcting his prejudices. The worst practical consequence of his faulty theory is that it prevents him from arriving at a conception of Shakespearean comedy *as drama*—such a conception as his theory does enable him to bring to the comedy of the Restoration. The very ability that serves Hazlitt so well in dealing with the tragedies now breeds confusion and distraction; for without the cue of tragic passion, his feeling for character leads him away, rather than toward, the dramatic center of the plays. Whenever character rises above the design, Hazlitt's portraiture (in the essays on the comedies and the histories in *Characters*) is likely to be as telling as ever: his masterpiece in this vein is his full-length, six-page sketch of Falstaff, and so brilliant is this portrait of comic exuberance incarnate ("He manures and nourishes his mind with jests, as he does his body with sack and sugar": 4.278) that we are likely to overlook the ultimate infidelity of the all-too-amiable figure that Hazlitt creates to Shakespeare's all-too-human Sir John. The trouble here, as in all his commentary on the comedies, is that Hazlitt does not know what to do with the characters after stamping their authenticity; they amuse or entrance him with their "humours," and he assumes that this can be their only meaning in "the comedy of nature." His vision of Shakespeare's comic world is of a riotous paradise of impulse, in which the flora and fauna of almost every known species of human foible and folly "shoot out with native, happy, unchecked luxuriance" (4.314), while their creator, like a benign English gardener, beams upon them and humors his own fond fancy as he does everything he can to "pamper" their whims (6.36).

This vision still has much persuasive force; we have here a primitive version of C. L. Barber's view of Shakespearean comedy as "festive" comedy, "concerned with the relation between man and the nature celebrated by holiday, not relations between social classes and types."[7] But what is clearly wrong in Hazlitt's praise is the judgmental conclusion to which he is pointing: that the comedies, happy and winning though they are, are "deficient," are not "great" as the tragedies are great; again the assumption is that comedy can be great only to the degree that it provokes either satiric or "amiable" laughter—and preferrably in that order of frequency. Shakespeare's Muse was "too good-natured and magnanimous"; "we sympathize with his characters oftener than we laugh at them." It was not that Shakespeare lacked talent for comedy ("He had an equal genius for comedy and tragedy": 5.56); it was rather that his other gifts over-

whelmed his comic powers and prevented their purely comic fruition. "Shakespeare was a greater poet than wit: his imagination was
the leading and master-quality of his mind, which was always ready
to soar into its native element: the ludicrous was only secondary and
subordinate" (6.30–35).

What, though, is Hazlitt really saying here? Is he saying that
Shakespeare's comedy suffered from an excess of his humor and
"fancy" at the expense of wit, or that there is a natural and, sooner
or later, exclusive antagonism between comedy and the sympathies
of poetic imagination? Reluctantly, Hazlitt seems to decide for the
latter alternative: "I do not, in short, consider comedy as exactly an
affair of the heart or the imagination; and it is for this reason only
that I think Shakespeare's comedies deficient" (6.38).[8] But Hazlitt's
comparison of Shakespeare with Ben Jonson suggests a different
reading. Although the author of *Volpone* clearly transcends this limitation, Jonson's characters are too "mean," his plots too "mechanical"; he has the comic "extravagance" but not the comic exuberance.
And how little Hazlitt is willing, in his specific judgments, to separate
wit and poetic imagination, whatever his theory may say, is clear
from his comment that Jonsonian comedy wants "that genial spirit of
enjoyment and finer fancy, which constitute the essence of poetry
and of wit" (6.38–45). The "disconnection" of our sympathies which
Hazlitt imputes to wit would therefore seem to be more apparent
than real, or a reference to the effects of wit on the audience, rather
than to its essence or to the process of its creation. Such, at least,
seems the most obvious way of reconciling the foregoing with Hazlitt's general conclusion: "Wit, as distinguished from poetry, is the
imagination or fancy inverted, and so applied to given objects, as to
make the little look less, the mean more light and worthless; or to
divert our admiration or wean our affections from that which is lofty
or impressive, instead of producing a more intense admiration and
exalted passion, as poetry does" (6.15).

"Admiration": again that word may help us absolve Hazlitt from
confusion. He believes that comedy finds its generic consummation
in satire, yet he is unable or unwilling to postulate a clear continuity
in imagination between humor and wit; and one reason why he cannot or will not do so is that all the instincts of his upbringing tempt

him to conceive of that continuity as moral and historical, rather than "natural"—rather than as a tendency inhering in given values and powers of the mind. Since, we remember, the sympathy of poetic imagination is with "power" as well as value, that "admiration" needs continual chastening; and Hazlitt sees wit, "the eloquence of indifference" (6.15), as imagination correcting its errors and excesses of "admiration" by "inverting" or "diverting" its sympathies. But the power to do so cannot properly exist in the mind, that is, can have no proper function, until the original sin of "aggrandizing" worldly power beyond its value has actually been committed in the world, and on a scale that thoroughly confuses the motives of power and value in society. This for Hazlitt is the ultimate function of comic genius in the cause of "humanity": not merely to expose and censure, in the Augustan way, the grossness or pettiness of vice and folly, but to challenge and counterbalance the idolatry of power which is latent in all imagination and which even the greatest poetic genius tends in some degree to flatter—witness Shakespeare's in *Coriolanus* (4.214). Here we see the role of comic theater, and especially of "comedy of manners," in Hazlitt's myth of "progress" through genius: while the other arts foster pleasure and passional sympathy, comedy converts antipathy to virtue, through farcical exaggeration or merciless ridicule of false power: "I think that comedy does not find its richest harvest till individual infirmities have passed into general manners, and it is the example of courts chiefly [as in the Stuart Restoration], that stamps folly with credit and currency, or glosses over vice with meretricious lustre" (6.36).

But by this account "wit," and by extension all comic invention which aims at more than "fancy," remains anti-poetic, essentially negative and inhumane, untrue in itself—in a word, purely reactive, dependent for meaning on its emotional contrary and its moral effect, expressing the incongruous only by making it appear more contemptibly absurd. And by this reasoning, too, modern comedy must die when its countervailing delusion in society dies. This is the mythic logic that nominally governs the progression of the *Lectures,* and we shall find that Hazlitt can make much of it sound persuasive, even at this remote distance. He is, however, finally too intelligent, has too much love and respect for the great wits of English litera-

241

ture—and perhaps too much also for his own powers of wit—to let this solemn fiction stand as his final judgment on the "truth" of wit. In "On Wit and Humour" Hazlitt had reaffirmed the Augustan distinction between "true" and "false" wit, but he had done so in very general terms, by likening "true" wit and its powers of "detection" to acuteness of reasoning or "subtle observation" (6.19–22)—a truth of content rather than one inhering in form, in the processes of wit itself; wit is seen as departing from reason, and thus from truth, in its distinctive attraction to "accidental" or "verbal combinations" (6.19–22). Not until a late essay, "Definition of Wit" (1829), does Hazlitt return to the question, and there his account of wit, although largely the same, differs in precisely this particular: the metaphoric play of wit is seen now, not as a projection of images and verbal novelties designed to "mock" or "belittle," but as an act of "discursive" imagination, dissolving habitual "aggregates" in the mind and recombining their ideas (as we would say today, condensing and displacing them) so as to reveal otherwise undetected truth, some contradiction or "double meaning" that we would otherwise be unable or unwilling to acknowledge. Rescued at last from the role of playing the jolly or mischievous fool to the king of "lofty" poetry, wit is now defined as "one mode of viewing and representing nature, or the difference and similitudes, the harmonies and discords in the links and chains of our ideas of things at large" (20.352–62).[9]

Characteristically, Hazlitt admits to no disparity between the two accounts of wit. Yet, in another sense, he was right not to do so, for most of his 1819 *Lectures,* or at least those dealing with the Restoration and the comic tradition thereafter, do faithfully present a vision of "truth" as inhering either in the comedic form itself or in the historically dynamic relationship of a changing form with a changing subject matter. And nowhere does this enlarged vision of the comic emerge more strongly than in Hazlitt's unprecedented account of the novel and of its enormous potential for greatness as a form. We recall, at the start of this chapter, Hazlitt defending the originality of his comic sense "in forming an estimate of passages relating to common life and manners." It is this change of direction emerging in the later lectures—a change from comedy in its classical function as a "test" of truth by ridicule to comic "truth" as having its own substantial existence in the processes of experience, a sense of "truth" which anticipates also many of the attitudes known to a later generation as *realism*—that will prove most important to trace here for our purposes, as it signals a major shift in Hazlitt's understanding of what is "modern" in literature and in life.

༝༝༝

Among the major English critics Hazlitt stands alone in his unstinting praise of the Restoration as "the golden period of our comedy" (6.37). All that had glittered treacherously in the reigns of the later Stuart kings became for this Dissenter pure gold—unalloyed "wit and pleasure"—in the mirrors of Restoration comedy:

> In turning over the pages of the best comedies, we are almost transported to another world, and escape from this dull age to one that was all life, and whim, and mirth, and humour. . . . We are admitted behind the scenes like spectators at court, on a levee or birthday; but it is the court, the gala day of wit and pleasure, of gallantry and Charles II! What an air breathes from the name! What a rustling of silks and waving of plumes! What a sparkling of diamond ear-rings and shoe-buckles! What bright eyes, (ah, those were Waller's Sacharissa's as she passed!) what killing looks and graceful motions! . . . Happy, thoughtless age, when kings and nobles led purely ornamental lives; when the utmost stretch of a morning's study went no farther than the choice of a sword-knot, or the adjustment of a side-curl; when the soul spoke out in all the pleasing eloquence of dress; and beaux and belles, enamoured of themselves in one another's follies, fluttered like gilded butterflies, in giddy mazes, through the walks of St. James Park." (6.70).

This is from one of Hazlitt's finest bravura set-pieces, but the passage must also be characterized as an indulgence in sentiment that suppresses much unsavory truth about Restoration comedy. We are given no hint whatever here of the arrogant cruelty, not excluding even an occasional willingness to murder, that lurked in some of those "killing looks"; and we may wonder why Hazlitt, predisposed to moral censure in other literary contexts, should so willingly overlook the shameless hedonism of that "happy, thoughtless age." Indeed, it seems but a step from Hazlitt's evocation of "another world"

to Lamb's view of Restoration comedy as wholly "artificial," a world
of its own emancipated from moral reality—"the Utopia of gallantry,
where pleasure is duty, and the manners perfect freedom" (Lamb,
Works, 2.143). Yet there is still an important difference between Hazlitt's view and that of his friend, alike in tenor though they are. No
doubt it is true that in concentrating attention on the Millamants and
Fopling Flutters, both Hazlitt and Lamb were disarming the prudish
conscience of their time—and perhaps their own consciences. But
that Hazlitt was rationalizing away, as Sir Herbert Read contends, a
"cynical realism" that Romanticism could not confront is an accusa-
tion demonstrably false,[10] as we learn soon enough if we attend to
what Hazlitt actually says of comic vision in the plays of Congreve,
Wycherley, Vanbrugh, and Farquhar.

His lecture on these writers is among the more enduring
chapters in Hazlitt's criticism, and it is so because he seldom loses his
sense of what is historically real and what is only comically "true" in
their plays. If he tries always to say the best that can be said about
them, this at least is a best seldom even acknowledged as possible by
critics determined to discover the worst. Nor is the best that Hazlitt
sees limited to what L. C. Knights has called the "myth" of Restoration wit—the belief that brilliance of style redeems it from triviality
and cynicism.[11] That apology appears only in Hazlitt's account of
Congreve, who "had by far the most wit and elegance, with less of
other things." Of the dialogue in *The Way of the World,* he writes: "It
is an essence almost too fine; and the sense of pleasure evaporates in
an aspiration after something that seems too exquisite ever to have
been realized." Hazlitt is thinking here mainly of the repartees of
Millamant with her suitors; and much as he admires this heroine, he
is prepared to concede that her "fine essence" is nothing if not "theatrical." For Hazlitt this quality is always the key to Congreve's style:
his wit is not, nor was it meant to be, subtle perception; its "sense
and satire" lie in its "artful raillery," modelled on courtly conversation, but now made more "polished and pointed" for its theatrical effect as a "new conquest over dullness." Millamant "is the ideal
heroine of the comedy of high life, who arrives at the height of indifference to every thing from the height of satisfaction; to whom
pleasure is as familiar as the air she draws . . . who has nothing to

COMEDY AND THE NOVEL

hope or to fear, her own caprice being the only law to herself, and rule to those about her." As such she represents the "finest idea" possible of her type, "the accomplished fine lady," translated from all its sins and blemishes in society to radiant sovereignty on the comic stage. True, Congreve "has done no more" than create one of the most artificial of artificial characters—but "if he had [attempted more], he would have done wrong" (6.71–75).

Now this is not, as I understand it, Lamb's defense of Restoration comedy. Hazlitt's point is rather that "meretricious" manners, when comically "embellished" in a spirit that seeks only to enhance and magnify them, make their own satiric comment on themselves, even though we may come to that awareness through our delight in the extravagant frivolity or cleverness of the characters. And if not in Congreve, Hazlitt does find moral issues variously present in the other dramatists. His Wycherley, unlike Lamb's, is a writer fiercely angry at "duplicity," at least as the creator of Manly and Olivia in *The Plain Dealer* (6.78). And Farquhar implants "high principles of gallantry and honour" in the generous feelings of his otherwise "rattle-brained, thoughtless" heroes. But it is Vanbrugh who for Hazlitt most honestly—or blatantly—typifies the ambiguity of a comedy capable of moral dimension without, or with very little, moral purpose. Vanbrugh is seen as not unlike his favorite characters—"knavish, adroit adventurers," engaged in a "predatory warfare on the simplicity, follies, or vices of mankind." Yet this "cunning impudence" results in "happy and brilliant contrasts of character" (6.81–85)—and in such "opposing" of characters Hazlitt sees the satiric dialectic at work, unconscious though it may be in serving its end. The three classes which for Hazlitt comprise nearly all the characters in Restoration comedy ("artificial elegance and courtly accomplishments" in one class, "the affectation of them" in another, and "absolute rusticity" in the third: 6.37) criticize each other simply by being what they are; and out of this "conscious self-satisfaction and mutual antipathy" (6.150) grows the satiric awareness, in the mind of the audience if not of the author, which finds all of them wanting as human beings.

Hazlitt's view still seems to me the most credible apology that can be offered for Restoration comedy, for it does not reduce these writers to aesthetes or entertainers, or to philosophical intellectuals, or to secret lovers of virtue.[12] Hazlitt succeeds, I think, in demonstrating that the dramatic power (which perhaps he generally overrates) of these comedies is owing to their flirtation with the vices they "expose," and that this purely dramatic virtue had to be—and should be, under such circumstances—the primary if not the sole regard of the dramatist. The motives to satire in the theater of this age were, and could only be, motives which the satirist shared with his society: the aspiration to mannered "refinement," the most obvious sign—or test—of which is the detection and artful reproof of false pretensions. Yet to see human vanity as being mocked in these plays by a subtler variant of itself is not to acquiesce in cynicism; for Hazlitt suggests that in the very depth of the "weakness" exposed in these plays lies a transcendent source of value which survives unimpaired. As he says of a scene which reveals the "hateful" vindictiveness of Farquhar's Lady Lurewell, "The depravity would be intolerable, even in imagination, if the weakness were not ludicrous in the extreme" (6.86). The saving "salt" of humor that Hazlitt finds in this comedy, its redeeming element of intersubjectivity, lies simply in the magnetism of sex, however gross, prurient, or morally ambiguous its expression. In his opening lecture Hazlitt had remarked that "there is another source of comic humour which has been but little touched on or attended to by the critics—not the infliction of casual pain, but the pursuit of uncertain pleasure and idle gallantry"; and he estimates that "half the business and gaiety of comedy turn upon" this "attraction" to "a subject that can only be glanced at indirectly . . . a sort of forbidden ground to the imagination, except under severe restrictions, which are constantly broken through." Eros, even in its most arrogant corruption, is Eros still; and Hazlitt does not hesitate to express his delight in all comic manifestations, farcically broad or delicate, of the only force of "nature" to remain unconquered by the "artificial" power of the Restoration court. Hazlitt was one son of Puritanism who did not identify, as Macaulay would, the "depravity" of the Restoration with its lust and sensuality; as we have seen, in his psychology the brutality and malice of man have their origin in the passions of the will, not in the desires of the body as such. This conviction enables Hazlitt to see in Restoration salaciousness not a fever of moral disease but a force that constantly humanizes the contempt of wit and dissolves cruelty of will into some laughable blindness or vulnerability of feeling: it is this sympathetic grace of instinct which "makes Horner decent and Millamant divine" (6.14).[13] True, in a world where "vice," that is, libertinism, was "worn as a mark of distinction" (6.35), comedy was bound to degenerate at times into lustful intrigue or bawdy ribaldry; yet for all the rascality and "duplicity" that this state of affairs produces, the sense of erotic—and thus of comic—pleasure is never lost (6.153). Indeed, Hazlitt would seem to be of the opinion (though he does not expressly make the comparison) that there is more "cynical" feeling and "biting" malice toward women in Ben Jonson's comedy—in *The Silent Woman,* for instance, where the women exhibit "an utter want of principle and decency, and are equally without a sense of pleasure, taste, or elegance" (6.43–44).

Living in an age of mounting middle-class "cant," Hazlitt recognized that neither the comic spirit nor a genuineness of moral feeling could endure if humor wholly turned its back on its original "resources" in erotic "gallantry": "Our old comedies would be invaluable, were it only for this, that they keep alive this sentiment, which still survives in all its fluttering grace and breathless palpitation on the stage" (6.15). And even if the fluttering heroine should prove to be, more often than not, a wanton and a hypocrite, and if the gallant at her side should turn out to be no better than a lecherous knave, this reversal, too, is no mere jest of the Restoration but holds an everlasting lesson for moralistic critics: "One benefit of the dramatic exhibition of such characters is, that they overturn false maxims of morality, and settle accounts fairly and satisfactorily between theory and practice" (6.85–86).

⁂

The sudden decline of Restoration comedy did not tempt Hazlitt to doubt its merit but confirmed him in his view of its excellence. The Restoration theater itself, by the very excellence of its satiric portraiture, had played no small role in furthering the process of its dissolution: "It is not the criticism which the public taste exercises upon the stage, but the criticism which the stage exercises upon public manners, that is fatal to comedy, by rendering the subject-matter of it tame, correct, and spiritless." If we look upon "the stage" here as meaning the entire theatrical tradition in its cumulative effect, as it modifies and merges with the influence of all literature upon opinion, we can still find wisdom in Hazlitt's generalization that comedy "destroys the very food on which it lives." "Comedy naturally wears itself out. . . It holds the mirror up to nature; and men, seeing their most striking peculiarities and defects pass in gay review before them, learn either to avoid or conceal them" (6.149–50).

The myth of decadence was perhaps even more commonly applied to comedy in Hazlitt's time than to poetry—and with good reason, for the dearth of good comedies after Sheridan was a fact that no sophisticated theatergoer would have wished to deny. Hazlitt had been proclaiming the death of modern comedy since 1813, and he was even more adamant in this prophecy than in his melancholy prognoses for painting and poetry. He dates the decline of English comedy "from the time of Farquhar," but he is too fond of that author to indict him as the first offender. Comedy had taken its fatal turn for the worse in "those *de-me-good,* lack-a-daisical, whining, make-believe comedies" of Richard Steele and others of like mind in his generation, who, bowing to the influence of Jeremy Collier and his pious denunciations, elected to write comedy "with a view not to imitate the manners but to reform the morals of the age" (6.89–90, 157–58). Some of the "good-natured malice" of the Comic Muse returned in the author of *The School for Scandal* ("perhaps the most finished and faultless comedy which we have"), but Sheridan was the "Hesperus" of a dying tradition, and even his powers could not consistently sustain—keep free from caricature—the truly "humorous, or that truth of feeling which distinguishes the boundary between the absurdities of natural character and . . . gratuitous fictions" (6.164–65, 9.66). Insofar as humor, in scattered moments, did manage to survive on the contemporary stage, it was made subservient to farce or mixed with the "amiably mawkish"—inspired by the wish, no longer in the least to hold manners up to ridicule, but to flatter the attitudes of the audience. As Hazlitt wrote of one popular specimen, Cherry's *The Soldier's Daughter:* "We are reminded of our own boasted perfections both as men and Britons: —or if any of our follies and weaknesses appear, they are sure to lean to the favorable side—*too much* good-nature, *too much* gaiety and thoughtlessness, *too much* unsuspecting frankness . . ." (9.71, 77).

Yet Hazlitt is advising no attempt to revive the old "humorous" perception. The "originals" who alone could inspire the art have vanished with the masters who understood them; and perhaps all that might be hoped for is that the theater honestly learn to know its bias toward sentiment for what it is—as modern man's habitual "abstraction" from the given reality of self. The fault did not lie merely in the fact that the characters of men in society have been disciplined into uniformity; for moral perception itself had been changing in that process. Men who are habitual readers no longer see each other as individuals in some "concrete" situation of "action and circumstances," but observe each other's differences with an eye to general sentiments or, among men of reflection, to "universal truths," which are "applicable in a degree to all things, and in their extent to none." And how therefore could one still hope to see comic character realized distinctly and concretely on the stage? A form essentially more abstract is needed to satisfy modern sensibility: "We accordingly find that to genuine comedy succeed [prose or verse] satire and novels, the one dealing in general character and description, and the other making out particulars by the assistance of narrative and comment" (20.8–10).

It is thus no caprice on Hazlitt's part that his lectures on the essayists and the novelists should immediately follow that on the Restoration, or that Steele should be praised for his attempt in the *Tatler* "to wed the graces to the virtues" and reprobated for the same intention on the comic stage (6.157–58). Hazlitt's criticism of the essayists will be deferred to the subsequent chapter, but it is logical to deal here with his account of Swift, despite the fact that England's greatest master of prose satire is missing from these lectures, Hazlitt having dealt with the author of *Gulliver's Travels* in the preceding series on the poets (where Swift also wins some rare praise for his verse). Nothing more emphatically shows Hazlitt's instinctive resistance to the fashion of the "amiable" than his steadfast admiration of Swift, at a time when other influential voices in criticism—Johnson, Jeffrey,

Coleridge—were disparaging *Gulliver's Travels* as either too "mechanical" or too "misanthropic."[14] Hazlitt's willingness to enjoy Swift, like his pleasure in Pope or in the Butler of *Hudibras* (6.62–67), is based on the recognition that literary satire is distinct from other forms of the comic, and is redeemed from its want of sympathetic pleasure by its comparative "abstraction." Many of the "disagreeable" qualities that he had castigated in Ben Jonson's comedy are welcomed as virtues in Swift, since they appear now in a form no longer grounded in a sense of individual character. Yet Hazlitt's defense of Swift's "abstraction" is not the usual line of defense for the Gloomy Dean: Swift went mad because he could not "get rid of the distinction between right and wrong," but this "constitutional preference of the true to the agreeable" was not the result of a rationalist's idealism or an ascetic's demand for moral purity but of a "literal, dry, incorrigible tenaciousness of . . . understanding" which gave him "his soreness and impatience of the least absurdity." Hence the "playful" element in Swift is his "sensible" irony about the deceptive appearances of "sense," and his only fancifulness—or all that his genius needed—was "the sparkling effervescence of his gall" as he withdrew from reality to devise a consistent counter-world of his own, one that would expose "the prejudices of sense." And in this enterprise Hazlitt discerns, without adverting to the culture of the period, the secret affinity of Swift's satire with modern science: "He has tried an experiment upon human life, and sifted its pretensions from the alloy of circumstances; he has measured it with a rule, has weighed it in a balance, and found it, for the most part, wanting and worthless—in substance and in shew." Was the result, then, "misanthropy?" "What presumption," Hazlitt sardonically answers, "and what *malice prepense,* to shew men what they are, and to teach them what they ought to be!" Hazlitt might well have paused to explain just how that last teaching survives so pessimistic a demonstration as Book Four of the *Travels;* but at least his reading of Swift anticipates most scholarly consensus today that the satire of the *Travels* was designed, not to ridicule man's suppressed animality, his want of reason or conscience as such, but "to shew the insignificance or the grossness of our overweening self-love"—of man's "empty pride." "It is," Hazlitt concludes, "an attempt to tear off the mask of imposture from the world; and nothing but imposture has a right to complain of it" (5.109–11).

Hazlitt had always insisted that "the proper object of ridicule is *egotism*" (6.151), whether worldly or intellectual; and to note this constant theme in his praise of satire—and in his own satire, we might add—is to be made aware again of the political motive in his willingness to see traditional comedy die. Why lament the passing from the theater of genuinely dramatic characters, with their laughable bagwigs and swords, if the same historical process has "driven our fops and bullies off the stage of common life?" (17.329). There might remain "the same fund of absurdity and prejudice in the world as ever" (6.151), but the very force of self-love in mankind, now made sensitive to the novel "power" of such ridicule as Swift's or Voltaire's (5.110 ff.), would insure that the selfishness of "arbitrary" power could never again seduce human consciousness into sanctioning, or accepting without question, the systematic or prescriptive violation of the rights of self-love in others. In this thought we may discern why Hazlitt prizes satire and "comedy of manners" over "comedy of nature"; and indeed we begin to understand now that Hazlitt sees essentially the same continuity of moral tendency in all phases and modes of comedy. The process by which individual humors had passed in the Restoration into uniform "pretensions" of class superiority was also a process of "enlargement" mediated by a "generalization" of taste whose counterpart is the modern "diffusion" of knowledge (6.37). And the growth of sentimental comedy and prose satire was symptomatic of a more advanced phase of the same expansion of consciousness into a force of "public opinion" which transcends class lines and transforms "manners" into norms of conduct no longer based on "dress" and modes of speech but on "private sentiment and public morals," that is, intersubjective values (17.328 ff., 6.150 ff.). However uncreative, or averse to genius, all this "abstraction" might be, it accords with "the natural progress of things . . . with the ceaseless tendency of the human mind from the *Finite* to the *Infinite*" (20.304, and see also 13.51 n.).

Hazlitt would not, however, always take so benign a view of the human comedy's triumph over itself. A greater evil than "egotism" might be breeding in the world, a peculiarly modern evil of inwardly "levelling" uniformity whose consequences for the quality of life and thought might be far worse than the mere "want of character" in modern imagination. Something of this fear is heard—although, being mixed with Hazlitt's inherited myth of history, there is still no suggestion, as there will be in the twenties, that the "levelling" tendency is virulent and destructive of civilization—in this brilliant hail-and-farewell to the comedy of "character":

> It is, indeed, the evident tendency of all literature to generalise and *dissipate* character, by giving men the same artificial education . . . so that . . . all men become alike mere readers—spectators, not actors in the scene, and lose all proper personal identity. The templar, the wit, the man of pleasure, and the man of fashion, the courtier and the citizen, the knight and the squire, the lover and the miser—[and here follows a long list of names of famous specimens of these and other types in comic literature] . . . have all met, and exchanged common-places on the barren plains of the *haute littérature*—toil slowly on to the Temple of Science, seen a long way off upon a level, and end in one dull compound of politics, criticism, chemistry, and metaphysics! (6.151)

This was written in 1813, and although the prophecy was repeated in the last of the lectures on comedy, it is by no means Hazlitt's last word on the future of "character" in modern literature. For this was conceived before the advent of Scott's novels, and Hazlitt was to learn from the regeneration of the novel in his time to discover some unexpected and redeeming benefits for literary imagination in the continued ascendancy of science and other forms of modern "abstraction".

※※※

In his lecture "On the English Novelists" (much of which repeats a long review-essay written for the *Edinburgh* in 1815), Hazlitt is still content to describe his critical effort, in this relatively unfrequented "department of criticism," as one "toward settling the standard of excellence, both as to degree and kind, in these several writers"—writers still assumed to be, however philosophical, "comic writers," engaged like their fellows in the humorous or satiric depiction of "manners," though in "the airy medium of romance"

(6.106–08; cf. 16.5 ff.). Clearly Hazlitt in these words is still accepting the traditional identity of the novel as an impure form of comedy or romance—or, in Johnson's description, as "the comedy of
romance"—and only in incidental observations does the lecturer
begin to move toward that original conception of the novel, emerging in fragments and by slow degrees over the next ten years, for
which Hazlitt has never been given sufficient credit. And how original for its time that conception was may be inferred from a remark
of his three years hence: "Good novels are . . . the most authentic as
well as most accessible repositories of the natural history and philosophy of the species" (12.231). The novelist had often been called a
"historian," but it was breaking new ground to suggest that the modern writer of fiction might also be a kind of scientist, a philosophical
experimenter refining upon his observations in the laboratory of fictional invention.[15] Here was a comparison which is no longer, as in
Hazlitt's praise of Swift, a mere analogy; here it points the way toward the modern independence of the novel from other forms, as a
genre with its own laws of character development and its own
methods of representing "truth."

Hazlitt had learned from Fielding to begin an account of the
novel with Cervantes. Although Hazlitt places *Don Quixote* in the category of "comedy of nature," Cervantes is praised as "the inventor
of a new style of writing," for "there is no work which combines so
much whimsical invention with such an air of truth." "The whole
work breathes that air of romance, that aspiration after imaginary
good, that indescribable longing after something more than we possess, that in all places and in all conditions of life,

> '—still prompts the eternal sigh,
> For which we wish to live, or dare to die!' "

And Hazlitt then proceeds to contrast this spirit of "romance" with
the more purely comic genius of Fielding, who does not draw "lofty
characters or strong passions," and whose nearest approach to a
"romantic" character is Parson Adams in *Joseph Andrews*. Hazlitt remarks that the Don and Sancho "do not so much belong to, as form
a class by themselves," and being no less "original" than "ideal," they
"identify themselves more readily with our imagination," with the

result that "the blows and wounds" incurred by this pair in their grotesque adventures haunt the memory and have exercised throughout Europe a "healing influence" on "many a hurt mind." But after hinting at this unprecedented intimacy of relationship between fictional character and the self of the reader, Hazlitt obscures his insight by resorting to the language of his comic theory. He describes "truth" in *Don Quixote* as perfect "keeping in comic character," or "consistency in absurdity" (6.11)—essentially the same in principle as truth of "the ludicrous" in stage comedy, the principal difference being, presumably, that humor in Cervantes invariably relates to imaginative aspiration (6.108–12).

Clearer signs of Hazlitt's feeling for the distinctive powers of the novel begin to emerge when Fielding is compared with Smollett. The humor in Smollett, Hazlitt observes, "arises from the situation of the persons, or the peculiarity of their external appearance," almost never, as in Fielding, from some surprising but inevitable fitness of the incidents to the characters of the persons involved. Smollett "exhibits the ridiculous accidents and reverses to which human life is liable," but Fielding reveals "the stuff of which it is composed." Fielding's "subtlety of observation on the springs of human conduct . . . is only equalled by the ingenuity of contrivance in bringing those springs into play, in such a manner as to lay open their smallest irregularity." Again Hazlitt draws the parallel with modern science: "The detection is always complete, and made with the certainty of skill of a philosophical experiment, and the obviousness and familiarity of a casual observation." Fielding's excellence is thus neither great wit nor humor but "profound knowledge of human nature," and especially of "what may be called the *double entendre* of character," surprising us—as in the case of the "demure" but "equivocal" Mrs. Bennet in *Amelia*—"no less by what he leaves in the dark (hardly known to the persons themselves) than by . . . [his] unexpected discoveries" (6.113–17).

Hazlitt in these perceptions is on the verge of breaking through to the distinctive psychological potential of the novel, but the comic-satiric tradition of "truth" is still too strong in his mind. He speaks of the "vast variety" of life in *Tom Jones,* but the phrase barely hints at the epic quality of that novel; and Hazlitt, determined to regard his author as using "incident and situation only to bring out character," fails to discern the purely novelistic relationship between Fielding's hero and the novel's panoramic vision of English society. Hazlitt was never quite happy with Tom as a hero: he confessed to "a lurking suspicion that Jones was but an awkward fellow" (6.113–14), a slave to "headlong impulse," and perhaps not very admirable except for "a morality of good-nature which in him is made a foil to principle" (17.250). What Hazlitt fails to see is that the conflict between principle and natural impulse, between the morally heroic and the unheroic, is the true dialectic of the novel that Cervantes and Fielding had discovered: the progress toward discovery of this truth of experience by the hero—or by the reader, but most often by both —constitutes the true "development" of the story. For unlike the hero of pure romance, who embodies an ideal of virtue that society already admires, the hero of the novel is made to undertake his journey through society in order to learn the difference between ideal and fact, between inward virtue or truth and its outward simulation—or (to use Lionel Trilling's terms) between reality and appearance.[16] The relative weakness of this dialectic in the eighteenth-century novel helps to explain Hazlitt's uncertain grasp of it; and we should note that his dissatisfaction with these novelists points to precisely this weakness. He had spoken of the power of imagination in Cervantes as an "involuntary unity of purpose" (6.109); and his objection to all the eighteenth-century novelists is that their "energy of purpose" (6.115) is either, as in Fielding, too slight or, as in Richardson, too conscious of its ends. When he praises Richardson for "intense activity of mind" and a power of "reasoning imagination" capable of linking character to "ideal forms," he comes close to recognizing in these qualities a significant advance beyond Fielding's essentially theatrical conception of the novel. *Pamela,* for instance, is described, but only in passing, as the educational biography of a self: "The interest of the story increases with the dawn of understanding and reflection in the heroine." Hazlitt is distracted from pursuing this insight by the lesser problem of Richardson's epistolary method, whose excessive rationalism lures our critic into the mistake of judging Richardson by the standards of Fielding's realism. No doubt it is true that Richardson fallaciously endows his characters with "the presence of mind of the author," but, as Hazlitt himself concedes, the entire and complex "chain" of motive, event, and consequence—the "wonderful chain of interest"—is brilliantly revealed by this artifice, so that "everything is brought home in its full force to the mind of the reader also." Hazlitt looks no farther into the paradox of this "artificial reality"; and his remarks trail off in wonder at the "peculiarity" of a writer who could create such miracles of moral interest as Clarissa and Lovelace yet "systematically prefer" to both so monstrous a moral coxcomb as Sir Charles Grandison (6.117–20).

Hazlitt's comments on the author of *Tristram Shandy* are brief and slight, but he does capture the essential paradox in Sterne: "a vein of dry, sarcastic humour, and of extreme tenderness of feeling," which merge in a wit that is "poignant, though artificial." What chiefly interests Hazlitt in the non-heroic, "hobby-horse" whimsy of Sterne is its cultural aspect, its expression of its time. Hazlitt asks himself now why "our four best novel-writers" should have appeared in the same period with Hogarth, the first periodical essayists, domestic tragedy and "the middle style" in stage comedy. Waiving more general causes, he gives a political explanation: after 1688 and the Hanoverian Succession, "it was found high time that the people should be represented in books as well as in Parliament." Hazlitt's own politics tend to color this account, but essentially he sees, and is the first critic to see, the new direction in literature as a middle-class phenomenon: "In despotic countries, human nature is not of sufficient importance. . . . The *canaille* are objects of disgust rather than curiosity; and there are no middle classes." Uncle Toby and his creator could now appear in the world of English fiction because, under a dispensation that secured "person and property," the English individual "had a certain ground-plot of his own to cultivate his particular humours in." This insight into the shaping of literary forms (not merely of their intellectual content) by the cultural milieu represents one of the birth moments of a genuinely historical criticism: Hazlitt here, as Tave remarks, "seizes the central fact" (p. 97), though we must note that the change in sensibility is dated somewhat too late. And when he turns to the novels of his own time, Hazlitt's historical sense is even more apparent, although its articulation is more troubled and ambivalent. He is aware that such new departures as Gothic fiction had challenged "the ancient *regime* of novel-writing" (16.123 and n.) but how deep that innovative challenge was, or could become, he himself was slow to learn, as his judgments here on Scott suggest.

This first report on the Waverley Novels is favorable but scarcely enthusiastic. Hazlitt deplores the absence in the "author of Waverley" (not yet identified as Scott) of the Cervantesque "ideal" quality ("the author has all power given him from without—he has not, perhaps, an equal power from within"), and he misses, too, the mediating sympathy of a Fielding, perhaps even the conscience of a Richardson: "In the midst of all this phantasmagoria, the author himself never appears to take part with his characters, to prompt our affection to the good, or sharpen our antipathy to the bad" (6.128). Behind this complaint there lurks, too, a prejudicial aversion that Hazlitt had felt to Shakespeare's history plays ("Something whispers us that we have no right to . . . turn the truth of things into the puppet and plaything of our fancies": 4.306), and this prejudice had led Hazlitt in 1816 to declare outright: "We do not like novels founded on facts" (4.152). It is, in short, "imagination and passion" that he looks for in Scott and fails to find in any intense degree: he fails, that is, to see and appreciate the mode of their presence, although he is probably right about the limited degree of their power. Yet five years later, in *The Spirit of the Age,* Hazlitt very differently balances the same account. What had hitherto been reckoned a deficiency in endowment now becomes the distinguishing mark of Scott's genius and its wealth of resources: a generic weakness has bred an original and compensatory strength. Novelistic imagination is here no longer conceived as bound to the "ideal" imagination of romance; indeed, Scott's genius is seen now as a power justly rebelling against the dominion of standards borrowed from poetry: "Sir Walter has found out (oh, rare discovery) that facts are better than fiction; that there is no romance like the romance of real life; and that if we can but arrive at what men feel, do, and say in striking and singular situations, the result will be 'more lively, audible, and full of vent,' than the fine-spun cobwebs of the brain." Scott is still described as "only the amanuensis of truth and history," but now Hazlitt adds: "It is impossible to say how fine his writings in consequence are, unless we could describe how fine nature is." But it is the commentary on Scott's characters that chiefly registers Hazlitt's change in attitude. He had said in his lecture that the characters of this novelist "appear like tapestry figures . . . the obvious patchwork of tradition and history," but now we are told that by this method Scott "has enriched his own genius with everlasting variety, truth, and freedom." And as proof Hazlitt offers a stunning pageant, two pages in length, of more than forty Scott characters, which he summons individually from his memory, citing for each some quality or act or association which makes them unforgettable. This new catalogue has the air of a Homeric roll-call; it is a conscious tribute to the epic range of Scott's knowledge of humanity. "What a host of associations!" Hazlitt exclaims in his peroration; "What a thing is human life! What a power is that of genius! What a world of thought and feeling is thus rescued from oblivion!" (11.62–64; cf. 6.128–29).

In this sense of a novelistic "world," of a perspective on "human life" distinct from or transcending the individual life, Hazlitt was at last responding to the dimension of "truth" peculiar to the novel, or at least to the nineteenth-century novel. What we have in this praise is essentially a vision of the novel as the Balzacian *comédie humaine*—a "comedy" as different from comedy in the old sense as from romance, for this is the creation of a "world" which no longer depends for its interest on a poignant blend of pathos and humor rooted in individual character, or on some preconceived judgment of the congruity or rationality of human behavior. It is significant that Hazlitt no longer taxes Scott with moral indifference to his characters; that indifference, indeed, is now seen as inseparable from Scott's unique merit as a novelist—"the candour of Sir Walter's historic pen." Scott "treats of the strength or the infirmity of the human mind, of the virtue or vices of the human breast, as they are to be found blended in the whole race of mankind." Hazlitt never dwelt long enough on this insight to note its implicit challenge to eighteenth-century precedents, or to relate it to his own myth of history as progressive "abstraction"; but if he had, he might have seen how the novel was escaping from the dilemma posed by the modern atrophy of the sense of concrete individuality. What modern "abstraction" had really been producing, in Scott as in his greatest contemporary critic, was a historical sense of society and a cultural sense of personality. Mind-

COMEDY AND THE NOVEL

ful always of Scott's Toryism and his Caledonian pride, Hazlitt preferred to see only the pastness, the primitivism, the nostalgia in
Scott's created world; and this is why he continues to speak of the
historical element in the novels, not as their very center, but as the
"background," again by implied analogy with a painter's canvas
(11.64–65).[17] And Hazlitt continues also to call attention to the
weakness of the dramatic foreground, even though Scott "is the
most dramatic writer now living" (11.72). Hazlitt vigorously pro-
tested the contemporary habit of likening the Great Unknown to
Shakespeare (see 12.340 ff.); and he noted that Scott's heroes, all too
reminiscent of the "insipid" heroes of popular romance, "do not act,
but are acted upon" (17.252). That, no doubt, is Scott's limitation,
but it was surely also his originality to represent for the first time the
individual will as being acted upon, in the very depths of the mind
and heart, by historical forces. And there was, too, another kind of
force operative in Scott which linked in an original way the historical
changes of the past to the timeless world of romance—and, by indirect reaction in the reader's imagination, to the modern world. If we
wonder what, in terms of Hazlitt's own psychology of the self, the
new dimension of inward power was that so forcibly struck him in
his reading of Scott sometime after 1819, we shall find it, I think, in
this passage from "On the Pleasure of Hating" (1823):

> The secret of the *Scotch Novels* is . . . [that] they carry us back
> to the feuds, the heart-burnings, the havoc, the dismay, the
> wrongs and the revenge of a barbarous age and people—to the
> rooted prejudices and deadly animosities of sects and parties in
> politics and religion, and of contending chiefs and clans in war
> and intrigue. We feel the full force of the spirit of hatred with
> all of them in turn. As we read, we throw aside the trammels of
> civilization, the flimsy veil of humanity. 'Off, you lendings!'
> The wild beast resumes its sway within us, we feel like hunting-
> animals, and as the hound starts in his sleep and rushes on the
> chase in fancy, the heart rouses itself in its native lair, and
> utters a wild cry of joy, at being restored once more to freedom
> and lawless, unrestrained impulses. (12.129)

No one could wish for a clearer recognition in Hazlitt's time of
the role of the repressed unconscious self in shaping modern literary

imagination. It should go without saying how far this vision of modern delight in fiction differs from Hazlitt's earlier picture of the bemused reader of Sterne—the middle-class Hanoverian Whig, congratulating himself on his escape from Popery and content to cultivate the garden of his amiable humors. Hazlitt has here put firmly behind him the aura of benevolist sentimentality that occasionally hangs over his aesthetic principle of "sympathy"; here his dissatisfaction with Fielding's ethic of "good-nature" finds potent articulation. And perhaps the growth of Hazlitt's admiration of Scott's novels may be most simply explained as the realization that, even in their tendency to glorify the loyalties of the barbarous past, their author was serving the cause of sympathetic imagination more purely than any of his liberal and nobly self-conscious contemporaries. What for Hazlitt redeems the fascination with "lawless" violence in Scott is not only the enlargement of the sense of "humanity" but its constant accompaniment, on the conscious level, with manifestly empirical fact: the love of power is here not indulged in Gothic fantasy but made to enforce the sense of inescapable reality. Only indisputably known and sharply realized facts, or those things of lore and legend which wield the power of fact in popular memory— something whose existence is still relevant to national or to historical consciousness, yet securely removed from the conscious temperings of modern will—could enable that will truly to go out of itself, whether in reader or writer. "Fiction," Hazlitt cautions in a late review (1829), "to be good for anything, must not be in the author's mind, but belong to the age or country in which he lives" (16.320; see also 20.144–45).

Charles I. Patterson, who judges Hazlitt's criticism of the novel to be "the first clear and well-defined conception of fiction from a great English critic," has aptly interpreted his doctrine for the novel to mean that "the actual condition the conceptual" in the author's imagination.[18] But I would add to this formulation the corollary that for Hazlitt the conceptual in fiction ought to function, or functions best, as a conception *of* the actual—or, more precisely, of the factual, of some recorded or observed "circumstance" which is or once was real (or believed to have been real) in the world of events, and which provides the novelist with an incontestable substance, a "material" basis, for his inventive experiment. There is a brief essay of 1829 which corroborates this point: the essay stands as Hazlitt's last known comment on Scott, and in it the impact of the Waverley Novels at last takes the form of some theoretic generalizations about novelistic imagination. Hazlitt was answering an objection made to Scott's recent habit of appending to his novels historical and other notes, which a writer in the *London* had deplored as an ugly unveiling of "machinery" that must spoil the imaginative effect. The question, Hazlitt saw, involves the entire problem of the relation of the novelist's art to life:

> Fiction is not necessarily the mere production of fancy, although much fancy is to be found in works of fiction; nor is it essential that fiction should be untrue. . . . It is not a stage illusion, nor a magic lantern, presenting shadows and spectacles that either burlesque or flatter humanity; but a transcript from nature, in which the truth is preserved not *literally,* but *poetically.* . . . The plain fact will not constitute a novel; there must be the creative spirit to work up all its parts into an embellished picture, and superadd such matters as, although not actually true, are deducible from that which is, and are relatively consistent. . . . The question then is, how far our pleasure will be interrupted by the assurance that certain portions are real, and how far our confidence in the rest will be thereby shaken. To know that [in *The Heart of Midlothian,* which Hazlitt thought Scott's finest novel: 19.91] Effie Deans lived and was accused is not likely to produce a disbelief in the remaining parts of her story, *which if not literally true might have been so, and seem as if they could not be dispensed with without violating the congruity of the whole* [my italics]. Her history is not the less touching because historical evidence does not attest it scene by scene; while its appeal to our feelings is enhanced by our knowledge that the main incident did happen, from which all the other details and circumstances appear to spring naturally. . . . To be vexed at the shock our first enthusiasm might receive [from the notes] would be weakness or vanity; we should have known that there was a secret process going forward; if we did not know it, it is our vanity that is hurt at the exposure. . . . A true relish for nature can neither be deceived by a bad fiction, nor dissipated by the most prosaic illustrations. (20.232–33)

With this formulation of the novel's distinctive "truth," no longer to be confused with that of romance or comic theater, Hazlitt may be said to have provided aesthetic warrant for new creative possibilities that would soon appear in nineteenth-century fiction to belie his prophecy of the necessary inanition of modern literature. Hazlitt has here fully adapted to conditions of imagination in the novel his aesthetic of intersubjective sympathy: we should note that sympathy not only with the leading characters but with the "creative spirit" of the novelist makes the "'secret process" go forward: we not only are but *should* be aware of the authorial presence just as—to cite an analogy that Hazlitt draws in the same essay—we are and should be aware of the puppet-master's strings and of the wood and paint of his figures, for it is that awareness which makes their actions seem both pleasurable and real to imagination. This, then, is Hazlitt's modification of the parallel with a scientific experiment: the "process" differs from its cultural model in being one in which the observer participates. The novel, in short, is neither more nor less objective than any other form of art; its function is not to reveal a truth in a world conceived as existing entirely beyond art but an aspect of truth implicit in all the arts; its "poetic" process differs from poetry in being not merely the symbolic intensification of value, but the symbolic articulation of historical and other "plain fact" in its significance for value.

Obviously there are delicate problems in relating realistic to symbolic "truth" in the novel that Hazlitt's theory ignores; he would have been a very clairvoyant critic, indeed, if he had detected and isolated such problems so early in the century. Like so much of his speculation, his vision of the novel is left undeveloped in its own right, but less, I suspect, because of habitual imprecision than because of the pressure of other issues that could not be denied their claims upon his waning time and energies in his final decade. The transition we have been observing in his theory of fiction from perspectives of "nature" and "ideal" imagination to perspectives of "real life," of history and necessities of "the age," was not something precipitated, as perhaps I have so far suggested, by the impact of Scott's genius; rather, his growing sense of Scott's importance expresses the deepening aggravation of the passional conflict in himself—a conflict that had been growing steadily more complex and demanding, both in its inward stresses and in its effects upon his career and his life in society. The transition in theory becomes one, therefore, in its motivating logic, with the transformation, after 1819, of the public lecturer into the personal essayist—into a writer performing his own experiment on "human life," in order to understand and save, once and for all, his living gifts of power from neglect or attrition by an increasingly hostile world, as well as from the estranging piety of a myth of moral "truth" that had hitherto dominated his sense of identity.

Chapter Eight

The Essays:
A Criticism of Life

THE last of Hazlitt's *Lectures on the Dramatic Literature of the Age of Elizabeth*, delivered in November and December of 1819, ends on a note of severe pessimism. An author, he remarks, "thinks that the attainment of acknowledged excellence will secure him the expression of those feelings in others which the image and hope of it had excited in his own breast, but instead of that, he meets with nothing (or scarcely nothing) but squint-eyed suspicion, idiot wonder, and grinning scorn." Here is Hazlitt's first public confession of the bitter disgust and despair that had been welling inside him during two years of unrelenting persecution by the Tory press. His lament, however, for the fate of literary excellence is not confined to its fate in an indifferent or hostile world; for what most appals him now is "not the despair of not attaining, so much as knowing there is nothing worth obtaining." It is "the fear of having nothing left even to wish for that damps our ardour and relaxes our efforts. . . . We stagger on the few remaining paces to the end of our journey; make perhaps one final effort; and are glad when our task is done" (6.364).

The "final effort" of *Table-Talk* (1821) launched a career as personal essayist that once more brought Hazlitt popularity and secured his fame; indeed, the "few remaining paces" would lead to the production of nearly two-thirds of his life work! It is little wonder, then, that Hazlitt's biographers should prefer to regard his despondency as a transient state of imbalance brought on, and made acute in the early twenties, by the mounting pressure of adverse circumstances: his persecution and the threat it posed to his very livelihood, his worsening health, his separation from his wife in 1819, and, not least, the miserable love affair with Sarah Walker recorded in *Liber Amoris* (1823). *Liber Amoris,* though, is something more than the record of a middle-aged man's infatuation with a girl; it is less the story of man hopelessly fallen in love than of a writer struggling to come to terms with an unfulfilled dream of destiny and with the hopeless conviction of his incurable lovelessness—a conviction that at times became the suspicion of his essential strangeness and hatefulness, not only in the eyes of the "respectable" world but even among his erstwhile friends. It is this aspect of the Sarah Walker episode, not a mere coincidence in time, which links it inseparably with his vilification in the Tory journals. We are accustomed to think of Hazlitt, in contrast to the weaponless Keats, as a battle-hardened partisan fighter who at last beat his attackers into silence (or into more respectful retaliation), and whose only enduring wound from the fray was a sense of moral outrage. But for all his deft control of himself in the combat (as witnessed in the brilliance of *A Letter to William Gifford* and *A Reply to Z*), Hazlitt was bleeding internally, and for a time saw himself as mortally wounded. The *Blackwood's* affair, he confided to Leigh Hunt in 1821, "put me nearly under ground," and at the end of the same letter we glimpse the depth of the wound: "I want to know why every body has such a dislike to me" (Howe, pp. 321–22). Peter George Patmore, who, although often an unreliable witness, perhaps saw more of Hazlitt than anyone else at this time, speaks of his "morbid sensitiveness," his fancying that every stranger he passed in the street was secretly recognizing him or covertly pointing him out as "the gentleman who was so abused last month in *Blackwood's.*"[1] All of Hazlitt's behavior after the attacks confirms this paranoiac tendency: his retirement to the loneliness of the inn at Winterslow, his scorn or distrust of his friends for not leaping to his defense, and especially his determination to exacerbate and prolong his duel with his persecutors, instead of scoffing at their slander as a low-life farce—which was Leigh Hunt's wiser tactic. But the most direct evidence lies in the personal essays themselves, which offer portraits of their author as a "self-tormentor," a "morbid egotist" (12.167, 238), a creature doomed to be *sui generis* ("a species by myself"), forever exiled from "the courts of love" (8.237). Nor could Hazlitt wholly conceal from himself the urge to self-abasement that impelled him to make a public display of his feelings in long rages of "misanthropy" which he knew would only provoke further abuse from his enemies. "All the former part of my life," he told North-cote, "I was treated as a cipher; and since I have got into notice, I have been set upon as a wild beast. When this is the case, and you can expect as little justice as candour, you naturally in self-defense take refuge in a sort of misanthropy and cynical contempt for mankind. One is disposed to humour them, and to furnish them with some ground for their idle and malevolent censures" (11.318).

The pain of his lovelessness, the sense of his spectral aloneness in an alien world, might have been less acute if Hazlitt's Puritan conscience had been able to look upon his fate as a martyrdom for the future; but events had conspired to deprive him of even this consolation. In the uniquely potent Preface that he wrote in 1819 (the year of "Peterloo" and the repressive Six Acts) for *Political Essays,* he takes coolly angry, often scornful leave of his hopes for a constitutional reform in his lifetime. Here the hater of apostasy turns his satirical lash upon all parties in the state—"the insolent Tory, the blind Reformer, the coward Whig," as he roundly sums them up elsewhere (12.135)—and now it is the lasher's own party that takes the worst licking. The pleas for unity in the *Yellow Dwarf* had manifestly gone unheeded (the weekly itself collapsed after a life of only six months), and Hazlitt's former tones of monitory invective now give way to disdainful valediction. "Henceforward," as Howe remarks, "he was to do no more journalism avowedly political; his connection with the daily and weekly organs of the press was severed, and was never in the same spirit of henchmanship to be resumed" (p. 281). And in the first years of the new decade, as the course of events continued to worsen with his own experience, Hazlitt came close to recanting his faith in the ultimate modern triumph of "public opinion." Briefly in 1820 had come joyful news that Spain was rising "from the tomb of liberty" (8.156), but the revolt against Ferdinand was soon crushed by French intervention; and early in 1821 came word of the death of Buonaparte on St. Helena. The event, however, which called forth Hazlitt's most pessimistic prophecy for the world was one that we might least expect him to take seriously—the divorce trial of Queen Caroline. This affair was a "popular farce," a "rag-fair of royalty" in which "the cant of loyalty, the cant of gallantry, and the cant of freedom" were thrown together "in delightful and inextricable confusion"; and even stalwart radicals (Hone and Thelwall among them) were to be seen rushing to kiss the hand of a Queen deprived of her rights. "What a scene," exclaims our grieving Buonapartist, "for history to laugh at!" The entire episode "gave a deathblow to the hopes of all reflecting persons with respect to the springs and issues of public spirit and opinion. . . . Truth has no echo, but folly and imposture have a thousand reverberations in the hollowness of the human heart" (20.136–38).[2]

The note of self-dramatic hyperbole in these pronouncements is not to be missed, but there can be no doubt that one of his most cherished beliefs was dying in Hazlitt's mind. "So far then," he writes in "On Living to One's-Self" (1821)—in explicit contradiction of the doctrine advanced in "What is the People?" (1818)—"is public opinion from resting on a broad and solid basis, as the aggregate of thought and feeling in a community, that it is slight and shallow and variable to the last degree . . . [and] we may safely say the public is the dupe of public opinion, not its parent" (8.98). Hazlitt does not stint from recognizing that this conclusion cuts the ground from under the Louvre-inspired faith—his faith in a community of freedom and democracy mediated by a sympathy with the power of genius and other "excellence"—on which his criticism had so far been based: "I used to think," he writes in late 1823, "better of the world. . . . I thought its great fault, its original sin, was barbarous ignorance and want, which would be cured by the diffusion of civilization and letters. But I find (or fancy I do) that as selfishness is the vice of unlettered periods and nations, envy is the bane of more refined and intellectual ones. Vanity springs out of the grave of sordid self-interest" (12.87). And surely one could not ask for a more unequivocal confession of his doubts of, and disgust with, his former "opinions"—of all that I have called Hazlitt's "myth" of modern "humanity"—than this statement in "On the Pleasure of Hating" (1823):

> As to my old opinions, I am heartily sick of them. I have reason, for they have deceived me sadly. . . . Instead of patriots and friends of freedom, I see nothing but the tyrant and the slave, the people linked with kings to rivet on the chains of despotism and superstition. I see folly join with knavery, and together make up public spirit and public opinions. . . . Seeing all this as I do, and unravelling the web of human life into its various threads of meanness, spite, cowardice, want of feeling, and want of understanding, of indifference towards others and ignorance of ourselves—seeing custom prevail over all excellence, itself giving way to infamy—mistaken as I have been in my public and private hopes, calculating others from myself, and calculating wrong; always disappointed where I placed most reliance; the dupe of friendship, and the fool of love; have I not reason to hate and to despise myself? Indeed I do; and chiefly for not having hated and despised the world enough. (12.135–36)

The tones of a "good hater" (4.103) are seldom darker than they are here—and perhaps it is the very darkness of tone, the note of conscious rhetorical extravagance, contrasted as this is with a genial lightness of tone elsewhere in the personal essays, which has led us to suspect that Hazlitt is not really in moral and intellectual earnest when he writes his testimonials of despair. Scholarship may point, moreover, to the fact that, after 1823, Hazlitt increasingly reaffirms a faith—although, as we shall see, a highly qualified faith—in the progressive tendency of modern opinion. But does this return to more hopeful attitudes prove that his pessimism is no more than an affliction of mood, a transient seizure from which he quickly recovers—and after which he goes his old ways once more, unchanged except for some wear and tear?[3] On the contrary, the pattern of loss and recovery of faith suggests to me that the writing of the personal essays, the majority of which are written in this same four-year period, 1820–23, was a process of self-exploration which enabled Hazlitt not only to confess but to confront, understand, and master his pessimism, and thus ultimately to strengthen a faith that had been tested—and reshaped—in the crucible of self-doubt. That, after all, is what the word *"essai"* once meant, in its original Montaignian signification—a venturesome "testing," the "trying out" in experience of ideas, beliefs, and values.[4]

There is more than a biographical significance in this essayist's "experiment," just as there was always more than personal despair in Hazlitt's pessimism. This is not the defiant, self-assertive pessimism of the Byronic Hero but one of disorientation, of dissatisfaction with man's will and with one's own habitual consciousness, and thus of alienation from the world but not from life or existence itself (though Hazlitt does, as we shall see, briefly experiment, and by no means casually, with a radical pessimism). Hayden V. White has remarked that Romanticism in general, "as it grew older," grew "dissatisfied with its own achievement"; and he goes on to suggest that Historicism and Realism, both "the heirs of Romanticism," draw their animus from this dissatisfaction, although without disavowing the "family" inheritance, a common stock of fundamental premises about reality.[5] Hazlitt may seem far removed from these Continental movements—although his friendship and correspondence with Stendhal in the later years of this decade is evidence of direct contact and close affinity, if not of influence.[6] In any case, we miss both the distinctive flavor and the true originality of his *Table-Talk* essays unless we recognize in them a sharp and pivotal break from antecedent Romanticism—an approach to the mentality, although not to the methods, of early Realist literature (the fiction of Balzac and Stendhal, the social criticism of Tocqueville). Read any twenty pages from Lamb or De Quincey and then follow them with twenty pages of *Table-Talk,* and the difference in attitude is at once apparent: all three writers may be "Romantic" in theme and sensibility, in language and in a stylistic manner oriented in some way to poetry, but the decisive difference is that Hazlitt, although he too loves and delights in imagination, no longer identifies with its powers, but seeks continually to penetrate its illusions, as of all other subtle deceptions of the passional self. (In this respect Hazlitt actually shows a much closer resemblance to that rambling familiar essayist in verse, the author of *Don Juan*—and the striking coincidence in time may also be no accident.)

In recent years there has been considerable controversy about the precise relationship of Realism to Romanticism, but the leading authorities, while at odds on specific issues, seem agreed that the change is not to be explained as primarily a shift to methodical objectivity or to a scientific model for society but as the transition from a relatively simple (or "monistic") to a complex (or "pluralistic") view of causal forces in their relation to values—a shift, to recall our own terminology, from cause as "power," by analogy with organic "genius" and individual will, to causation as multiple "process," involving many different kinds of causal reality. The Romanticists, too, of course, often invoked the concept of process, but always as *power* culminating in *value* (or anti-value): hence its assimilation, as in Hazlitt's case, to the logic of myth. And it is precisely this easy assimilation, this assumption that the imaginative mind, in its presumed transcendence, always *knows* what value or power or "truth" is, that our essayist now begins consistently to question. Hazlitt, it is true, remains instinctively a Romanticist in that he continues to oppose individual power, as the source of value, to "power" in the world;[7] the new direction of his interest in society and history is not in the world-process as such but in man's *consciousness* of society and history. And he continues to conceive of man's shared consciousness, even when he speaks of "the age," as being always more intersubjective than objective in character. Indeed, this is the basis of his confidence in the familiar essay as an instrument, no less flexibly faithful than the novel, of an enlarged awareness of human reality.

※✻※

Between 1818 and his death in 1830, Hazlitt wrote well over a hundred familiar essays—116, by my reckoning—and this figure does not include the sketches in *The Spirit of the Age* and various periodical contributions written in much the same familiar style but too brief, or too analytical and impersonal, to fall properly in this category. All but about forty of the essays were written before 1827, and over half of them within the four-year period, 1820–23, when Hazlitt's essays were winning their greatest popularity in the columns of the *London* and *New Monthly* magazines. The first volume of *Table-Talk* (1821) was an immediate success; a second volume apeared a year later, a second English edition in 1824, and a Paris edition (with new material) in 1825. *The Plain Speaker* followed in 1826, and by the time of his death there were enough uncollected essays to have formed (as in Howe's edition) another substantial volume—which would, however, in any event have been Hazlitt's last, for in a number of these a weary and spent essayist is bidding conscious farewell to the genre (e. g., 17.313 ff.).

There are more than chronological reasons for excluding from this phase of Hazlitt's career in prose the essays of *The Round Table* (1817), which are "familiar" enough in the sense of being casually informal but are never intimately personal in the manner of *Table-Talk*. The originality, however, of his essays in the twenties is not to be understood by taking our cue from other contemporary experiments in the genre—from Lamb's *Essays of Elia* and De Quincey's *Confessions,* both of which began appearing together with the early specimens of *Table-Talk* in John Scott's *London Magazine*. Thanks to the rapid growth of the reading public, the development of steam printing and improved facilities of distribution, magazines multiplied in this decade and became appreciably larger; and this condition, with the consequent demand of editors for more, and for more original, material, gave the essayist license to ramble as never before.[8] To this greater freedom Hazlitt would respond in ways that differ demonstrably, despite superficial resemblances, from the innovations of Lamb and De Quincey. The most popular of Hazlitt's essays in our anthologies—"My First Acquaintance with Poets," "The Fight," "On Going a Journey"—suggest an affinity with his fellow contributors to the *London* that is not confirmed by the great majority of the pieces in *Table-Talk*. Indeed, when Hazlitt's interests as an essayist are compared with those of the great essayists of the past, it is remarkable how traditional in orientation his work in the genre appears. Friendship, love, happiness, solitude, youth and age, duty, ambition, fame, travel, superstition, the fear of death—these and other perennial topics of the essay appear and reappear, and are most often addressed directly, not tangentially encountered as in Lamb. "On the Conduct of Life," "On the Spirit of Obligations," "On the Qualifications Necessary to Success in Life"—such titles alone are enough to suggest that for the ultimate ancestry of his essays we should look back, beyond both Bacon and Montaigne, to the less celebrated Renaissance moralists in prose, the compilers of "maxims" and writers of "meditations"—whose purpose, as they had learned from their models among the Ancients, was to teach *sapientia,* wisdom for the soul in private life, and *prudentia,* the wise conduct of affairs in the public world.[9] If we set aside the overt didacticism of this tradition, we have terms that still serve to describe Hazlitt's most constant concerns—the perennial problems of common experience and moral understanding—problems more interpersonal than personal, examined anew for his age in the light of a non-rationalistic psychology of the will.

Hazlitt was fully aware of the evolution wrought in the essay's ethical motivation by Bacon and Montaigne; and again he associates this change, as in his other descriptions of modern prose literature, with the rise of science. In his lecture "On the Periodical Essayists," he defines the familiar essay as "that sort of writing . . . which consists in applying the talents and resources of the mind to . . . that mixed mass of human affairs" which no "regular" art or science can properly encompass and which can only be understood as it "comes home [he here adapts a phrase of Bacon's] to the business and bosoms of men." The method of the essayist "is in morals and manners what the experimental is in natural philosophy, as opposed to the dogmatical method. . . . It inquires what human life is and has been, to shew what it ought to be" (6.91–92). The same analogy appears in his excellent character of Bacon, which reminds us of Hazlitt's own "metaphysical" ambition: "He was master of the comparative anatomy of the mind of man, of the balance of power among the different faculties. He had thoroughly investigated and carefully registered the steps and process of his own thoughts, with their irregularities and failures . . . and he applied this self-knowledge on a mighty scale to the general advances or retrograde movements of the aggregate intellect of the world." But Bacon is for Hazlitt too much the "judicial" philosopher (6.327) to stand as the father of the modern familiar essay; that honor Hazlitt grants only to Montaigne, "the first who had the courage to say as an author what he felt as a man." Montaigne "began by teaching us what he himself was"; he was a moralist "by merely daring to tell us whatever passed through his mind, in its naked simplicity and force." Whether turned inward or outward, this *"morale observatrice"* was Montaigne's gift to his successors; and Hazlitt goes so far as to say that "there has been no new impulse given to thought since his time." Hazlitt recognizes no real difference in kind—here he unforgivably neglects the importance of La Bruyère and the English "character" writers—between Montaigne and the periodical essayists of the eighteenth century. Addison and Steele "applied the same unrestrained expression of their thoughts to the more immediate and passing scenes of life, to temporary and local matters; and in order to discharge the invidious office of *Censor Morum* more freely . . . assumed some fictitious and humorous disguise, which, however, in a great degree corresponded to their own peculiar habits and character" (6.92–95).

The crucial difference between phases of the essay tradition that Hazlitt is here minimizing may be said to correspond roughly to the unconfessed contrast of his own more conventional essays in *The Round Table,* which were still cast in the eighteenth-century mold, with the new, more Montaignian departures of *Table-Talk.*[10] In the earlier series the pronoun "I" seldom occurs, being almost always subsumed in the "we" of the *Examiner,* and over this pronoun constantly hovers the presiding spirit of Leigh Hunt. Twelve of the fifty-two pieces in *The Round Table,* as originally published, were by Hunt; indeed, the whole enterprise, including the very name of the series, appears to have originated with the *Examiner*'s editor, who wished to inspire his readers with "philosophic gallantry." "Table-talk" was the name that Hunt at first (in 1813) proposed for such a series, and he explained that "under this head, we may be considered as sitting with the very best and pleasantest part of our readers over a glass of old port or a cup of coffee." The idea of a club that would, as in the *Tatler* or *Spectator,* include correspondents (whether real or imaginary) soon disappeared,[11] but the clubby "we" remained in a more fundamental sense: here the pronoun does not mean, as in Hazlitt's later essays, his contemporaries or human beings in general—or does so only as this larger plurality is assumed to coincide in spirit with the "we" of the *Examiner* and its cultural program for English opinion. It was the intention of the series "to expose certain vulgar errors" (4.1), and the preponderance of literary and theoretic themes over more common and familiar concerns—a proportion reversed in *Table-Talk*—is an index to this programmatic emphasis.

On the whole, the essayist of *The Round Table* pitches his style too consistently to the Huntian keynote of Pleasure, of Cheerful Opinions; and what we miss in his prose here are precisely those darker, sharper modulations of voice which were then to be heard emerging in Hazlitt's political contributions to the *Examiner*. This is not to discount the many moments in this series of deft insight and appealing gusto; but the charm we feel is the deliberate charm of a fledgling writer still in his "honeymoon of authorship" (8.292), and rather too consciously planning and executing his effects. We sense, moreover, that the brief *Spectator* format is constantly thwarting the multi-directional movement of Hazlitt's mind: held to a limit of three or four short columns, he tries in every paragraph to be at once analytical, illustrative, witty, eloquent, and ingratiating; and the result, more often than not, is that either the writing loses its freedom and thrust or the idea is denied a convincing fullness of development.

The author of these essays was, in short, writing more as an author than as a man; and that, by Hazlitt's own theory, is a fatal impurity in the familiar essay. We may see the difference plainly if we pause to compare two passages—one early, one late—on the same subject. The first is from "On Manner" (1815):

> What any person says or does is one thing; the mode in which he says or does it is another. The last of these is what we understand by *manner*. In other words, manner is the involuntary or incidental expression given to our thoughts and sentiments by looks, tones and gestures. Now, we are inclined to prefer this latter mode of judging of what passes in the mind to more positive and formal proof, were it for no other reason than that it is involuntary . . . .

Hazlitt then quotes Lord Chesterfield for support, and proceeds rapidly to apply his idea of involuntary revelation to various contexts—to writing and to the actor's art as well as to ordinary social intercourse (4.41–47). But none of these contexts is vividly evoked, for Hazlitt is interested in them only as illustrative means for making his point. Observe now how differently he pursues the same theme in "On the Knowledge of Character" (1822):

> There are people whom we do not like, though we may have known them long, and have no fault to find with them. . . .
> There is a coldness, a selfishness, a levity, an insincerity, which

275

we cannot fix upon any particular phase or action, but we see it in their whole persons and deportment. One reason that we do not see it in any other way may be that they are all the time trying to conceal this defect by every means in their power. There is, luckily, a sort of *second sight* in morals: we discern the lurking indications of temper and habit a long while before their palpable effects appear. I once used to meet with a person at an ordinary [i. e., tavern], a very civil, good-looking man in other respects, but with an odd look about his eyes, which I could not explain, as if he saw you under their fringed lids, and you could not see him again: this man was a common sharper. The greatest hypocrite I ever knew [this is Sarah Walker of *Liber Amoris*] was a little, demure, pretty, modest-looking girl, with eyes timidly cast upon the ground, and an air soft as enchantment; the only circumstance that could lead to a suspicion of the true character was a cold, sullen, watery, glazed look about the eyes, which she bent on vacancy, as if determined to avoid all explanation with yours. I might have spied in their glittering, motionless surface, the rocks and quicksands that awaited me below!

Clearly the superiority of this passage lies in its dramatic quality: the thought does not develop by logical reference to a pre-defined concept ("manner") but is made to inhere in, and unfold from, the process of observation itself. And this process is made manifest not only by the apt use of metaphor but in the very rhythms of the sentence structure, which reenact the impact of experience as the mind and its preconceptions meet the shock of concrete truth. Yet there is still another aspect to the dramatic force of this "personal" method: the writer himself proves to be as full of surprises as he has shown life to be. Just as the reader of this passage is settling into the assurance that he may trust his instinctive response to people, Hazlitt surprises him with the reflection that a reliance upon feeling in judging another's character may be every bit as deceptive as our abstractly reasoned inferences. In "On Manner" we were told that the "cordiality" of a man's handshake in conferring a favor, whatever his voice may say, "does not admit of misinterpretation," but Hazlitt now offers a far subtler version of the difference between appearance and reality:

I know a person [himself, perhaps?] to whom it has been objected [very probably by Leigh Hunt] as a disqualification for friendship, that he never shakes you cordially by the hand. I own this is a damper to sanguine and florid temperaments, who abound in these practical demonstrations and 'compliments extern.' The same person, who testifies the least pleasure at meeting you, is the last to quit his seat in your company, grapples with a subject in conversation right earnestly, and is, I take it, backward to give up a cause or a friend. . . . The most phlegmatic constitutions often contain the most inflammable spirits—as fire is struck from the hardest flints. (8.305–06; cf. 4.42)

Such turns or reversals of feeling in the later essays would not seem, then (if this instance is typical, and we shall see that it is), to arise from a wantonness of mood in Hazlitt but from a tension of feeling that has developed between his thought and his sense of the reader's response. Bonamy Dobrée has recognized something of this tension in Hazlitt; he remarks that when Hazlitt "is amusing, as he often is, it is not seldom at our own expense. . . . To read him . . . is like bathing in the sea on a fine clear day; but the water is cold, even a little rough; and there is plenty of salt in it."[12] A healthier respect for the reader's resistance to an idea or a judgment was, I suspect, the decisive lesson that Hazlitt had learned as a writer from the vicissitudes of his career in the previous decade. As if in express disavowal of the technique of The Round Table for exposing "vulgar errors," he remarks in Table-Talk: "The best way to instruct mankind is not to show them their mutual errors, but to teach them to think rightly on indifferent matters, where they will listen with patience in order to be amused, and where they will not think . . . a syllogism the worst insult that can be offered them" (8.38).

Since this element of tension between writer and reader holds, I believe, the clue to the stylistic originality of Hazlitt's "experiment," it may be worth our while to consider at this point the increasing emphasis that he places upon "conversation" in his comments on prose style in general. In a preface written for the Paris edition of Table-Talk he describes the novelty of his essays as an attempt to "combine . . . two styles, the *literary* and *conversational;* or after stating and enforcing some leading idea, to follow it up by such observations and reflections as would probably suggest themselves in discussing the same question in company with others. This seemed to me to promise a greater variety and richness, and perhaps a greater sincerity,

than could be attained by a more precise and scholastic method"
(8.333). Here a dimension of "method" has been added to "conversational style" that cannot be clearly discerned in his earlier criticism,
where "a pure conversational prose-style" (such as that found in
"Swift, Arbuthnot, Steele, and the other writers of the age of Queen
Anne") is conceived mainly in terms of diction and sentence structure, and is opposed, in these terms, to the "florid and artificial style"
of Doctor Johnson, with its antithetically balanced periods and *ses-
quipedalia verba.*" Perhaps Hazlitt in 1824 is still thinking of Johnson
when he speaks of "scholastic method," for we should not underestimate the magisterial spell that the author of the *Rambler* still exercised over all prose, whatever the occasion: "At present," Hazlitt
complains in 1818, "we cannot see a lottery puff or a quack advertisement pasted against a wall, that is not perfectly Johnsonian in style"
(5.104–05). Yet Hazlitt believed that the degeneration of the eighteenth-century essay had not begun with Johnson but with Addison,
whose "regular dissertations" first departed in form and spirit from
"the dramatic and conversational turn" which was "the greatest
charm" of the *Tatler* and of the *Spectator* at its best. Steele's "reflections" were "more like the remarks which occur in sensible conversation, and less like a lecture. Something is left to the understanding of
the reader." And Hazlitt suggests that what is left for the reader to
understand is "the dramatic contrast and ironical point of view to
which the whole is subjected"—an effect which arises from the
"piquancy" of the movement back and forth between various descriptions of the same world and critical reflections upon that world
by an author who pretends to be merely another character in the
world he describes (6.95–97).

I submit that something of the same "ironical point of view" survives in the style of Hazlitt's essays—with the great difference being
that the conversational dialectic has penetrated more deeply into the
writer's self-consciousness and can no longer be quite so simply or so
amiably resolved. What Hazlitt does, as we shall understand better in
a moment, is to adapt the ironic tensions and contrasts of this dialectic to the greater seriousness and abstraction of converstional subject
matter in his time—a change in English habits also prefigured in Addison and fostered by his example and Johnson's: "The style of our

THE ESSAYS: A CRITICISM OF LIFE

common conversation has undergone a total change from the personal and *piquant* to the critical and didactic; and, instead of aiming
at elegant raillery or pointed repartee, the most polished circles now
discuss general topics, or analyze abstruse problems" (16.216). Here
is an observation which suggests how narrow the gap was in Hazlitt's
age between sophisticated conversation and prose discourse ("Everyone," he remarks, "now affects to speak as authors write":
5.106)—and the 'familiar style" of *Table-Talk* might be described as
the attempt of a lover of argument and animated talk to make the
actual table-talk of his time more truly conversational, and to make
the written idiom of intellectual discourse more colloquial in spirit,
less committed to formal and doctrinal rigidities. Just as ordinary
conversation in society tends to degenerate into polite ventilation of
"no opinions but what will please," so the mentality of "authorship"
is subject to its own complacencies: "Men of the world have no fixed
principles, no ground-work of thought: mere scholars have too
much an object, a theory always in view. . . . By mixing with society,
they rub off their hardness of manner. . . . In the confidence and
unreserve of private intercourse, they are more at liberty to say what
they think, to put the subject in different and opposite points of
view, to illustrate it more briefly and pithily by familiar expressions,
by an appeal to individual character and personal knowledge—to
bring in the limitation, to obviate misconception, to state difficulties
. . . and answer them as well as they can. This would hardly agree
with the prudery, and somewhat ostentatious claims of authorship"
(12.30–33).

Now in one sense, of course, this comment shows us a Hazlitt
who is still too much the Addisonian "author" in his conception of
"conversational" style, which is here being viewed as a vehicle for
"argument" and its apt illustration. And again he fails to acknowledge the difference between "personal" and merely "familiar" essay-
writing. But Hazlitt's terminology will still suffice to encompass this
difference if we remember that his conversation with the reader is
always also a conversation with himself—a dialectic of the "opposite
points of view,"[13] both moral and intellectual, that had developed in
his own mind since his persecution in 1818–19 and his consequent
reaction from his former myth-oriented habits. So far it has been

sufficient in this study to distinguish two alternating voices in Haz-litt—Prig and Boy, Dissenter and rebellious son, rationalist and pas-sionalist—but now, since he is in revolt from his own intellectual past as well as from the world of established privilege, the old polarity changes form and direction—its alignment vis-à-vis the world—in the most characteristic essays of this period. Indeed, it is now that Hazlitt himself appears conscious for the first time of the contending voices—no longer as generic "contradiction" merely, nor only as the difference between "painter" and "metaphysician" (see 17.311), but as the discrepancy between the tenor of his professed ideals and beliefs and the darkly violent urgings of his passional being. To me-diate between these conflicting halves of his nature the author of *Table-Talk* finds it necessary to speak with another, a third voice—one not without precedent in his earlier prose, but whose accents in the previous decade were never heard so distinctly as we have just heard them in the passage from "On the Knowledge of Character." And we shall see now that this stylistic change is accompanied, and perhaps made possible, by an intellectual change—by Hazlitt's will-ingness to put to the dialectical test, to revise drastically without wholly surrendering, some of the most cherished convictions of his youth.

❧

To understand this "conversational" voice as an attitude of mind, we must first be clear about the stylistic interaction in the essays of Hazlitt's more habitual voices; for it is only as the emotional successor and dialectical moderator of these earlier attitudes that the third voice appears, or appears at its purest. The voice that posterity prefers to remember from the essays is the amiable voice of "On the Pleasure of Painting" (the first essay in *Table-Talk*): here is the freedom-loving Boy in Hazlitt, at last willing to escape the solemn conscience of "Liberty," happy in his memories of youth, generous and enthusiastic (indeed, often sentimental) in his responses to both art and life, content to forget his quarrels with the world and live only "to himself" (8.90 ff.). When, however, this vein of reminis-cence leads Hazlitt to contemplate his solitariness as an enforced withdrawal from the world, the style is likely to modulate rather sud-

National Portrait Gallery

7. HAZLITT IN THE *Table-Talk* YEARS. A REPLICA BY WILLIAM BEWICK
(SIGNED 1825) OF HIS CHALK-DRAWING OF 1822.

denly into the violent rhetoric of the second voice: the gusto and exuberance then translate into an acrimonious and often sulfurous
contempt for a society, or a dastardly humankind, that has made a
mockery of his aspirations, by its treachery or indifference to "truth"
and "excellence." Readers of *Political Essays* will have no trouble
recognizing the antecedent life of this darker voice. All the saltiness
and spleen that had hitherto characterized his political satire—the
heaping up of epithets in invective or mock praise, the grotesque yet
penetrating analogies, the relentless *reductio ad absurdum,* the ironic
interrogations, the staccato of short, stabbing sentences which follow
or build up to some massive, wide-sweeping, hydra-like sentence a
page or two long, or longer—these weapons of "the good hater" are
now turned upon all his smouldering hatreds, including not a few
things which Hazlitt had hitherto treated with indulgence or even
with affection. Here, in short, is the censorious mentality of the Prig,
but without the shield of his former optimism, inflamed now less by
righteous will than by the bewildered, bleeding rage of despair, and
directed as much—and with almost equal violence—against his
former habits of deceptive hope as against the treacherous world.
"On the Pleasure of Hating" shows us the savage voice at its most
brilliant, and there the reaction from his youthful benevolism is
given its most extreme statement in the essays: "We revenge injuries;
we repay benefits with ingratitude. . . . Love and friendship melt in
their own fires. We hate old friends: we hate old books: we hate old
opinions; and at last we come to hate ourselves" (12.130). One would
think, from this emphasis, that Hazlitt's despondent "hate" could go
no further, but there is evidence from a fragment written in this
same bitter year, 1823, that his "misanthropy" very nearly extended
to existence itself: "Happy are they that can say with Timon—'I am
Misanthropos, and hate mankind!' They can never be at a loss for
subjects to exercise their spleen upon. . . . Let them cast an eye on
that long disease, human life, [or] on that villainous compound,
human nature, and glut their malice." And then follows surely the
longest and most caustic sentence Hazlitt ever wrote, cataloguing
more than eighty ills that flesh and spirit are heir to—more than
enough, he concludes, "to feed the largest spleen and swell it, even
to bursting!" (20.132–33).

To consider such an outburst as yet another instance of Romantic self-indulgence, as a kind of Byronism in prose, is to mistake the *Table-Talk* enterprise; for such moments form only part, and by no means the dominant or decisive phase, of Hazlitt's ongoing "experiment" with life. George Barnett has brought to light an unpublished review of *Table-Talk* by Lamb, which reveals an interesting opinion of one great essayist about another: "Lamb believes that Hazlitt is not really the discontented man he appears to be in *Table-Talk,* but that he has assumed this character to give 'force and style to his writing.' "[14] Perhaps Lamb when he wrote this review did not know just how embittered his friend had become, but the lasting truth in his remark lies in its suggestion that Hazlitt's pessimistic stance is no more to be confused with his essential personality, even at the time of writing, than "Elia" is with Lamb or Manfred and Cain with Byron. Yet if this is so, then neither is Hazlitt's affable personality in the essays any more or less a persona: both exist in self-dramatic tension with each other, and it is doubtful that we would have had the Hazlitt of amiable pleasure without the antagonist voice of negation. Hazlitt himself recognizes the principle of this truth when he observes (although he is not referring specifically to his own experience): "Misanthropy is not the disgust of the mind at human nature, but with itself" (17.89). To revert to Hazlitt's psychological theory, we may say that his rhetoric of "hate" represents the experimental effort of his mind to gain "conscious power" over his negative emotions—"to know," as he had stated the principle earlier, "the worst we have to contend with, and to contend with it to the utmost" (5.7). Thus a movement of feeling that would seem to lead only toward emotional imbalance actually induces a restoration of balance: it imperceptibly revives and releases, by reaction, the organic will to pleasure and at last generates, under optimum conditions when the restored equilibrium itself becomes a feeling, that reflective serenity of mind which is the characteristic tone of Hazlitt's third voice at its strongest and purest.

That the process worked as self-therapy there can be no doubt; for Hazlitt did "come on [his] legs again" (12.123), and the pessimistic strain becomes noticeably less frequent and intense in the essays written after *The Plain Speaker.* The process of stabilization, however, had always to be repeated, and the regrettable aspect of the process is that its polarization of feeling tended to manifest itself in his thought as a regression to the old moral dualism of self and world— the habitual bias of Dissent that his critical thought in previous years had outgrown. Now that his myth of "progress" had been badly shaken, Hazlitt instinctively fell back on the ritual patterns of moral response that he shared with his father (and we should not overlook the impact of his father's death in 1820 in aggravating his distrust of both himself and the world). Whenever Hazlitt falls into this antithetic pattern, the thoughts of the essayist verge on the tedious and truistic, even at times on the banal, as he tirelessly rings the changes on his favorite antitheses—independence and servility, genius and fashion, honesty and vanity, humanity and courts, the individual and "corporate bodies" (8.264 ff.), and so on. Dissociated from the political myth that had promised a resolution of them, these dualisms tend to produce an impasse in thought and a stalemate in feeling; and many a promising Hazlitt essay ("On Living to One's Self," for instance, where the first two voices confront each other in alternate solo, overwhelming the thinker: 8.90 ff.) falls victim to this compulsive ritual.

But an antithetic stalemate is characteristic of the essays only when he forgets or neglects his reader—and this Hazlitt seldom does. Normally his style solicits or encourages in the reader a mood keyed to a certain kind of critical observation—to that state of mind which is typical of the self in its response, not to "the world" in its strangeness or impersonality, but to a world of *others,* of other selves. It is to this watchful, defensive aspect of the ego in the give and take of conversation, tacitly engaged in maintaining its own identity in a tension of sympathy or antipathy with others, that Hazlitt's third voice appeals; and at its best his style succeeds in sustaining this disposition in an unmilitant and relaxed, lively yet reflective mood which lies somewhere between a comic or satiric sense of irony and a tolerant philosophical moralism. And this "tension with otherness," as I like to call the distinctive pitch of his style—a tension that was always present in his earlier prose, but without acquiring a feeling-tone of its own—becomes a new and original mode of thought when it shows itself willing not only to confess emotionally the dualism of self and world on which it rests but to challenge and undeceive the pride and moral despair that tempt us to accept this dualism as final.

In effect, this phase of the "experiment" becomes a return to the problem of self-love, although no longer a return to the point of view of the apostolic defender of "disinterestedness." Our best clue to the new awareness of self in the essays lies in a little book that Hazlitt published in 1823—*Characteristics; In the Manner of Rochefoucauld's Maxims*. This neglected volume, which consists of 434 apothegms—or aphoristic reflections, for some extend to a sizable paragraph—is of considerable interest, not only in its own right as a late and worthy specimen of a vanishing genre, but as a compendium of the leading ideas, and especially the moral ideas, of the essays. It is a measure of Hazlitt's capacity for growth that by 1823 he had learned to regard Rochefoucauld not as the cynical spokesman of a jaded French aristocracy but as one of the world's great moralists, not unlike Pope or Swift—or Shakespeare—in recognizing that the first business of morality is to expose and chasten the moral vanity of the will. How far Hazlitt had travelled from his youth may be seen at once if we compare his earlier thoughts on the nature of envy with one of his aphorisms on the same theme in *Characteristics*. In 1814 Hazlitt had argued that "there is no such thing as envy," for what we call envy does not arise from a jealousy of superiority but simply from uncertainty that the excellence imputed to another is real: once remove that doubt—as in the case of the well-established reputation of the great dead—and "envy" ceases (20.37–38). Compare now this quite different reflection on envy (elsewhere called at this time "the ruling passion of mankind": 20.280) in *Characteristics*: "Mankind are so ready to bestow their admiration on the dead because the latter do not hear it, or because it gives no pleasure to the objects of it. Even fame is the offspring of envy" (9.228). Nothing demonstrates more emphatically than this aphorism the change in his conception of the sympathy of imagination with value: he is not recanting his belief that there is a real sympathy with value *as* value, but he now insists that this sympathy, even in the case of an "ideal" object, is likely to provoke an equally natural reaction in the self against the claims of value, insofar as the excellence in question is felt to inhere in a value or power distinct from the sense of value or power that sustains one's own identity. This bondage of the mind's sympathetic response to the sense of identity, the conscious or unconscious resistance of our individual character to some countervailing otherness, is what Hazlitt now means by "self-love." The crusader against mechanistic hedonism who had once contended for the primacy in feeling of "disinterested" imagination now writes: "Our self-love, rather than our self-interest, is the master-key to all our affections" (12.82).

The self-love of an apostate-hating metaphysician forbids express acknowledgment of a lapse from his former convictions, but the change is apparent in nearly every essay of the *Table-Talk* period. Hazlitt had always been willing to grant that self-love, insofar as it implies a need for the approbation of others, supports and even enlarges the sympathies of "opinion" in society (4.93 ff.), but he is now prepared to recognize that the converse is equally true: our sympathy with the minds of others also intensifies self-love and makes it morbidly "exclusive," by tempting us to court their admiration, to place an inordinate value on our good opinion of ourselves, and thus to resist or minimize the competing claims of others.[15] "We *are* very much what others *think of us*" (9.221): this was the lesson that Hazlitt had learned from his loss of self-respect under the stress of his persecution. And insofar as our sympathy with other minds does seek or pretend to remain "ideal" in character, it may lead to consequences nearly as bad, in their sum total, as those of common selfishness: it makes us dissatisfied with our actual condition in life and diminishes our sympathy with all otherness except our own inward, unattainable ideals of imagination. "Even the very strength of the speculative faculty, or the desire to square things with an *ideal* standard of perfection (whether we can or no) leads perhaps to half the absurdities and miseries of mankind. We are hunting after what we cannot find, and quarreling with the good within our reach" (12.137 n.). And again: "Instead of being delighted with the proofs of excellence, and the admiration paid to it, we are mortified with it. . . . By being tried by an *ideal* standard of vanity and affectation, real objects and common people become odious or insipid" (12.87).

That last comment seems to me to epitomize perfectly the paradox of Hazlitt's attitude in the essays toward all human "vanity." We have seen in previous chapters an "ideal" model of creative or intellectual power gradually giving way in Hazlitt's mind to "dramatic," or passionally interactive, power as his standard of literary excellence; and now in the *Table-Talk* phase we witness the turning point where "ideal" excellence ceases to be conceived as an essentially *transcendent* power—that is, a power of mind communicably free of its source in a conditioned self—or is so only in genius and the context of art, not in life beyond the aesthetic experience. "In reading we always take the right side, and make the case properly our own. Our imaginations are sufficiently excited, we have nothing to do with the matter but as a pure creation of the mind, and we therefore yield to the natural, unwarped impression of good and evil. Our own passions, interests, and prejudices out of the question, or in an abstracted point of view, we judge fairly and conscientiously. . . . But no sooner have we to act or suffer, than the spirit of contradiction or some other demon comes into play, and there is an end of common sense and reason" (12.136–37 n.). Yet if the intersubjective communion of art and literature is impossible to translate back into life, that very limitation holds the potential for another kind of "abstraction" from self, one that does not surrender the power of the "real"—the possibility of a purely "conversational" intersubjectivity, a communion less of sympathetic hearts or souls than of inescapable egos, willing to compare notes on the tragicomic servitude of their mutual bondage to the fate of self-love.

A "respect for others" has thus come to mean for Hazlitt not merely a sympathetic response to the passions of "the human heart" but to those impulses in the heart of another which make it an alien other, and with which we can only sympathize as we acknowledge the equivalent alienation, with all its possibilities for intolerance, in ourselves. "Nature (the more we look into it) seems made up of antipathies; without something to hate, we should lose the very spring of thought and action" (12.128). Moral judgment of others is, in short, valid only as it implies at the same time a judgment passed upon one's own potential for malice or weakness. Hazlitt does not shrink from recognizing that admitting an ineluctable self-love means admitting also that the antinomian principle is inevitable in society: "Every man, in his own opinion, forms an exception to the ordinary rules of morality" (9.217). And it is in counteracting the more sordid, brutalizing, and envy-provoked effects of this principle that human vanity reveals its redeeming moral function. The antipathies of the will to power are softened by the pleasures of vanity; and society becomes tolerably humane precisely because vanity *does* sympathize with human vanity—not with another's ego but with its expressions of pleasure in itself. As long as there is no direct affront to our self-love, we naturally welcome in others an egotism that in its easy resolve and serene assurance of success confirms our own pretensions to be the best judge of our merits. Vanity is thus entitled to its praise as "the elixir of human life" (12.107); some degree of "affectation" is said to be "as necessary to the mind as dress to the body" (8.304; 9.192); and even "modesty" is now brought under suspicion as either an "excess of pride" or as really the concealment of weakness which others instinctively take it to be (12.196). A "gentleman" is defined by our essayist as someone "who understands and shews every mark of deference to the claims of self-love in others, and exacts it in return from them" (12.217–19); and the same "compromise" of vanities helps to make a charity of conscience, a mutual forgiveness of sins, possible in the world.

Hazlitt's second voice, however, will tolerate only so much of this tolerance: sooner or later he breaks in with some tart reminder (for example, "Mankind are a herd of knaves or fools": 9.202) that the world has precious little regard for the human self as either mind or soul. But if the world of inward vision is no less trustworthy, if "the heart is deceitful above all things" (17.297), and if, as Hazlitt wrote in 1819, "life is a struggle to be what we are not and to do what we cannot" (6.364)—then what surcease or hope is there for a self with an inveterate passion for "excellence"? The Hazlitt of *Table-Talk* has discovered a new function for "ideal" feeling: not one of impelling the will to realize its values in either the world or the individual future, but one of securing "continuity of impression" (17.318) between our past and our present, of sustaining what he calls our "ideal identity" in time, even though that identity is not to be "domesticated" and must always stand in contradiction to the "destiny" of our "actual" identity in the world (8.189). This "personal" function leads our essayist to a new appreciation of art and literature, and before we can follow his "experiment" further as a criticism of life, we must pause to consider some rather striking changes in his literary criticism.

❧

There is scarcely a page in the essays without several quotations from, or allusions to, literature, but of literary criticism there is surprisingly little—only sixteen essays focus directly upon an aesthetic or literary topic—and the author of this criticism is not always recognizable as the critic of the previous decade. With two conspicuous exceptions,[16] we meet with no more antithetic contrasts and multiple comparisons of genius, nor does Hazlitt develop further the contradistinctions drawn in the *Lectures* among genres, styles, and historical periods. Much of our knowledge of his theory comes from certain essays in *Table-Talk*, but we no longer have the sense of a critic building up, from carefully laid theoretic foundations, a "temple of true Fame" (6.176) to enshrine the genius of the past for future modern ages. Instead, our essayist of this decade speaks of "waking from the dream of books at last," and the dream seems (at least in 1823) to have left behind no compensating truth of vision: "The object of books is to teach us ignorance; that is, to throw a veil over nature, and persuade us that things are not what they are, but what the writer fancies or wishes them to be" (20.126). In contrast to the respect shown for classical learning and even for "pedantry" in the *Round Table* series, now we are told that "the description of persons who have the fewest ideas of all others are mere authors and readers," and that "any one who has passed through the regular gradations of a classical education, and is not made a fool by it, may consider himself as having had a very narrow escape" (8.70–71; cf. 4.80 ff.).

The reaction from "ideal" power would seem to have been extended here to all literature, but the comment just quoted suggests that we must make a distinction between intrinsic power in literary art and the bookish world of the *literati*, "mere authors and readers." Precisely this distinction proves important in understanding the *Table-Talk* essay "On Criticism." The most curious thing about this essay is its detachment, its avoidance of autobiography: it seems to have been written by a man who had never himself mounted the

critical rostrum—or perhaps, more accurately, by a man who may
have wished that he never had. Hazlitt deplores here, among other
things, the fashion of "subtle metaphysical distinction or solemn didactic declamation" that prevails in contemporary reviews, where the
critic's object "is not to do justice to his author, whom he treats with
very little ceremony, but to do himself homage and to show his acquaintance with all the topics and resources of criticism." Hazlitt
includes the *Edinburgh*, "the most admired of our Reviews," in this
rebuke; and one of Jeffrey's better-known hands would seem to be
not wholly excepting his own past performances when he describes
the prevailing method as one in which "the author is reduced to a
class . . . the value of this class of writing must be developed and as-
certained . . . the principles of taste, the elements of our sensations,
the structure of the human faculties, all must undergo a strict scrutiny and revision. The modern or metaphysical system of criticism,
in short, supposes the question, *Why?* to be repeated at the end of
every decision; and the answer gives birth to interminable arguments and discussion." Then Hazlitt reveals his satiric point: this in-
finity of "dialectics and debatable matter" is precisely the usefulness
of such criticism for its readers, for their "object is less to read the
work than to dispute upon its merits, and go into company clad in
the whole defensive and offensive armor of criticism." A perpetual
flux of controversy is, he grants, only to be expected; for not only is
criticism "an art that undergoes a great variety of changes, and aims
at different objects at different times," but there seem also "to be
sects and parties in taste . . . coeval with the arts of composition."
There would always be a contentious difference between critics who
extol "simplicity" and others who demand "elegance"; those "of a
decided and original, and others of a more general and versatile
taste"; those who are pedantic precisians ("word-catchers") and "oc-
cult" critics (he is perhaps glancing here at both Lamb and Coleridge) who "discern no beauties but what are concealed from superficial eyes" (8.214–26).

"On Criticism" may best be summed up as a plea for the tolera-
tion of a necessary diversity of views in critical opinion—not because
a multiplicty of views is of value in itself but because it promotes recognition that the true community of purpose in criticism is the love,

enjoyment, and understanding of works of art, not the theoretic formulation of taste except as this communicates and fosters a greater responsiveness to diverse works of genius. "The end of criticism," Hazlitt writes in 1825, "is to direct attention to objects of taste, not to dictate to it" (10.222). Hazlitt had always deplored the sectarian principle in criticism, but now, instead of combatting it frontally with his own polemic for a "catholic faith" (19.29), he seeks to reduce the virulence of dogmatism by pleading for acknowledgement and conscious control of its presence as a necessary impulse in the mind—as the necessary sublimation of the self-love rooted in the critic's personal character (see also 12.164, 324). Hazlitt's own capacity for intolerance, his instinct for argumentative capacity, is now turned upon all symptoms of critical intolerance: "We hate comparisons or the *exclusive* in matters of taste," he writes in 1829, "and reject, abjure and renounce all decisions and systems of criticism founded upon them." This plea for magnanimity does not, as the word "hate" may remind us, come with an entirely happy grace from a critic who had once delighted in the invidious contrast of Turner with Claude Lorraine, of Wordsworth with Milton, of Dryden with Chaucer or Boccaccio, of French with English tragedy. "Why must every thing have a foil?" he now asks rhetorically (20.262), and the question perhaps confesses his own uneasiness about his former use of the comparative method, with its inevitable temptation to antithetic contrasts.

His weariness with theoretic contention goes back at least as far as the Elizabethan lectures of 1819; for there Hazlitt pauses to deliver an extended rebuke to dogmatic formulation, in an aside which has more than once been wrenched from context to convict his own criticism of a methodless impressionism.[17] His intention, he says, "in this and in former cases, is merely to read over a set of authors with the audience, as I would do with a friend, to point out a favourite passage, to explain an objection, or if a remark or a theory occurs, to state it in illustration of the subject, but neither to tire him nor puzzle myself with pedantic rules and pragmatic formulas of criticism that can do no good to any body." And he concludes: "In a word, I have endeavoured to feel what was good, and to 'give a reason for the faith that was in me' when necessary, and when in my power.

This is what I have done, and what I must continue to do" (6.301–02). No, this is not quite what the lecturer had done in "former cases," for he had done much more, and from more purposeful motives: his theory had not then been confined to incidental "illustration." But this is a faithful statement of what the lecturer so often enjoyed doing in his last performance, and of what he would continue to do, at greater leisure, in several of the essays (e.g., "On Milton's Sonnets": 8.174 ff.).

Although this change from his former habits develops by emotional reaction, it is by no means inconsistent with his former theory, and indeed follows almost predictably from Hazlitt's major premises. In his earlier criticism (and still, in those passages of *Table-Talk* devoted to theory) he had been concerned to establish, in more or less conventional modes of discourse, the intersubjective character of all art and literature, but now he has himself embarked on what is an intersubjective creation of sorts, and the criticism therein changes accordingly. The act of criticism has become the personal appreciation of certain decisive aesthetic experiences in his life, rather than again (although this, of course, naturally occurs), the description or judgment of aesthetic experience itself in its distinctive intensity. Hazlitt's evaluations are now almost always made with explicit reference to personal memory—to the memory, most often, of his first encounters with genius or works of genius, and to the modification or deepening of that memory by other experiences of kindred value or intensity of power: "The excellence that we feel, we participate in as if it were our own—it becomes ours by transfusion of mind—it is instilled into our hearts—it mingles with our blood" (12.101). There can be, I think, no better defense than this statement affords of Hazlitt's inveterate habit of casual literary quotation—a habit which, however wanton or excessive at times, confirms and illustrates his theme of the necessary interweaving of uniquely private feeling with imaginative "association," necessary to sustain that "ideal" continuity of identity which is the only secure basis of our self-love (indeed, seen in this light, his frequent *mis*quotations serve all the better to reinforce the theme!). Let us note, here, moreover, his word "transfusion," for it suggests the distinction that Hazlitt constantly maintains between the "characteristic" power of a work of literature and the developing impact of that power on the self and its life in time. The reading of Rousseau, for instance, is one of our essayist's most hallowed memories; but Rousseau himself has long since become for Hazlitt a "paradox-monger" (5.163) and—interestingly enough, in its bearing on this point—a man whose "intense consciousness of his own existence" circumscribed his imagination (4.88 ff., 8.42). It is this quality of intense self-absorption which makes Rousseau appeal to the feelings of youth; and the same quality remains his lasting value in the continuity of our personal lives, even when experience and the reading of other literature have revealed his deficiencies. The distance of time, the contrast between the dreams of young imagination and the truths of experience, is always a factor in Hazlitt's sentiment for an "old favourite"; and he sees no contradiction whatever in cherishing a deep-seated love and respect for works that he would now quarrel with intellectually—Goethe's *Werther,* for instance, or Mrs. Inchbald's novels. The degree of worth of books in themselves and their perspective effect upon our lives are distinct in thought but inseparable in feeling; for in both dimensions, books become—and note the necessary doublet of terms—"*landmarks and guides* in our journey through life" (12.221 ff.; my italics).

Now there is a sense in which this new mode of valuation is—as the essays in general have been accused of being—"anti-intellectual."[18] For all his fidelity to "genius," Hazlitt's insistence that "books do not teach the use of books" clearly runs counter to the Promethean faith of so many of his contemporaries in the power of the creative, or at least the poetic, Word; and beyond this distrust of prophetic pretension, his animus in the essays holds an implicit challenge also to the entire nineteenth-century tradition, then just emerging, of *Kultur*—that faith in the progressive interdependence of individual and general "culture" which descends from Kant, Goethe, and Schiller, through Coleridge and Arnold, down to Leavis and other critics in our own time.[19] What I have called Hazlitt's "Religion of the Louvre" may be described as a variant of the same tradition, and he is never to depart so far from his Unitarian heritage as to question the premise that rational intelligence requires educational development; but now more than ever he insists upon the inevitable "abstraction" of the intellectual faculties—that is, on their

distinction, however inseparable the connection, from "moral" powers, which properly inhere in feeling and are modified by the life of
action and the sympathies of self-love with "opinion" rather than by
"thought" as such. Hazlitt's rediscovery of self-love has led him, as
we have seen, to the recognition that there neither is nor should be
an indefinitely progressive sympathy in the individual mind with
varieties of value; there is and can only be an innate sympathy with
value (a given predisposition to certain values and not others), and
any attempt to force this sympathy beyond the limits and degrees inherent in individual bias must necessarily produce a hostile and self-
defeating reaction. On this question Hazlitt appeals to what he calls
the law of "negative merit"—that a man's success in any pursuit is
likely to derive as much "from the qualifications which he wants as
from those he possesses." The will to excellence and its realization
are seldom in proportion to a "greater enlargement of comprehension or susceptibility of taste," and in fact may be fatally inhibited by
them: "There is a balance of power in the human mind, by which
defects frequently assist in furthering our views, as superfluous excellences are converted into the nature of impediments"
(12.195–97).

Hazlitt was not abandoning, though, his solicitude for "standards." Rather, his concern now is that value judgments become
"catholic" in a more fundamental sense—that truly "universal" cri-
teria no longer be confused with "ideal" or purely intellectual standards. In the Regency years he had been alarmed by the vulgarization of taste, but he had now been compelled to recognize clearly for
the first time that the challenge to genuine art in culture comes not
only from indifference or jealousy of superiority but from an instinctively reactive defense in non-intellectual natures of various
other, and no less necessary, values. The abstract community of the
arts, his Louvre vision of the continuity of values in imagination by
which one genius defines, complements, and fulfills another, is not
the same as the community of values in society—and far from con-
ducing to such community, may itself depend for its survival on the
strength of a more elementary bond of values in the wills of men
(see 11.231). Another criterion in our judgments of excellence is

needed to combat the evils of envy at their source in self-love—to
prevent the resistance to otherness, "the spirit of contradiction,"
from becoming a hostile reaction against the "ideal" in those who are
unable, or merely pretend, to find their identity in the world of art
and thought. "The less excellent must be provided for, as well as the
most excellent" (12.163): standards, in short, must be provided that
make for community itself—for a community of shared experience
available to every self. And these standards are necessarily distinct in
society, and should be kept distinct in every mind, from the "comparative" standards of value (20.386) that make for the no less necessary
community of intellectual culture.

"There is," he remarks in 1829, "an endless variety of excellence, *nearly equal in different ways,* if we had but the sense and
spirit to enter properly into it" (20.263; my italics). Hazlitt was to die
before he could work out a coherent resolution in principle of the
two standards, egalitarian and intellectual, of community in culture,
but there is one essay which does unforgettably demonstrate the
"sense and spirit" that his own mind could bring to the appreciation
of diverse, even opposing, modes of excellence. "The Indian Jugglers" has won frequent acclaim as perhaps the classic statement in
English of the difference between "intellectual" and "mechanical,"
imaginative and non-creative excellence; yet the memorableness of
the essay consists also, as I shall now try to demonstrate, in the reciprocity that Hazlitt discovers between these modes of power, not
only in their contradistinction.

※※※

Perhaps more than any other nineteenth-century essay, "The
Indian Jugglers" anticipates, and has helped to establish, the struc-
tural pattern of the informal literary essay as it is still being written
today. We have, first, the introductory anecdote or event, vividly described; then a series of general reflections upon it and related matters; and lastly, a return in some way to concrete experience not
unlike the opening episode in feeling or circumstance, but rein-
terpreted now or infused with symbolic meaning in the light of the
intervening reflections. It is by following this pattern as Hazlitt de-

295

velops it here, making it a dialectic, a "conversation" between two points of view, that we are best able to understand the unity of vision informing his apparent waywardness of mood and attitude.

We should note, first of all, how careful Hazlitt is from the start not to minimize the "mechanical" achievement of the Jugglers. Their "dexterity" is described as almost "miraculous," almost divinely effortless in its consummate ease and grace: "It is skill surmounting difficulty, and beauty triumphing over skill." Hazlitt will tolerate no intellectual condescension toward this skill as a "trifling" display of power, and to make his point he mocks his own writing, when measured against the juggler's flawless command of power, as a graceless hash: "What errors, what ill-pieced transitions, what crooked reasons, what lame conclusions!" And no critic has to pay for his errors in judgment as the juggler must do if he fails to catch his knives: "I can make a very bad antithesis without cutting my fingers." From this point of view, mechanical skill is not only equal but superior to intellectual achievement: in "complete mastery of execution," in the "self-possession" it demands and the perfect, instantaneous satisfaction it gives to the will of the performer, mechanical excellence is a perpetual challenge to all other pretensions; it directly confronts the sloth and piques the self-love of the beholder as the arts of the mind cannot. Hazlitt is therefore by no means joshing when he exclaims: "It makes me ashamed of myself. I ask what there is that I can do as well as this? Nothing. What have I been doing all my life? . . . Is there no one thing in which I can challenge competition, that I can bring as an instance of exact perfection, in which others cannot find a flaw? The utmost I can pretend to do is to write a description of what this fellow can do." And indeed Hazlitt's response to the challenge, his depiction in his opening paragraph of the juggler's art, is one of the most beautifully wrought—and poetically profound—passages in the entire range of his writing (and here, as will be obvious, all his stylistic voices are speaking in concert):

A single error of a hair's-breadth, of the smallest conceivable portion of time, would be fatal: the precision of the movements must be like a mathematical truth, their rapidity is like lightning. To catch four balls in succession in less than a second of time, and deliver them back so as to return with seeming consciousness to the hand again, to make them revolve around him at certain intervals, like the planets in their spheres, to make them chase one another like sparkles of fire, or shoot up like flowers or meteors, to throw them behind his back and twine them round his neck like ribbons or like serpents, to do what appears an impossibility, and to do it with all the ease, the grace, the carelessness imaginable, to laugh at, to play with the glittering mockeries, to follow them with his eye as if he could fascinate them with its lambent fire, or as if he had only to see that they kept time with the music on the stage—there is something in all this which he who does not admire may be quite sure he never really admired any thing in the whole course of his life. (8.77–80)

From the resonances of the imagery here it is clear that Hazlitt intends the juggler's virtuosity to loom as symbolic, in its pure moment of "beauty," of all excellence—and perhaps not only of human excellence but of its ultimate source, that Power of God or Nature which creates and sustains the mathematical harmony and living grace of all bodies and all energies, celestial or earthly. But whatever the penumbra of suggestiveness in this praise, there can be no doubt of Hazlitt's immediate critical purpose, which is to stun his "intellectual" reader into humbly acknowledging the juggler's "perfection." Or to state the point in expressly democratic terms, as he does elsewhere, "there can be no true superiority but that which arises out of the presupposed ground of equality" (8.208). And only after, by contrast with this achievement of the body's powers, the fallibility and the dangers of snobbery in intellectual effort have been unforgettably established is Hazlitt ready to suggest that the relative imperfection of the arts of the mind is itself the measure of their finally greater value. The manual performer undertakes to do what he knows he *can* perform; but the artist of imagination has always an "abstract, independent standard of difficulty or excellence" that lies beyond certainty of demonstration in some inward and "obscure" region of thought or invention where there is no manifest knowledge of success or failure, and where "the power of human skill and industry" may become not only impotent but fatal to excellence if it persists in emulating only itself. Hence Sir Joshua Reynolds, cited at the start of the essay as a bungling hand in executing his colors when compared with the faultless precision of the juggler, reappears now as the artist of superior "grace." For his is an art where power is gained only through a strength which constantly risks the unforeseeable betrayal of weakness; here was an excellence which it takes sympathy with human feeling and aspiration to conceive or understand, and which only the artist's willingness to look beyond self yet to trust to his unique feelings as a man could have created. And on this basis Hazlitt proceeds to develop the familiar Romantic distinction between talent and genius, as the difference between "voluntary" (educable, improvable) and original or "involuntary" power.

But Hazlitt is not forgetting his original irony about the "ambiguous" character of intellectual power: there must be a further and unmistakable trial of the merit of genius before it can be considered "great." "Admiration, to be solid and lasting, must be founded on proofs from which we have no means of escaping"—a proof no less surely real than that which the juggler demonstrates but one that never ends, that can never be summed up. "Greatness is great power, producing great effects," and these effects are great only insofar as they persist in time and become themselves causes of energy in other men. It is in this respect that the "idea" we have of the great individual differs from the natural "truth" of individual genius: "It is in the nature of greatness to propagate an idea of itself, as wave impels wave, circle without circle." With the elucidation of this principle Hazlitt would seem to have reached the climax of his theme; but he has another surprise in store for those readers willing to conclude that all greatness is finally "intellectual" in its meaning. Hazlitt suddenly cuts short these reflections as a "digression"—and proceeds to end the essay with a eulogy on one John Cavanagh, a recently deceased hero of the London fives-courts! Now this might seem to be one of those "ill-pieced transitions" and "lame conclusions" of which our essayist had spoken earlier. But as W. P. Albrecht observes (and Baker makes a similar point), in Cavanagh's skill there was "a self-forgetting consummation of power that attained a kind of greatness."[20] Perhaps we may go further and say that Cavanagh differs from the Indian Juggler in that his excellence, although of nearly the same kind in form, *does* "propagate an idea of itself." "There are hundreds at this day, who cannot mention his name without admiration, as the best fives-player that perhaps ever lived (the greatest excellence of which they have any notion)—and the noisy shout of the ring happily stood him in stead of the unheard voice of posterity!" And this "idea" is all the more true to the spirit of greatness because it is free of reference to a self-conscious love of greatness; for greatness of any kind can be achieved only by a love of the otherness of excellence and not by the will to greatness itself: "A really great man has always an idea of something greater than himself." Or as Hazlitt more bluntly makes the point elsewhere: "No really great man ever thought himself so" (12.117). When Hazlitt says of Cavanagh that there was no "affectation" in his ability, that "he saw the whole game, and played it," that his "blows" were not "lumbering like Mr. Wordworth's epic poetry, nor wavering like Mr. Coleridge's lyric prose . . . nor foul like the *Quarterly,* nor *let* balls like the *Edinburgh Review,*" it is clear why this eulogy is a just ending to the essay; for Cavanagh emerges as a heroic symbol of the pure fidelity of the self to its native gifts of power. Here is a portrait, not of a genius, but nonetheless of a man with a more than mechanical talent—an artist of sorts, but one whose great good fortune it was not to know himself an artist, whose only "style" was his love and knowledge of the game (8.81–89).

There is a melancholy as well as sardonic note in this ending; for the innuendo is clear that only in the innocence of sport, where the test of power and the rewards of power merge in one and the same event, has excellence a chance to remain unblinded by self-love. And this thought, too, is in the spirit of Hazlitt's critical theme and of the essay form as he conceives it. For perhaps it is the mission of the essayist to remind us, as other artists cannot, that all art remains flawed by its humanity and that only this frailty of the self makes us love perfection; that the intellect of man, like his conversation, reaches no lasting conclusions; and that where the power of all art and thought ends, life goes on its unpredictable, inscrutable, but always venturous way once more. "Man, thou art a wonderful animal," Hazlitt exclaims at the start of this essay, "and thy ways past finding out! Thou canst do strange things, but thou turnest them to little account!"

With this essay Hazlitt was, in effect, bidding goodbye to the concept of "intellectual" greatness as individual transcendence—to the heroic notion of genius as capable of realizing and propagating its "truth," its "idea" in the world through individual power alone, or through the sympathies of individual minds as such. Like Byron in *Don Juan,* like Stendhal and Balzac, like other Romanticists who in this decade were moving toward the attitudes of Realism, Hazlitt was learning to understand that only the life of society "turns" value and power "to account"—or fails to. "Great acts grow out of great occasions," he writes elsewhere in *Table-Talk,* "and great occasions spring from great principles, working changes in society, and tearing it up by the roots" (8.108). Just how well the energies of a revolutionary age, enamored of an ideal of individual greatness, had met the challenge of its own "great occasions" is the issue that Hazlitt proceeds to confront in his last two attempts to capture the changing character of "power" in his time—in *The Spirit of the Age* and *The Life of Napoleon Buonaparte.*

Chapter Nine

Portraits of an Age

"I SHOULD not be surprised," wrote H. W. Garrod of *The Spirit of the Age,* "if, a hundred years hence [he was writing in 1923], when Criticism makes up her jewels, she accounted this book her brightest ornament."[1] This elegant praise is likely to seem a quaint prophecy in the light of critical fashion today; we no longer believe in a timeless Muse of criticism, and the staunchest admirer of the book today must be content to hope that posterity will continue to honor it as the crowning ornament of Hazlitt's career, and as one of the lasting glories of nineteenth-century criticism. Garrod's prophecy, indeed, must appear ironic when we measure our dutifully repeated praise of this book against its persistent neglect (until very recent years) by literary scholarship. The book has been often enough consulted as a brilliant series—to recall the subtitle—of *Contemporary Portraits,* but only in this character has it become a classic; seldom has it won the scholar's interest or admiration as a work with an integrating theme and purpose of its own, as a study of *The Spirit of the Age.* Admittedly, once the title page is turned, Hazlitt's portraits encourage no such expectations; here, without prologue or epilogue, are twenty-five sketches of the leading philosophers, politicians, and literary men of the time—presented in a sequence which exhibits a pattern of contrasts but which in all other respects seems a random affair, impressive in total effect but without apparent design.[2] "There is," René Wellek concludes, "little analysis of the reigning spirit of a time. The plan is static, and there is hardly any continuity between the essays" (p. 207).

This opinion could not, I believe, be more mistaken, all appearances in its favor notwithstanding. The book's unity or want of unity must be demonstrated within the context, not of systematic *Geistesgeschichte,* but of its own tradition—one scarcely a generation old when Hazlitt wrote his book but already well enough established that he had no choice but to work within its prescribed format. The tradition of the "sketch" or "portrait" (or what we now know, in enlarged form, as the "profile") evolved from a merging of the old "character" essay with the *ad hominem* style in contemporary reviewing and with the more compendious critical-biographical essay of the later eighteenth century (as in Johnson's *Lives of the Poets*). It is the tradition, to cite only immediate antecedents, of *The Monthly Magazine*'s "Contemporary Authors" (1817), of John Scott's "Living Authors" in the *London* (1820), of Leigh Hunt's "On the Living Poets" in the 1821 *Examiner*.[3] In none of these predecessors is there much attempt at thematic continuity or at a synoptic vision of the time, as there is in Hazlitt's early Victorian successors—and precisely, one suspects, because they are his successors: F. D. Maurice in a series in the *Athenaeum* (1828), George Gilfillan in *A Gallery of Literary Portraits* (1845), R. H. Horne in *A New Spirit of the Age* (1844). These were all, as Horne's title suggests, attempts to repeat Hazlitt's success, but they signally failed to grasp the secret of his book's own "spirit," of his critical relationship to his time. Although willing enough to attack popular idolatries, theirs was not a vision which dares to undercut with stylistic irony the reader's pleasure or pride in, or to challenge the very motives of his curiosity about, the pieties and confident aspirations of the "New Age." Hazlitt alone in nineteenth-century England deserves to join the company of Sainte-Beuve and Baudelaire in France as a critic who succeeds in lifting an inglorious, if not always a time-serving, tradition of the journalistic marketplace for a moment above itself.[4]

There are signs that Hazlitt had a low or indifferent opinion of the tradition when he came to it, and that he saw its critical possibilities only after, with some reluctance, he was fairly embarked upon his series of sketches. When approached after John Scott's death to continue the "Living Authors" series, he begged off after contributing one essay (on Crabbe), saying that he much preferred to continue writing *Table-talks*. Early in 1824, however, whether on his own or another's initiative, he began publishing a series in the *New Monthly* under the heading, "The Spirits of the Age"; and it may be significant that the first of these, "Mr. Bentham," makes only a glancing reference to the age in general. No doubt Hazlitt intended from the first to make a book out of the series, but from internal evidence it is clear that his book (completed and published anonymously late in 1824, though dated 1825) had changed its character as it grew under his hand. "The Spirits of the Age" had become, in a more than nominal sense, *The Spirit of the Age*—a phrase which did not acquire the emphasis of capitals and italics until the third and fourth essays of the five written for the *New Monthly*, and then continued to be prominently featured in most of the other (and presumably later) essays on the major figures, together with an increasing incidence of commentary about "the age." Nor had it taken Hazlitt long to become involved emotionally with his theme: "You can hardly suppose," he confided to Landor, "the depression of body and mind under which I wrote some of these articles."[5] Whatever his bodily ills, the "depression" of mind almost certainly refers to the painful realities that he found himself confronting when he wrote the essays on the much-altered friends and mentors of his youth— Godwin, Coleridge, and Wordsworth. Since 1819 Hazlitt had not dealt in any large way with contemporary literature or politics, and in the Regency years he had confronted the two subject matters together only as susceptible to the same blight of Tory "legitimacy," not as animated by one and the same "spirit." What he now found himself examining was nothing less than the question of the reality or unreality of his myth of modern "progress" (and by implication also, of modern aesthetic decadence); and presumably it is when he recognizes this confrontation to be inevitable that he begins to think of his sketches as linked in one extended design—not as studies simply of individuals, each to be set in its own frame, but as passages in a landscape-with-figures.

What emerges is a composite portrait of the age, whose unity of character is now seen to inhere precisely in its inconsistencies, in the dramatic logic of its discords—a polarity of conflict often very different in its motives from the tensions and contentions of the age as the combatants themselves were defining them. Yet the essential irony in this vision will not be understood so long as we continue to confuse Hazlitt's sense of the unity of the age with the connotation that his title phrase has acquired today. However we explain the elusive concept of a *Zeitgeist*—whether we think of it as a "stream" or "atmosphere" or "symphony," a "collective unconscious," a "dynamic system of attractions and repulsions"[6]—we are likely to be making certain assumptions about cultural change that derive from post-Hegelian historicism, and that were still alien to the conceptual framework of the Romantic age, at least in the England of the eighteen-twenties. Friedrich Schlegel, describing "the ordinary sense" of the term *Zeitgeist,* said that "it signifies the spirit which has originally arisen out of the age itself, and in its sphere brilliantly predominant, but which at the same time transcends in some way that sphere, either blending itself with some equally great, if not still more exalted, past, or with some new and future era." Shelley, too, saw the "spirit" of his time as an "electric fire" leaping from one creative mind to another, and kindling especially the minds of poets, who "are the hierophants of an unapprehended inspiration; the mirrors of the gigantic shadows which futurity casts upon the present. . . ."[7] In both statements we see unmistakably the mythic-proleptic character of the *Zeitgeist* concept at this period of its birth. The idea belongs in this phase to the category of "apocalyptic" myth, of "end-determined fictions" of history (to borrow Frank Kermode's language), and is therefore not to be reduced, as it so often is, to an identity with the "spirit" of a single event, the French Revolution, which was less the source of the age's *Geist,* of "the flame of liberty, the light of intellect" (11. 37), than the event, the "dawn," which marks the fiery transition of this "light" from the world of thought to the world of will and action, its emergence into fully public consciousness. *Geist* or "spirit," then, in Romantic usage is no mere metaphor but signifies a tendency of mind which is itself a power—an "intellectual" force *moving through* the age and transforming it, not a unity of tendency bred, shaped, or determined by the age itself. Only an understanding of Hazlitt's title-phrase in this sense will enable us to see why he omits from his book celebrities on whom he had written extensively elsewhere—Turner and Edmund Kean, for example. These figures, like many others of equal note, are excluded because, although representative men of genius, they are not spirits of original "intellect" who mediate significantly between ideas and opinion; indeed, their presence would have puzzled readers of a book with this title—readers who knew well enough that "the spirit of the age" could only mean, for better or (if one's politics were Toryish) worse, "the march of mind."[8]

In the eighteenth century the phrase "spirit of the age" was not unknown, and the growing self-consciousness of the Enlightenment certainly helped to generate what Jaspers calls "epochal consciousness."[9] But there is nonetheless a crucial difference between assuming that "the age" is governed by a bias to a certain activity (a "commercial spirit," a "philosophical spirit," that is, some timeless trait or disposition which it shares, in whatever degree, with other ages), and the Romantic assumption that all minds (or creative minds) in an age participate interactively, by virtue of the sympathetic nature of all thought and imagination, in an emerging pattern of expressive consciousness which is organically unique to the "spirits" of that time and unprecedented in history. Hazlitt had by no means outgrown the older assumption, for at times he speaks of his time's "spirit" in terms indistinguishable from the logic of earlier usage: "A bias to abstraction," he remarks in 1820, "is evidently the reigning spirit of the age" (18.305). But a more characteristic sense of his time in history appears in his way of understanding this "bias." As we have learned in other contexts, Hazlitt is extending his reference here beyond the abstractions of reason and science; he has in mind several other kinds of "abstraction" from the reality of self, and especially, as Park points out (pp. 76 ff.), the highly generalized, dubiously "poetic" anti-empiricism of Coleridge and other Transcendentalists.[10] Hazlitt had no use, it is clear, for the new ideas of the *Zeitgeist* flowing in from Germany; and he had singled out for special abuse "the holy Arndt"—Ernst Moritz Arndt, whose anti-Napoleonic pamphlet *Geist der Zeit* (1805, 1813; Part One first translated, 1808) was chiefly instrumental in introducing those ideas to the English public. This "metagrabbalist" of "the High Dutch school" had sought to identify the new spirit of freedom with the reawakening of national feeling and medieval faith, and Hazlitt ridiculed this argument as merely another sophistry to divide and conquer the cause of Liberty by divorcing it once again from universal Reason (19.177). We begin to see, therefore, what informs Hazlitt's irony about the ambiguity of the Time-Spirit; for in an age of "abstraction," the will to abstraction can assume innumerable forms, can even be turned against abstract thought itself; the *Zeitgeist* could thus be readily enlisted—and often enough had been—in the service of its latent contrary, that inertia of established Power hostile or indifferent to the values of intellect and to the freedom which is the necessary condition for attaining "truth." Yet we shall see also that Hazlitt, in pursuing this irony, does not wholly abandon faith in a transcendent power of mind at work in the troubled "spirits" of the age. What he calls "the revolutionary movement of our age" (11.87) obeys an irreversible dynamic greater than any of its partial manifestations, and even the resistance of "prejudice" may be contributing to the very process of change that its voices wish to arrest or destroy. It is this dialectic of conflict that emerges on the one occasion when Hazlitt pauses to offer a definition of his title phrase (not, alas, in the book itself, but in an essay of the previous year): "the spirit of the age," he explains in a parenthesis, is *"the progress of intellectual refinement, warring with our natural infirmities"* (12.128; my italics).[11]

The importance of understanding the structure of Hazlitt's book is that it enables us (although we will need the continued assistance of other writings from this decade) to complete the logic of his definition, that is, to understand what necessary connection he sees between the "progress" and the "warring" of his time, and what hope, if any, he finds in the modern future for a happier resolution of the struggle. Conversely, that structure will yield its unity of vision only if we recognize the method of his portraiture—only if we recognize that Hazlitt is not here playing the usual game of discourse; his critique of "abstraction" would lose its very reason for being if he, like so many of his subjects, were engaged in developing one more thesis about the *Zeitgeist*. With this book especially, the analogy with painting is by no means casual; for *The Spirit of the Age* is one of those rare works of criticism which really do approach to the character of a work of art. Meaning must be sought here not only in statement and logical inference but in image and counter-image—in echoes and repetitions, in parallels and hidden likenesses lurking within apparent contrasts, in *leitmotifs* of tone and phrase—in all those particulars which for Hazlitt constitute the web of *symbolic* meaning, "truth" to the imagination. This continuity, and no apology for incoherence, was perhaps what he had in mind when he combined title with subtitle, and perhaps especially when he chose his epigraph (adapted from *Hamlet,* v.2.146): "To know another well were to know one's self." Not unfaithful to paternal faith in "progress" but even more loyal to Shakespearean truth, the essayist of *Table-Talk* was again speaking to the passional self—but now through the projection of a "mirror" less personal than dramatic, to "show the very age and body of the time its form and pressure." [12]

꿍

As befits a period of "intellectual refinement," the first three portraits—of Bentham, Godwin, and Coleridge—are studies of the most representative philosophers of the age. Then follow two sketches (of Edward Irving and Horne Tooke) which have a transitional function in the design, namely, to reveal the intrusion into intellectual polemic of "our natural infirmities," and especially those of self-love, which the heady abstractions of the intellect would fain deny or forget. Such infirmities, insofar as they remain "natural," are then seen becoming one with passional or creative strength, although seldom happily wedded to intellectual power, in the central group of portraits, the four most influential figures of literary genius—Scott, Byron, Southey, and Wordsworth. After this point, the essays lose (at least for us) some of their intrinsic interest as Hazlitt proceeds to the lesser celebrities—the politicians and editors, followed by the minor poets and men of letters.[13] Yet it is only in this second half of the volume, where human weaknesses, unredeemed by genius, resume their triumphs over the self and compromise the faltering intellect, that Hazlitt's vision reaches fully ironic perspective and the "warring" of the age emerges in its starkest and most definitive clarity. And only here, too, are modern infirmities shown to possess—although, again, only insofar as they remain "natural"—a redeeming power of their own, and one perhaps not wholly irreconcileable with the saner aspirations of the *Zeitgeist*.

It was logical to begin the series with Bentham, not only because he was then the philosopher in the ascendant, but because in his thought the impulse to "intellectual refinement" is seen in its blandest confidence of "progress," pretending to both a speculative and a practical triumph over hitherto crippling infirmities of human prejudice. Hazlitt's portrait is a good-humored but ironic study of the degree to which the modern philosopher, and the modern intellectual generally, has been "abstracted . . . from himself" (18.305). Bentham has found his identity in the making of constitutions "for the other side of the globe" and is scarcely known to his neighbors in Westminster, where for the past forty years he has lived "like an anchorite in his cell, reducing law to a system, and the mind of man to a machine." Hazlitt vividly records here his York Street memories of Bentham bustling about in his garden as he entertains some philosophical visitor—"his walk almost amounting to a run, his tongue keeping pace with it . . . negligent of his person, his dress, and his manners, intent only on his grand theme of UTILITY." Bentham would talk of, and listen to, "nothing but facts," but he is blind to the facts of his own immediate being: "His eye is quick and lively; but it glances not from object to object, but from thought to thought." Hazlitt then proceeds to make delightfully ironic sport—to a fault, certainly—of Bentham's felicific calculus as a principle of legislation, arguing that its denial of the depth and contradictoriness of passion and prejudice misrepresents the real motives of men, whether to virtue or to crime. The doctrine of Utility expresses only Bentham's willful naïveté and his innocence of the world, not "his natural humor, sense, spirit, or style"—not the spirit of the man whose face bears no slight resemblance to Milton's, who loves to play the organ, and who relishes the art of Hogarth. The living Jeremy Bentham who enjoys these pleasures offers the world no augury of the future triumph of the pleasure principle as mechanical Utility, of "dull, plodding, technical calculation," except perhaps as Mr. Bentham occasionally pauses, "for exercise," to turn "wooden utensils in a lathe . . . and fancies he can turn men in the same manner" (pp. 5–16).

The principle that Benthamism ignores, of "fluctuation and reaction" in human motives, is seen taking prompt and thorough revenge on philosophy in the next essay. Here the *Zeitgeist* makes its first explicit appearance, and the introduction it is given is scarcely flattering: "The Spirit of the Age was never more fully shown than in its treatment of this writer [Godwin]—its love of paradox and change, its dastard submission to prejudice and to the fashion of the day." So changeful an age would prefer not to remember its origins in the French Revolution, and Hazlitt makes sure now, with some vivid reminiscences of opinion in the nineties, that his liberal readers do not again suffer a convenient loss of memory. In the reasoning of *Political Justice* there was nothing, he insists, so paradoxically extreme as the first heady adulation of Godwin's disciples, nor so immoderate as their headlong retreat from, and contemptuous disavowal of, their former "oracle." Not Godwin but his mockers and former idolaters—often the same persons—should be accused of "having trampled on the common feelings and prejudices of mankind"; for Godwin's speculative errors were not sins against reason or conscience but against the frailty of our self-love, which is never more sorely affronted than when we are "complimented on imaginary achievements to which we are wholly unequal." The distinctive significance of *Political Justice* does not lie in its vanished Utopian vision but in the unintended demonstration, by the honest error of his rigorous logic, that "reason alone is not the sole and sufficient ground of morals." That reason did possess such potential dominion over the will, that "*the Just and the True were one,*" was a traditional prejudice of philosophy that had to be experimentally tested—like the geographer's dream of the Northwest Passage—by a bold and lonely voyage to the extremes of moral possibility. Godwin's failure is really his lasting glory; and that achievement is not to be obliterated by the "worse error" of believing that either fanciful sentiment or the material sense-values of man's "physical nature" (here is the glance back at Bentham) can or should supplant the rational judgment of nature's values as the "principal," if not the sufficient, ground of morality (pp. 16–23).

No doubt the fact that Coleridge had once succeeded Godwin as Hazlitt's philosophical mentor helps to dictate the transition to the third essay, but there is thematic logic in this sequence as well. For in Coleridge the abstraction of thought from self has reached the point where "intellectual refinement" is no longer directed to practical ends in the world of action but has become an end in itself—an impulse that is its own object. "The present is an age of talkers, and not of doers"; and the general cause that Hazlitt proposes for this condition is that knowledge and the arts have progressed so far in their complication and multiple interrelatedness that "the variety of objects distracts and dazzles the looker-on." Coleridge, with " 'a mind reflecting ages past'," epitomizes for Hazlitt the modern embarrassment of cultural riches, which here for the first time has met its counterpart in an individual mind, a spirit doomed to a fate of endless speculative wandering by the very multiplicity and "cross-purposes" of his talents and interests. Hazlitt had introduced in the previous essay the image of a thinker voyaging alone in his "frail bark"; and now for three brilliant pages Hazlitt reviews the saga of Coleridge's voyage through strange seas of thought—an odyssey destined to end in the impotence of a will to infinitude that is able to express its knowledge only in perpetual, freely ranging, evanescent sallies of talk. The same image of Coleridge as the mist-enshrouded voyager through speculative infinitudes was to be brilliantly developed by Carlyle in his famous portrait of the sage of Highgate; but the simile in Carlyle is edged with a practical moralist's sneer at a visionary "haze-world,"[14] while in Hazlitt the image remains purely symbolic of Coleridge's dialectical versatility, of the "subtlety and susceptibility" of an intellect by no means fogbound in its flights or remote from truth, however far removed from the world of action. Indeed, although the image still echoes Hazlitt's caricatures of Coleridge in the previous decade as a dreamer virtually "without will" ("with neither purposes nor passions of his own": 7.115–17), the voyager image no less often suggests—and in this regard Hazlitt is, of course, drawing upon the suggestiveness of the poet's own Ancient Mariner—Coleridge's tragic loneliness as a versatile thinker, his inevitable alienation from the various causes he has served with his varying theories. But what the image is finally intended to convey is a sense of Coleridge's fidelity to the "uncompelled and free" ways of his own spirit. It is the irrepressible love of an original mind for the freedom of speculative thought—the positive converse to the profligate mismanagement of his genius—that Hazlitt, in this farewell tribute, finally salutes, even as he accuses Coleridge of mapping out for his fellow poets their devious route back from the wilds of the Revolution to the gates of the Tory Establishment, the same that had once scorned and persecuted their genius. "They are safely inclosed there," but their forlorn guide could not or would not enter with them, "pitching his tent upon the barren waste without [that is, at Highgate], and having no abiding place nor city of refuge" (pp. 28–38).

It is Hazlitt's constantly insinuated inference, in all three of these sketches, that the failure of the philosophers of the age is a failure of self-knowledge: the war between intellectual and institutional power which really determines their thought has remained all but unknown (or, in Coleridge's case, subtly misrepresented) in its radical and inescapable form as a conflict in the passional self. Bentham remains oblivious to "contradiction and anomaly in the mind and heart of man" (p. 9); the author of *Political Justice* "gives no quarter to the amiable weaknesses of our nature" (p. 19); and in Coleridge "the individual is always merged in the abstract and general" (p. 31). Instead of learning from the fate of the Revolution that the relative powerlessness of the intellect in society must itself become the basis for the moral authority of reason over the will, all three philosophers, even when chastened by experience, have typically persisted in the tendency, as he says of Bentham, to "think the mind of man omnipotent" (p. 16)—to recognize almost no power in man and no aspect of the human condition that is not, or cannot be made, amenable to the constructions, whether visionary or mathematical, of the intellect. It is this dream of the age, first brought to self-conscious life by Godwin and grotesquely disfigured by the "facts" of Benthamism, that Hazlitt sees perishing in the fate of the opium-driven Coleridge, reduced to "swallowing doses of oblivion and . . . writing paragraphs in the *Courier*.—Such, and so little is the mind of man!" (p. 34). In the greatest intellect of the age, the greatest dream of the age (its "towering aspirations after good": p. 23) is seen drifting back to its original inwardness in imagination—still a dream of limitless power, but now unwilling to confess its origin in time or its fate in the dreamer, so that dream and dreamer, concealing each other, have become one—"sunk into torpid, uneasy repose, tantalized by useless resources, haunted by vain imaginings, his lips idly moving, but his heart forever still, or, as the shattered chords vibrate of themselves, making melancholy music to the ear of memory!" (p. 34).

The next sketch, although its subject has long since vanished into limbo, is important for helping Hazlitt's reader to understand what the age's philosophers, given their characteristic "abstraction," could not: namely, how "the war between power and reason" in society (p. 37) emanates from, or reacts upon, the internal "warring" of contemporary thought or "refinement" with unconscious "infirmities" of the self. Carlyle's friend Edward Irving (1792–1834) had recently created a sensation in London with his dazzling sermons. Eminent men of letters, Members of Parliament, and elegant lords and ladies were all to be seen crowding into a small Calvinist chapel in a shabby corner of London to hear this robustly handsome, literate, eloquent, brilliantly explosive Scots minister deliver his prophetic message—a warning to a faithless world to prepare for the imminent Advent of Christ. An admirer of Wordsworth's poetry and at least a partial convert to the philosophy of Coleridge—who in turn hailed the young preacher as a reformer with more "of the genial power of Martin Luther than any man now alive"—Irving had attained, since his arrival in London in 1822, a rapid celebrity by daring to denounce a proud and sanctimonious age as an "age of expediency, both in the Church and out of the Church." Irving did not hesitate to name chapter and verse in his indictment of a money-grubbing "prudence" infecting nearly all of British society: he made direct allusion to the dicta of Jeremy Bentham, to speeches in Parliament, to sermons that hollowly repeated "moth-eaten and undervalued creeds." But why then did so many celebrities of the age flock to hear their various notions, habits, and life-styles insulted to their faces? This is the anomaly that Hazlitt undertakes to explain in this essay (and in two other, in some ways superior, pieces on Irving); and he finds his answer in the visible ironies of the scene in the Caledonian Chapel. The age of secular fashion that Irving has denounced is really, with its "preposterous rage for novelty," responsible for Irving's success; and the novelty in this case does not consist in bold flights of original genius but simply in "a transposition of ideas." In this pulpit stands no dessicated Calvinist parson delivering some coldly rational vindication of the doctrine of eternal punishment—but a fiery orator with the physique of a pugilist and the dark good looks, noble bearing, and sonorous voice of an actor in a romantic drama at Drury Lane. A barbarous belief had here taken on the attractions of barbarism: superstitious prejudices were again to be seen "backed" by a "Patagonian" pair of shoulders; but there was nothing that could be called vulgar or benighted in these invocations of hellfire, "kindled anew with the very sweepings of sceptical and infidel libraries," and delivered in rolling periods, handsomely punctuated with a "turn of his head and wave of his hand." Hazlitt, with characteristically ruthless regard for the truth, seizes on Irving's one physical defect, a squint from a cast in his right eye, and finds in this "distortion of sight" a more than literal meaning—"a portentous obliquity of vision." If one eye of Irving's imagination (I now crudely spell out what Hazlitt leaves to inference) looks up to a wrathful God cast in his own image, "endowed with all his own . . . irritable humors in an infinitely exaggerated degree" (20.224), the other is always squinting askew at the prestigious image of Edward Irving reflected in the gaze of his fashionable audience—and especially in the rapt admiration of "the female part of his congregation" (pp. 38–43). No critic, of course, could then have predicted the imminent and unjust persecution of Irving (only a few years hence he would be stripped of his ministry and, in effect, driven to his death by heresy-fearing elders of the Church of Scotland), but our sympathy with his heroic defense of his beliefs in that ordeal ought not to obscure the just penetration of Hazlitt's analysis, which even the grieving Carlyle would (for the most part) confirm in his account of his friend's years in London.[15]

Yet the more elusive significance of the Irving phenomenon, for an understanding of the *Zeitgeist,* comes into view only from the vantage point of the next essay. That Irving has "a *radical* taint in him" (20.122)—is a child of his time without knowing it—is precisely the point of the contrast with Horne Tooke, an eighteenth-century radical, once a clergyman, whose thought and literary style exhibit "none of the grand whirling movements of the French Revolution." Dead in 1812 at the age of seventy-six, this non-contemporary is introduced as one of the "connecting links between a former period and the existing generation. His education and accomplishments, nay, his political opinions, were of the last age; his mind, and the tone of his feelings, were *modern.*" Tooke represents, then, an older, pre-Revolutionary tendency in modern attitudes, one no longer sanctioned by fashion but which nonetheless persists beneath "the tumultuous glow of rebellion." "Parson Horne," the reformer who attained his greatest celebrity in the days of Junius and Wilkes, stood temperamentally apart from his later counterparts in the almost entire "absence of passion and enthusiasm" from his mind, which, though lively, had always a "matter-of-fact" cast and, indeed, "had no *religion* in it." Tooke committed himself to radicalism and to the materialism of "the modern philosophy," not through disinterested conviction or sympathy with a public cause, but because such opinions enabled him (and this was true even of his original, and unjustly neglected, discoveries in the theory and history of language) to indulge his "delight in contradiction"—a delight in shocking the prejudice or wounding the self-love that he saw always lurking in the opinions of others. Although in his manners and speech "a finished gentleman of the last age," Tooke no longer believed in the Augustan values, except as wit, urbanity, and consummate self-possession could be fused in a single weapon of power, "a polished bow of steel," with which he shot satiric barbs at all "sounding commonplaces and sweeping clauses," even when the attack threatened injury to his own party. In Parliament, as in private conversation, Tooke "represented nobody but himself." The motive of his "patriotism" (that is, reformism) was not "principle" so much as "spleen or the exercise of intellectual power" (pp. 47–57).

By his very alienation, then, from the spirit of the new age in its enthusiastic forms, Tooke illustrates a motive in the *Zeitgeist* that "the bias to abstraction" conceals—the tendency, namely, to hold an opinion by reaction, to believe, deny, or affirm something simply because it is not, or can be opposed to, another man's opinion, or because it enables the ego to keep its sense of power "impenetrable" to external authority, to whatever is felt to be the "general bias" of society or of mankind in general. The difference, in this respect, between Tooke and all other figures in the book is that in him the thrust to "intellectual power" remains in "negative" phase and never becomes a positive identification with something both in and beyond himself. But this negativism is precisely what is most "modern" in Tooke's sense of power, and Hazlitt's later sketches will reveal this unconsciously "defensive" stance of the will (pp. 52 ff) to be the secret affinity between all "paradox" (here again used in the old, rhetorical sense of something contrary to "commonplace") and militant "prejudice" in the age. The likeness of motive in the two extremes lies in their being both reactions from or against what is imagined to be a countervailing otherness: in either case, the reaction is not simply (as Mill's theory of historical "spirit" would later suggest) to social change as such [16]—that is, a rebellious embracing of the new or a falling-back upon the old—but a recoil of the self from another form of self-consciousness, or from ideas and institutions as they are imagined to favor one form of self-consciousness rather than another. The symbolic character of all the portraits that follow lies in their being representative instances of these patterns of consciousness in the *Zeitgeist,* as they activate, merge in imagination with, or define themselves against each other.

If Tooke was a man with "not one particle of deference for the opinion of others" (p. 48), Sir Walter Scott logically appears next in the sequence as the voice at the other pole of the contemporary dialectic—the man who in an age of revolution "dotes on all well-authenticated superstitions" and "shudders at the shadow of innovation." Yet Hazlitt makes us aware at once of the latent affinity of consciousness beneath the apparent contraries. For all his devotion to antiquarian lore, Scott's genius belongs to an age of science; he, too, is "a learned, a literal, a *matter-of-fact* expounder of truth," and is finally as unpoetic in his own way as Tooke and Bentham are in theirs. The clinging to the practical and the palpable takes the form in Scott of "retentiveness of memory"; his is a mind incapable of "reacting on his first impressions" in flights of imagination or in bold Godwinian voyages into unknown regions of "the speculative understanding," from which Scott's genius "mechanically shrinks back" as from a precipice. "Sir Walter would make a bad hand at a description of the Millennium, unless he could lay the scene in Scotland four hundred years ago." The Tory, the man, and the novelist in Scott are one in believing "that nothing *is* but what *has been*—that the moral world stands still, as the material one was supposed to do of old." This, as we have intimated earlier, does not do justice to Scott's sense of history; but the necessary amendment to Hazlitt's critique does not, I think, invalidate his main charge that Scott's sense of history is conditioned by his mode of expressive reaction from contemporary norms of opinion. More specifically, Hazlitt is intent on dispelling the Legitimist mystique surrounding Scott's genius: "Does he really think of making us enamoured of the 'good old times' by the faithful and harrowing portraits he has drawn of them?" The attraction to the past in Scott's romances proceeds directly from the spirit of the age: from its demand for knowledge, its impulse to transcend inherited attitudes, its desire for something "new and startling"—and especially for the novelty of a primitive world of violent action that offers relief from the "fastidious refinement" of the modern mind, "rarefied as it has been with modern philosophy, and heated with ultra-radicalism." In short, the moral and imaginative appeal of the novels lies in the fact that they are read and written at so great a distance from the state of society they describe. Hazlitt cannot bring himself to believe that Scott has no suspicion of this truth—no inkling that his success depends on the liberal ideal of "humanity"—and he therefore charges Scott with suppressing this awareness and willfully turning against it in political cabal. "The most humane and accomplished writer of the age" is none other than "the man who would fain put down the Spirit of the Age"—whose devious hand is to be seen organizing, subsidizing, and helping to concert the scurrilous policies of several pro-Government journals (the *Quarterly*, *Blackwood's, John Bull, The Beacon*), through whose pages he "has repaid the public liberality by striking a secret and envenomed blow at the reputation of every one who was not the ready tool of power" (pp. 61–68, and Howe's n. 68, p. 335).

"Frailty, thy name is *Genius!*" So Hazlitt had exclaimed in his essay on Coleridge (p. 34), and the same complaint becomes, with variations, the dominant *leitmotif* in this central group of essays on the leading writers of the age. The frailty, though, that is calling forth several flashes of ill-temper in these essays is really, I suspect, the infirm tenure in Hazlitt's own mind of his former faith in the transcendent power of genius. By the standards of his myth of "truth," genius, being the offspring of "nature," should be above the stresses and strains of opinion that it is destined to lead; and by this standard Scott is found to have "degraded" his gifts (p. 68), although Hazlitt knows better than to suggest—having just demonstrated the organic reciprocity of the Tory and the novelist in Scott—that the Author of Waverley would have been a better writer had he been a less militant partisan. And in the essay that follows on Byron, we witness an even more acute disparity between the logic of Hazlitt's insights and the rhetoric of the Prig-Dissenter, who cannot abide the possibility that the genius of a poet might owe its power, if not its very being, to the fact of his being a haughty Lord. Indeed, so anxious is Hazlitt to defend his faith that he summons Scott, only a moment before on trial himself, as a model witness in the prosecution of Byron's sins of egotism: "The object of the one writer is to restore us to truth and nature: the other chiefly thinks how he shall display his own power, or vent his spleen, or astonish the reader" (p. 70).

But even as he says that "no two men can be more unlike," Hazlitt begins to suggest that Scott and Byron are both children of the age in yielding to negative impulses of reaction, however different their purposes. "Lord Byron, who in his politics is a *liberal,* in his genius is haughty and aristocratic: Walter Scott, who is an aristocrat in principle, is popular in his writings, and is (as it were) equally *servile* to nature and to opinion." Both men, in short, are notoriously inconsistent in relating their political identities to moral and literary values, and they are able to maintain this inconsistency only by virtue of a habitual escape into the past, or into some other exotic world. In

Scott's novels "the veil of egotism is rent" and "he goes back to old prejudices and superstitions as a relief to the modern reader," while the poet of *Childe Harold's Pilgrimage* "seems to cast himself indignantly from 'this bank and shoal of time,' or [from] the frail tottering bark that bears up modern reputation, into the huge sea of ancient renown. . . . His contempt of his contemporaries makes him turn back to the lustrous past, or project himself forward to the dim future!" Hazlitt may be right in attributing Byron's affectation of "superiority," his pretended disregard of opinion to his self-consciousness of titled rank, with the ironic result that this exiled and rebellious poet becomes one "who panders to the spirit of the age," as he "goes to the very edge of extreme and licentious speculation." But Hazlitt fails to see that much of Byron's "extravagance" is also the revolt of an ego struggling to free itself from an externally imposed identity in order to confront honestly the reality of death—a theme which Hazlitt sees as obsessive in Byron's melancholy but which he fails to relate clearly to that special "intensity" of voice, the "electric force" of an inward "demon," which is the "great and prominent distinction of Lord Byron's writings." Nor does Hazlitt recognize, even while acknowledging the power of *Don Juan* and its parodic character as a "poem about itself," that this poem is precisely a satire on self-love—on the inability of the self in this age finally to escape its self-consciousness, or the sense of its own vanity and insignificance, even in its rare and intense moments of love and suffering. Hazlitt can sympathize with Byron's honest scorn of contemporary "cant," but the poet of *Don Juan* seems to him to find in the present world, as distinct from the past, no remedy but a self-indulgent relief from cant: "A classical intoxication is followed by the splashing of soda-water, by frothy effusions of ordinary bile." Rightly or wrongly, Hazlitt sees no victory over despair in the comic Byron—perhaps because Hazlitt still needs to see Byron in the image of that pessimism against which he himself had been struggling in recent years, and which he had been able to subdue only by equating "misanthropic" attitudes with a morbidly disguised vanity. Perhaps this need of his own reactive impulses explains why he is determined to see only "love of singularity" and mere inversion or darkening of "common-place" in Byron's "paradoxes," and why he is so ready to praise Scott as the superior genius by any standards, political or literary. For the novelist is, in spite of his politics, helping to emancipate the age from "bigotted prejudices," while "Lord Byron is the greatest pamperer of those prejudices, by seeming to think there is nothing else worth encouraging but the seeds or the full luxuriant growth of dogmatism and self-conceit" (pp. 69–78).

Interesting though the sketch of Southey is as the study of a Jacobin poet turned Tory enthusiast—of an inveterate idealist of power who, having "missed his way in Utopia . . . has found it again at Old Sarum" (p. 79)—we must pass it over to reach the portrait of Wordsworth and its more significant contrast with Byronic egotism. Hazlitt recognizes only two peaks of literary achievement in the age, the Waverley Novels and Wordsworth's poetry, but only the latter's genius wins acclaim as being thoroughly expressive of its time, "a pure emanation of the Spirit of the Age." The love of novelty and "paradox" having now been traced, not to the "vanity" of modern writers as individuals, but to the Time-Spirit itself, Wordsworth can be praised for having turned to creative account tendencies that in his contemporaries, while proceeding from the same self-consciousness, remain bound to a negative polarity—dependent on the negation or suppression of a contrary—and so produce either an unresolved discord between, or (as in Scott) a false separation of, political and literary values which are really continuous in the *Zeitgeist.* Wordsworth has reacted only, or mainly, from "the pride of art" in the age, and in doing so has kept imaginative faith with a more profound impulse in the "bias to abstraction." This deeper impulse is the impulse to "equality"; and we should note how careful Hazlitt is now to relate democratic "simplicity" in Wordsworth to the major theme of modernity, "abstraction": "He takes the simplest elements of nature and of the human mind, the *mere abstract conditions* inseparable from our being, and tries to compound a new system of poetry from them" (my italics). Wordsworth's genius thus transcends "the revolutionary movement of our age" by restoring the hitherto abstract values of equality to the intercourse of personality with nature, where reflection on universals ceases to be an abstraction from the identity of the living self.

Hazlitt had described Bentham as "one of those who prefer the artificial to the natural in most things," and it is this polarity that Hazlitt sees Wordsworth as having returned to its true historical energies, by restoring the age's demand for freedom through knowledge to the original sense of "fact" in the self, to a sense of elemental "things" as they truly interest "the heart of man." "In a word, his poetry is founded on setting up an opposition (and pushing it to the utmost length) between the natural and the artificial; between the spirit of humanity, and the spirit of fashion and of the world!" This again may strike us as jaded Rousseauist-liberal rhetoric; but Hazlitt goes on to make it clear that Wordsworth has expressed this "opposition," not by a willed identification with one contrary or a simple rejection of the other, but by daring to look beyond politics—to discover that the rebellious impulses of the self, if pursued through memory and imagination to their roots in the life of identity, lose their negativism and become a new sympathy with being:

> Prevented by native pride and indolence from climbing the ascent of learning or greatness, taught by political opinions to say to the vain pomp and glory of the world, 'I hate ye,' seeing the path of classical and artificial poetry blocked up by the cumbrous ornaments of style and turgid *commonplaces* . . . he has turned back partly from the bias of his mind, partly perhaps from a judicious policy—has struck into the sequestered vale of humble life, sought out the Muse among sheep-cotes and hamlets and the peasant's mountain-haunts, has discarded all the tinsel pageantry of verse, and endeavoured (not in vain) to aggrandise the trivial and add the charm of novelty to the familiar. No one has shown the same imagination in raising trifles into importance: no one has displayed the same pathos in treating of the simplest feelings of the heart. . . [t]o the author of the *Lyrical Ballads,* nature is a kind of home; and he may be said to take a personal interest in the universe.

Critics of Wordsworth are still divided on the question that Hazlitt here was the first to raise (or to raise fairly, as Jeffrey had not)—the question of whether the ethos of the French Revolution was essential (not merely contributory) to the poet's imagination. But however we resolve the issue, we should not oversimplify Hazlitt's position: he is not reducing Wordsworth's genius to the spirit of "equality."[17] Hazlitt's Wordsworth represents, fully as much as

Byron, the proud self-consciousness of the age: "He tramples on the pride of art with greater pride." And Hazlitt now insists that it is this peculiar character of pride in Wordsworth, a "proud humility," which differentiates his poetry from the tradition of Shakespeare and Milton. For the first time Hazlitt makes it unequivocally clear that Wordsworth *is* a sublime poet—and sublime *because* he is also a "levelling" poet. The great and the small in the poet's experience are not being reduced, as Hazlitt had hitherto intimated, to the mood-levels of personal association, but are made to reveal, in a new way, their character and interdependence in nature: Wordsworth is able to invest his description of the lowliest daisy "with the majesty and sublimity of the objects around him." Seldom has what Keats called "the egotistical sublime" in Wordsworth, the intercourse of his imagination with its symbolical correlatives in nature, been better described: "The tall rock lifts its head in the erectness of his spirit; the cataract roars in the sound of his verse. . . . There is little mention of mountainous scenery in Mr. Wordsworth's poetry; but by internal evidence one might be almost sure that it was written in a mountainous country, from its bareness, its simplicity, its loftiness and its depth!"

Hazlitt, however, still does not regard Wordsworth, by the specifications of *Biographia Literaria,* as preeminently a "philosophical" poet. There is, indeed, "inspired reflection" in his poetry, but its appeal is to "the lonely and retired student of nature"—to a small minority of humanity, and only to that portion of the lives of this minority which is passed in solitude. The fact, then, that Wordsworth's poetry emanates from the *Zeitgeist* is for Hazlitt no indication whatever of the power of his poetry to react upon it or to modify and guide modern "spirit" in the future. The closest Hazlitt comes in this book to an express recantation of his dying Louvre myth of Genius as the deliverer of humanity is in this passage—which may also serve to suggest that his new tolerance of a former adversary was purchased at the cost of relinquishing some long-cherished hopes:

> It happens to him, as to others, that his strength lies in his
> weakness; and perhaps we have no right to complain. . . . We
> should 'take the good the Gods provide us': a fine and original
> vein of poetry is not one of their most contemptible gifts, and

the rest is scarcely worth thinking of, except as it may be a mor-
tification to those who expect perfection from human nature;
or who *have been idle enough at some period of their lives, to deify
men of genius as possessing claims above it.* But this is a chord that
jars, and we shall not dwell upon it. (my italics; pp. 86–94)

But once the forlorn hope is silenced, there seems nothing in
Hazlitt's remaining pages to promise a resolution of the discords of
the age. "The personal always prevails over the intellectual," he remarks in the essay on Lord Eldon, "where the latter is not backed by
strong feeling and principle" (p. 145). If the passion of creative genius and the systematic "principle" of philosophy have both failed
the test of strength needed to save the fallen *Zeitgeist,* what hope is
there in men of lesser gifts? Mackintosh, Malthus, Gifford, Jeffrey,
Brougham, Burdett, Eldon, Wilberforce, Canning—the general
dimness today of these erstwhile luminaries offers a measure of
Hazlitt's despair for the regeneration of public opinion in an age
when "spirits" of this magnitude were its most influential shapers
and arbiters. What seems most to worry Hazlitt is the debilitating effect that the polemicists and the more popular writers of the age
were having on language—on both the spoken and the written
tongue.[18] Often in the earlier sketches, too, he was concerned to expose the corruption of language that afflicts an age of revolution
which is also "an age of talkers"—when the forms, conventions, and
rhythms of sophisticated discourse tend to acquire an autonomy in
consciousness which serves the will as a ritual substitute for firm
belief, resolute action, and sincerely responsive feeling. Such abuses
of idiom are seen reaching a near-perfection of perversity in the
evasive rhetoric of the "political rope-dancer," George Canning
(1770–1827), then Foreign Minister and once the famous parodist
for the *Anti-Jacobin.* Canning's successes "are strong indications of
the Genius of the Age, in which words have obtained a mastery over
things, 'and to call evil good and good evil,' is thought the mark of a
superior and happy spirit" (pp. 154–57). And it is interesting to note
that several of the terms used to disparage Canning's oratory return
to describe the most popular poetry of the time: Thomas Moore's
Lalla Rookh is also said to be "glossy," "dazzling," and "meretricious."
Just as Canning's rhetoric serves to conceal the roots of political

issues in death and suffering, so Moore's *"cosmetic* art" serves to distract the sensibility of the age from self-knowledge of its motives and from a candid, morally rational awareness of social reality. Beneath the demand for the brilliant, the sensuous, and the exotic in contemporary taste lurks the impulse to deny or escape the extremes of social inequality, the manifest injustice that haunts the insecure pieties of the age of Malthus and Wilberforce. And this unpleasantness "the artificial taste of the age" seeks continually, if not to shun, to "relieve" or displace, in its attraction to poetry and romance, onto remote and less disturbing objects. "The craving of the public mind after novelty and effect is a false and uneasy appetite that must be pampered with fine words at every step—we must be tickled with sound, startled with shew, and relieved by the importunate, uninterrupted display of fancy and verbal tinsel as much as possible from the fatigue of thought or shock of feeling" (pp. 169–71).[19]

Indeed, only two of the lesser writers escape this censure, and the fact that they are not poets testifies to Hazlitt's conviction—stated elsewhere but strongly intimated in the essay on Scott (pp. 58, 62)—that literary leadership in the modern world is inevitably passing from poetry to prose.[20] The "picturesque and dramatic" vision (8.52–53) that he fails to find sustained in the minor poets of the time (in Campbell, Crabbe and Hunt), he finds quickening the prose of Cobbett and Lamb—and especially in the essays of "Elia," notwithstanding Lamb's occasional lapses into "mannerism." It may seem inapposite that Hazlitt's panorama of the *Zeitgeist* should end with glimpses of a crotchety bibliophile indulging an eccentric taste for literary antiquities at a bookstall in an alley off Fleet Street. But precisely this contrast with the public world of political London serves to make Hazlitt's critical point. The figure of Elia represents in the symbolic landscape of the age those least tractable but deeply natural "infirmities" of man which, ignored by, when not wholly invisible to, the humorless self-abstraction of modern pride, will never be made to yield to "the progress of intellectual refinement." Here, too, personality prevails over intellect, but it does so—and this makes all the difference morally—because the writer's ego dares to be truly personal, to find, without defensive reaction, the ways of his own mind reflected in the infirmities of others. Man's weaknesses not only appear in Lamb undisguised in their frailty but are frankly confessed, even shamelessly valued as such: the characters in his essays (Mrs. Battle, for instance) are "lasting and lively emblems of human infirmity." We should note the deliberate contrast with nearly all the preceding figures in the volume when Hazlitt describes his friend as "shy of all imposing appearances," immune to "the turbulence or froth of new-fangled opinions"—one who has learned to rediscover "the spirit of life" in whatever smacks of mortality, who "has succeeded not by conforming to *The Spirit of the Age*, but in opposition to it," and who is, indeed, so little enamored of the vanities of his time that he "would fain 'shuffle off this mortal coil' " (pp. 178–82).

Is Hazlitt recommending, then, a life of withdrawal from the "modern" life of the age—from the world of "opinion" and its obsession with "change"? From a comment elsewhere we learn that he intends no such conclusions to be drawn: "Let us," he writes later in this decade, "make the most of the spirit of our times. We may direct, but we cannot arrest the progress of knowledge" (17.330). But the meaning of "knowledge" is what Hazlitt's book has been calling in question; clearly such "progress" must now include self-knowledge, and the ironic condition of such knowledge may be recognition of the possibility that the age has reached an impasse, a siege of contraries that is virtually hopeless for all combatants, although perhaps only *as* combatants. Hazlitt was aware that this is a clarity of "truth" without much radiance, and that to accept it is to give up the mythic consciousness of "progress" as essentially "intellectual"—precisely such consciousness as had given birth to the simple legend of the *Zietgeist* as the Spirit of Freedom. This was the burden of his final quarrel with another liberal believer in the Time-Spirit, Shelley; and a review that Hazlitt wrote in this same year (1824) of Shelley's *Posthumous Poems* offers perhaps the clearest summation we have of Hazlitt's altered vision of his time. Shelley is depicted here, not unsympathetically, as a victim of the age's most lethal disease, "the rage of paradox": this poet-reformer's reaction from "established opinions" had become "a species of madness," a revolt from reality itself: "He shook off, as an heroic and praiseworthy act, the trammels of sense, custom, and sympathy, and became the creature of his own will." Yet the public, too, is cautioned to learn something from Shelley's martyrdom; and the lesson that Hazlitt proceeds to read to his age admirably sums up nearly all the judgmental themes in his book:

> He gave great encouragement to those who believe in all received absurdities, and are wedded to all existing abuses: his extravagance seeming to sanction their grossness and selfishness, as theirs were a full justification of his folly and eccentricity. The two extremes in this way often meet, jostle—and confirm one another. . . . Opinion thus alternates in a round of contradictions . . . and leaves a horrid gap, a blank sense and feeling in the middle, which seems never likely to be filled up without a total change in our mode of proceeding. The martello-towers with which we are to repress, if we cannot destroy, the systems of fraud and oppression should not be castles in the air, or clouds in the verge of the horizon, but the enormous and accumulated pile of abuses which have arisen out of their continuance. . . . To be convinced of the existence of wrong, we should read history rather than poetry: the levers with which we must work out our regeneration are not the cobwebs of the brain, but the warm, palpitating fibres of the human heart. It is the collision of passions and interests, the petulance of party-spirit and the perversities of self-will and self-opinion that have been the great obstacles to social improvement—not stupidity or ignorance; and the caricaturing one side of the question and shocking the most pardonable prejudices on the other, is not the way to allay heats or produce unanimity. (16.268–69)

※※※

Although Hazlitt alludes to it as the one "sterling work" by which his name should be remembered (8.325; Howe, p. 420), the four-volume *Life of Napoleon Buonaparte* (1828–30) need not detain us long. As a work of historical and biographical research, the book was unoriginal even when it appeared: Robinson's study has shown that only about a fourth of its pages (240 out of 1,049) can claim to be entirely Hazlitt's own, the rest—the historical narrative as distinct from the commentary—being largely paraphrases of passages in memoirs and in earlier (mainly French) histories.[21] And if we expect to find in this commentary a philosophy of history and a comprehensive vision of the future prospects of society and civilization, we are soon disappointed. Far from being the autumnal fruit of his wisdom, Hazlitt's most ambitious book is the least characteristic, the least radically critical, of his works in this decade. Here, as if in reaction from his ironic attitudes in *The Spirit of the Age,* his inherited myth of Truth is permitted its last—if no longer a hopeful—triumph over his mature sense of dialectic.

The *Life* is, in short, notwithstanding his admonition to his age, more "poetry" than "history"; it is less a biography than a hero-epic in prose, although an epic far closer to tragedy—and this point cannot be too strongly emphasized—than to heroic "idolatry." Remarking on the grief of Napoleon's soldiers as they pass, during the retreat from Moscow, the battlefield of Borodino (not long before, the site of a heroic but costly victory), Hazlitt exclaims: "And *there* not only they [the battle dead] but the whole human race surrendered up their moral being and their vital breath, and can only henceforward as in a charnel-house drag out a mutilated and dishonored existence—bodies without a living soul, the forms without the freeborn spirit of men! A fit inscription for that ghastly spot would make mad the survivors, and set free the world" (15.83). The modern Armageddon that Hazlitt's Puritan sense of history had taught him to expect in his lifetime—the ultimate battle between Truth, or the Power of Liberty and Genius, and the princely Powers of the world—here at last takes place in a world of compensatory rhetoric; and the very failure of history—of the record of events—to conform to the myth is twisted into a kind of revelation. The Apocalypse of Liberty is now seen as the total defeat of Liberty by the ancient powers of darkness, whose evil, however, has thereby been more clearly and universally revealed to posterity than ever before. Liberty can now be served honestly only by worshipping at "the tomb of Liberty" (8.238), and the only sincere apostle of Liberty is he who is willing to recognize that its death at Waterloo may be "eternal" and that its grave in Bourbon France may be the tomb of "the human race" (cf. 13.38; 14.76, 98).

It is this hyper-melancholy logic of the book, its strenuous militancy of resentment without hope, that has made so many readers turn away from it as a fulsome exercise in self-pity or as a chauvinistic rationalization (Chauvinistic, indeed) for a Buonapartist's life of blind prostration before his idol. Yet in acknowledging his regressive mentality, we should not slip into the error of assuming that Hazlitt has been writing his defense of Buonaparte in pathological isolation from the mainstream of English opinion. The *Life* was in part conceived as a corrective to Scott's biography; but we should also be aware that Scott's work, in turn, was intended to check a tide in opinion that was turning strongly in Napoleon's favor. As Albert Léon Guérard observes, "About 1824, Liberalism everywhere was assuming a Napoleonic tinge";[22] and Hazlitt had therefore judged the time to be ripe for a book that would present Napoleon not as the perifidious Caesar of the French Revolution but as its "child and champion" (13.ix).

There were limits, even in his own mind, to the credibility of his hero as a "liberal" champion, and we must be very clear about the role that Hazlitt assigns to Napoleon in his mythic drama. Hazlitt does not so much identify Napoleon's wars with the French Revolution as the Revolution with the Napoleonic wars; for by "the Revolution" he primarily means the movement of ideas and events in France as determined by the struggle with the ancient tyranny of courts, not as defined by the Utopian imagination of "Liberty" in the early nineties. Hazlitt sympathizes with the Girondists and he refuses to condone the policy of the Jacobins in the Reign of Terror, with its "*demonism* of political orthodoxy" (13.144–54); but he also insists that some such phase of bloodshed, of both internecine strife and foreign war, was inevitable, as the only possible resolution—by force—of a "fatal" conflict whose antagonists, given the French history of "servitude," could never have been peaceably reconciled (13.77 ff.). And by the latter years of the decade, when the victorious General Buonaparte arrives on the scene, there was no longer a viable cause of republican government for the ambitious Napoleon to betray. Buonaparte's role was largely fashioned for him by circumstance: it was one of translating the self-assertive will of "Jacobinism" from abstract ideology into institutional forms which, by borrowing the power-symbols but not the substance of monarchist tradition, would appeal also to the self-love of men hitherto averse or indifferent to liberal ideas. His rule was popular not in an ideal sense, but as the incarnate expression or satisfaction of unconscious motives, active in every self at that time, of sympathy or "fascination" with power—motives compounded variously of combative idealism and vengeful contempt for idealism, of fear, envy, baffled pride, and the identification of the impotent with compensatory or oppressive strength—motives which had hitherto often worked to destroy the Revolution and which, under the circumstances, were indispensable energies for a concerted resistance to the Counter-Revolution. Hazlitt's Napoleon, therefore, is not—and here he most conspicuously departs from "the Napoleonic Legend" emanating from St. Helena—the faithful "saviour" of the Revolution who first rescues it from anarchy and then "perfects" it in a system of law.[23] The self-crowned Emperor remains the "champion" of the Revolution only in the sense of preserving its ethos of "independence" as the will to resist at all costs the return of its implacable antagonist, the "slavery" of hereditary monarchy and aristocracy (14.46–95).

Hazlitt does not deny that Napoleon's regime was, in many respects, a tyranny; nor does he palliate the Emperor's will to conquest even as he holds Britain and the Allies chiefly responsible for conditions which continually justified a policy of imperial expansion. Hazlitt once praised Milton for never surrendering his "erectness of understanding" in his loyalty to Cromwell (8.178); and we need only glance at some of Hazlitt's comments on his hero to learn that he maintains his critical grasp of character in the very heat of his admiration:

> He vaulted into the empty seat of a government as a wild Arab throws himself on the back of a horse without a rider. . . . A popular government was to him as chimerical an idea as a herd of centaurs; and he hated what he had no faith in. (13.326)

> We see a soul of fire without water or clay, that nothing could tame, could soften, or deter. It is not a question of degree, but a total separation in principle and an antipathy in nature to the ordinary and cherished weaknesses of human nature. (14.120)

> To contrive and to will were the first necessities of his soul; to succeed, unless by extraordinary and arduous means, was only the second. (14.22)

> So far from propagating new principles of civilisation in the East, it was his object to crush and neutralise them at home. (14.30)

328

The dead bodies [slain by the mob in the Tuileries in 1792] were many [seemed unbelievably numerous to Buonaparte], because they were there without his knowledge or connivance: had they served to swell his triumphs, or to furnish proofs of his power and skill, they would have seemed too few! (13.18 n.)

We must doubt, then, that Hazlitt can be justly accused of a "sentimental view of Caesarism" (Baker, p. 330) or of exonerating Napoleon as "a noble-intentioned champion of the emancipation of mankind."[24] On the contrary, it is precisely because Buonaparte has an "iron will" (14.53) with a coldly Machiavellian intelligence to match—because his will to power is largely free of humane deterrents—that he is, in Hazlitt's view, a fit "champion" to rival the strength of prejudice that sustains upholders of the *ancien régime*. For Hazlitt, we remember, the will to liberty as well as the impulse to tyranny is rooted in the necessary love of power in the self; and for him Napoleon's redeeming greatness is that he succeeded in stripping the aura of inviolable sanctity from traditional authority and in revealing to men everywhere that the source of all power, in politics as in art and culture, lies nowhere but in themselves. Whatever his sins and limitations, "the greatest man in modern history" (8.230) remains great because he has left an idea of his genius behind him, an idea that has enlarged immeasurably man's conception of the capacity of the individual mind and will to understand, penetrate, transform, and master in action the actual *world:*

To use means to ends, to set causes in motion, to wield the machine of society, to subject the wills of others to your own, to manage abler men than yourself by means of that which is stronger in them than their wisdom, *viz.* their weakness and their folly . . . to foresee a long, obscure, and complicated train of events, of chances and openings of success, to unwind the web of others' policy and weave your own out of it . . . to see latent talent or lurking treachery, to know mankind for what they are, and use them as they deserve, to have a purpose steadily in view and to effect it after removing every obstacle, to master others and be true to yourself, asks power and knowledge, both nerves and brain. (8.107–08)

Now this passage may seem to strike not a few chords reminiscent of the Nietzschean *Übermensch*, but Hazlitt differs from almost all other Napoleon-worshippers in his century in remaining convinced that the future of the modern world, if it ever has one distinct from its present "slavery," lies with democracy, and that Napoleon's mastery lay precisely in his command of the modern ethos of equality—the principle of "equality of pretension" being "the chief maxim of his reign" (13.8).[25] This view does not, of course, begin to define the relationship of Napoleon's government to other democratic legacies of the Revolution—a relationship that would soon be clarified by Tocqueville, who saw Napoleon as successfully turning the popular demand for Equality against principles of Liberty, thereby establishing a new and ominous form of modern dictatorship.[26] Hazlitt insists that Napoleon "owed his ruin" to "barbarism" and not "to his running counter to the liberal maxims and spirit of the age" (14.166); but in this defense he refuses to consider the larger historical issues transcending those of strategy. For to do so, to raise his sights, might call seriously in doubt the cogency of his myth—and especially the consistency of his mythic identification of Napoleon as Liberty's tragic champion with his larger myth of civilization as "progress," of which we are still given a few fleeting glimpses through the darkening rhetoric. "The tendency of the human understanding," we are told early in the *Life* (though only in a footnote), "is from the *concrete* to the *abstract,* in institutions, in religion, in literature, in life, and manners, in all cases in which the experience and reflection of civil society can be supposed to receive a gradual enlargement; and this marked and unavoidable tendency points, for the most part, to the greatest quantity of truth, and, I should hope, of good" (13.51 n.). Hazlitt is not entirely forgetting this premise when he acquiesces in a hereditary Buonapartist dynasty—as a kind of interregnum until the modern "enlargement" of opinion should have its proper effect on European society—and he recognizes that he must therefore write himself down as a "Revolutionist" rather than "Republican"; he believes, that is, in but one principle as absolute, namely, the right of a nation "to change its government and its governors," even if that right finds its one visible proof in "the heraldry of its [the nation's] kings" (14.236–37). What Hazlitt is unwilling to recognize is that the fundamental issue now, after the failure of both the Revolution and Napoleon, is no longer the purely political issue of sovereignty: the greater question—as Napoleon himself understood with brutal clarity—is whether the democratic ethos is capable of developing, without autocratic rule, its own aristocracy of talent and intellect, or whether modern "equality of pretension" must not continually degenerate, as the author of *The Spirit of the Age* would seem to suggest, into an anarchy of "contradiction."

Perhaps it is wrong to expect much clear thinking in the *Life,* for the condition of its being written at all is that here the Boy and the Prig find their perfect reconciliation—the one celebrating the "glory" of defiant Genius, the other mourning the fallen Power of Liberty. Yet this farewell homage is not wholly a conspiracy against Hazlitt's mature honesty; for the act of writing the *Life* must be seen also, in its elegiac anti-optimism, as a ritual slaying of the paternal myth, a belief being honored now *because* it is no longer a viable prophecy. And this act serves to release, however briefly, from its antiquated political conscience Hazlitt's critical genius, enabling the dialectical thinker in our essayist to put on record, elsewhere in these same years, his own prognosis of the democratic future.

※※※

Tocqueville and Mill are usually recognized as the first liberal theorists to expose an unprecedented threat to intellectual freedom in the modern democratic state, but Hazlitt, in a review (of William Ellery Channing's *Sermons and Tracts*) written for the *Edinburgh* in 1829, anticipates their worst fears:

> And here we will state a suspicion, into which we have been led by more than one American writer, that the establishment of civil and religious liberty is not quite so favourable to the independent formation, and free circulation of opinion, as might be expected. . . . In a monarchy, or mixed government, there is an appeal open from the government to the people; there is a natural opposition, as it were, between prejudice, or authority, and reason: but when the community take the power into their own hands, and there is but one body of opinion, and one voice to express it, there can be no *reaction* against it; and to remonstrate or resist, is not only a public outrage, but sounds like a personal insult to every individual in the community. It is

differing from the company; you become a *black sheep in the flock*. . . . Opinions must march abreast—must keep in rank and file, and woe to the caitiff thought that advances before the rest, or turns aside! This uniformity, and equal purpose on all sides, leads (if not checked) to a monstrous ostracism in public opinion. (16.325)

Hazlitt had never before suggested that the "levelling" uniformity of modern "progress" might, when thoroughly democratized, become a conformism that would tend to annihilate, not merely weaken, true liberty of thought and expression. In the Regency decade his misgivings about the homogeneous "abstraction" of modern culture had been confined to complaints of *ennui*, mediocrity, and spiritless "refinement"; and the worst fate he had then imagined for civilization was that "there will be nothing left, good nor bad, to be desired or dreaded, in the theatre or in real life" (4.194). The prosy dullards of the distant future would at least be free of the inhumane virulence of passion: in this way Hazlitt had consoled himself with the thought that literary decadence is compensated by social and political, if not moral, progress. And he continued to believe that "the influence of books," together with the profusion of goods made possible by the Industrial Revolution, would make modern society a better and more humane world to live in, at least by comparison with the poverty, ignorance, and licensed cruelty of the feudal past (17.321–31). "It may be laid down as a general rule," he decides in 1821, "that mankind improve, by means of luxury and civilization, in social manners, and become more depraved in what relates to habits and character." "We may," he concludes in the same essay, ". . . look forward to a decent and moderate, rather than a thorough and radical reform. . . . I conceive we may improve the mechanism, if not the texture of society; that is, we may improve the physical circumstances of individuals and their general relations to the state, though the internal character, like the grain in wood [and here Hazlitt strangely forgets the worsening "depravity" cited only five pages before] . . . may remain nearly the same" (12.235–41).

That "depravity" is precisely what Hazlitt does not forget in the closing years of this decade, when at last he begins to leave behind the convenient fiction of "public" and "private" worlds of the mind, of "external" progress and "internal" decadence—a division which perhaps had never been anything more than a vague compromise of the conflict we have traced in himself between conditioned conscience and reactive will. The vision of the dialectic of contemporary character that informs *The Spirit of the Age* becomes generalized in these twilight years, with the result that the principle of inward reactivity, of "paradox" and "contradiction," comes to be seen as the dominant force in shaping future changes in civilization. Indeed, what bothers him most now as he contemplates the democratization of society is not so much the danger of majority tyranny—that remains for Hazlitt a remote peril—but almost the contrary prospect, the degeneration of English individualism into a corrosive pluralism which is steadily losing its capacity for class-transcendence and intersubjective understanding. His comments now on the relationship of modern literature to society scarcely warrant his hope that literary culture might still create a "Catholic spirit"—a "common creed," which in 1829 he insists is more urgently needed than ever (20.284–85)—to withstand and moderate the welter and collision of wills and interests. Now he doubts that there can ever be "a common language or medium of understanding . . . between those who judge of things from books or from their senses." That awakening to "nature" which the *Lyrical Ballads* had once promised looms now, in retrospect, as wishful illusion: "I have made this capital mistake all my life, in imagining that those objects which lay open to all, and excited an interest merely from the *idea* of them, spoke a common language to all. . . . Not so. The vital air, the sky, the woods, the streams—all these go for nothing, except with a favoured few. The poor are taken up with their bodily wants—the rich, with external acquisitions. . . . Both have the same distaste for *sentiment*" (17.271–72). And even among the *literati,* there seems to be "no common bond of union or interest," such as the institutions of religion had once afforded: "Where there is no frame-work of respectability . . . the jarring pretensions of individuals fall into a chaos of elementary particles, neutralising each other by mutual antipathy, and soon become the sport and laughter of the multitude." The very diffusion of the idea of genius might actually be crippling, at its source, respect for true genius: "Where the whole [of excellence] is referred to intrinsic, real merit, this creates a standard of conceit, egotism and envy in everyone's own mind, lowering the class, not raising the individual" (11.231).

The gloomy conclusion that a hater of class-consciousness had been reluctant to reach in his battle with the Malthusians becomes, as early as 1825, explicit: there is "little . . . in common between the different classes of society," and it seems "impossible . . . ever to unite the diversities of custom and knowledge which separate them" (8.310). And even if literacy should become universal and material prosperity reach unprecedented heights, this very triumph might breed still another threat to "public spirit"—the enervation of "principle" and "intellectual energy" from habits of "luxury." The Americans, he speculates, "will perhaps lose [their liberty] when they begin fully to reap all the fruits of it; for the energy necessary to acquire freedom, and the ease that follows the enjoyment of it, are almost incompatible" (10.257). It is not merely that the powers and aspirations of the mind are dissipated as wants of the flesh are satisfied, but that the instincts and processes of the body have thereby become indistinct or confused in modern consciousness. Men are more "voluptuous," more "effeminate" in sensibility (20.342; 8.328); mothers aspire to resemble their daughters; youth (at least in London) is more sophisticated but also more childlike in its expectations of pleasure; and scarcely any one, male or female, is content to "grow old," to be thought "venerable" (12.73–74; 20.350). And so far is literature from checking such tendencies that it shows, on the contrary, every indication of surrendering to the levelling tide—of either conforming to the norms of fashion or of courting, in the manner of Byron and Shelley, a notoriety of "shock"; for the typical "modern artist" would rather "be disgusting and extravagant than . . . be charged with a want of genius and originality" (16.279). "Our literature," Hazlitt prophetically observes in 1825, has "descended . . . from the tone of the pulpit to that of the court or drawing-room, from the drawing-room into the parlor, and from thence, if some critics say true, to the kitchen and ale-house. It may do even worse than that!" (12.323).

The logical thrust of these thoughts could not long be denied, and in one of his last essays ("The Spirit of Controversy," 1830)

Hazlitt gives the lie forever to his inherited myth of history as "the progress of truth":

> No sooner is one out-work of established faith or practice de-
> molished, than another is left a defenceless mark for the
> enemy, and the engines of wit and sophistry immediately begin
> to batter it. Thus we proceed step by step, till, passing through
> the several gradations of vanity and paradox, we come to doubt
> whether we stand on our head or our heels, alternately deny
> the existence of spirit and matter, maintain that black is white,
> call evil good and good evil, and defy any one to prove the con-
> trary. As faith is the prop and cement that upholds society by
> opposing fixed principles as a barrier against the inroads of
> passion, so reason is the *menstruum* which dissolves it by leaving
> nothing firm or unquestioned in our opinions to withstand the
> current and bias of inclination. Hence the decay and ruin of
> states—then barbarism, sloth, and ignorance—and so we com-
> mence the circle again of building up all that it is possible to
> conceive out of a rude chaos, and the obscure shadowings of
> things, and then pulling down all that we have built up, till not
> a trace of it is left. Such is the effect of the ebb and flow and
> restless agitation of the human mind. (20.311)

Not the least startling among the surprises here is that Hazlitt seems not to be batting an eye as he shifts from a linear-progressive to a cyclical theory of history.[27] The cyclical pattern is, of course, not without precedent in his thought; indeed, all its phases are pre-figured in his theory of the rise and decline of art—all but the last and darkest phase, that which swings the cycle back to "barbarism." Hazlitt had speculated once before that it is "the extreme tendency of civilization" to "dissolve all moral principle" (4.88), but here that extreme possibility is regarded as inevitable, and as, moreover, a fatality that inheres in the very nature of human intellect, not merely as the consequence of an over-civilized "refinement." How, then, are we to account for the equanimity of tone that accompanies this otherwise dire vision of the human future? From our reading of the *Table-Talk* essays we should recognize this tone of voice: it is the dialectical thinker speaking, and for once he is in full command of a subject—"truth," its nature and history—which had hitherto been the exclusive preserve (to be divided between them) of Hazlitt's myth-obsessed voices. Hazlitt now rejects the simple alternatives of

335

hope or despair; the question we should ask, when confronted by the seeming futility of controversy, is not, *"What does it all come to?"* but rather, *"What would [men] have done without it?"* Men can only pursue truth with an "end" in view; but the very fact that such pursuit demands intense will and energy should make us wonder whether "an end is only of value in itself, and not as it draws out the living resources . . . of human nature." For "truth" has, and can have, no termination; its relations change, or change their meaning, with the seeker's point of view; it is not therefore something whose mysteries can be resolved, by analogy with war and physical conflict, by a triumphant act of power that crushes a simple adversary, "error." And because "truth is not one thing," it is—and these are strange words coming from a veteran satirist—"nearer akin to charity than the dealers in controversy or the declaimers against it are apt to imagine" (20.306–07).

The tenor of this remark should take us back to the lesson Hazlitt read to his contemporaries in *The Spirit of the Age;* he is repeating that lesson here and, with somewhat more allowance for hope, in this exhortation of 1829, called forth by the arrogance of the more dogmatic Benthamites:

> The principle of all reform is this, that there is a tendency to dogmatism, to credulity and intolerance in the human mind itself, as well as in certain systems of bigotry and superstition; and until reformers are themselves aware of, and guard carefully against, the natural infirmity which besets them in common with all others, they must necessarily run into the error which they cry out against. Without this self-knowledge and circumspection, though the great wheel of vulgar prejudice and traditional authority may be stopped or slackened in its course, we shall only have a number of small ones of petulance, contradiction, and partisanship set a-going . . . in its place: or (to vary the figure) instead of crowding into a common stage-coach or hum-drum vehicle of opinion to arrive at a conclusion, every man will be for mounting his own *velocipede,* run up against his neighbours, and exhaust his breath and agitate his limbs in vain. (20.264)

An "intellectual refinement" that might itself become a knowledge of the "natural infirmities" with which it is warring—this would appear to be Hazlitt's last and modest hope for a progressive "humanity," if not for truly liberal democracy, in the marches and counter-marches of opinion in his time. At least Hazlitt in recording his prophecy of "barbarism" does not expressly deny this sober exception for hope in the short-term future of "truth." Yet it would be wrong to imagine Hazlitt as having altered to the point of counselling a spirit of compromise—as anticipating the favorite Victorian gospel of *via media*. For although awareness of the dialectic of "truth" demands a willingness to learn from the enemy and to make "concessions" (20.306), it even more fundamentally presupposes the ineluctability of contraries—the inevitable polarity of "reaction" that all human passion generates, and without which there can be neither honest antipathy nor truly sympathetic understanding. Although weary of his mythic battle, and with most hope gone in its promised "end," an "incorrigible" Dissenter would brook no loss of faith in the need for controversy itself, however interminable: "If reform were to gain the day, reform would become as vulgar as cant of any kind. We only shew a spirit of independence and resistance to power, as long as power is against us. . . . Had events taken a different turn in 1794, who can predict what the popular cry would have been? This may point out how little chance there is of any great improvement in the affairs of the world. Virtue ceases with difficulty; honesty is *militant*." And Hazlitt ends this train of thought with a paradox that penetrates to one of the best-kept secrets of the age: "It is essential to the triumph of reform that it should never succeed" (20.333–34).

Chapter Ten

*Conclusion:
The Faith of the Centaur*

THERE is a sense in which it would not be wholly fanciful to say that Hazlitt never returned from his European tour of 1824–25. When he boarded the packet at Brighton in September of 1824, he was a not unprosperous author, still a contemporary in spirit and again a man with a will to the future—the most obvious sign of which was the presence of a new wife by his side, a handsome widow named Isabella Bridgewater, who is said to have fallen in love with him "on account of his writings." [1] Their itinerary was a familiar version of the Grand Tour: Paris first, then Italy—Florence, Siena, Rome; then north again through the Umbrian towns to Padua and Venice; then a long rest in Switzerland, followed by the voyage down the Rhine to the Low Countries, whence Hazlitt returned to London in October 1825. But from the start—from the time he re-entered the Louvre shrine of his "eternal regrets" (4.120, 10.106)—it was less contemporary Europe that Hazlitt visited than the lost Europe of his youthful imagination; and this contrast between fact and memory became the melancholy theme of *Notes of a Journey through France and Italy* (1826). At some point during his travels (or not long after), Hazlitt began planning *The Life of Napoleon,* research for which would twice more call him back to Paris—and, inwardly, draw him ever deeper into seclusion and spiritual exile from the contemporary world. Before his second sojourn in Paris was over (in the summer of 1827), the mysterious Isabella had departed from his life—into the oblivion whence she came and where she has remained ever since—and Hazlitt himself all but disappears from view, drifting in obscure poverty (though not in destitution) from one lodging house to another until his death, in a room in Soho, on September 18, 1830.

The cause of his alienation from the world in his last years does not lie solely in declining health and the melancholy will of this essayist to dwell in the past. The new England emerging in the later twenties—the world of Huskisson and Peel, of doctrinaire Benthamism, of steam packets and iron railways, of *Fraser's* and the *Athenaeum,* of the young Bulwer's novels and the young Macaulay's reviews—was rapidly leaving Hazlitt behind, even while it could still read and enjoy *The Spirit of the Age.*[2] The waning of his reputation in a changing culture is seen in the fact that more and more of the essays now appear anonymously and, after *The Plain Speaker* (1826), fail to reappear in book form. He did succeed in bringing out one more book that won considerable admiration—*Conversations of James Northcote* (1830), parts of which had been appearing in magazines at intervals since 1826. In these dialogues with "a divine old man" (11.186), a painter who was the last notable survivor from the age of Johnson and Reynolds—dialogues which, however, were not seldom an exercise in ventriloquism—Hazlitt continued to find an outlet for his ideas in a form that cost him little effort in the writing and that answered to the tastes of a novel-reading, fact-demanding, increasingly history-conscious public. Otherwise he was often hard-pressed to make a living in a literary marketplace that his name had not long ago commanded. When the four-volume *Life of Napoleon,* which began appearing in 1828, failed to bring him the sum needed to pay the debts incurred in writing it, Hazlitt was reduced to writing anonymous fillers ("Maxims," "Queries and Answers," "Memorabilia": 20.239 ff.) for the weekly newspapers. He was acutely aware that the easy-going and intimate manner of his former critical successes was no longer in demand; the *Edinburgh Review,* for instance, heavy with theory and encyclopaedic knowledge, now came up to town less "like a pleasure-yacht" than "like a coal-barge" (20.245). Under its new editor, Mac-Vey Napier, the *Edinburgh* in 1829 did invite Hazlitt to contribute again, after four years of exclusion; but four well-paid reviews could not prevent his arrest for debt in the last year of his life, after the publishers of the Napoleon biography (of its first two volumes) went bankrupt. To the end he was so strapped for money that when he fell ill in 1830, Hazlitt was forced to be eloquent—in one of his last and most engaging essays, "The Sick Chamber"—even about his fatal illness.

It is little wonder, then, that in these years he felt his "substantial" identity vanishing from him (17.197), and that his only real being lay in the historical and the personal past. Yet enveloped though he was in the shadows of memory, Hazlitt's thought in this twilight phase is not a nostalgia-haunted reiteration of earlier ideas and attitudes. For one thing, he knew that he was dying; that "organic disease of the stomach, of many years' standing" (as a friend described it: Howe, p. 418)—its exact nature remains unclear: an ulcer? a cancer?—was now returning with ever more painful frequency, no doubt aggravated by his European tour and Parisian sojourns. As far back as *Table-Talk* Hazlitt could see Death "coming to meet" him (8.325), and a number of passages in the later essays seem, quite consciously, attempts to compose his mind for that dread encounter. One effect of this death-awareness was to lessen the tension between Boy and Prig, to remove the essayist further than ever from a political consciousness of his identity—especially since he was simultaneously, as we have seen, providing due memorial for that consciousness in *The Life of Napoleon.* Hazlitt can also be observed, in the last three years of his life, putting his intellectual house in order: he composes a series of brief essays that he calls "Outlines" ("Outlines of Taste," "of Morals," "of the Human Mind," etc.: 20.376 ff.), with a view, of course, to turning past capital into present profit (again he was unsuccessful: they went unpublished), but also, one suspects, as a way of insuring that certain neglected parts of his intellectual estate should not be lost to posterity. Conservation, though, and the retrieval of cherished memory are not the whole of his retrospective interests at this time. His obsessive longing for the past

341

brought with it also a fresh appreciation of the time dimension in human experience; and this awareness, which has its counterpart in Hazlitt's changing sense of history, leads also, as we shall see in this chapter, to a deepening interest in religion and in the mystery of the ultimate nature of man's being. But the theme most often provoked by the near approach of death remains, perhaps predictably for our essayist, the thought of the close of life as the closure of identity—the finality that demands from the self a final reckoning. "I have thought and suffered too much to be willing to have thought and suffered in vain": this questioning of the self, this protest against futility, against "emptiness and desolation" (8.325–26) persists in all the later essays of reminiscence, with innumerable tones and variations—at times serenely resigned, at others embittered, but never with the decisive reassurance that the questioner seems in search of. What judgment was now to be made of a life drawing toward an end so different from its beginnings—indeed, so contrary to its dreams and expectations of life?

By one kind of evidence, Hazlitt did arrive at an answer, a resolute judgment delivered at the very moment of the dread encounter. As reported by his son, Hazlitt's last words, shortly before he expired, were these: "Well, I've had a happy life." Catherine M. Maclean found it so difficult to credit Hazlitt's famous deathbed utterance that she refused to include the words in the text of her biography, and in a note she explains that the words "seem to us to have a touch of *panache,* very foreign to Hazlitt" (p. 408, n. 357). Ralph M. Wardle, although not entirely convinced, more wisely accepts the authenticity of the utterance (as do Howe, p. 419, and Baker, p. 469), and he invites doubters to consider the "world of meaning in that *well.*" Deathbed scenes, of course, as Wardle reminds us (pp. 484–85, with n. 42), were indispensable staples of nineteenth-century biography; but rather than simply viewing with askance these reported miracles of moral nobility, we should rather consider how the dying would conceive and enact their roles in the cultural ritual. Hazlitt was surely aware that his was one of the first literary lives to be lived without professed adherence to the "consolations" of religion; and his valediction, conceived with the knowledge that his father before him had made a "gracious" end (see 8.373), may be seen as, in one

CONCLUSION: THE FAITH OF THE CENTAUR

respect, another quietly rebellious answer to the paternal creed (*this* life is the life of happiness) and, in another sense—and more importantly to him now—as an equally gracious assurance to his family that he was not forsaking ancestral virtue in his own fidelity to man and "nature." Hazlitt knew, moreover—however remote such things must have seemed to him in his last hours—that in the world beyond the sickroom door were voices waiting to pay their last disrespects to a radical-reformer's memory: these voices would not hesitate to warn of the law of retribution, recently manifest in the early or violent or otherwise miserable ends (*vide* Shelley's) to which all such spirits must come. But in his own case Hazlitt would have been surprised to learn just whose those voices would prove to be. Coleridge wrote a rather rancid verse epitaph for his erstwhile protégé, describing a man "thankless" of God's gifts, who "died like one who dared not hope to live." And Carlyle would place "poor Hazlitt" among "the Unblest on burning deserts," who "passionately dig wells . . . draw up only the dry quicksand . . . and die and make no sign."[3]

Hazlitt did not depart without a "sign"—it is there, or waits to be found, in his last works, if not in his dying words—although it is one which both his contemporaries and his Victorian successors were reluctant to recognize, and which even his remoter posterity have been loath to credit as a mark of wisdom. Hazlitt died, I believe, with a firm faith in the goodness and worth of his life—not in the benevolent goodness of *man,* and certainly not in the happiness of his own unamiable nature, but in the ultimate goodness, joy, and wonder of *life;* for that, we should note, is what his dying statement is about. This faith is not a religion, but, as we shall understand better in a moment, it is best approached in terms of the traditional quest to discover the existence, nature, and meaning of God. Doubt, of course, and ironic doubt at that—flowing irrepressibly from his dialectic of "everlasting contradiction"—constantly attends this faith, at times gravely weakens it, but at last proves necessarily inseparable from it. And unless we are willing to admit the possibility that Hazlitt could attain to a difficult faith—to something more than a "personal" affirmation ("personal" being always translated in this context, of course, as uniquely emotional, intellectually incoherent)—we may never be able to arrive at our own judgment of the meaning of his life and career, or to understand why he remains, after innumerable insults, a candidate for greatness in criticism.

꽃

Conflicting evidence awaits the most careful effort to penetrate to Hazlitt's religious views.[4] One contemporary was confident that he remained a Unitarian believer (see Baker, p. 45), but Haydon called him a "sceptic" and put his face in a picture, *Christ's Entry into Jerusalem,* as someone "looking at Christ as an investigator" (Haydon, pp. 300, 306). The scholars complete the spectrum of divided opinion: Ian Jack concludes that Hazlitt "may be described as a deist," but Baker, more cautiously, stresses Hazlitt's "reticence" and the absence of proof "that he maintained his early faith" (p. 45). The only consensus, it is clear, is that Hazlitt, while he might have remained (in Henry Crabb Robinson's phrase for him) "an avowed infidel," had not become an avowed atheist.[5]

Curiously enough, no scholar has thoroughly sifted Hazlitt's own prose for a clue to resolve the discordant testimony. If statements about his own attitudes are rare and seldom unambiguous, the statistical incidence of references to religion is surprisingly high—at least sixty pages of the *Complete Works* are devoted to religious matters—and one's cumulative impression after reading and comparing these passages is of a mind not only often but intensely concerned with the history of religion, with its role in the lives of his contemporaries, and with the psychology of belief and its moral effect on the believer. With these questions we must begin, if we are to know what to look for, and no less importantly, what *not* to look for, in his personal beliefs.

We have seen, in our last chapter, Hazlitt endorsing a premise wholly contrary to his Unitarian upbringing: reason is the solvent of faith, not its God-given support and safeguard. Before this time, of course, he had often made allusion to the modern antagonism of faith and science, and never more vividly or extensively than in some comments in 1823 on a sermon of Thomas Chalmers (1780–1847), the influential Scots divine and theologian. Chalmers had been replying to an objection to Christianity, "its supposed inconsistency with the Newtonian philosophy," and "we ourselves," Hazlitt confesses, were staggered by the blow (either then or long before) and still gasp for a reply. . . . As we thought the universe turned round the earth as its pivot, so religion turned round man as its center, as the sole, important, moral and accountable agent in existence. But there are other worlds revolving in infinite space, to which this is a speck. Are they all desert, worthless? . . . Have we alone a God, a Saviour, revealed to us? . . . It can hardly seem that we alone have occupied the thoughts or been the sole objects of the plans of infinite wisdom from eternity—that our life, resurrection, and judgment to come, are the whole history of a wide-seeing Providence, or the loftiest events in the grand drama of the universe, which was got up as a theatre only for us to perform our petty parts in. . . .

Now this willingness to recognize man's reduction to a "pitiful, diminished perspective" (20.116–17) in the universe revealed by Bruno and Galileo was anything but common in Hazlitt's time and had strangely little precedent in previous generations. Far from confessing a shock to their powers of faith, most English intellectuals, even before the Newtonian synthesis restored order to the heavens, welcomed the new astronomical infinitudes—as further testimony to the infinite bounty and glory of a God of Plenitude, whose Creation could now shine forth with a boundless immensity which liberated imagination from its medieval confines and gave cosmological scope to the infinite aspirations of man's soul. Even Tom Paine, on most issues a science-minded sceptic, found in the new astronomy the "cheerful" idea of an infinite "society" of worlds;[6] and Hazlitt's response was no less further removed from that of his fellow Romanticists, most of whom limited their complaints of Newtonian science to its mechanistic formulation of cosmic energies. Perhaps only Lamb, Byron, Peacock, and the author of *Lamia* would have agreed with Hazlitt that "religious and poetical enthusiasm" have both, and both *necessarily,* suffered a loss of "visionary" power from "the progress of experimental philosophy." "There can never be," Hazlitt insists, "another Jacob's dream. Since that time, the heavens have gone farther off, and grown astronomical. They have become averse to the imagination, nor will they return to us on the squares of the distances, or on Doctor Chalmers' Discourses" (5.9). Chalmers might ingeniously argue that the telescope and microscope, by extending knowledge equally into regions of the universe above and beneath us, have left man just where he always was on the scale of being; but these apologetics are the abstract paradoxes of the speculative reason, as strange to imagination as the Newtonian orbits or the creatures in the microscopic depths. And by appealing to "pride of intellect" rather than "simplicity of heart," such arguments succeed only in showing "how impossible it is to reconcile the faith delivered to the saints with the subtleties and intricacies of metaphysics" (20.117–18).

It is this solicitude for imagination and the "heart" which best suggests how Hazlitt's scepticism, after its beginnings at Hackney College, came to differ from, and with, the scepticism of the Enlightenment. When he remarks that "faith is founded on the sleep of reason," he is not suggesting that reason is a faculty which necessarily negates the credibility of faith, but a faculty which, being based on the distinction between objects and feeling, tends to divide cognitions from ideals of the will, and so to make faith, once instinctive and unquestioned, increasingly conscious of itself as an act of imagination. Modern science has brought rational knowledge to the point where it is not only divided from imagination but "averse" to it; for man can no longer find *himself*—that is, his passions, his organic life as a self—imaged in the stars, or if he does believe that his faith is reflected in their infinitude, he does so by an act of "ideal" abstraction which sets aside, or wills to forget, the habitual life and expression of passion which constitutes the humanity of the soul on earth (14.131–32, 5.9). Yet the very logic which makes such a conclusion inevitable also strips modern reason of its pretensions to be the judge of faith. For reason is only one form of the "intellectual" principle, is not a power originally distinct from imagination, and becomes distinct from it only through object-knowledge (8.35). How far Hazlitt would depart, in this direction, from eighteenth-century scepticism becomes emphatically clear in his want of respect for Hume's attack on the credibility of miracles: "According to Hume's reasoning [Hazlitt is paraphrasing the only "observation" he ever found to admire in William Paley], miracles must be *equally* inadmissible and improbable, whether we believe in a superintending Providence or not. There must therefore be some fallacy in an argument which completely sets aside so material a consideration" (1.296 n.). I read this to mean that morality, will, and "natural" prejudice, as Hazlitt says elsewhere, play a part in all belief or assent (20.324–28), and consequently determine the degree to which an event will appear to be probable or consistent with human experience, however inconsistent the event may be with our rationally organized knowledge of causes and effects in society or in nature.

Hazlitt thus, despite his large concessions to science, comes to share some common ground with the Romantic defenders of Christianity. He, too, contends that man is to be defined as "the only religious animal," whose "greater power of imagination" continually projects his sense of existence and its consequences "into another state of being" (20.61). But that man's religious instincts are primal or irrepressible does not mean for Hazlitt that they are religiously sound. This is the issue that comes to acrimonious definition in his review, for the *Edinburgh Review,* of Coleridge's *The Statesman's Manual* (1816)—a review which greatly dismayed Coleridge, who preferred to believe that Hazlitt was not saying "what he himself really thought" (BL.2.214). "Reason and religion," Coleridge had argued, "are their own evidence," that is, do not depend on the credence given to miracles by the faculties of "sense and fancy," whose tendency, indeed, to oppose or obscure "spiritual truth" had made miracles necessary: "It was only to overthrow the usurpation exercised in and through the senses, that the senses were miraculously appealed to."[7] Citing this passage, Hazlitt replies: "Revelation utters a voice in the silence of reason, but does not contradict it: it throws a light on objects too distant for the unassisted eye to behold. But it does not pervert our natural organs of vision, with respect to the objects within their reach. Reason and religion are therefore consistent, but not the same, nor equally self-evident." Now it must be granted that this rejoinder, whatever the merit of its logic, does not come with a good grace from a critic whom we have just heard confessing that Christian belief and "reason" (and Hazlitt refuses to consider seriously the new Coleridgean semantic for that term) are anything but "consistent" in his own mind. And still less gracious is the charge of *"potential infidelity"* which our self-confessed sceptic dares to hurl at Coleridge in this review (16.106–08). But even in this sally Hazlitt is expressing, quite independently of a personal or political animus, what he felt to be the only honest explanation for Coleridge's religious philosophy. For Hazlitt was convinced that Coleridge was, at bottom, scarcely less of a sceptic in religion than he himself was. The only difference was that Coleridge, being a poetic sceptic, "lives in the belief of a perpetual lie" (7.116–17)—by which Hazlitt means, presumably, that Coleridge, taking his cue from the German Transcendentalists, had invented an independent faculty of faith whereby the mystery of the Incarnation need no longer be judged by its empirical credibility but by the "truth" of its desirability as an ideal (16.124; and see 17.29).

Coleridge's attitude was, however, no isolated anomaly: "The characters of poet and sceptic are now often united in the same individual, as those of poet and prophet were supposed to be of old" (12.252). How modern scepticism could thus react against itself and become, as Hazlitt says of Transcendentalism in general, a disposition "to *believe in all unbelief*" (12.18–19) was a mystery that he did not leave unexplored. He explains it by a psychology of belief which he saw confirmed in the history of Protestantism; and it is imperative to understand this psychology if we are not to misunderstand the non-dogmatic faith which at last emerges from his own scepticism.

Hazlitt distinguishes two kinds or modes of "belief," which he thought had been notoriously confused in religious debate. One sort is purely cognitive and involuntary, an assent to "incontestable truth," whether of material fact or mathematical axioms; but quite another belief operates when our judgments of truth or falsehood cannot be "so plain and palpable" and where "the ground of reason is preoccupied by passion, habit, example." All religious belief is primarily of the latter kind, that is, "voluntary," an assent not freely given from motives of pure thought or conscience but one subject to "the bias of the will" (20.363–66). Thus it is not impossible to "believe something to be true that we *know* to be false" (1.126); and indeed this is likely to be the case when a prejudice inherited from the past has never been sorely tried in controversy, or when passion and the will to defy or dominate others impel the mind to embrace mysteries which might otherwise be rejected as incredible. What has generated so much religious energy and furor since the collapse of medieval authority is not some instinctive faith or will to faith; it is rather "the spirit of controversy" that has generated all modern intensity of conviction. The zeal of Puritan England was kindled by "the fires of Smithfield," and once that persecution abated, so did the Puritan inspiration. And with the proliferation of sects, with the constant "collision" of heresies, men gradually learn to distrust all belief: fanaticism culminates in scepticism (20.100–03, 309–11).

Not only the rationalism bred by science, then, but the value placed by modern culture on reasoning itself has led to erosion of the Christian certainties: for "to give a reason for something is to breed a doubt of it" (12.266). Scepticism, to be sure, would never enjoy a universal victory, for past inertias of belief would continue to operate: "People stick to an opinion that they have long supported and that supports them" (20.365). But scepticism is becoming "general" in an unconscious sense: the symptom of its omnipresence is (as in the case of Coleridge) "cant," the affectation of "a greater admiration or abhorrence of certain things than we really feel"; and this condition is the counterpart in common opinion to the love of "paradox" cultivated by rebellious intellectuals like Byron and Shelley (16.269). With the spread of "liberal opinions" not only the clergy but all "religious persons" become "squeamish and jealous" of their doctrines: "As our interest in anything wears out with time and habit, we exaggerate the outward symptoms of zeal as mechanical helps to devotion, dwell the longer on our words as they are less felt, and hence the very origin of the term, *cant*" (17.348, 353).

Hazlitt was aware of what, in theological terms, this analysis of belief amounted to: namely, to denial of the doctrine of Justification by Faith. His objection to this doctrine, which he saw on the rise everywhere in the religion of the age, is one since made familiar by several generations of moralists: such doctrine mistakes piety for virtue, substitutes confession of sin and penitent avowels of faith for the obligation to act justly and with charity—and thus encourages, in a word, "hypocrisy." Yet we must also ask whether Hazlitt's attack on what he rather arbitrarily calls "Gnosticism" is not finally aimed at Christianity, and perhaps at religion itself, as organized "hypocrisy." Take, for instance, this passage: "Religion is, in grosser minds, an enemy to self-knowledge. The consciousness of the presence of an all-powerful Being, who is both the witness and judge of every

349

thought, word, and action . . . forces the religious man to practise every mode of deceit upon himself . . . for it is only by being wilfully blind to his own faults, that he can suppose they will escape the eye of Omniscience." Hazlitt is careful to qualify his indictment: the effect described does not take place when religion has its "proper effect," which is to make men "wise and virtuous" (4.128). Yet how are we to reconcile this profession of essential respect with a scathing remark made in *Political Essays:* "Religion is another name for fear" (7.150)? Hazlitt here would seem to be joining Blake and Shelley in unqualified repudiation of traditional religion as craven worship of a despotic Father-God. And some further remarks of his suggest that he was ultimately aiming his critique at the dubious moral perfection of an omnipotent Deity who dispenses rewards and punishments at a Last Judgment. "Shall we suppose," he asks scornfully, "the Divine Being, who is the great geometer of the universe, to be unable to endure or witness without emotions of intolerable loathing, those mixed results which he has contemplated from the beginning to the end of time, and ordained in their eternal and immutable progression?" (20.224–25). This is a blast at Calvinism, but the logic of Hazlitt's inference here seems to impugn, *a fortiori,* belief in an Eternal Judge of any kind.

Having arrived at a historical analysis of belief that strips faith of absolute content, and having advocated a morality of sympathetic "disinterestedness" which conceives of "good" as inhering in human persons as such (1.46–47), not in actions that can be judged absolutely (12.241), Hazlitt would seem to have severed the last bond between his humanism and his father's Christian eschatology. If there is a Divine Being who is not merely "the great geometer" but a personal and loving God, He must be One who demands no belief in moral and spiritual absolutes, not even the simple obedience of faith in Himself, all such faith having proved of dubious virtue, on earth if not in Heaven. This would seem to be the unspoken conclusion in Hazlitt's cautiously agnostic statement: "That we are here, and for our good, is all we are permitted to know, or bound to believe, in our present state" (16.169).

Yet just as we are ready to conclude that Hazlitt's scepticism is final, we come upon certain statements in the later essays that must give us pause. "If by the proofs of intellectual superiority," he writes in an essay of 1827, "we survive ourselves in this world, by exemplary virtue or unblemished faith, we are taught to ensure an interest in another and a higher state of being, and to anticipate at the same time the applause of men and angels" (17.198–99). Now how are we to account for this and several other hints in Hazlitt's later work of a willingness to believe in some kind of immortality? It is a note never struck in his earlier writing, where his sympathy with Christian sentiment is always abstract, ethical, and impersonal. There we find "the Christian religion" praised as "the religion of the heart," and Christ praised as a prophetic "teacher" who "alone conceived the idea of a pure humanity," who "made the affections of the heart the sole seat of morality, instead of the pride of the understanding or the sternness of the will" (6.184–85). We might still interpret Hazlitt's late expression of "interest" in immortal "being" as mainly rhetorical, a concession to the nostalgic pieties of his own once-Christian "heart," were it not accompanied by a remarkable shift in his critical attitude toward traditional religion. The change is most striking when we compare "On Religious Hypocrisy" (1814), the essay quoted at some length two paragraphs back, with "On Cant and Hypocrisy" (1828). In the former essay Hazlitt scoffs at Methodism as a nauseous example of religious hypocrisy, but now he exempts the devout Methodist from that charge ("hypocrisy," since it implies the real absence of the feeling professed, is here carefully distinguished from mere "cant"). And Hazlitt is now prepared also to find "more wit than philosophy" in the common legend of "the hypocrisy of priests." "We all wear some disguise . . . use some artifice to set ourselves off as being better than we are"—and why not extend this same tolerance to priests and parsons, "who may sometimes be caught tripping" but perhaps "also with greater remorse of conscience"? In his earlier criticism Hazlitt had been willing to trace the worldly "perversion" of religion to "the contradiction between the passions and the understanding—between what we are, and what we desire to be" (4.57). But the difference now is that institutionalized religion is no longer seen as necessarily a "perversion," a *pathological* expression of the "contradiction" between the imagined and real self:

> The contrariety and warfare of different faculties and dispositions within us . . . will account for many of the mummeries and dogmas both of Popery and Calvinism—confession, absolution, justification by faith, etc. . . . A person does wrong; he is sorry for it; and as he still feels himself liable to error, he is desirous to make atonement as well as he can, by ablutions, by tithes, by penance, by sacrifices, or other voluntary demonstrations of obedience, which are in his power, though his passions are not, and which prove that his will is not refractory, and that his understanding is right towards God. (17.352–54)

Here, it seems to me, is clear recognition that religion, as traditionally practiced, is no mere anachronism but performs an indispensable function in culture—one that is necessary because it inheres in, and is generated from, the dynamic of the "everlasting contradiction" which defines the nature of man (see 9.192). We are accustomed to think of pessimism and scepticism as corollaries in nineteenth-century sensibility; but the paradox of Hazlitt's scepticism is that it originally drew its inspiration from moral and political optimism; and when his confidence in the future gives way to a pessimistic sense of man's "contradiction," so does most of his opposition to traditional religion. It is true that his analysis in "On Cant and Hypocrisy" can still be read as simply a naturalistic account of religious motivation: guilt feelings are inevitable in human life and so therefore are religious institutions. But the naturalistic analysis of religion logically ends, as William James concluded—and Hazlitt here would seem to agree—in confessing the irreducibility of the "personal" standard of truth in judging religious experience.[8] And if this is so, then the tension between imaginative faith and rational doubt in the honest sceptic's mind may be seen as a contradiction to be defined, not in the terms of its own dialectic, but as the experience of a larger dynamic of conflict in human existence—of whose origins or ends, whether wholly psychological or ontological, that is, with correlatives in all being, the self can never be certain. "Here 'upon this bank and shoal of time,' the utmost we can hope to attain," Hazlitt concludes in this essay, "is a strong habitual belief in the excellence of virtue, or the dispensations of Providence; and the conflict of the passions, and their occasional mastery over us, far from disproving or destroying this general, rational conviction, often fling us back more forcibly upon it, and like other infidelities and misunderstandings, produce all the alternate remorse and raptures of repentance and reconciliation" (17.348–49).

Now is it possible to read this statement as testimony to a recovery of religious faith? Had Hazlitt, too, been "flung back" from former "infidelities," and all the more strongly because of "misunderstandings," upon a "conviction" of the essential truth of religious imagination—a return to faith that was not, and could not be, a "reconciliation" with the letter of his childhood's Christian belief, but with its spirit, its confidence that the soul, the essential being of man, is immortal, or in some way transcends temporal definition? Indeed, his emphasis on time in the passage just quoted may help us to understand why nearly all the Romanticists underwent some phase or degree of attraction to scepticism—not because, like the Victorians, they sought a firm faith or a heroic confrontation of their doubts, but because only the sceptical attitude, with its willing suspension of both belief and disbelief (and the aptness of the famous Coleridgean phrase in this context is no accident) made for the energized awareness, the creative tension of opposites they instinctively sought[9]— enabled them, that is, to confess freely the bondage of the self to time yet to explore that condition with the hope of regaining some transcendent deliverance from time's illusions through the temporal quest itself. Broadly speaking, Romanticism may be said to explore three kinds of experience which promise, singly or in combination, deliverance from the world of phenomenal flux: 1. sympathetic (or empathic) communion, through concretely organic sympathies, with a Soul or Spirit in Nature; 2. intuitive communion, through visionary imagination, with the Eternal and the Infinite as distinct from, or transcending, earthly Nature; and 3. expressive communion with the "divine" through the joy or symbolic vision of artistic creation, as distinct from the finite work of art which genius, in its purely human character, creates. What the seeker after Hazlitt's faith soon discovers to his chagrin is that Hazlitt sooner or later rejects or abandons all three of these routes of return to God, or to "a higher state of being," although we shall find also that each makes some contribution to his own vision of transcendence—to that paradoxical state of sceptical mysticism, as it might be called, which seems to me his closest approximation to religious "conviction."

We might expect a critic who pays devout homage to nature in his literary theory to be something of a pantheist in his personal sensibility, but the fact is that our former Wordsworthian "novice" (17.116) emerges in the later essays as something of an anti-pantheist. He accuses Tom Moore of "methodistical cant" in saying that the sight of Mont Blanc "convinced" him of the existence of God: "The poet himself, standing at the bottom of it, however diminutive in appearance, was a much greater proof of his own argument than a huge, shapeless lump of ice" (12.368 n.). Even the sublimity of the ocean fails to move Hazlitt to rapt admiration; what he feels as he stands before the reality of the sea is a sense of endless flux and remorseless oscillation of passion: "I hate to be near the sea, and to hear it roaring and raging like a wild beast in its den. It puts me in mind of the everlasting efforts of the human mind, struggling to be free, and ending just where it began" (20.132). A year later, it is true, Hazlitt felt a brief resurgence of his old sense of wonder at the sea, as he walked the beach at Brighton: "Still is it given to the mind of man to wonder at thee, to confess its ignorance, and to stand in awe of thy stupendous might and majesty, and of its own being, that can question thine!" Note that Hazlitt here still stands in quasi-religious "awe" of the mind's "being" even as he confesses the mind's helpless "ignorance" of the sea's enigma: its inspiring "majesty," its "devouring" depths (10.90). Other Romanticists, undismayed by the cruelty or indifference of nature, would learn to find in this very tendency of the mind to "question" nature's power, just as it questions its own mortality, sufficient manifestation of the soul's innate tropism toward the Infinite. Hazlitt grants that "the ceaseless tendency of the human mind [is] from the *Finite* to the *Infinite*" (20.304)—but do we therefore have reason to believe that this tendency, although it may define all thought, implies desire for the Infinite or Eternal, a will to a transcendent realm of being? More than once, Hazlitt returns an emphatic No to this question. Although an admirer of the *Immortality Ode,* he rejects, even as allegory, Words-

354

worth's Platonic "supposition of a pre-existent state"; for it is "our ignorance of the future . . . the obscurity spread before it that colors the prospect of life with hope, as it is the cloud which reflects the rainbow. There is no occasion to resort to any mystical union and transmission of feeling through different states of being to account for the romantic enthusiasm of youth; nor to plant the root of hope in the grave, nor to derive it from the skies" (4.250). Just as emphatically, Hazlitt scouts other versions of the belief that man has some instinctive awareness of "another world" or an instinctive desire for immortality. Our antipathy to death is simply our will as a self to prolong our identity, not a will to Heaven. "We have little interest in unalterable felicity" (17.254): every man would wish "to remain a little longer in this mansion of clay" rather than leave it for an existence which may be infinitely more blissful yet is not certainly his own, and only when there is no hope of escaping the grave has he "no objection (making a virtue of necessity) to put on angel's wings, to have radiant locks, to wear a wreath of amaranth, and thus to masquerade it in the skies" (17.354).

Much the same sense of an ineluctable bondage of the mind to time keeps Hazlitt from believing that artistic creation offers revelation of, or communion with, the Divine. But, as the remark above on Tom Moore may suggest, Hazlitt feels immense attraction to this possibility and is clearly reluctant to abandon it—if, indeed, we can be sure that he does. Speaking once with William Bewick about the persecutions and other sufferings which Homer, Dante, Michelangelo, and Milton had endured but which had not destroyed their will or power to create, Hazlitt was moved to express this hope: "May we not be permitted to look for aid and protection from the Creator of such rare and mighty minds—of beings, by comparison, almost superhuman?" (Landseer, 1.114–15). One would be more inclined to accept this thought as Hazlitt's firm conviction had we found it in his own prose; for there the closest approaches to a belief of this kind fall far short of a clear inference that great creative genius emanates from, or yields an intimation of, the Deity. "The contemplation of truth and beauty is the proper object for which we were created"—but this remark of Hazlitt's needs to be glossed by another, also from an essay on painting: "The union of truth with

355

beauty suggests the feeling of immortality" (10.7–8, 57). The operative words are "suggests the feeling"; and it is this constant emphasis on "truth" in art as "passion" and "feeling" which chiefly motivates his religiose vocabulary of aesthetic praise—"shrine," "votary," "temple," "altar"—all of which are the inert metaphors of a conventional sign-language, common enough in the age as a whole, and resorted to as a way of winning respect for the "intensity" of art and its elevation above the vanities of the world. At least most of the time this explanation suffices, but perhaps not always—not, it would seem, in this description of "gusto" in art: "As the objects themselves in nature would produce an impression on the sense, distinct from every other object, and having something divine in it, which the heart owns and imagination consecrates, the objects in the picture preserve the same impression, absolute, unimpaired . . ." (4.77). Yet even here, of course, there is ambiguity. Is the impression "divine" because it *is* divine in essence and origin, or is it so because it is what "the heart owns" and imagination, taking its cue from feeling, "consecrates"?

That ambiguity, however, may not be one of irresolute confusion but deliberate. Remarking how often precise explications of "points of faith" so often defeat their purpose, Hazlitt observes: "Nothing beyond [a] general and implicit conviction can be obtained, where all is undefined and infinite" (4.82). It should be clear by now that, despite the eighteenth-century cast of Hazlitt's language, this repeated emphasis on the "general" character of his "conviction" cannot be justly described as "deism"—not at least if we take that term in the strict sense as implying belief in a purely transcendent, not an immanent Deity. We have seen him rejecting the idea that "the Newtonian philosophy" reinforces religious faith, and while we have found him speaking of God as a "geometer," this equation of the Divine Being with "mind" or "intelligence" is still not to be identified with the concept of the Aristotelian Mover or First Cause; indeed, Hazlitt expressly refuses to admit the argument from a First Cause as a legitimate argument for the existence of God (2.190). It is precisely on this issue that Hazlitt's analogy of great art with "divine" power has its importance; for it serves to remind us that Hazlitt would not have been the influential Romantic thinker he was if he had not turned away from the notion of a wholly transcendent Mind governing "nature," just as he had repudiated the idea of a transcendent Reason in the self. His sense of man's "contradiction" still reflects the classical dualism of mind and body; but this is no longer a hieratic dualism of "higher" and "lower" spheres of being (although Hazlitt sometimes speaks as if it is) but a dialectic of equal and interdependent powers—of subject and object, consciousness and nature, feeling and perception—whose precise functions in the continuous "web" of experience must forever remain indistinguishable, "undefined" (see 1.70).

But that Hazlitt still found it possible to imagine a Deity informing this immeasurable dynamism, a God who would be at once Creator, "Providence," and indwelling "Power," is suggested (if no more than suggested) by his praise of the most "universal" of human creators, Shakespeare. Here was a supremely "disinterested" intelligence whose power to create was not from "above" nature but at once immanent and transcendent, boundless in his sympathy with human passion but nonetheless a "moralist" (although only in the sense of "shewing us the consequences of our actions"), yet sublimely, impartially "indifferent" to the happiness of his creatures in sustaining the "general design" and poetic glory of his created worlds.[10] Hazlitt never invokes, as Coleridge and De Quincey do, a "divine" Shakespeare—if only because he wants to stress the contrast of Shakespeare's dramatic with Milton's epic and religious imagination (5.56). Yet, whether or not he was conscious of it, Hazlitt's language in describing the God of Christian theism suggests a Shakespearean, rather than a Miltonic, model for the omnipresent yet unknowable Creator-God: the Christian God is "unlimited, undefined Power," a "universal, invisible Principle of all things" (16.66). Nearly all of Hazlitt's locutions for the Power of the Deity echo the familiar images and phrases of traditional theism—"the image of God in man," "the stamp of the Divinity" (7.33, 9.220)—and a particular favorite is the *"divinae particula aurae,"* that "ethereal fire . . . which nothing can extinguish," whose spark is found in all moments of profound passion that lift man's animality above itself, whether through intellectual creativity, heroic effort, or self-sacrificing love (17.196, 14.28). In the light of this emphasis we should read Hazlitt's insistence upon the necessarily "general" character of modern faith—not as envisioning a Deity who is less accessible to man because He is amoral or remote but because both His immanence and transcendence are more complex and "infinite" than earlier ages had imagined.

How determinate, then, can, or should, such a believer's faith be? Hazlitt seems to have found it difficult to sustain for long even the broadly adumbrated theism I have just described: "According to circumstances, and the frame of mind we are in, our belief varies from the most sanguine enthusiasm to lukewarm indifference or the most gloomy despair" (17.348). This comment is noteworthy as much for its indication that he really did worry about religion—did try to reach and maintain a stable faith—as for the equanimity of tone with which he contemplates the mutability of his mind. The remark is from the late twenties; and its lateness suggests that Hazlitt had finally come to regard the temporal bondage of consciousness not as something to be resisted or transcended but as something inseparable from the nature and genesis of faith. He still, to be sure, sought to escape from the ravages of time—but the author of the personal essays does so not by entering visionary states or worlds but by escaping into the past, and there he finds his mystical sense of the timelessness of the mind's being confirmed by time's own destroyings: *"That things should be that are now no more* creates in my mind the most unfeigned astonishment. I cannot solve the mystery of the past, nor exhaust my pleasure in it" (17.242). He does not sentimentalize the "mystery," for he recognizes that the condition of this dream-like pleasure in memory-images is the decay of the will to the future and a sense of the insubstantiality of personal identity. Echoing Prospero, Hazlitt is prepared to confess "the stuff of which our lives are made—bubbles that reflect the glorious features of the universe, and that glance a passing shadow, a feeble gleam, on those around them!" (12.301). Yet even the thought that all our experiences may be "dreams within the dream of life" (17.194) and that a man may be "an insect of the hour, and all that he is, or that others have been—nothing!" (20.156) feeds not only the pessimism lurking in his scepticism but his susceptibility to faith—his willingness to recognize both the primacy and finality of "imagination." If both the past and the future prove to be equally "ideal" and subject to "deception" (see

8.256), the seemingly real "present" moment of bodily sensation, since it comes to consciousness only as an "idea" (1.39), has no greater claim than impassioned imagination to ontological reality: "The *imaginary* is what we conceive to be: it is reality that tantalizes us and turns out a fiction—that is the false Florimel!" (12.93). While other Romanticists would, like Shelley, draw from the same awareness the conclusion that the temporal shadow-world disproves its own reality, Hazlitt learns quite a different lesson: not that a will to the ideal is the only true becoming, but that the ideal and the temporal are endlessly, and always ambiguously, confused in "imagination." As his mysticism about the immateriality of being deepened with his immersion in time, so—and for much the same reasons— did his scepticism, that is, his doubts about the capacity of any man's religious faith to clarify and resolve, not merely to express and placate, its contradictory motives.

Just how ambiguously compounded these motives could become in imagination is suggested by one of the most grimly sardonic passages Hazlitt ever wrote—in some "Aphorisms on Man," published posthumously in 1831. Hazlitt here re-opens the question, "What is the distinguishing characteristic of man?" and this time his answer is not that man is "the only religious animal" but *"the only animal that dresses."* Anticipating the theme of *Sartor Resartus,* Hazlitt speculates that "the tailor . . . makes both the gentleman and the man," but utterly unlike Carlyle's is Hazlitt's account of the symbol-clothing that man creates for his aspiring soul:

> He is the only being who is coxcomb enough not to go out of the world naked as he came into it; that is ashamed of what he really is, and proud of what he is not; and that tries to pass off an artificial disguise as himself. . . . Strange, that a reptile should wish to be thought an angel; or that he should not be content to writhe and grovel in his native earth, without aspiring to the skies! It is from the love of dress and finery. He is the Chimney-sweeper on May-day all the year round; the soot peeps through the rags and tinsel, and all the flowers of sentiment!

If Hazlitt had let these words stand unqualified, it would be difficult, I grant, to extract a particle of faith or hope from so damning an account of the human animal. But the very next aphorism makes us question our impression of cynicism: "The meaning of all which is, that man is the only hypocrite in the creation; or that he is composed of two natures, the *ideal* and the *physical,* the one of which he is always trying to keep a secret from the other. He is the *Centaur not fabulous*" (20.348–49). Now a centaur is a far different creature from a "reptile," and what this change of image adds, or restores, to Hazlitt's vision is precisely his Romantic awareness of the *organic* nature of human contradictions—the reciprocal interdependence of "ideal" and "physical" motives in the passions of the self, and which indeed makes the dynamic union of mind and body a conscious self. But is this, then, the principle of the soul's unity? Is it possible to conceive of the organic principle as existing apart from the world of time, growth, and process? Or do the engendering contraries, which he had earlier described as locked in "eternal competition for the mastery" (17.350), have their counterparts in the eternal world—since "the spirit of contradiction," as he once remarked, "is included in the very idea of all life, power, and motion" (19.303)? I am not suggesting that Hazlitt ever asked himself these ultimate questions; but to spell them out in this way is to learn why he was unable to reconcile his own, his Romantic sense of divine immanence with his inherited sense of eternal transcendence—or why he could do so only by embodying that enigma in the image of a new breed of centaur, a creature that may be said to exist only, as it were, in its own imagination. "Vanities, and jests, and *irony itself*—do these things go out with life?" Charles Lamb once asked ("New Year's Eve," 2.29)—a question asked whimsically, but it has a serious tension of awareness behind it; and of the English Romanticists perhaps only Blake was prepared to pursue its possibilities (although, again, only in symbolic images) toward a dramatic, dialectical conception of Deity itself.

We must conclude, I think, that Hazlitt did not really "believe in" personal immortality, or in any immortality of the soul as the self imagines it. But to reach that conclusion is also to remind ourselves that Hazlitt did not really believe in *belief*—in faith as "conviction" and "principle," yes, but not in the commitment of the will to religious doctrine. "The debasement of the actual through the elevation of the *ideal* part of man's nature" (10.215): this was Hazlitt's final objection to "Popery" and to all ritual-cum-dogma religions—as it was, in a different sense, to his Transcendentalist contemporaries who "take refuge in the spirit" (4.58) and thus divide the contraries which constitute man's bondage but also his only natural wholeness of being. As he neared death, Hazlitt seems not to have worried very much over the degree of his belief or disbelief in immortality; for by that time, if not long before, he had learned—as these words from "The Spirit of Controversy" (1830) suggest—to think of "the ends of being" (8.30) as values which were never meant for fruition at, or beyond, the termination of life, or at least as ends to be realized then only if loved as having equally real value now, here in man's life in time:

> By insisting on the ultimate value of things when all is over, we may acquire the character of *grave* men, but not of wise ones. *Passe pour cela.* If we would set up such a sort of fixed and final standard of moral truth and worth, we had better try to construct life over again, so as to make it a *punctum stans,* and not a thing in progress; for as it is, every end, before it can be realized, implies a previous imagination, a warm interest in, and an active pursuit of, itself, all of which are integral and vital parts of human existence, and it is a begging of the question to say that an end is only of value in itself, and not as it draws out the living resources, and satisfies the original capacities of human nature. (20.307)

⁘

We have now followed Hazlitt's mind through the four decades of his intellectual life. We have seen, I trust, ample evidence of change and growth. We have seen a young Dissenter transferring his allegiance to "truth" from the model of Reason to that of Genius; and then, as his theory of imagination and his psychology of the will move further beyond the shadow of his father's conscience, from benevolently "ideal" to expressively "dramatic" standards in his judgments of art and literature. We have seen his love of "ideal" imagination, always associated with the Louvre and Renaissance painting, increasingly turn for sustenance to the past, to both the historical and the personal past, while his sense of the "modern" in literature—in part reflecting the consciousness of his own growing power as a writer—moves continually away from the inward perspectives of poetry to the medium of prose, and especially to the more openly dramatic world of the novel, with its vision of both society and the individual life as process. This very gradual shift in his literary values does not emerge decisively until the end of the Regency decade, when, coinciding with both personal and political despair, it takes violently pessimistic form as a denial of his inherited myth of civilization as necessarily in progress toward greater freedom and "humanity." The pessimist, however, in turn gives way to the dialectical essayist of *Table-Talk,* and especially to the author of *The Spirit of the Age,* who has learned to accept the modern subjection of, in varying degrees, both the mind and the will to self-love, and even to discover in this awareness the possibility of a new ethos for the reform of "opinion," a more truly democratic sympathy, a non-ideal but also less abstract "humanity." And now we have learned from his last speculations that although religious faith is still honestly possible in the modern world—a faith, at least, in the transcendent nature of the mind's "being"—such a conviction, even when free from dogmatic "perversion," affords no resolution of the ironic battle of contradictory desires in man, of the modern "warring" between "intellectual" values and vitally reactive "power" in the passional self. Unlike most other Romanticists, and unlike in this respect even his protégé Keats, Hazlitt holds out no hope, in either the individual or the life of the species, for some harmonizing of nature's contraries— for a "higher" state of perfection, or an ultimate freedom of spirit. The one ideal that survives from the wreck of his hopes for "truth," for a progressive regeneration of consciousness in man, is the hope for "self-knowledge"; and even this ideal is at last, as we have seen, conceived less as understanding of one's own than of generic subjectivity, of the human "microcosm," of self as known only in the mirror of otherness.

Yet it goes against the grain—and against the grain of his style particularly—to think of Hazlitt's triumph over despair as a stoical, or simply tough-minded, resignation to human limitations. Still missing from our account of his mature faith in "life" is some statement of how this resignation becomes the valedictory judgment that his own life had been "happy." So far we have spoken about Hazlitt's thought in terms of "theory" and "dialectic" and "conviction," in short, on the level of abstraction where conceptualized reflection takes place. And we are inclined to forget that there is an entire and elementary dimension of his, and of any sensitive man's, intellectual life which must forever remain inaccessible to this study and perhaps to any study, whatever its method. This tacit dimension of the mind's life, extremely important in Romanticism, is the life of what might be called the *intensive moment,* the moment of intense experience whether in life or art,[11] and Hazlitt's idea of "gusto" is perhaps as close as the language of theoretic generalization has ever come to articulating the essentially concrete nature of the critical experience. We have been necessarily so much concerned to follow the evolution of the conflict in Hazlitt's thought between Prig and Boy that we have had to overlook an important fact about that conflict: that it disappears in the act of intensive perception, and that it arises only, as it were, the moment after the moment of response. Prig and Boy may disagree over the *reasons* for valuing or disvaluing what they have experienced, or they will prize different aspects of the same values, and the Boy is inclined always to prize the moment itself rather than the reflections that it may suggest. But the act of their unconscious fusion in perception—which Hazlitt knew as a "going out of" himself, that is, a leaving behind of his habitual conflicts—is obviously as essential to his criticism as the act of discourse, where the two sides of his nature come together in that inimitable dialectic which we can only call, in the inadequacy of language, "style," the speech of the fortunately unfabulous "centaur" that was Hazlitt's literary identity.

Hazlitt sometimes suggests that these moments of perception were his "happy" moments, and his comment, quoted above, that the "end" matters less than the "progress" of the journey, would seem to support the same conclusion. A mind in conflict, moreover, and resigned to that conflict, would seem to welcome and prize supremely those moments of restoration to unity of being when "pleasure" in value and delight in "power" again become one. But it should go without saying that I resist this conclusion; for to accept it is to accept again that unjust inscription on his critical tombstone, "Impressionist." Most people who credit Hazlitt's farewell to his "happy life" tend, I suspect, to accept it on this basis, or on some equivalent supposition, rather than as a judgment on his life in its entirety. And this is why the dissension surrounding Hazlitt's last words is no idle issue. For implicit in our hesitation is not only the question of what he believed the nature and purpose of life to be but of our conception of the nature and purpose of a literary career devoted to *criticism*—to criticism in its broadest sense, as concerned not only with the arts but with the entire experience of the mind, with intellectual culture in general. If this study is to leave the reader with a sense of having reached a revaluation of Hazlitt, or with greater means of estimating afresh his place and status in modern criticism, then we must ask ourselves again what we assume the nature of critical *judgment* to be—in its relation to knowledge and theory, on the one side, and to feeling and personality, on the other. Needless to say, we can only glance at a delicate and complex problem, but unless we do, unless we raise our sights to this ultimate issue, the relation of Hazlitt's thought to his sentient life, as it makes for what I take to be his greatest excellence as a critic, will remain not only imperfectly treated but perhaps even, from the more important angles, invisible.

Misrepresentation of the division of attitudes in Hazlitt's mind began in Victorian times, but we may find a suggestive clue to our own errors of assumption if we consider the rather surprising scope and extent of his Victorian reputation. If we reflect on the variety of the nineteenth-century writers in English who admired Hazlitt and acknowledged, or whose work unmistakably reveals, some degree of indebtedness—and it is an impressive list, including Carlyle, Macaulay, Thackeray, Dickens, Hood, Bulwer-Lytton, Froude, Ruskin, George Eliot, Bagehot, Henley, and Stevenson, along with Poe, Lowell, and Tuckerman in America—we soon learn, from the very range and diversity of that influence, what its common denominator was. Unlike Wordsworth and Coleridge, Hazlitt was not read, at least after mid-century, for his theoretic ideas—which, except in America, were largely discounted as suspect (insofar as they were uniquely his, not those shared with other leading Romanticists) because of his unsavory politics. Hazlitt was admired for the unrivalled energy of his prose, or more exactly, for certain attitudes believed to inhere in his style; for the style itself was too dangerously explosive, had too much "unhealthy heat," to suit Victorian taste. Yet this is not to say that the Victorians admired him only as an essayist, not as a critic; on the contrary, there was frequent and emphatic praise for his powers of judgment. Gilfillan spoke of his "unrivalled *critical* genius," and Thackeray called him "one of the keenest and brightest critics that ever lived."[12] The partisan "Jacobin" who could nevertheless honor and even champion the genius of Burke, Wordsworth, and Scott— this was the Hazlitt the Victorians were especially drawn to; for such judgments answered their need to believe in a literary, and ulti- mately a moral, continuity in culture above the reach of politics and social conflict. Hazlitt provided "the Victorian compromise"[13] with an image of itself which it could find nowhere else; here it could see itself as a pure integrity of sensibility or conscience free of class or ideological pride, expressing a sureness of judgment in a style that seemed anything but compromising in its self-reliance, its sinewy forthrightness, its thoroughly English delight in native resources of feeling. Augustine Birrell, writing just after the turn of the century (1902), testifies unequivocally to Hazlitt's pervasive influence on the literary education of almost every Victorian, early or late: "These lectures of Hazlitt's must have had many students. . . . He has man- aged to imbed . . . his ideas and opinions about the English poets into the clay of our compositions. Today all ordinary, well-read, sen- sible people . . . entertain as their own the lecturer's opinions about Chaucer and Spenser, Gray and Collins, Swift and Goldsmith."[14]

One great name, however, is noticeably missing from this list of Victorian tributaries to Hazlitt's genius. I have suggested more than once that Arnold is the nineteenth-century critic with whom Hazlitt, in his sense of the moral centrality of literature in society, has most in common, but Arnold makes not a single reference to Hazlitt by name.[15] All that we can infer with reasonable certainty of Arnold's opinion is that Hazlitt, too, stands indicted, in a famous essay, with his Romantic contemporaries for failing to "establish an order of ideas" to sustain their "premature" effort in poetry—such a "move- ment of mind" as only "a great critical effort," at once the anteced- ent condition and the accompaniment to great creativity, could have accomplished. "The Function of Criticism at the Present Time" marks a pivotal moment in nineteenth-century criticism, and not only the ways of Hazlitt and his generation in criticism (Coleridge perhaps excepted) are here being challenged and left behind as inadequate. Here the critic is no longer conceived as mediating a relationship between writer and reader that inheres in the nature of a given genre or work; rather the "function" of the critic is seen now as deriving from an authority that inheres less in literary power than in the intellectual ministry of criticism itself, that is, in the power of "ideas," in the quasi-religious authority of "culture" and its "study of perfection." And so successful and self-perpetuating has the Arnoldean revision been, at least in academic circles, that it has all but obliterated, long after its own faith in "culture" has waned, awareness of the possibility of any other basis than "knowledge" and "ideas" for the authority of critical judgment. Arnold's denigration of "the personal estimate" in criticism would insure the decline thereafter of such reputations as Hazlitt's,[16] and prepared the way for reclassification of his work as "impressionism," notwithstanding the fact that Walter Pater, continuing Arnold's silence, acknowledges no such affinity with Hazlitt (although he did with other Romanticists). The categorical likeness of two such alien temperaments in criticism has been wholly the invention of subsequent scholarship.

The nineteenth-century continuity is there, of course, and Northrop Frye has introduced a term that helps us to rediscover what it is. "Public criticism": this is Frye's broad and simple but indispensable term for the kind of criticism (the genus, not the mutational species) practiced by both Hazlitt and Arnold, and indeed by most nineteenth-century critics. I am less than happy, though, with Frye's rather arbitrary definition: he invidiously contrasts public criticism with "real" or "genuine" criticism, that which addresses itself to the study of "the whole of literature" as an "impersonal body of knowledge," rather than discriminating works of literature, in the manner of Hazlitt or Arnold, by comparative judgments of value. Frye does not minimize the importance of the public critic, whose "task" is "to exemplify how a man of taste uses and evaluates literature, and thus show how literature is to be absorbed into society." But Frye argues that this exercise of taste is always historically determined; its "rhetorical value-judgments" reflect an "imposed critical attitude," motivated not by the cumulative knowledge of literature but by the fashions and prejudices of the age; and he wittily likens the history of taste to an "imaginary stock-exchange" where literary reputations soar and crash crazily from one school, period, or critic to another. But it may be doubted whether the reputations he selects (of Donne, Milton, Shelley) are really typical.[17] We need only pass in mental review the names of almost all the other admired poets in English literature to be struck in each case by how little change there has been in our opinion of their degree of eminence, despite the many upheavals in taste over the past seventy years. And to what do we owe this constancy of eminence? To the influence of criticism— not as the changing expression of taste, but as a counterweight in culture to the variability of taste. Our standard valuations of the English classics today may be fairly described as the progressive balancing-out of the judgments, each correcting the other's errors or excesses, of the five most persistently influential critics—Dryden, Johnson, Coleridge, Hazlitt, and Arnold. And of these five, it is Hazlitt whose reputation has suffered most from our unwillingness to confess that our learned taste has been drawing unawares upon an inherited capital of critical wisdom. Without impugning the greatness of *Biographia Literaria,* we ought to remind ourselves that it was Hazlitt, not Coleridge, who actually got around to the urgent business of a public and comprehensive revaluation of the national achievement in literature. Indeed, it is high time we acknowledged that Hazlitt, by academic legend the most "personal" and emotionally biassed of critics,[18] stands unrivalled as the English critic with the best (that is, most consistently confirmed) record of judgment; with very few exceptions, his estimates of the writers of the English past and even, as Wellek points out (2.209), of his contemporaries—which is saying a lot—are still ours or once again are becoming ours.

Yet the fact that his criticism meets the surest test of time evidently holds little or no interest for us. And that this should be so suggests to me the rather terrible irony that today the word "criticism" is ceasing to mean judgment at all. Today we "interpret" a writer, we look for "structure" and "conventions" in his work, we "place" him in a "tradition," and we may wish to decide whether he is or is not "important for our time"—but all this judiciousness is not really judgment; for it is never a praise that is also willing, as Hazlitt's or Johnson's was, to damn. We no longer conceive of literature as inviting a judgment on its values, especially our fashionable values of "irony" and "paradox"; indeed, I suspect that all our celebration of the "autonomy" of the work of art means no more than that, an exemption from criticism in the old sense—from a public estimate of the writer's character. If Hazlitt can still "exasperate" us today (e.g., Baker, p. vii), it is, I believe, because he reminds us that criticism, no matter how systematic its methods of analysis may become, can never escape the risk of a personal judgment of another's mind in its personality. Ignore or deride him how we will, our memory of Hazlitt will always be there reminding us that literature and criticism, whatever else they may be, end in the act of reading, in a dialogue that ensues between a self that has actually written and a self that actually reads; and he reminds us that these selves have brought themselves to write and read in order to know and judge, not "art" or "reality" or "the modern self," but themselves.

Our greater knowledge of the sources and resources of literature has not altered a condition that inheres in the very nature of the printed word: all that has necessarily changed is our way of mediating the relationship of personality to literature, not the existence or the urgent force of that relationship, which requires at some point the express recognition of self-consciousness. The perennial problem of criticism since the Renaissance—since culture ceased to be the property of a uniformly educated Christian aristocracy—has not been the problem of disentangling the authority of criticsm from the arbitrary authority of fashion, but the problem of exercising and communicating judgment in a world without an established communal authority of any kind to which the critic may make appeal. Yet the waning of that authority did not necessarily divide judgment, as Frye assumes, into incommunicably "private" motives and socially conditioned attitudes;[19] on the contrary, the critical intelligence was thereby enabled to recognize more clearly than ever before—although at first only in practice, not in theory— that judgments of "character" are inescapable, and that this mode of judgment must inform and guide all other valuations.

The fundamental continuity of English criticism from Dryden

through Pope, Addison and Johnson to Hazlitt may be said to consist in the simple fact that these critics were all essayists, whether in prose or verse; they brought to their judgments, as distinct from their various theorizing about poetics, the same concern for the empirical study of character, and the same love for comparisons and contrasts of character, which defines the eighteenth-century growth of the novel and the familiar essay on manners. It is only with the Victorian critics, and most obviously with Arnold, that the comparative judgment of character ceases to be an end in itself, the practical exercise of reason in understanding "nature," and becomes programmatically directed to the establishment of authoritative standards for the moral and aesthetic (as distinct from cognitive-descriptive) judgment of character, that is, to ideal norms of "nobility" and the "perfection" of "the best self." Only at this time does critical prose consistently cultivate hortatory modes of style and become predominantly a "rhetoric," as the critic's sense of purpose becomes consciously divorced—although by no means always in his practice (we remember Arnold's parodic reiterations: "Wragg is in custody")—from the comic-satiric attitudes hitherto acquired from apprenticeship to his prose instrument. Even Arnold's dubious analogy of literature with religion might have suggested to him a function of criticism that he was almost wholly forgetting—a function whose medieval counterpart was performed by the priest not at the altar of belief but in the parish confessional. If the modern critic is to be the effective guardian of transcendence, of "the best that has been thought and said in the world," then surely he must first be the guarantor of moral and intellectual honesty. It may seem absurd to think of a critic introducing himself as father-confessor to his fellow intellectuals, but the analogy nevertheless suggests the ultimate irony, on the existential level, of every act of modern intellectual judgment, insofar as the object of judgment involves not merely an idea and a medium but a personality. Without apostolic sanction or benefit of clergy, the "public critic" launches his enterprise by an act of necessary arrogance which it is the art of his office to vindicate by the persuasiveness of his judgments and, more importantly, by making the reader a willing accomplice in his presumption.

Hazlitt enters criticism at a time when a new relationship with the reader was called for, when the last illusion of a privileged public authority in criticism—the throne of Right Reason occupied by Doctor Johnson—had crumbled away; but Hazlitt's response to this situation is again not to be confused with Coleridge's attempt (ancestor of Arnold's) to reconstitute the lost authority of critical judgment as an inward spiritual authority, as the law of an ideal harmony among the faculties of the self. Hazlitt is the only nineteenth-century English critic with a finally ironic awareness of man; and perhaps it is this dialectical awareness of conflicting but interdependent modes of value and power which has always made, and still makes, his style freshly readable; for it implicates the reader in the act of criticism more intimately than ever before, by that process of "tension with otherness," as I have called it, which was always latent in his prose and which came to full fruition in the personal essays. Hazlitt's "familiar" manner in criticism represents the recognition that, in a culture no longer grounded in universal authority, not merely the pretension of a theory to truth and the pretender to creative originality must be brought to trial in criticism but the reader's degree of responsiveness to original power as the communication of value. The critic, as Hazlitt exercises the office, must write with solicitude for values present in the reader's response though not in the object; but being also the representative of the creative mind, the critic must elicit these "associations" of the reader only to define the novelty of the work through them and against them, always at the same time acknowledging by his candid confession of feeling the implicit right of the reader to decide whether the judgment being delivered might not be dictated by some latent prejudice of the critic's own. What has been taken for Hazlitt's dissolution of methodically descriptive judgment into a "personal" or impressionistic response is therefore really a transaction in which every individual concerned—artist, reader, and not least the critic himself—is being judged even as each passes tacit or explicit judgment on the other's limitations.

Stylistically, Hazlitt's manner is an innovation; but is it really so very different in principle from the way the best English criticism, at least since Dryden, has always been written? When we read the great critics of the past, what makes us listen to their voices is not the art of their rhetoric—for to the degree that their manner of persuasion is rhetorical we may measure, as in Carlyle or Macaulay, the imperfectness of the criticism—but the forthrightness and fullness of conviction with which they present their judgments, so that the reader is given the wherewithal to form a judgment of the critic himself as a mind and temperament, if not (and this further dimension may be the true novelty of the Romantic critics, even of Coleridge) as a person. Hazlitt may be wrong about Donne, as Johnson is about *Lycidas* or as Arnold is about Pope, but *we* are never mistaken about their mistaken responses; we are always able to detect where the error lies, for an honest transaction between a distinct self and the distinct otherness of the work, as defined by that self, is going forward. And as we find ourselves responding to this rare experience of a genuine duality of otherness in relation to ourselves, we discover the pleasure, and the possibility of greater knowledge of our own attitudes, which the reading of great criticism—and perhaps only great non-contemporary criticism—can provide.

Now it might be said that we demand something more from great criticism; we want something to take away from the experience, to "use"; we crave "ideas." What we are really asking for is, I suspect, some reassurance about the continuing importance of what we are doing: some positive enlargement, such as Arnold demanded, of the idea of Criticism itself. I have tried to suggest throughout this study that Hazlitt does contribute positively to the intellectual capital of modern criticism, not merely in the idiom of his own time but in larger modern terms: his theme of sympathetic imagination amounts to the reconceiving of art and literature, and to some degree of all intellectual consciousness, as modes of *intersubjectivity,* continually modifying—and with the potential therefore of critically controlling or directing—the effective force of all "power" in the world, insofar as power requires the participation of human minds to realize its effect. And it is time now to recognize that not only Hazlitt's combative temperament but his very commitment to this idea compels him to adopt an adversary attitude toward other ideas of criticism in his time that were challenging—whether or not intending to do so—the primal values of passional sympathy in literature and in the mind itself. Hazlitt's later treatment of Coleridge's ideas has always exasperated scholars: in 1816, for instance, when

Coleridge was about to publish his *Lay Sermon,* Hazlitt "reviewed" the book before it even appeared, for the good reason, he said, that he saw no difference between this author's "published and unpublished compositions," since both were "immaculate conceptions," having nothing to do with any reality beyond Coleridge's own "voluntary self-delusion" (7.115, 123). Baker, like others before him, finds "malignity" and "vulgarity" in this attack (pp. 355–56); but within the limits and conventions of the neo-Theophrastan "character," which was still the principal English tradition in prose satire, is there a better way of suggesting what went wrong with Coleridge's mind—or, for that matter, with all of Idealist philosophy after Kant? No, it is not any blindness in Hazlitt—far from it—that so many intellectuals (and especially liberal intellectuals) have found offensive; it is rather his attack on the idea of an abstract purity: his refusal throughout his work to regard ideas, any ideas, whatever their moral tone or political color, as having their source or end in themselves, as free from personal bias, will, and circumstance.

Today we are ready enough to assent to this truth in principle— it is a staple of our ironic knowingness about human motives—but we curiously divorce this awareness from our habits in literary criticism, which is more reluctant than ever to confess, much less revive, its ancient affinity with comedy and satire. That sense of the "comic frame of motives" which, if Kenneth Burke is right,[20] is germane to all perceptive criticism has all but vanished from our critical prose, where it survives only in frills of wit to decorate or relieve the heaviness of analytical hermeneutics. Our comic sense today is gloomily bound to our sense of irony, to our love of detecting ambivalences and ambiguities; and this irony seldom modulates out of abstraction because it has lost the comic awareness of, and love for, the "character" of minds—which is really to say that the critical intellect in our time has lost the ability to discern and confess, let alone enjoy, its own inordinate vanities, the willingness, as Hazlitt once stated the principle, to "pay [one's] share of the public tax upon character" (17.230). This is not to suggest that literary culture can afford to do without the methodical semantic analysis and conceptual precision that Coleridge introduced to criticism; but it is to suggest that his tradition in criticism and Hazlitt's "character" criticism need again to be brought into mutually corrective balance. We shall never lack for critics who are able to deal with literary and aesthetic ideas on their own terms, for that entails no sacrifice but the patience to school a talent; but there may always be a shortage of critics like Hazlitt who are willing to risk exposure of their own characters, in order to penetrate to the peculiar vanity of "intellectual power," and the defensive resistance to all other power, that lurks beneath the abstract lineaments of logic and language.

※※※

Once we recognize that Hazlitt's gift for criticism is, in its combination of powers, of a special kind—that, unlike his four great compeers, he brings to criticism the intelligence of the novelist rather than, to borrow his own idiom, the more "ideal" bias of a poet—we should also be prepared to recognize that he may be a great critic precisely because he lacks those qualities which we have learned to associate with greatness in literature. Certainly, for all his range and versatility, Hazlitt wants the largeness of soul, the immunity from meanness, the magnanimity of passion or vision which constitute the classical—I had almost said, the Goethean—hallmarks of literary greatness. But it is no less true that Hazlitt lacks, or surrendered at an early age, the ambitious will to greatness, and this want of ego idealism may be, to recall one of his more important principles of character, his "negative merit" as a critic. Hazlitt had the love of power as intellectual "excitement" (20.44), but not the will to power as authority; as he himself acknowledged, "I have little ambition 'to set a throne or chair of state in the understandings of other men' " (8.6–7). "No really great man," he firmly believed, "ever thought himself so" (12.117): but regardless of whether this is true, it was the condition of Hazlitt's potential for greatness that *he* could not for a moment think of himself as great—that he had to live, think, and write as a "plain man" (17.312) who could lay claim to only one transcendent superiority, the ability to discern and admire greatness, or approaches to greatness, in others. And it may, in fact, be the very absence in his judgments of the will to power as authority—so strong a motive in Johnson, in Coleridge, in Arnold—which endows his criticism, in its entirety, with something like that seminal power of an implicit "idea" which was his own standard of greatness (8.84). For the most original and lasting value of his work in its entirety lies, I believe, in its unprecedented vision of the psychology of modern equality—of the tension of self with otherness in all experience of "power," or of value as power. For many of us the vivid suppleness of movement, the enduring freshness of his style, as—to borrow words of admiration that he himself applied to Burke's prose—it "rises with the lofty, descends with the mean, luxuriates in beauty, gloats over deformity" (12.10) will seem sufficient justification for the freedom of his "gusto" from even the inward authority of an ideal of Love.

"Life is indeed a strange gift, and its privileges are most miraculous" (17.191). Loveless Hazlitt may have been, but the truth is, I suspect, that few human beings have ever enjoyed more, or more intensely, the "privileges" of human sentience than he did. Is it really his dying statement, or is it not rather something in ourselves that we doubt, in our readiness to assume that a life like his of militant judgment must finally pay an ironic price for its proud will to freedom—must end by turning in upon itself in lonely anguish or embittered resentment? What we forget is that a life of protesting and opposing power in the world may also be a life of celebrating, renewing, and imparting power—that whatever "has power over the human mind" may indomitably awaken, even be itself convertible into, the pleasure and power of the mind's own life. Hazlitt's fellow Shakespearean, Keats, had no trouble understanding this paradox of impulse in the critic he called "your only good damner." After copying out in a letter a long extract from one of Hazlitt's most virulent invectives (*A Letter to William Gifford*, 1819: 9.33 ff.), Keats calls delighted attention to "the sort of feu de joie" that Hazlitt's style "keeps up."[21] And indeed the life of Hazlitt's style *is* a celebrant joy: it is life often angry at itself, at times hating itself for abuse of its powers, yet often, and in the same breath, amused at its "consistency in absurdity" (6.11)—never contemning, never losing graphically sentient touch with its dramatic variety and its greatest "privileges" of impassioned desire and sympathetically responsive consciousness. Even at his most priggishly nasty and defensive, Hazlitt never lost his painter's sense of the givenness of life as a *givingness* (see 8.8–10);

374

and perhaps it was this sense of life's largesse which enabled his love of life to include at last the contrarieties of power in his own contrarious character.

"Well, I've had a happy life." Not long before his death, he had written: "The last pleasure in life is the sense of discharging our duty" (12.310). Was this last pleasure, then, another loyal performance of his duty to the past? But if so, it was also William Hazlitt's last act of criticism, and was no less honest, no less characteristic than its ampler predecessors, which remain its best explanation.

Concise Chronology of Hazlitt's Life

1778	Born April 10 in Maidstone, Kent, son of a Dissenting (Presbyterian) minister, William Hazlitt (1737–1820).
1783–87	With his family in America (mainly in New York, Philadelphia, Boston, and vicinity); his father's zeal for Unitarianism, conflicting with Calvinist orthodoxy, compels, after three years, return to England.
1787–93	Grows up in village of Wem, Shropshire; educated by father.
1793–94	A subsidized student for the ministry at the Unitarian New College at Hackney, near London. Revolutionary fervor at its height; Godwin's *Enquiry concerning Political Justice* (1793) especially influential.
1794–97	Probably in his sixteenth year (perhaps at Hackney) makes "metaphysical discovery" of sympathetic imagination, the mind's "natural disinterestedness" (unselfishness); withdrawal in 1795 from Hackney College, abandoning ministerial career; returns to Wem, tries unsuccessfully to write philosophical essay.
1798	"First acquaintance" with Coleridge, Wordsworth, and *Lyrical Ballads*.
1799–1801	At Orleans Collection in London (winter 1798–99), sees for first time original paintings by Italian Renaissance masters; visits country-house collections of art; begins,

377

under his brother John's instruction, apprenticeship to portrait painting.

1802–03   Portrait painting in Manchester and Liverpool; his portrait of his father accepted for Royal Academy exhibition, 1802; in Paris (October 1802 to February 1803) during the Peace of Amiens, studying and copying paintings in *Musée Napoleon* (the Louvre).

1803   Meets Charles Lamb (March). An itinerant portrait painter, he visits, in summer and early fall, Wordsworth and Coleridge in the Lakes; sojourn ends in perhaps traumatic episode (flees a village mob after spanking a girl who spurned his advances).

1804–08   Residing mainly in London; period of greatest intimacy with Lamb; increasingly despairs of success in painting. "Metaphysical discovery" appears in *An Essay on the Principles of Human Action* (1805). Begins compiling, editing various works for publishers (see *infra*, Contents of Volumes in the Centenary Edition, Vols 1–3); collects anti-Malthusian articles in *Reply to the Essay on Population* (1807).

1808–12   Marriage to Sarah Stoddart, May 1, 1808; living in Sarah's cottage at Winterslow, near Salisbury, with frequent periods in London; only surviving son (William) born (1809).

1812   Lectures on English Philosophy, delivered (January–April) in London. In October hired as Parliamentary reporter for the Whig *Morning Chronicle*.

1813–14   First journalistic successes: reviews of art and theater for the *Chronicle;* champions Edmund Kean's acting. Probable author of satiric verses in the *Chronicle* (April 1813) on Wordsworth's appointment as Stamp-Distributor. Discharged from the *Chronicle,* mainly for political reasons, begins writing (in early 1814) essays and criticism for two weeklies, John Scott's *Champion* and John and Leigh Hunt's *Examiner*.

1815–16   Mounting celebrity, both as critic and political satirist; contributes to *Edinburgh Review*. After grief over Waterloo and the Settlement of Vienna, intensifies attack on political "apostasy" of the Lake Poets.

378

1817   *The Round Table* (familiar essays, criticism); *Characters of Shakespear's Plays.*

1818   *Lectures on the English Poets; A View of the English Stage.* Height of his influence on Keats. *Blackwood's* includes Hazlitt (July–August) in attack on "Cockney School."

1819   *Lectures on the English Comic Writers;* collects his political journalism in *Political Essays;* answers his Tory attackers in *A Reply to 'Z'* and *A Letter to William Gifford, Esq.*

1820   *Lectures on the Dramatic Literature of the Age of Elizabeth* (delivered in previous autumn). Contributes "table-talks," essays in more personal, expansive, Montaignian style, to *London Magazine.* Death of his father (July). Living, since sometime in 1819, apart from his wife; infatuated at first sight (August) with Sarah Walker, daughter (in her late teens) of his lodging-house keeper in London.

1821   *Table-Talk* (vol. 2, 1822; second edn., 1824; Paris edn., 1825).

1822   Journeys twice to Scotland (Edinburgh) to obtain divorce (granted, July); despairs of Sarah Walker when he returns to find her still indifferent, involved with other lodgers.

1823   *Characteristics* (aphorisms); *Liber Amoris,* anonymous, imaginatively modified narrative of the Sarah Walker affair.

1824–25   *Sketches of the Principal Picture-Galleries in England* (1824); *The Spirit of the Age* (appearing late 1824, dated 1825; Paris and second English edns., 1825). European tour (begun September 1824), accompanied by his second wife, Isabella Bridgwater (married April 1824). Friendship with Stendhal in Paris; returns in October 1825.

1826–29   *Notes of a Journey through France and Italy* (1826); *The Plain Speaker* (1826), more "conversational" essays. Two more visits to Paris for research toward *The Life of Napoleon Buonaparte* (4 vols., 1828–30). Separation from Isabella in 1827; financially hard-pressed; declining health, increasing isolation.

1830   *Conversations of James Northcote.* Lives to see the restored Bourbons deposed in the July Revolution. Dies in lodgings in Soho, London, September 18.

Contents of Volumes in the Centenary Edition

(See *ante,* Short Forms of Titles. The arrangement of the edition is, through the first fifteen volumes, broadly chronological; cf. my Concise Chronology.)

CONTENTS OF THE CENTENARY EDITION

Notes

1. PURITAN FATHERS, UNITARIAN SONS

1. "William Hazlitt," in *Hours in a Library*, 2d ed. (London, 1899), 2.84; Cecil, "Hazlitt's Occasional Essays," in *The Fine Art of Reading* (Indianapolis: Bobbs-Merrill, 1957), pp. 247–48.

2. For various statements, variously qualified, on Hazlitt's presumed lack of development see Albrecht, p. 27; Baker, pp. 142, 147; Wardle, pp. 24, 85; Park, p. 96 (who, however, sees Hazlitt reaching stable "maturity" as a critic by 1812). On "the sympathetic imagination" see Bate, *Criticism*, p. 283. It is well to remember that, although this phrase accurately reflects Hazlitt's idea, the phrase itself (as distinct from its root terms) is ours, not his.

3. Letters quoted in Howe, pp. 31–35.

4. Qu. in H. McLachlan, *The Unitarian Movement in the Religious Life of England* (London: Allen and Unwin, 1934), 1.285.

5. See W. Carew Hazlitt, *The Hazlitts: An Account of their Origin and Descent* (Edinburgh: Ballantyne, Hanson, 1911), pp. 16, 509; also his *Memoirs of William Hazlitt* (London, 1867), 1.269.

6. See Baker, pp. 21–22, and Maclean, pp. 34–36, 41–42.

7. *Collected Letters*, ed. E. L. Griggs, 2 (London: Oxford University Press, 1956), 990.

8. For the somewhat confused facts, and for a similar view of them as suggesting "adolescent rebellion," see Wardle, pp. 38–39.

9. See Moyne, p. 32; Howe, p. 28.

10. Raymond V. Holt, *The Unitarian Contribution to Social Progress in England*, 2d ed. (London: Lindsey Press, 1952), p. 305. The account that follows of the evolution of English Presbyterianism in indebted to Holt, pp. 283–316; Olive M. Griffiths, *Religion and Learning: A Study in English Presbyterian Thought* (Cambridge: Cambridge University Press, 1935), pp. 1–53; Anthony Lincoln, *Some Political and Social Ideas of English Dissent, 1763–1800* (Cambridge: Cambridge University Press, 1938), pp. 80–96; H. McLachlan, *English Education under the Test Acts* (Manchester: Manchester University

Press, 1931), pp. 1–40 et passim; J. Estlin Carpenter, *Unitarianism: An Historic Survey* (London: Lindsey Press, 1922); and Earl Morse Wilbur, *Our Unitarian Heritage* (Boston: Beacon Press, 1925), pp. 316–38.

11. *A Thanksgiving Discourse Preached at Hallowell [Maine] 15 December 1785* (Boston, 1786), p. 16.

12. Jerom Murch, *A History of the Presbyterian and General Baptist Churches in the West of England* (London, 1835), p. x.

13. *Sermons for the Use of Families* (London, 1808), 1.285.

14. Neal, *The History of the Puritans* (New York, 1843), 2.293, 318, 343, et passim. See also Edmund Calamy, *The Nonconformist's Memorial*, 2d ed. (London, 1778), pp. 37 ff. The idea that "truth" is "one and entire" yet is revealed only progressively to the finite understanding of individuals and generations was a staple of Puritan doctrine, and seems to have originated with the first Socinians in England: see William Haller, *The Rise of Puritanism* (New York: Columbia University Press, 1938), pp. 97–99. Clarke Garrett, in *Respectable Folly: Millenarians and the French Revolution in France and England* (Baltimore: Johns Hopkins University Press, 1975), offers further evidence that belief in the Apocalypse of the Book of Revelation was still, or became again, common doctrine among professedly "rational" Dissenters (pp. 121 ff.). Some idea of the Apocalyptic connotations that the word "truth" would always hold for Hazlitt is conveyed by the prediction of a Unitarian reformer in 1789 that England's corrupt institutions would "melt like snow before the sun of truth" (Garrett, p. 165).

15. *Sermons*, 2.126.

16. G. P. Hinton, "The Reverend William Hazlitt," *The Monthly Repository*, 15 (November 1820), 677.

17. Anon., "Joseph Hunter on the Hazlitts," *Notes and Queries*, 4 (June 1957), 266.

18. Moyne, pp. 4–5, 41–43, 127, 148 (". . . fine preacher").

19. Letter, Hazlitt to MacVey Napier, July 21, 1829, British Museum Additional MS. 34611, f. 128.

20. Moyne, pp. 9–13, 51, 81–82.

21. *Sermons*, 1.27–60, 157; "An Explanation of 1 Peter iii.19, 20," *Theological Repository*, 3d ed. (London, 1795), 2.444–49. For the identification of this and other contributions (see below) by the elder Hazlitt to the *Theological Repository* see Francis E. Mineka, *The Dissidence of Dissent* (Chapel Hill: University of North Carolina Press, 1944), p. 40; J. T. Rutt, *Life and Correspondence of Joseph Priestley* (London, 1831), 1.159, 174; and Wardle, p. 5, n. 3. See also Basil Willey, *The Seventeenth Century Background* (Garden City, N.Y.: Doubleday, 1953), pp. 139–43 (on "candle," etc.).

22. "An Answer to Bereanus on the Pre-existence of Christ," *Theo. Repos.*, 2.433–36 (on grace); "An Explanation . . . ," pp. 443–49 (on ancients); *Sermons*, 1.59, 114, 156, 261, and 2.92; *Discourses for the Use of Families on the Advantages of a Free Enquiry and on the Study of the Scriptures* (London, 1790), pp. 10, 22, 52, 37–38, 70, 120, 153; "Some Thoughts on Praying in the Name of Christ," *Theo. Repos.*, 2.167–68.

23. "An Answer . . . ," pp. 433–36 (on "pre-existence"); *Discourses*, p. 37; *Sermons*, 1.270 (". . . disinterested").

24. "An Explanation . . . ," p. 449; see also *Discourses,* p. 190.

25. *Discourses,* p. 102; *Sermons,* 1.77, 2.23; Joseph Priestley, *An Essay on the First Principles of Government,* 2d ed. (London, 1771), p. 116; and for William Paley's theological utilitarianism, see Leslie Stephen, *History of English Thought in the Eighteenth Century,* 3d ed. (New York: Putnam, 1902), 2.121–25.

26. *Discourses,* pp. 17–18, 29, 39; *Sermons,* 2.232 ("not to . . ."); Cf. *Institutes* 7.4–5 in Calvin, *On the Christian Faith,* ed. J. T. McNeill (New York; Bobbs-Merrill, 1957), pp. 22–26.

27. *Discourses,* pp. 39–40 ("endeavour . . ."), 121, 136–37, 157.

28. "Appendix," *Discourses,* n. p. ("Infidelity . . ."); *Sermons,* 2.9. The son, in historically general terms, recognized the irony: "The Dissenters, in carrying their point against the Church of England, did not dream of that crop of infidelity and scepticism which, to their great horror and scandal, sprung up in the following age, from their claim of free inquiry and private judgment" (20.311).

29. Hazlitt recalls these events and the political atmosphere of the time in 3.141–42; 8.152; 13.122–68.

30. *PJ,* 1.81–83; 2.114–211 passim, 283 ff., 431 ff., 498–509. Coleridge, *Complete Poetical Works,* ed. E. H. Coleridge (Oxford: Oxford University Press, 1912), 1.86 and n.

31. See Baker, pp. 23–26.

32. See Ben Ross Schneider, *Wordsworth's Cambridge Education* (Cambridge: Cambridge University Press, 1957), pp. 222–24. The intimate relationship, which I assume in the account that follows, of the young Hazlitt's thought with Godwin's has never been sufficiently recognized. A letter to his father from London in 1796, after Hazlitt's "discovery" of disinterestedness, speaks of his theory as founding "the propriety of virtue on its coincidence with the pursuit of private interest" (Howe, p. 45); and this language seems to echo *PJ,* 2.79 ("coincidence of virtue . . . with private interest"). But perhaps the strongest evidence comes from the entry in Godwin's diary (in the Abinger Collection, Duke University, quoted here by permission of Professor Lewis Patton) for May 18, 1802: "Hazlitt calls (reads)." If he was reading to his friend from the MS that became *An Essay on the Principles of Human Action* (1805), the only work that Hazlitt is known to have been writing at the time, then perhaps a young metaphysician was enjoying the satisfaction of submitting his ideas to the philosopher who had first inspired his faith in "disinterestedness."

33. For the relative philosophical positions see, among other accounts, L. A. Selby-Bigge's introduction to *British Moralists* (Oxford, 1897), l.xi–lx; Stephen, *History* (see n. 25 above), 2.33–55; and Hazlitt's own comments in 1.2–7.

34. *Émile,* Everyman ed. (London: J. M. Dent, 1950), esp. pp. 180–84, 249; 1.17, 26, 70–72. For other influences see Leonard M. Trawick, III, "Sources of Hazlitt's 'Metaphysical Discovery'," *Philological Quarterly,* 42 (April 1963), 277–82, which strangely ignores Rousseau.

35. *Émile,* pp. 228–78, esp. p. 276 ("Without faith . . ."); and for Hazlitt's admiration of the Vicar and his thought see 2.157 and Jacques Voisine,

J.-J. Rousseau en Angleterre a l'époque romantique (Paris: Didier, 1956), pp. 347 ff, and 118–27 (on the vogue of Rousseau in the Revolutionary decade).

36. *Système de la Nature* (London, 1770), pp. 301–04. Just when and where Hazlitt made his "discovery" is a matter of some doubt. I follow Maclean, p. 83, and Hazlitt's own suggestion, quoted earlier, about the intellectual importance of his sixteenth year (17.22–23), in locating the "discovery" at some point in his second and last year at Hackney College, perhaps sometime in the early months of 1795. Howe (p. 44) and Baker (p. 28) are less decisive, and Wardle seems to assume that the discovery occurs in 1796, after the departure from the college (pp. 46–47). But whether coming before or after his decision to give up a ministerial career, the "discovery" would have served Hazlitt well as self-vindication (whether or not consciously intended as such)—a motive which his biographers have been curiously loath to recognize, in view of Hazlitt's own emphasis on the sense of liberation that followed his "discovery": "From that time I felt a certain weight and tightness about my heart taken off, and cheerful and confident thoughts springing up in the place of anxious fears and sad forebodings" (9.58). And we should note also the strong sense of quasi-religious, Godwinian commitment: "I owed something to truth, for she had done something for me. . . . I had laid my hand on the ark, and could not turn back!" (9.51).

37. Hazlitt would have been aware of Priestley's idea that personal identity is reconstituted in eternity by a recomposition of the "corporeal soul" after the body has been decomposed in death. Hazlitt had read widely in Priestley (see 1.62; 20.337) and perhaps heard him lecture on Natural Philosophy at Hackney before Priestley's departure for America in April 1794: see Anne Holt, *A Life of Joseph Priestley* (Oxford: Oxford University Press, 1931), p. 175, and pp. 117 ff. (for a review of Priestley's ideas of identity and immortality). On Hartley, Priestley, and "natural theology" see Basil Willey, *The Eighteenth Century Background* (Boston: Beacon Press, 1961), pp. 136–54, 168–204.

38. "William Hazlitt," in *The Common Reader, First and Second Series* (New York: Harcourt, Brace, 1948), pp. 177–78. To note the difference from my own account that follows: the "thinker" in her view of Hazlitt is the "inquiring boy," while the "artist" is "the sensuous and emotional man" (p. 178).

39. Some precedent for this contrast and its terms comes from Elisabeth Schneider, who—in "William Hazlitt," *The English Romantic Poets and Essayists: A Review of Research and Criticism,* 2d ed., ed. C. W. and L. H. Houtchens (New York: Modern Language Association, 1966), p. 85—detects a "paranoid and almost priggish strain in Hazlitt," following a suggestion that she finds in Maclean's comments (perhaps esp. pp. 58–60). A view somewhat (only somewhat) closer to my own is in Kathleen Coburn, "Hazlitt on the Disinterested Imagination," in *Some British Romantics,* ed. James V. Logan, J. E. Jordan, and Northrop Frye (Columbus: Ohio State University Press, 1966), where the "creed" of "disinterestedness" is seen as becoming a "compulsion" (p. 186), a "whip for his prejudices and private conflicts" (p. 188).

40. Letter to Napier, July 21, 1829, cited above in n. 19.

41. For other instances of, or correlatives to, this process of "naturaliz-

ing" Protestant Millennarianism, see Ernest Lee Tuveson, *Millennium and Utopia* (Berkeley: University of California Press, 1949), esp. pp. 112, 130–66, and M. H. Abrams, *Natural Supernaturalism* (New York: Norton, 1971), esp. pp. 13, 66.

42. "As for Hazlitt, it is not to be believed how the destruction of Napoleon affected him; he seemed prostrate in mind and body: he walked about unwashed, unshaved, hardly sober by day, and always intoxicated by night, literally, without exaggeration, for weeks . . ." (Haydon, pp. 249–50). Haydon does exaggerate, but perhaps not without some assistance from his subject.

43. See 8.181 ff. ("On Going a Journey"), and for a clear indication from Hazlitt's own conversation (as recorded by his wife) of his frequent intimacy with "girls of the town," see *The Journals of Sarah and William Hazlitt, 1822–1831,* ed. W. H. Bonner, University of Buffalo Studies, Vol. 24, No. 3 (Buffalo, 1959), pp. 245, 247.

2. THE METAPHYSICIAN: MIND AND NATURE

1. Mead, *Movements of Thought in the Nineteenth Century* (Chicago: University of Chicago Press, 1931), pp. 17, 25–29; and see B. Sprague Allen, "The Reaction against William Godwin," *MP,* 16 (1918), 225–43.

2. See Basil Willey's account of these changes in *The Eighteenth Century Background* (Boston: Beacon Press, 1961), pp. 235–39.

3. See Bertrand Evans, *Gothic Drama from Walpole to Shelley* (Berkeley: University of California Press, 1947), pp. 86–89; Peter L. Thorslev, Jr., "Wordsworth's *Borderers* and the Romantic Villain-Hero," *SIR,* 5 (1966), 87–93; Goethe, *Autobiography,* trans. A. J. W. Morrison, 2 (London, 1849), Bk. 19.141–42; Bk. 20, 158–59; and see Roy Pascal, *The German Sturm und Drang* (Manchester: Manchester University Press, 1953), pp. 137 ff.

4. *PJ,* Bk. VIII, Chs. 8–10, in Vol. 2, 495 ff., esp. p. 506 (on resorting to "solitude" for "the purest delight"). "Our second duty is tranquillity" (p. 548).

5. Wordsworth, Preface (1800), *Pr W,* 1.126–40; "Lines left upon a seat in a Yew Tree". 55–64, "Tintern Abbey". 45–46, "Intimations" Ode. 182, in *Po W,* 1.92, 2.260, 4.279.

6. See the excerpts of reviews in Wardle, pp. 85–86.

7. See 2.288–93 (Howe's notes); and see Howe, pp. 133 ff., Baker, p. 185.

8. The legend of Hazlitt's philosophical failure, or incompetence, was perhaps first established by Augustine Birrell, *William Hazlitt* (London: Macmillan, 1902), pp. 71, 77, citing Leslie Stephen, *Hours in a Library* (London, 1899), 2.72; and Hazlitt is still being described as a "failed metaphysician" in John Gross, *The Rise and Fall of the Man of Letters* (London: Weidenfeld and Nicolson, 1969), p. 15.

9. Walter Jackson Bate, *John Keats* (New York: Oxford University Press, 1966), pp. 255 ff.; Hunt, *LC,* p. 278; De Quincey, *Collected Writings,* ed. David Masson (Edinburgh, 1889), 3.82 (on Lamb). Other testimonials cited and more of the same tenor may be found in 9.249 (n. 3, quoting Cole-

ridge); Howe, pp. 96, 145, 249; Baker, pp. 200, 236 ff., 247 ff.; and in W. C. Hazlitt, *The Hazlitts* (Edinburgh: Ballantyne, Hanson, 1911), pp. 500 ff. (Talfourd's). Ian Jack, "De Quincey Revises his *Confessions*," *PMLA*, 72 1957), 133 n., believes that the reference in the 1821 text is "undoubtedly to Hazlitt"; cf. De Quincey, *Collected Writings*, 5.230–36.

10. See 17.203 n. (on Plato), 20.18–21 (on Kant); and René Wellek, *Immanuel Kant in England, 1793–1838* (Princeton: Princeton University Press, 1931), pp. 165–67.

11. Qutoed from *The Doctor* (1834) by Howe in 7.391, n. 187.

12. For this distinction see D. H. Monro, *Godwin's Moral Philosophy* (Oxford: Clarendon Press, 1953), pp. 14 ff.

13. Moore, *Principia Ethica* (Cambridge: Cambridge University Press, 1929), pp. 7–42; Butler, Preface to *Sermons*, in *The Whole Works of Joseph Butler* (London, 1835), pp. vi ff. Hazlitt admired this work of Butler's: see 17.113.

14. See the discussion of this issue by L. A. Selby-Bigge, Introduction, *British Moralists* (Oxford, 1897), 1.xi–lx.

15. See Lewis White Beck's Introduction to his edition of Kant's *Critique of Practical Reason* (Chicago: University of Chicago Press, 1949), p. 44; and Austin Duncan-Jones, *Butler's Moral Philosophy* (London: Penguin Books, 1952), pp. 59–65.

16. See Smith, *The Theory of Moral Sentiments*, 6th ed. (London, 1790), 1.3–10. Hazlitt's difference from Smith on this point is overlooked by Roy E. Cain, "David Hume and Adam Smith as Sources of the Concept of Sympathy in Hazlitt," *Papers on Language and Literature*, 1 (1965), 133–40.

17. *The Nature of Sympathy,* trans. Peter Heath (London: Routledge and Kegan Paul, 1954), pp. 40–50, 244–53, et passim.

18. Locke, *An Essay concerning Human Understanding,* Everyman ed. (London: J. M. Dent, 1947), Bk. II, pp. 119 ff.; Spinoza, *Ethics*, Pt. III, Props. 6–9 in *Philosophy of Benedict de Spinoza,* trans. R. H. M. Elwes (New York: Tudor, n.d.).

19. Butler, Sermon XI, *Works*, pp. 104–09; and see H. D. Aikin, Introduction, *Hume's Moral and Political Philosophy* (New York: Hafner, 1948), pp. xix–xxiv.

20. For a somewhat different analysis, though one which similarly insists that Hazlitt's "discovery" makes an "original and provocative" contribution to speculation on the nature of personal identity, see James Noxon, "Hazlitt as Moral Philosopher," *Ethics*, 72 (1963), 279–83. See also my entry on Hazlitt in *The Encyclopedia of Philosophy* (New York: Macmillan, 1967), 3.428–29.

21. The six extant of the ten Lectures are (in their relative positions in the original sequence): "On the Writings of Hobbes," "On Locke's *Essay*," "On Abstract Ideas," "On Self-Love," "On Liberty and Necessity," and "On Tooke's 'Diversions of Purley'." On the missing lectures see Howe's notes, 2.292–93; much of the original Lecture VI probably survives as the essay "Mind and Motive" (20.43–53).

22. The "greatest" was Hobbes (mainly for his originality and consistency), then Berkeley, and "after them come Hume and Hartley." After

1812 Hazlitt's admiration for Hartley seems to have waned considerably, whereas he continued to admire, with "relish," Hume's *Treatise* (17.113). "Compared with these Locke was a mere common practical man" (2.180 n.).

23. Locke, *Essay*, Bk. II, p. 26; Berkeley, *Of the Principles of Human Knowledge*, in *A New Theory of Vision and Other Writings*, Everyman ed. (London: J. M. Dent, 1910), p. 100. See the well-informed discussion of Hazlitt's view of abstract ideas in Park, pp. 95–104, though I think Park drives too deep a wedge between Hazlitt and his eighteenth-century predecessors.

24. Alfred North Whitehead, *Science and the Modern World* (New York: New American Library, 1948), pp. 52 ff. (this resemblance has been pointed out by Bate in *Criticism*, p. 291); and Whitehead, *Process and Reality* (New York: Macmillan, 1936), p. 85 ("logical simplicity"). Hazlitt's critique clearly anticipates later objections to Lockean empiricism: see C. R. Morris, *Locke, Berkeley, Hume* (Oxford: Clarendon Press, 1931), pp. 72–85. Park rightly calls attention to the endorsement of Hazlitt's emphasis on "individuation" in twentieth-century theories of perception, but in doing so obscures or underestimates the importance of "generalization" in Hazlitt's view of the process of perceiving (p. 99, n. 7).

25. See 2.116–17; and Coleridge, *Philosophical Lectures*, ed. Kathleen Coburn (New York: Pilot Press, 1949), pp. 84–85.

26. Wellek, *Kant in England*, points out that the Kantian synthetic judgments *a priori* are not "notions," as Willich's bad translation would have led Hazlitt to think, but "functions of unity" (pp. 164–66).

27. Quoted and discussed by J. H. Muirhead, *Coleridge as Philosopher* (London: Allen and Unwin, 1930), p. 92. This *organic* principle, as I go on to suggest, seems to me the link between "generalization" and "abstraction," and thus between Hazlitt and Coleridge, that Park's account ignores (p. 103).

28. *An Abridgment of the Light of Nature Pursued* (London, 1807), Bk. III, pp. 73–74.

29. Berkeley, *Principles*, p. 116; James, *A Pluralistic Universe* (New York: Longmans, Green, 1947), p. 219. Hazlitt's repudiation of Kant first appears, not in the *Lectures* where he is still highly praised, but in an essay of 1814 (20.18–22), presumably after Hazlitt had made his first direct acquaintance with Kant's theory through Willich's translation.

30. See C. E. Pulos, *The Deep Truth: A Study of Shelley's Scepticism* (Lincoln: University of Nebraska Press, 1954), pp. 27–66; Donald H. Reiman, *Shelley's 'The Triumph of Life': A Critical Study*, University of Illinois Studies in Language and Literature (Urbana: University of Illinois Press, 1965), p. 5; Earl R. Wassermann, Introduction, *Shelley's Prometheus Unbound* (Baltimore: Johns Hopkins University Press, 1965), pp. 4–5, n. 3.

31. Baker has also characterized Hazlitt as "a kind of vitalist" (p. 143) but does not enlarge upon his use of the term.

32. See Hume, *A Treatise of Human Nature*, Everyman ed. (London: J. M. Dent, 1911), 1.153–72.

33. Edwards, *A Careful and Strict Enquiry into . . . Freedom of Will* (London, 1790), pp. 20–22, 281–90, qu. by Hazlitt in 2.262–66.

34. Hazlitt quotes extensively (2.246–59) from Hobbes, "On Liberty

and Necessity," *Tripos,* in *English Works,* ed. W. Molesworth, 4 (London, 1840), 272–78; from Locke, *Essay,* Bk. II, pp. 115 ff.; and alludes to a "demonstration" in Spinoza that may refer to Ethics, Pt. I, pp. 65–69, and Pt. II, pp. 118–19.

35. See H. W. Piper, *The Active Universe* (London: University of London, Athlone Press, 1962), pp. 18 ff.

36. Tucker, *Abridgment,* Bk. III, pp. 233–39. The *Monthly* letter was first identified and discussed by Geoffrey Carnall, *Times Literary Supplement,* June 19, 1953, p. 397.

3. IMAGINATION AND THE WORLDS OF POWER

1. Wardle, pp. 103–32; Howe, p. 159; Robinson, 1.57–70.

2. Élie Halévy, *The Growth of Philosophic Radicalism,* trans. Mary Morris (Boston: Beacon Press, 1955), pp. 250–55; and see Park's discussion of the decline of philosophy (pp. 9–13).

3. G. D. H. Cole, *The Life of William Cobbett,* 3d ed. (London: Home and Van Thal, 1947), pp. 90–180; Michael Roberts, *The Whig Party: 1807–1812* (London: Macmillan, 1939), pp. 149–299.

4. Preface, *Examiner,* 1 (1808), in *Prefaces by Leigh Hunt,* ed. R. Brimley Johnson (Port Washington, N.Y.: Kennikat Press, 1967), p. 37; "Buonaparte: His Present Aspect and Character" (1811), *Leigh Hunt's Political and Occasional Essays,* ed. L. H. and C. W. Houtchens (New York: Columbia University Press, 1962), pp. 128 ff. E. Tangye Lean, *The Napoleonists* (London: Oxford University Press, 1970) typically emphasizes psychological rather than intellectual motives among Buonaparte's supporters (pp. 202 ff.).

5. See the contrast with Wordsworth in Maclean, pp. 158 ff.

6. See also 7.10 ff., 8.174 ("Iron Crown"); Godwin, *Thoughts Occasioned by the Perusal of Dr. Parr's Spital Sermon* (London, 1801), where Napoleon is hailed as an "auspicious and beneficent genius" (p. 6).

7. "Beyond Good and Evil," *The Philosophy of Nietzsche,* trans. Helen Zimmern, Modern Library ed. (New York: Random House, 1927), pp. 554–57. We find Hazlitt in 1803 approving of Lamb's remark in conversation, "Give me man as he is *not* to be" (17.122).

8. Hazlitt, it is true, can be found praising "faith in the natural goodness of man" (6.165), but he means by "natural" in this context precisely a kind of goodness that cannot be effectively translated into political society. And if "goodness" is natural, so also is perversity: as early as 1807 he speaks of "the perverse nature of man" (1.198). Crane Brinton could not be more wrong when he describes Hazlitt as a believer in "the old doctrine of . . . natural goodness" who "thinks too well of his fellows": *Political Ideas of the English Romanticists* (London: Oxford University Press, 1926), p. 129.

9. "Pitt and Buonaparte," repr. from *The Morning Post* (March 19, 1800) by Hazlitt in 7.326 ff.; also in Coleridge, *Essays on His Own Times* (London, 1850), 2.319–29.

10. "Essay Supplementary to the Preface" (1815), *Pr W,* 3.82. On "power" in *The Prelude* see R. D. Havens, *The Mind of the Poet* (Baltimore: Johns Hopkins University Press, 1941), pp. 46–47, 472–73.

11. De Quincey, "The Poetry of Pope," *Collected Writings,* ed. David Masson (Edinburgh, 1889), 11.54–60, and see also "Letter to a Young Man . . . ," 10.48 ff. Perhaps the best brief general statement on the pervasive idea of "power" in this period is in Jacob Bronowski, *The Ascent of Man* (Boston: Little, Brown, 1973), pp. 280–86.

12. On eighteenth-century ideas of the love of power, see Lester G. Crocker, *An Age of Crisis: Man and World in Eighteenth Century French Thought* (Baltimore: John Hopkins University Press, 1959), pp. 282–320. Juvenal, Satire x.3.54–113, in *Juvenal and Persius,* Loeb Classical Library (London, 1918).

13. See Howe, pp. 90–149 (Coleridge quoted, pp. 91, 98); Baker, pp. 128–39, 152–81; Maclean, pp. 246 ff. In some jesting correspondence with Lamb and Joseph Hume in 1808, Hazlitt promised to "leave off wenching": Wardle, p. 106.

14. Preface (1800), *Pr W,* 1.130.

15. The conversation that Hazlitt recalls is possibly the same as that recorded in 1803, quite differently, by Coleridge, in *Notebooks,* ed. Kathleen Coburn, 1 (New York: Pantheon Books, 1957), Series 1616–1620, 1622. On Coleridge's theory see *BL,* 1.97, 202; *Philosophical Lectures,* ed. K. Coburn (New York: Pilot Press, 1949), pp. 90–92, 115, 358–64; Humphry House, *Coleridge* (London: Rupert Hart-Davis, 1953), pp. 44 ff.

16. In citing these resemblances, I do not wish to obscure the fact that Hazlitt habitually uses the word "unconscious" in its traditional, purely adjectival sense as referring to feeling or expression which is un-*self*-conscious, or not distinctly recognized by the mind. There can be no doubt, however, that Hazlitt, as Philip Rieff remarks, "anticipates many of Freud's principles": see Rieff, *Freud: The Mind of the Moralist,* 2d ed. (Garden City, N.Y.: Doubleday, 1961), pp. 149, 380.

17. *Beyond the Pleasure Principle,* trans. James Strachey (London: Hogarth Press), pp. 39–45.

18. While he acknowledges some affinity of his idea with "doctrines of original sin, grace, election, reprobation, or the Gnostic principle that acts do not determine the virtue or vice of the character," he nonetheless insists that there is a redeeming "salvo" in his return to these traditions (12.241).

19. "Art and Neurosis," *The Liberal Imagination* (New York: Viking Press, 1950), p. 178.

20. Rieff also cites this passage as "proto-Freudian" (p. 380).

21. Alfred Adler, *The Practice and Theory of Individual Psychology,* 2d ed. (London: Routledge and Kegan Paul, 1950), pp. 7–13. Nietzsche's view is far less individualistic: see Walter Kaufmann, *Nietzsche,* 2d ed. (Princeton: Princeton University Press, 1956), p. 215.

22. *A General Introduction to Psycho-analysis,* rev. ed., trans. Joan Rivière (Garden City, N.Y.: Doubleday, 1935), pp. 352–53.

23. See, for example, Schneider, *Aesthetics,* where this passage is attributed to "an erratic moment" (p. 99).

24. Advertisement on end-page of "The Queen's Matrimonial Ladder," in Hone, *Facetiae and Miscellanies,* 2d ed. (London, 1827), n. p.

25. *Examiner,* Aug. 13 and Aug. 27, 1813, pp. 514, 522.

26. "On Mr. Wordsworth's Appointment," *Morning Chronicle*, April 20, 1813, p. 3; *Examiner*, April 25, 1813, p. 265. The remaining quatrains are:

> Since poets are *but* men, 'tis said
> The question may be well disputed,
> If they can eat Corruption's bread,
> And still continue unpolluted.

> With dangerous friends, and dangerous foes,
> O whither, whither do we tend us!
> May Heaven in mercy interpose,
> And from the shafts of both defend us.

Further reasons for the attribution to Hazlitt are given in my article, "Hazlitt as Poet: The Probable Authorship of Some Anonymous Verses on Wordsworth's Appointment as Stamp-Distributor," *SIR*, 12 (1973), 426–35. Stanley Jones, who in 1968 first called attention to the poem (but without speculating on its authorship), has recently challenged my attribution and proposes Thomas Moore, who had published verses in the *Chronicle*, as a likelier candidate: see "Regency Newspaper Verse: An Anonymous Squib on Wordsworth," *Keats-Shelley Journal*, 27 (1978), 87–107. But Jones is able to offer no firm evidence that Moore at this time had sufficient acquaintance with, or interest in, Wordsworth's poetry; and I think I have demonstrated in my article that only someone with an intimate knowledge of the poetry could have written these lines, which contain a variety of Wordsworthian allusions. Nor can Jones point to a number of direct echoes of the poem in Moore's later writing, such as I have found in Hazlitt's; indeed, nearly *everything* in the poem was to find restatement—and, in some instances, with the identical vocabulary—in Hazlitt's later criticism of Wordsworth. And in order to make a case for Moore (who had hoped for a "place" from government if the Whigs came to power), Jones is compelled to interpret the poem's sardonic irony as "worldly cynicism, a glib lax flippancy" (p. 94)—and this in a poem that expressly protests the relaxation of poetic virtue!

27. Wordsworth, *Po W*: "Guilt and Sorrow" ("Female Vagrant") 1.94 ff.; "September, 1802; Near Dover" .13–14, "Ode: 1815" in 3.115, 155 n. (lines 106–09 in 1816 ed.); "Ode to Duty".1, in 4.83. Coleridge, *BL*, 1.122; *The Statesman's Manual* (1816), in *Political Tracts*, p. 27. Wordsworth's "Ode: 1815" was published in the *Champion* several months after the massacre of republicans and Buonapartists at Nîmes in the Rhone valley: see B. Bernard Cohen, "William Hazlitt: Bonapartist Critic of *The Excursion*," *MLQ*, 10 (1949), 163; and for the background of events, M. D. R. Leys, *Between Two Empires* (London: Longmans, 1955), pp. 53 ff. See also, on Wordsworth's "martial" emphasis, Carl R. Woodring, *Politics in English Romantic Poetry* (Cambridge: Harvard University Press, 1970), p. 140.

28. Southey, *Poetical Works*, 10 (London: Longman, Rees, n.d.), 141, qu. by Hazlitt in 7.91.

29. Coleridge, *A Lay Sermon* (1817), in *Political Tracts*, p. 68.

30. See William H. Wickwar, *The Struggle for the Freedom of the Press, 1819–1832* (London: Allen and Unwin, 1928), pp. 15–45, which needs modification by the less critical, more detailed account in A. Aspinall, *Politics and*

the Press, 1780–1850 (London: Home and Van Thal, 1949), esp. pp. 6–98.

31. Hazlitt insists that he wishes to "maintain the system itself," not its "corruptions and abuses" (7.196). "There is no sympathy between Kings and their subjects, except in a constitutional monarchy like ours, through the medium of Lords and Commons" (7.285). The delicate, libel-avoiding ambiguity of that last statement, however, is to be noted. See Anthony Lincoln, *Some Political and Social Ideas of English Dissent, 1763–1800* (Cambridge: Cambridge University Press, 1938): "The Dissenters were a Hanoverian bodyguard" (p. 23).

32. "As for politics, I think *poets* are *tories* by nature, supposing them to be by nature poets": William Shenstone, letter to the Rev. R. Graves, April 6, 1746, in *Letters,* ed. Marjorie Williams (Oxford: Basil Blackwell, 1939), p. 101; qu. by Hazlitt, 19.255.

33. "Isaac Babel," *Beyond Culture* (New York: Viking Press, 1965), pp. 139, 143; and see "The Princess Cassamassima," in Trilling, *The Liberal Imagination* (New York: Viking Press, 1950), pp. 181–82.

34. Hobbes, *Leviathan,* ed. Michael Oakeshott (Oxford: Basil Blackwell, n.d.), ch. 13–14, pp. 82–85.

35. See George H. Sabine, *A History of Political Theory* (New York: Henry Holt, 1937), esp. pp. 528–93.

36. Hazlitt began his anti-Malthusian campaign in 1807, with a series of letters to Cobbett's *Political Register* which he republished later that year, with additions, as a *Reply to the Essay on Population.* A subsequent letter, which I came upon in the *Monthly Magazine,* 27 (April 1809), 250–53, has the value of being Hazlitt's own summary and evaluation of his arguments in the rather rambling *Reply.* Much revised, the letter reappeared in the *Political Register* in 1810 and in *Political Essays,* 7.357–61. I review these revisions, and the changes they reflect in his thinking on the population issue, in " 'Philo' and Prudence: A New Hazlitt Criticism of Malthus," *Bulletin of the New York Public Library,* 59 (1965), 153–63.

37. Boner, *Hungry Generations: The Nineteenth-Century Case against Malthusianism* (New York: Russell and Russell, 1955), pp. 60, 67; and see similar assessments in W. P. Albrecht, *William Hazlitt and the Malthusian Controversy* (Albuquerque: University of New Mexico Press, 1950), p. 63, pp. 104 ff., and Kenneth Smith, *The Malthusian Controversy* (London: Routledge and Kegan Paul, 1951), pp. 76 ff., 325.

38. This account of the issues draws on Guido Ruggiero, *The History of European Liberalism,* trans. R. G. Collingwood (London: Oxford University Press, 1927) pp. 60 ff.; G. M. Young, *Victorian England: Portrait of an Age,* 2d ed. (London: Oxford University Press), pp. 51–53 (on Macaulay); and A. V. Dicey, *Law and Public Opinion in England during the Nineteenth Century,* 2d ed. (London: Macmillan, 1914), pp. 95 ff., 215–17.

39. See *Quarterly Review,* 17 (1817), 369–403; the less qualified conversion of the *Edinburgh* may be said to date from the review of Hazlitt's *Reply* in 16 (1810), 464–76, in which Malthus might have had a hand; see James Bonar, *Malthus and His Work,* 2d ed. (London: Macmillan, 1924), p. 329 n.

40. See Simon Maccoby, *English Radicalism, 1786–1833* (London: Allen and Unwin, 1955), pp. 322–48; M. W. Patterson, *Sir Francis Burdett and his Times,* 2 (London: Macmillan, 1931), 420 ff; Cole, *Life of William Cobbett,* pp.

204–24; Élie Halévy, *A History of the English People in the Nineteenth Century,* trans. E. I. Watkin, 1 (New York: Peter Smith, 1949), 15 ff.

41. *Yellow Dwarf,* No. 6 (Feb. 7), p. 44; see also No. 4 (Jan. 24), p. 25, and No. 13 (March 28), p. 97; and see Howe, p. 254.

4. A NEW AESTHETIC FOR OLD MASTERS

1. *Boswell's Life of Johnson* (London: Oxford University Press, 1953), p. 1312. See Osbert Sitwell and Margaret Barton, "Taste," and Andrew Shirley, "Painting and Engraving," in *Johnson's England,* ed. A. S. Turberville, 2d ed. (Oxford: Clarendon Press, 1952), 2.37–40; 2.55–58, 65–66. On the rise and spread of art journalism in Hazlitt's time see J. D. O'Hara, "Hazlitt and Romantic Criticism of the Fine Arts," *JAAC,* 27 (1968), 73–79. On the transformation of the older and cruder pictorialism (*ut pictura poesis*) to a less objective, more imaginative version of the analogy, see Park, pp. 104–21. See also Jean H. Hagstrum, *The Sister Arts* (Chicago: University of Chicago Press, 1958), pp. 138 ff.

2. See J. E. Hodgson and F. A. Eaton, *The Royal Academy and its Members* (New York: Scribner's, 1905), pp. 178–82; Shirley, pp. 63–71; Ian Jack, *Keats and the Mirror of Art* (Oxford: Clarendon Press, 1967), pp. xix–xxii; R. H. Wilenski, *John Ruskin* (London: Faber and Faber, 1933), p. 199 (on the Dulwich Gallery); Haydon, pp. 33–48; Joshua Reynolds, *Discourses,* World's Classics ed. (London: Oxford University Press, 1907), Disc. 1, 13, 15, pp. 9, 212, 241; and for the contrast with Napoleonic France, see *Examiner* (Nov. 28, 1813), p. 767.

3. E. g., *Examiner,* (Feb. 28, 1913), p. 141.

4. See Hodgson and Eaton, p. 180; the prints in William T. Whitley, *Art in England, 1800–1820,* (Cambridge: Cambridge University Press, 1928), passim; and Hazlitt on exhibitors' "tricks," 4.385.

5. The strong opposition of certain members of the Royal Academy to these exhibitions was expressed in an anonymous satiric pamphlet, the *Catalogue Raisonnée,* issued in three parts, 1815–16, which Hazlitt promptly attacked (4.140 ff.). See also Whitley, *Art in England,* pp. 247–54.

6. The journalistic history of Hazlitt's art criticism—first as critic for the *Morning Chronicle* (1814), then for *The Champion* (1814–15), and then, his reputation well-established, as occasional essayist—is summarized in Howe's note, 18.421. The fullest, most detailed account of Hazlitt's youthful experience of art is in Maclean, pp. 129–87; and see also Baker, pp. 264–70.

7. Clarke Olney, *Benjamin Robert Haydon: Historical Painter* (Athens: University of Georgia Press, 1952), pp. 66–99. Although in his *Autobiography* Haydon scorns Hazlitt's despair for English art (p. 187), a remark of his, in 1816, best suggests the general aesthetic importance that many of his contemporaries found in Hazlitt's art criticism: "He practised Painting long enough to know it; and he carries into Literature a stock which no literary man ever did before": *Diary,* ed. W. B. Pope (Cambridge: Harvard University Press, 1960–63), 2.65.

8. Mario Praz, *The Hero in Eclipse in Victorian Fiction,* trans. A. Davidson (Oxford: Clarendon Press, 1956), pp. 101–02.

9. Coleridge, *The Statesman's Manual* (1816), in *Political Tracts,* p. 7; cf. Hazlitt, 17.326.

10. Hazlitt's account closely parallels Vasari's: see J. R. Hale, *England and the Italian Renaissance* (London: Faber and Faber, 1954), pp. 60–69, 76–81, et passim.

11. See John D. Schiffer, "The Idea of Decline in Literature and the Fine Arts in Eighteenth-Century England," *MP,* 35 (1936), 155–78; and Walter Jackson Bate, *The Burden of the Past and the English Poet* (Cambridge: Harvard University Press, 1970), pp. 46 ff.

12. The anticipation of De Quincey was first pointed out by Schneider, *Aesthetics,* p. 118 n.

13. Landseer, 1.130–33; the technical information is from W. G. Constable, *The Painter's Workshop* (London: Oxford University Press, 1954), esp. pp. 85–101.

14. Christopher Hussey, *The Picturesque* (New York: Putnam's, 1927), pp. 51, 246 ff.; Samuel Redgrave, *A Century of British Painters,* ed. Ruthven Todd (London: Phaidon, 1947), pp. 44–163, 251–70 (innovations in color technique). A. J. Finberg, *The Life of J. M. W. Turner* (Oxford: Clarendon Press, 1961) says that Hazlitt alone in his time reports Turner using blues and yellows in this way (pp. 246–47).

15. He does not identify the painting; it might have been *View on the Stour,* also exhibited, but was, more probably, *The Hay Wain,* which excited much comment in Paris at the time: see Graham Reynolds, *Constable* (New York: Schocken Books, 1969), pp. 96–97.

16. See Hagstrum, p. 158; Park, pp. 131 ff.

17. On Blake and Reynolds as artists deriving a conception of "ideal form" from classical sculpture, see Stephen A. Larrabee, *English Bards and Grecian Marbles* (New York: Columbia University Press, 1943), pp. 102–10. For views which emphasize what Hazlitt and Reynolds have in common, see Baker, p. 272, and Leonard M. Trawick, III, "Hazlitt, Reynolds and the Ideal," *SIR,* 4 (1965), esp. p. 242.

18. Blake, "Annotations to . . . Reynolds," pp. 638–41; Reynolds, *Discourses* 4, 10, 11, pp. 45–46, 146–47, 159, 163–65.

19. *Discourse* 3, pp. 24, 37; Schneider, *Aesthetics,* pp. 43–45, 174. Addison (*Spectator* No. 416) and other writers had similarly defended "imitation": see Bate, *Criticism,* p. 298.

20. "Hazlitt as a Critic of Art," *PMLA,* 39 (1924), 189–93.

21. Eugene C. Elliott, "Reynolds and Hazlitt," *JAAC,* 21 (1962), 78.

22. Ruskin evidently knew Hazlitt's *Sketches of the Principal Picture-Galleries of England* (10.55 ff.) and *Conversations with James Northcote* (11.186 ff.): see *Modern Painters,* I, II, in *Works,* ed. E. T. Cook and A. Wedderburn (London: G. Allen, 1903), 3.350, 4.253 ff. Whether the coincidence of their criticism on certain points indicates a direct influence is problematical: see Henry Ladd, *The Victorian Morality of Art: An Analysis of Ruskin's Aesthetic* (New York: R. Long and R. R. Smith, 1932), pp. 79–80, 215; and William C. Wright, "Hazlitt, Ruskin, and Nineteenth-Century Art Criticism," *JAAC,* 32 (1973), 509–23 (esp. pp. 519–23, for specific evidence of influence). On Ruskin and "organic form," see Wilenski, pp. 210, 239–40.

23. See Trawick, pp. 243–44; and Frederic Will, "Two Critics of the Elgin Marbles: William Hazlitt and Quatremère de Quincy," *JAAC*, 14 (1956), 462–74.

24. *Mirror*, p. 135; and see also O'Hara, pp. 77–78.

25. Albert S. Gérard, *English Romantic Poetry: Ethos, Structure and Symbol in Coleridge, Wordsworth, Shelley and Keats* (Berkeley: University of California Press, 1968), pp. 60–63. Others who have noted Hazlitt's emphasis on symbolism are Albrecht, *HCI*, p. 83; Wellek, 2.201; and Park, pp. 65–68, 128.

26. This view of aesthetic symbolism as value-language finds some general confirmation in speculation today, especially in such theoretic arguments as those of Charles W. Morris, "Science, Art and Technology," in *A Modern Book of Aesthetics*, ed. Melvin Rader, 3d ed. (New York: Holt, Rinehart and Winston, 1960), pp. 241–48; and of Morris Weitz, *Philosophy of the Arts* (Cambridge: Harvard University Press, 1950; rpt. New York: Russell and Russell, 1964), esp. pp. 59–60, 105–49. Their discussion helps to clarify the relationship of traditional theories of "expression" to "linguistic" conceptions of art variously advocated by Cassirer, Susanne Langer, and others.

27. On the general problem at this time of reconciling the beautiful and unbeautiful in art, see Lionello Venturi, *History of Art Criticism*, trans. C. Marriott, rev. ed. (New York: Dutton, 1961), pp. 190–209. For a view which stresses the continuity of beauty and sublimity in Hazlitt, as I do their difference, see W. P. Albrecht, *The Sublime Pleasures of Tragedy* (Lawrence: University Press of Kansas, 1975), pp. 118–19.

28. See Blake, "A Vision of the Last Judgment," pp. 544 ff. and Haydon, *Lectures on Painting and Design* (London, 1844), 1.7–8. The idea is found much earlier in Bellori, Shaftesbury, and Dennis: see Hussey, pp. 53–55.

29. See also 16.187, 12.290, and 5.10.

30. Wölfflin, *The Art of the Italian Renaissance* (New York: Putnam's, 1963), p. 55.

31. Clark, *Landscape into Art* (Boston: Beacon Press, 1961), pp. 67–68; Read, "The Art of Art Criticism," *The Tenth Muse* (New York: Horizon Press, 1958), p. 7. Graham Hough, *The Last Romantics* (New York: Barnes and Noble, 1961), p. 2 ("more warmth . . ."); Zabel, *The Romantic Idealism of Art, 1800–1848* (Chicago: University of Chicago Press, 1938), p. 226.

5. SHAKESPEARE AND TRAGEDY:
THE VIEW FROM DRURY LANE

1. *The Critic* 1.i.22–23, in *Plays and Poems of Richard Brinsley Sheridan*, ed. R. C. Rhodes, 2 (Oxford: Clarendon Press, 1928), 195.

2. See Thomas Noon Talfourd, Introduction, *Literary Remains of the late William Hazlitt*, ed. William Hazlitt [Jr.], 1 (London, 1836), cxiv-v. I have followed Baker (p. 285) in regarding the *Beggar's Opera* review as Hazlitt's first, but there is strong internal evidence for believing that he wrote most of a long and rather turgid review of the Drury Lane production of Coleridge's *Remorse* in January 1813: see 18.462–64 (where Howe recants his earlier opinion in the *Life* that the review was by another hand). For the theatergoing of his youth see 5.424; 8.292–93; and Baker, p. 285.

3. This is Hazlitt's spelling of the poet's name—without the terminal *e*—except in *The Round Table* (1817), *Lectures on the English Poets* (1818) and *Lectures on the English Comic Writers* (1819), where the name is spelled with the first *e* omitted, but with a terminal *e: Shakspeare*. After the *Lectures,* he returns to his spelling in *Characters.* For an account of the impact of Kean and of Hazlitt's reviews of Kean on the theater world see Harold Newcomb Hillebrand, *Edmund Kean* (New York: Oxford University Press, 1933), pp. 104–20; and for the belief that Hazlitt "saved" Drury Lane see Archer's Introduction (p. xx) to *Hazlitt on Theatre* (New York: Hill and Wang, n.d.), originally published as *Dramatic Essays,* ed. William Archer and Robert W. Lowe (London, 1859). Macready is quoted in Howe's notes (5.420, n. 334).

4. Disagreements, mainly political, with his editors account for the transfer of Hazlitt's talents as a reviewer, first (in the spring of 1814) from the *Chronicle* to John Scott's weekly, the *Champion,* and then from the *Champion,* in early 1815, to the *Examiner. A View of the English Stage* does not include most of the reviews written for the *Times* in the latter half of 1817, after which Hazlitt ceased to write reviews for the daily and weekly press: see Howe's note, 18.442. His last stint as a theater critic was in 1820, mainly for the *London Magazine* (see 18.271–374). Leigh Hunt's *Critical Essays on Performers of the London Theatres* (1808) was the only collection of its kind prior to Hazlitt's: see Hunt, *Dramatic Essays,* also ed. Archer and Lowe (London, 1894), pp. 16–17.

5. Shaw, *Our Theatres in the Nineties,* II, in *Collected Works,* 24 (London: Constable, 1932), 169; and Bentley's statement, on the cover of *Hazlitt on Theatre,* introduces the reissue of the Archer-Lowe selection. Bentley's metaphor must not be taken to mean that Hazlitt's criticism—or that of the other possible "father," Leigh Hunt—is without historical precedent; for their criticism, especially in its achievement of independence from "venal puffing," culminates a long and gradual evolution in eighteenth-century journalism: see Charles Harold Gray, *Theatrical Criticism in London to 1795* (New York: Columbia University Press, 1931; rpt. New York: Benjamin Blom, 1964), esp. p. 310.

6. M. C. Bradbrook, *Themes and Conventions of Elizabethan Tragedy* (Cambridge: Cambridge Univ. Press, 1957), pp. 50–52.

7. Lamb's essay "On the Tragedies of Shakespeare" (*Works,* 1.107 ff.) was first published in 1811. Cf. Hazlitt: "In [reading] Shakspeare we do not often think of him [Kean] except in those parts which he constantly acts, and in those one cannot forget him" (6.229). On contemporary literary opinions of Kean see Bernice Slote, *Keats and the Dramatic Principle* (Lincoln: University of Nebraska Press, 1958), pp. 78–91.

8. Here, and throughout this chapter, I am indebted to a number of general studies, but especially to Ernest Bradlee Watson, *Sheridan to Robertson: A Study of the Nineteenth Century Stage* (Cambridge: Harvard University Press, 1926, rpt. New York: Benjamin Blom, 1963), pp. 6–96; Allardyce Nicoll, *A History of Early Nineteenth-Century Drama, 1800–1850,* 1 (Cambridge: Cambridge University Press, 1930), 7–139; and George C. D. Odell, *Shakespeare from Betterton to Irving,* 2 (New York: Scribner's, 1920), esp. pp. 3–114. Rather surprisingly, Hazlitt only once mentions (20.284) the "O.P." (Old Price) Riots of 1809, when mobs of demonstrators forced the Covent Gar-

den management to abandon its attempt to raise prices—a "triumph of democracy" which helped to assure the increasing vulgarization of theater programming (see Watson, pp. 9 ff.).

9. Details from 5.222, 235–38, 254; 8.277–78; 18.288, 295–97, 379, 385; 20.206.

10. Thomas Barnes, "Theatrical Examiner," *Examiner* (July 25,1813), p. 477.

11. 18.212, 400 ff., 218 (Liston); 5.319 (farces).

12. 5.253, 302, 136–37; 4.270; 18.409.

13. 5.275, 378; on Kemble, 5.342–44, 350; and see Odell, 1.95 (staging of *Pizarro*, which Sheridan adapted from Kotzebue), 108–09 (on Kemble).

14. The casualness of Hazlitt's attitude is confessed in 18.239, 272, 357, 369.

15. See 18.272–73; 20.287–88; 12.77; 8.266 n.

16. 5.171–73, 231 (on sustaining illusion), 291, 302, 351, 367.

17. Bentley, *Hazlitt on Theater* (see my n. 5); Archer, *The Old Drama and the New* (Boston: Small, Maynard, 1923), p. 244 (where the period 1810–35 is said to be the "very barrenest" in English drama); and see Alvin Whitley, "Hazlitt and the Theater," *University of Texas Studies in English,* 34 (1955), 89, where Hazlitt's criticism is seen as allied to, and abetting, "the star system."

18. Kemble is quoted in Hillebrand, p. 333. It is often assumed that the tradition of concentrating on "hits" or "points" or histrionic "moments" necessarily produced a discontinuity of effect, or a sacrifice of "the character to the passion": see Arthur Colby Sprague, *Shakespearean Players and Performances* (Cambridge: Harvard University Press, 1953; rpt.; New York: Greenwood Press, 1969), pp. 74–75. Kean himself insisted that his acting was not "impulsive" but "studied"—see *Actors on Acting,* ed. Toby Cole and Helen Krich Chinoy, rev. ed. (New York: Crown, 1970), pp. 327–28—and since Hazlitt seems to have had some personal acquaintance with Kean (see 5.400), we may surmise that his analysis of Kean's acting in part reflects the actor's own views. He had only scorn for those young actors of the time who "caricatured" Kean by supposing "that to be familiar or violent is to be natural, and that to be natural is the perfection of acting" (5.299). His position, as summed up in 12.297–98, would seem to be close to William Archer's, who argued in *Masks or Faces?* (London, 1888) that deep emotional identification with the role need not preclude, and may indeed foster, aesthetic control and presence of mind (pp. 70 ff.).

19. See R. W. Babcock, *The Genesis of Shakespeare Idolatry* (Chapel Hill: University of North Carolina Press, 1931), esp. pp. 28–41, 135 ff. But few if any scholars today would agree with Babcock's conclusion that the Romantic critics "merely echoed" the character critics of the eighteenth century (p. 226), and the rest of this chapter will provide further reasons for disagreement. Hazlitt acknowledges his reading of William Richardson, and he records his indebtedness to Thomas Whately's comparison of Macbeth and Richard III (4.171), but there is no firm evidence that Hazlitt had read, or was appreciably influenced by, any other eighteenth-century studies of this kind. He shows only a slight and indirect acquaintance with the best of these critics, Maurice Morgann: see Stuart M. Tave, "Notes on the Influence of Morgann's Essay on Falstaff," *Review of English Studies,* 3 (1952), 371–72.

20. The exception: "Sir Walter Scott, Racine, and Shakespear," 12.336 ff.

21. The remainder of this chapter is adapted from my article, "Hazlitt and the 'Design' of Shakespearean Tragedy: A 'Character' Critic Revisited," *Shakespeare Quarterly*, 28 (1977), 22–39.

22. See, among numerous accusers, Bradbrook, as cited in my n. 6 above, and L. C. Knights, "How Many Children Had Lady Macbeth?," in *Explorations* (New York: New York University Press, 1964), pp. 28–30.

23. The considerable reputation of *Characters* in England and America is well-known, but the book won distinguished admirers on the Continent as well. "*Il l'avait dépassé*," was A. W. von Schlegel's appraisal of Hazlitt's Shakespeare criticism as compared with his own: qu. in Introduction, *Hazlitt on English Literature*, ed. Jacob Zeitlin (New York: Oxford University Press, 1913), pp. liv–lv. See also Kenneth Hayens, "Heine, Hazlitt, and Mrs. Jameson," *Modern Language Review*, 17 (1922), 42–49; and Robert Vigneron, "Stendhal et Hazlitt," *MP*, 35 (1938), 389 ff.

24. The general neglect of Hazlitt's concern with Shakespeare's "art" is perhaps to be explained as a reluctance to distinguish his own sense of the term "art" from its late eighteenth-century connotation of "artificial," to which his usage does, but only as context warrants, sometimes conform (see his own comment on the word "art" in "Pope, Lord Byron, and Mr. Bowles," 19.72–78, and see my notes 25 and 26 below). Only Arthur M. Eastman, in *A Short History of Shakespearean Criticism* (New York: Random House, 1968), has given adequate emphasis to Hazlitt's "sense" of the "unity" of certain plays (pp. 104–05), but he too makes the traditional mistake of assuming that Hazlitt "cares very little" for "dramatic means" or "ends" (p. 101). The word "design" itself does not obtrusively appear in *Characters* (4.184, 201, 210, 241), but the book abounds (one would never know this from most scholarly accounts of it) in statements about Shakespeare's "art," "management," "skill," "logic," "invention," "mastery," "arrangement of scenes," etc. (4.226, 255–60, 268, 293, 300, 311, to cite only the most emphatic).

25. "To give us nature, such as we see it, is well and deserving of praise: to give us nature, such as we have never seen, but have often wished to see it, is better, and deserving of higher praise. He . . . who, by his 'so potent art,' can . . . join the regions of imagination (a new conquest) to those of reality,—who teaches us not only what nature is, but what she has been, and is capable of being,—he who does this, and does it with simplicity, with truth, and grandeur, is lord of nature and her powers; and his mind is universal, and his art the master-art!" ("On a Landscape of Nicholas Poussin," 8.169).

26. To illustrate: Imogen's fidelity is repeated in lighter or darker hues—takes on wise or foolish, benign or malign form—in the persistence of strong feeling or resolve in the other characters—e.g., the faithfulness of the servant Pisanio, Cloten's relentless "importunities," Iachimo's "persevering determination," the Queen's "incorrigible wickedness," the King's "blind uxorious confidence." Hazlitt adds that as this "impression exists unconsciously in the mind of the reader, so it probably arose in the same manner in the mind of the author, *not from design,* but from the force of natural association, a particular train of thought suggesting different inflections of the same

predominant feeling, melting into, and strengthening one another, like chords in music" (4.179–84; my italics). Here, it will be noted, "design" is used in its pejorative sense, as connoting the "artificial," the imposition upon nature of an abstractly conceived "set purpose" ("Hamlet," 4.233). But Hazlitt, it is clear, is not denying that a "design," in effect, exists; he is simply insisting that a creative "design" need not imply a "design" of the will.

27. See 12.54–55: "Each man is a microcosm . . ."

28. In Hazlitt's opinion, only Kemble's sister, Sarah Siddons, "united both extremes of acting . . . that is, all the frailties of passion, with all the strength and resources of the intellect" (5.211).

29. Joseph W. Donohue, Jr., *Dramatic Character in the English Romantic Age* (Princeton: Princeton University Press, 1970), p. 286.

30. Elmer Edgar Stoll, *Art and Artifice in Shakespeare* (Cambridge: Cambridge University Press, 1933), pp. 77 ff.

31. Quotations from Shakespeare are from *Complete Works,* ed. Irving Ribner and George Lyman Kittredge (Waltham, Mass.: Ginn, 1971). Hazlitt, trusting too much in memory, slightly misquotes these lines.

32. Knight has acknowledged, in a general way, his kinship with Hazlitt, Coleridge, and A. C. Bradley: *The Wheel of Fire,* 5th ed. (New York: Noonday Press, 1957), pp. vi, 2.

33. The account that follows, however, differs considerably from his, which is not principally concerned with the themes of "contrast" and "power."

34. "No one ever hit the true perfection of the female character, the sense of weakness leaning on the strength of its affections for support, so well as Shakespear . . ." (4.180).

35. This perhaps is Hazlitt's most notable difference from Bradley, who, while stressing the "fatal imperfection" in Shakespeare's heroes, continually places his strongest emphasis on their "exceptional," "good," morally "innocent" and "noble" qualities: *Shakespearean Tragedy,* rev. ed. (New York: Noonday Press, 1955), esp. pp. 26–27, 37, 144–45. For Hazlitt the tragic passion is for "power," for power over weakness and evil; for Bradley, it is "a passion for perfection" (p. 39).

36. Ralph Berry, "Pattern in *Othello,*" *Shakespeare Quarterly,* 23 (1972), 8.

37. Perhaps because he was accused of calling Desdemona a "lewd woman" (*A Reply to 'Z',* 9.9), Hazlitt omitted this analysis from his essay in *Characters,* where it is only dimly suggested (4.208).

38. Coleridge, *SC,* 1.34 et passim; A. W. von Schlegel, *Lectures on Dramatic Art and Literature,* trans. John Black, rev. trans. A. J. W. Morrison (London: Henry G. Bohn, 1846), pp. 45–46; Shelley, "A Defence of Poetry," *Complete Works,* ed. R. Ingpen and W. E. Peck, 7 (London: Ernest Benn, 1930), 121. The legend that Hazlitt in his Shakespeare criticism was the disciple of Coleridge or Schlegel or of both is most readily put to rout by his own testimony in 16.76 ff. and his remarks in Collier's diary on Coleridge's abstractness and occasional "ignorance" of Shakespeare: *Coleridge on Shakespeare: The Text of the Lectures of 1811–12,* ed. R. A. Foakes (Charlottesville: University Press of Virginia, 1971), pp. 61–63.

39. "On the Tragedies of Shakespeare," *Works,* 1.107.

40. For an ably developed view, one which differs from mine in finding values of "order" in Hazlitt's conception of tragic "power," see W. P. Albrecht, *The Sublime Pleasures of Tragedy* (Lawrence: University Press of Kansas, 1975), pp. 122 ff.

41. "On sitting down to read *King Lear* once again," *Poems*, p. 277; *Letters*, 1.192–93, 2.101–04. I am indebted to, while at times disagreeing with, Alfred Harbage's discussion of Keats's and Hazlitt's ideas of tragedy in "The Fierce Dispute," *Conceptions of Shakespeare* (Cambridge: Harvard University Press, 1966), esp. pp. 85–98.

6. POETRY: THE ENGLISH MUSE

1. *Blackwood's*, 3 (1818), 71–76, 303–06; and see Howe, pp. 248 ff.; Baker, pp. 251 ff.; Wardle, pp. 191 ff.

2. T. M. Raysor, Introduction, Coleridge, *SC*, 1.li. The derivation from Wordsworth is argued by Wellek, 2.188–89. "Hazlitt is Coleridge's most immediate disciple," write Daniel G. Hoffman and Samuel Hynes in their anthology, *English Literary Criticism, Romantic and Victorian* (New York: Appleton-Century-Crofts, 1963), p. vi.

3. "Young Poets," *Examiner*, Dec. 1, 1816, p. 761; review of Keats's *Poems* (1817) in *Examiner*, June 1, July 6 and 13, 1817, pp. 345, 429, 443; Preface to *Foliage* (1818) in *LC*, pp. 129–36; and see John O. Hayden, *The Romantic Reviewers, 1802–1824* (Chicago: University of Chicago Press, 1968), pp. 77 ff., 176–90.

4. *Blackwood's*, 2 (1817), 38–41, 201 ("Cockney School"); and on Hazlitt, Vols. 3 (1818), 200 (incl. Keats), 453–56, 550–52; 12 (1822), 59, 159. See Howe, pp. 266 ff.; Baker, pp. 370 ff.; Wardle, pp. 229 ff.; and Alan Lang Strout, "Hunt, Hazlitt and 'Maga'," *ELH*, 4 (1937), 151–59 (for more on "pimpled Hazlitt"). Hazlitt was clear-skinned and was possibly the victim of a vague report reaching *Blackwood's* about another William Hazlitt—his father, whose face was "scarred by the small-pox" (8.12).

5. Hazlitt generalizes his attack and extends it especially to Byron and Shelley, in 16.279, where "modern poetry" is said to be in danger of being "eaten up with personality." See Coleridge, *BL*, 1.56–65 and Hazlitt's challenge, in his review of *Biographia*, to Coleridge's insistence (I give Hazlitt's paraphrase) that there is "nothing peculiar about" Wordsworth's poetry and that the idea of a "new" school is wholly a misunderstanding (16.721–22). Hazlitt further dissociates himself from Wordsworth's "school" and its "metaphysical doctrine" in 9.12.

6. "When to the Attractions of the Busy World" .80; and see also *The Excursion*, Bk. 1.77–91, in *Po W*, 2.122, 5.10–11. For the remainder of this section I am adapting, with a few minor changes, parts of my article, "Hazlitt, Keats, and the Poetics of Intersubjectivity," *Criticism*, 19 (1977), 1–12.

7. "Athenäums-Fragmente," *Kritische Schriften* (Munich: Carl Hanser, 1964), pp. 38–39. Schlegel introduces the term to describe a program for modern poetry ("Die romantische Poesie ist eine progressive Universalpoesie. . . .") but at the end of the same aphorism he virtually equates "Romantic" poetry with poetry in essence: "The Romantic genre of poetry is

the only one which is more than a genre, and which is, as it were, poetry itself. . . ." The translation is that of Ernst Behler and Roman Struc, in their edition of Schlegel's *Dialogue on Poetry and Literary Aphorisms* (University Park: Pennsylvania State University Press, 1968), p. 141; and see their comment on the close affinity of Schlegel's "universal poetry" to English Romantic theory, pp. 15–18.

8. *What is Literature?*, trans. Bernard Frechtman (New York: Harper and Row, 1965), pp. 34–35.

9. Although Coleridge here is discussing language in poetry, his comment on the proper function ("property") of passion confirms the central theme of this chapter (17) in *BL*, that poetry is *"essentially ideal and generic"* (2.28, 33, 42). Coleridge does not deny that "the heat of passion" may generate "new connections of thoughts or images," but "the terms of their conveyance must have preexisted," being inherent in, and dependent upon, "general truths," and these expressive terms of language "are only collected and crowded together by the unusual stimulation" (p. 42). And Coleridge goes on to insist in Ch. 18 that when imagination orders and unifies this collocation of elements, the creative "fire" in the process emanates from the imagination of "genius" rather than from the passions expressed: "The very act of poetic composition itself is, and is allowed to imply and to produce, an unusual state of excitement, which of course justifies and demands a correspondent difference of language, as truly, though not perhaps in as marked a degree, as the excitement of love, fear, rage, or jealousy. . . . The wheels take fire from the mere rapidity of their motion" (p. 56).

10. "What makes his [Coleridge's] view a one-sided one is, that in it the artist has become almost a mechanical agent: . . . the associative act in art or poetry is made to look like some blindly organic process of assimilation. The work of art is likened to a living organism. That expresses truly the sense of a self-delighting, independent life which the finished work of art gives us: it hardly figures the process by which such work was produced." In "Coleridge," *Appreciations* (London: Macmillan, 1931), pp. 80–81.

11. E. g., Abrams, *Mirror*, pp. 49–50, 54, and see my n. 2 above. The most balanced account of his indebtedness to Wordsworth's Prefaces (1800, 1815) is in Albrecht, *HCI*, pp. 75–86.

12. See Bate, *Criticism*, pp. 285 ff.; "The Sympathetic Imagination in Eighteenth-Century English Criticism," *ELH*, 12 (1945), 144–64; and his *John Keats*, rev. ed. (New York: Oxford University Press, 1966), pp. 254–59.

13. This account (and what follows) will, I hope, help to clarify the role of Hazlitt's theory of the principle of "association," which several commentators regard as central or definitive (e. g., Albrecht, *HCI*, pp. 73–86). Pre-existing "associations" make the poetic process possible, but do not make the process what it is; for the intensive "movement" *transforms* antecedent, empirical relations into new and "unknown" relations, "shapes and combinations of power" (5.4, 9). The shaping links are now those of image-feeling-word-sound (see 5.7)—are, in short, *passional* in their imaginative "association"; and only in that sense can these relations be said to have a potential pre-existence, i.e., as inhering in the self, not as an anterior tendency to "coalescence" in recurrent "experience" as such (even though imagination in

another mode, that of "tacit reason" or "common sense," actively contributes to that experience: 8.31 ff.). As Park makes the paradoxical point: "Imagination is associative [he cites Hazlitt's comment that imagination is "an *associating* principle": 12.51], but cannot be explained in terms of association" (p. 64).

14. I cannot stress enough that the distinction between poem and poetry, product and process is mainly of importance, where Hazlitt is concerned, in enabling us to understand, or not to mistake, his sense of poetic transcendence. Such phrases in Hazlitt studies as "loss of self" or "absence of self" (e. g., Park, pp. 164–68) will only confuse us unless we clearly recognize them as metaphors, and the intersubjective principle helps us to understand in what sense they are metaphorical.

15. "John Dryden," *Selected Essays* (New York: Harcourt, Brace, 1932), p. 268.

16. "The Metaphysical Poets," *Selected Essays,* pp. 247–50.

17. The contrast of "natural" and "artificial" as poetic categories was first developed in Hazlitt's time by William Lisle Bowles in his controversial *Observations* on Pope (1806), but the contrast is clearly prefigured, as Bowles himself suggests, in such distinctions as Johnson's between a poetry of "general nature" (or of "passion") and a poetry of "manners": see *The Poets and Their Critics: Chaucer to Collins,* rev. ed., ed. Hugh Sykes Davies (London: Hutchinson, 1960), pp. 192–94. Hazlitt seems, however, to have been the first critic to describe the contrast as one of "styles." Hazlitt's contribution to the Bowles-Campbell-Byron controversy over Pope, erupting a year or so after the *Lectures,* is one of his major critical essays and ought to be better known: see "Pope, Lord Byron and Mr. Bowles" (1821), 19.62 ff.

18. J. Middleton Murry, *The Problem of Style* (London: Oxford University Press, 1922), pp. 14 (where Flaubert is quoted), 34, 46–47.

19. The method is usually identified as, or with, "the comparative method": see J. W. H. Atkins, *English Literary Criticism: Seventeenth and Eighteenth Centuries* (New York: Barnes and Noble, 1951), pp. 142 ff.; and see the discussion of "comparison" and "character" criticism in Jean H.Hagstrum, *Samuel Johnson's Literary Criticism* (Minneapolis: University of Minnesota Press, 1952), pp. 28–29, 38 ff.

20. Coleridge, *Miscellaneous Criticism,* ed. Thomas Middleton Raysor (Cambridge: Harvard University Press, 1936), p. 165. See *The Poets and Their Critics,* pp. 121, 150, for the obvious derivation of Eliot's principal objection to Milton ("the hypertrophy of the auditory imagination at the expense of the visual and tactile") from Coleridge's insistence on Milton's "musical" and "artificial" style. James Thorpe alludes to this derivation in Introduction, *Milton Criticism* (New York: Rinehart, 1950), p. 9. References to Milton's poems in what follows are to *Works,* ed. F. A. Patterson (New York: Columbia University Press, 1931), 1.i, 2.i; and Keats's line is in "On a Lock of Milton's Hair." 1, *Poems,* p. 257.

21. Keats, *Letters,* 2.12; Arnold, "The Study of Poetry," *Complete Prose Works,* ed. R. H. Super, 9 (Ann Arbor: University of Michigan Press, 1973), 171 ff. There are, however, significant differences between the Romantic and the Victorian Milton—the Romanticists being less inclined to divorce the

man and thinker in Milton from the artist, as Wittreich points out: see *The Romantics on Milton,* ed. Joseph Anthony Wittreich, Jr. (Cleveland: Western Reserve University Press, 1970), pp. 7 ff.

22. See Coleridge, *BL,* 2.20: "All things and modes of action shape themselves anew in the being of Milton; while Shakespeare becomes all things, yet forever remaining himself." Patricia M. Ball rightly calls attention to the significance of this statement in understanding the "creative duality" in Romantic poetry, which is "at once Miltonic and Shakespearean," both "egotistical" and engaged in "sympathetic excursion from self," though I think that she minimizes the conflict between these modes: see *The Central Self: A Study in Romantic and Victorian Imagination* (London: University of London, Athlone Press, 1968), pp. 2–14. Hazlitt couples the poets as exemplars of the most "disinterested" genres and finds their common quality in "grandeur" of "conception" (20.304–05), but he was also willing to confess grave limitations in Milton's range of awareness (e. g., "nature and every thing in it" not seldom become in Milton "but a temple and an image consecrated by the poet's art to the worship of virtue and pure religion": 6.256).

23. "The Four Ages of Poetry," in *Thomas Love Peacock: Memoirs of Shelley and Other Essays and Reviews,* ed. Howard Mills (London: Rupert Hart-Davis, 1970), pp. 117–32; and see Walter Jackson Bate, *The Burden of the Past and the English Poet* (Cambridge: Harvard University Press, 1970), pp. 54, 61 ff.

24. Hazlitt has the distinction of editing (with some help from Lamb) the first anthology of poetry to be organized on historical principles (*Select British Poets,* 1824), but neither in its organization nor in his notes does Hazlitt emphasize the "gradations" of "decline" here described (9.233 ff.). Some earlier collections, of the popular "Specimens" type—such as those edited by Lamb, Southey, Ellis, and Campbell—had been broadly historical in conception or arrangement, but none were as comprehensive or as programmatically historical as Hazlitt's. For more on the anthology and its legal troubles after publication, see Baker, pp. 429–31.

25. In this series Hazlitt may be seen amplifying suggestions that Lamb had first adumbrated in *Specimens of English Dramatic Poets* (1808; Works, 3.3 ff.); and this is especially true of Hazlitt's remarks (6.203–74) on Marlowe, Heywood, Chapman, Dekker, Middleton, Webster, and Tourneur. His judgments, however, even when he is content to reinforce Lamb's praise, are more fully developed and are always based on his own theory of the drama. Massinger's characters lack the dialectical reality of "mixed motives" (6.269); and his greatest objection to Beaumont and Fletcher is to the general absence in their tragedies of a genuine "progress" of passion—a want, in short, of Shakespearean perspective and "gradation" (see 16.97; 6.249). And Hazlitt regards as finally meretricious two tragedies that Lamb admired—*The Maid's Tragedy* and Ford's *The Broken Heart* (6.251, 273).

26. Hazlitt expresses his scepticism about Coleridge's distinction in 16.121 ff. and 18.370 n. See also the thorough discussion of "fancy" in Albrecht, *HCI,* pp. 106–10. Generally, "fancy" in Hazlitt's usage signifies bold, sometimes frivolous metaphor and playful invention, "the figurative . . . exercise of the imagination" (8.42 n.), but without much depth of sympathy or

intensity of passion. He least values "fancy" when it appears in Metaphysical "wit," and he quotes with approval (6.49) from Johnson's "Life of Abraham Cowley," *Lives of the English Poets* (London: J. M. Dent, 1925), 1.11.

27. Unlike many revaluations of Pope at this time, Hazlitt's critique neither disparages the poet's gifts as an Augustan wit nor attempts especially to discover in his work qualities more consistent with Romantic fashion—warmth of affection, love of concrete nature, fresh responsiveness to beauty. See Upali Amarasinghe, *Dryden and Pope in the Early Nineteenth Century* (Cambridge: Cambridge University Press, 1962), pp. 150–54, 162–65, 185–86; and *The Poets and Their Critics*, pp. 165–74, 203–15. Hazlitt alone among his major contemporaries (Byron excepted) rated Pope above Dryden.

28. See Baker, pp. 342–50; Bate, *John Keats*, pp. 265–73; and for another possible cause of Wordsworth's hostility, as early as 1814, to Hazlitt's critical reputation—namely, the poet's suspicion of Hazlitt's authorship of the 1813 verses (discussed in Ch. 3)—see my article, "Hazlitt as Poet," *SIR*, 12 (1973), 431.

29. Keats, *Letters*, esp. to Reynolds, Feb. 3, 1818, 1.224; and to Woodhouse, Oct. 27, 1818, 1.387. This paragraph and the two paragraphs preceding are adapted, with some alterations, from my article, cited above (see n. 6) in *Criticism*, 19 (1977), 12–16.

7. THE MODERN DIFFERENCE:
COMEDY AND THE NOVEL

1. Byron, letter of Dec. 19, 1816, *Letters and Journals* (London: John Murray, 1922), 4.23; Shelley, as quoted by Peacock in Newman Ivey White, *Shelley* (New York: Knopf, 1940), 1.522; *Marriage of Heaven and Hell,* Proverbs of Hell. 60, in Blake, p. 37.

2. Introduction, *Wit and Humour,* rev. ed. (London, 1890), pp. 34–35. In his 1819 *Lectures* Hazlitt, undaunted, repeats (6.54) his objection to this line from Marvell's "The Character of Holland" .30, in *Complete Poems,* ed. A. B. Grosart (London, 1872, rpt. New York: AMS Press, 1966), p. 243.

3. The lectures were delivered, again at the Surrey Institution, between November 1818 and early January 1819. This time, however, the series was not so well attended—perhaps because of injury done by the Tory press to Hazlitt's reputation, but also, I suspect, because the subject was not one to stir the conscience of middle-class Londoners intent on "improvement" of the mind: see Howe, pp. 251, 276 ff.

4. *The Amiable Humorist* (Chicago: University of Chicago Press, 1960), pp. ix, 91 ff. My sense of the conflicting claims of "wit" and "humour" in Hazlitt's mind is partially indebted to Tave, especially to pp. 217, 245.

5. The originality, however, is considerable, for Hazlitt's distinctions were not precisely or consistently developed by his predecessors, and much, if not most, eighteenth-century theory leaves in indiscriminate confusion the "degrees" and other terms that Hazlitt differentiates: see John W. Draper, "The Theory of the Comic in Eighteenth-Century England," *Journal of English and Germanic Philology,* 37 (1938), 207–23. The affinity to Hugh Blair's theory is noted by Wellek, 2.208, and Tave points out precedents in Hartley,

Tucker, Corbyn Morris, Beattie, and Campbell (pp. 76 ff., 139, 192, 205). Hazlitt himself makes favorable reference to Isaac Barrow, Addison, Campbell, and James Harris (6.19, 22, 26–27, 62).

6. Just as the theory originates in Aristotle's emphasis on the comic as the "low" or "ugly" (aesthetic or ethical incongruity), so there are later modern variants of the same reductive fallacy: Bergson, for instance, identifies the source of the comic as the "mechanical" (incongruity with the vital). But in all these variations the motive remains the same: by deriving the comic impulse from something else, to deny it the status of being real in itself. See the review of theories in Allardyce Nicoll, *The Theory of Drama*, rev. ed. (London: Harrap, 1931), pp. 193–213. I should add that Hazlitt does later qualify, in an incidental observation, his general adherence to the theory: see my n. 9 below. A recent, philosophically oriented defense of the incongruity theory is in Marie Collins Swabey, *Comic Laughter* (New Haven: Yale University Press, 1961), esp. pp. 7–25.

7. "From Ritual to Comedy," in *Shakespeare: Modern Essays in Criticism*, rev. ed., ed. Leonard F. Dean (New York: Oxford University Press, 1967), pp. 145–47.

8. Hazlitt is being forced into diminishing the greatness of the comedies by his determination to refute Johnson's contention that Shakespeare's "natural" and greater gift was for comedy rather than tragedy: see "Preface to Shakespeare," in *Shakespeare Criticism*, ed. D. Nicoll Smith, World's Classics ed. (London: Oxford University Press, 1916), p. 86. Hazlitt leaves us in no doubt, though, of his opinion that "there are scenes or whole characters in Shakespeare equal in wit and drollery to any thing upon record"—Falstaff, for instance. Nevertheless Shakespeare was, he insists, excelled in certain aspects of comedy by Molière, Rabelais, and Cervantes, whereas no writer excelled him in any aspect of tragedy (6.31–32).

9. The analogy of king and jester is in part suggested by Hazlitt's discussion of Lear and the Fool, "the sublimest instance I know of passion and wit united" (6.24). In the 1829 essay he comes close to confessing the inadequacy of the incongruity theory (though almost in the next breath after reaffirming it!): the "constant recurrence" of wit suggests that the "contradiction" on which it turns "is less to what we find things than to what we wish them to be" (20.362). This puts "the serious" upon a far different footing from the mere congruity of experience as such—the "connection" of our ideas, the "habitual . . . expectation of a given order of events" (6.7)—and makes his theory of the comic at last more conformable with his general theory of intersubjective imagination.

10. "The Definition of Comedy," in Read, *Reason and Romanticism* (London: Faber and Gwyer, 1926), pp. 127–28. Cf. Bonamy Dobrée, *Restoration Comedy* (Oxford: Clarendon Press, 1924), who rightly sums up Hazlitt's view as the awareness "that although this comedy might have no reference whatever to the world that is, it was very like a society that had been" (p. 23). Dobrée's study also provides, however, a good review (pp. 18–22, 28) of the realities in that society that Hazlitt prefers to overlook. Yet his tolerance was not based on ignorance: he had read (see 18. 206) the most revealing document of Restoration social history then available, Anthony Hamilton's *Mem-*

oirs of the Comte de Gramont, recently re-edited by Walter Scott in 1811. Compare the entire indifference to history in Lamb's essay: "On the Artificial Comedy of the Last Century," *Works*, 2.143–44. The difference from Lamb becomes unmistakably clear if we take note of the fact that Lamb opposes the "artificial" in comedy to morality and its categories, whereas Hazlitt contrasts "artificial" comedy with "nature" and "comedy of nature," not with social-historical reality or moral experience as such. His use of "artificial" therefore remains a good deal closer than Lamb's to the meaning of the term as applied to Congreve's comedies by Johnson, Kames, and other earlier critics, who used the word to suggest, not fantasy, but the distortion of nature to produce certain effects of "art" and "wit" peculiar to a condition of "manners" removed from common life: see the critical opinions cited in Emmett L. Avery, *Congreve's Plays on the Eighteenth-Century Stage* (New York: Modern Language Association, 1951), esp. pp. 11–13.

11. "Restoration Comedy: The Reality and the Myth," in Knights, *Explorations* (New York: New York University Press, 1964), pp. 149–68.

12. Of the later critics I have read, Joseph Wood Krutch seems closest to Hazlitt in his view of Restoration comedy in general: see *Comedy and Conscience after the Restoration*, 2d ed. (New York: Columbia University Press, 1949), esp. pp. 44–46, 243.

13. As Hazlitt conceives it, the intersubjective sympathy of imagination does not preclude but tempers or "suspends," i.e., subordinates to humane response and understanding, our moral judgment of character in drama, even an adverse judgment of characters that are morally "deformed." He says of such characters in Shakespeare: "We pity as much as we despise them; in spite of our disgust we like them, because they like themselves, and because we are made to sympathise with them; and the ligament, fine as it is, which links them to humanity, is never broken. . . . By forming a part of our personal consciousness, [they] claim our personal forgiveness, and suspend or evade our moral judgment, by bribing our self-love to side with them. Not to do so, is not morality, but affectation, stupidity, or ill-nature" (6.33). (Here, by the way, is additional proof, if any such is needed at this point, that Hazlitt conceives of character in drama as being highly individualized without being "objective.") Undoubtedly another factor assisting Hazlitt's moral tolerance was his theatrical experience—in his younger years at least; for after about 1815, Restoration comedies were fast disappearing from the London stage: see Avery, pp. 150 ff. It is obvious that Macaulay, for instance, had little knowledge or appreciation of Restoration comedies in the theater: see "Comic Dramatists of the Restoration" (1841), in *Miscellaneous Essays* (New York, 1860), 4.350 ff.

14. Hazlitt alludes to the adverse criticisms by Johnson and Jeffrey—see *Edinburgh Review*, 27 (1816), 44–45—and glances, I believe, at Coleridge when he speaks of canting moralists who deplore Swift's satire and "write unmeaning panegyrics on mankind" (5.110–11). Compare Coleridge's estimate of Swift in *Miscellaneous Criticism*, ed. T. M. Raysor (Cambridge: Harvard University Press, 1936), pp. 128–30.

15. See the review of theories of fiction in Lionel Stevenson, *The English Novel* (Boston: Houghton-Mifflin, 1960), pp. 109–58. Hazlitt's stress on the

analogy with science cut against the grain of most contemporary formulations of the nature of fiction, which tended to re-emphasize the "romance" aspect of the novel: see Alexander Welsh, *The Hero of the Waverley Novels* (New Haven: Yale University Press, 1963), pp. 2–24.

16. "Manners, Morals, and the Novel," *The Liberal Imagination* (New York: Viking Press, 1950), pp. 207 ff.

17. Scott's sense of history has been defended from Hazlitt's (and other) accusations by Francis R. Hart, *Scott's Novels: The Plotting of Historic Survival* (Charlottesville: University Press of Virginia, 1960), esp. pp. 337 ff. For some other weaknesses of Hazlitt as a critic of Scott, see James T. Hillhouse, *The Waverley Novels and Their Critics* (Minneapolis: University of Minnesota Press, 1936), pp. 125–41.

18. "William Hazlitt as a Critic of Prose Fiction," *PMLA*, 68 (1953), 1001, 1015–16.

8. THE ESSAYS: A CRITICISM OF LIFE

1. Quoted by Richard LeGallienne in Introduction, *Liber Amoris* (London, 1893), p. iv; and for the letter to Hunt see Howe, pp. 321–22. Hazlitt's biographers have proved strangely inadequate in dealing with the affair narrated in *Liber Amoris* (9.95 ff.): compare Howe's abrupt indifference (pp. 337 ff), Maclean's sentimental pathos (pp. 415 ff.), Baker's disdain for a "mind diseased" in a "shabby liaison" (pp. 410 ff.), Wardle's patient documentation (pp. 269–336) of a "tragic farce" (p. 347). Hazlitt more than once hinted, in retrospect, that his strongest passion in the affair was not unrequited love (even in the sense of erotic obsession) but "mortified pride" (12.23, and see also 17.263). Perhaps Robert Ready, though treating *Liber Amoris* less as a confession than as a study of "character," as literature rather than biographical document—and viewing therefore its protagonist "H" as a semi-fictional and rather willful character, not one simply identical with Hazlitt—has succeeded in throwing most light on the significance of this unique and original-minded little book in its author's life: see "The Logic of Passion: Hazlitt's *Liber Amoris*," *SIR*, 14 (1975), 41–57.

2. An exception to Hazlitt's general political pessimism at this time may be found in a passage in 8.153–56, but this brief reversion to a moderate optimism seems mainly the effect of his short-lived hope (8.156) for the Spanish uprising of 1820.

3. E.g., Baker, p. 395 ("nothing really new in these essays").

4. See Erich Auerbach's suggestive remarks on Montaigne's method and the meaning of *"essai"* in *Mimesis*, trans. Willard Trask (Garden City, N.Y.: Doubleday, 1957), pp. 254–56.

5. White, "Romanticism, Historicism and Realism," in *The Uses of History: Essays in Intellectual and Social History*, ed. H. V. White (Detroit; Wayne State University Press, 1968), esp. pp. 49–51, 57.

6. Stendhal had been sufficiently impressed, mainly by Hazlitt's Shakespearean criticism, to make contact with the author, and the two men found, when they met in Paris in 1824, that they had strong mutual interests— Buonaparte and politics, painting, theater, and, among other matters of

theory, the psychology of love (and by contemporary standards, that psychology, as found both in *De l'amour* and *Liber Amoris,* might well be described as realistic). They seem to have met again several times on Hazlitt's Parisian sojourns after 1824. See Robert Vigneron, "Stendhal et Hazlitt," *MP,* 35 (1938), 375–414; Howe, p. 373; Baker, p. 443. Just as we speculate that Keats, had he lived, might have become a dramatist, so we have some warrant to conjecture that Hazlitt, had he survived into Victorian times, might have tried his hand at becoming, like his "friend Mr Beyle," a novelist.

7. My understanding of the transition to Realism is based mainly on Auerbach, *Mimesis,* pp. 400–30; White, pp. 46–48 (including summary of contending views), 54–57.

8. See George L. Barnett, *Charles Lamb: The Evolution of Elia* (Bloomington: Indiana University Press, 1964), pp. 26–36.

9. See Elbert N. S. Thompson, "The Seventeenth-Century English Essay," *University of Iowa Humanistic Studies,* 3 (1926), 10–70.

10. This transition in Hazlitt, together with a parallel development in the essays of Lamb and Hunt, has been carefully documented by Melvin R. Watson, *Magazine Serials and the Essay Tradition, 1746–1820* (Baton Rouge: Louisiana State University Press, 1956), esp. pp. 82–86. Watson, like some other commentators, would reserve the term "familiar" for the kind of essay that did not fully develop until the eighteen-twenties, in contrast to "the social and moral essay" of the traditional eighteenth-century serials (pp. 69–70). But I prefer, following Hazlitt's lead, to extend the term "familiar" (as in "familiar style": 8.242 ff.) to the Addison-Steele type of essay (which was often "familiar" in manner and tone, if not in subject-matter) and to describe the mature Romantic essay as not only "familiar" but "personal." As I go on to suggest, the essence of the "familiar" in essay writing lies in the manner of approaching and engaging the reader, not always in intimate revelation of the writer's personality.

11. "Advertisement," *The Round Table,* 4.n.p.; *Examiner,* Jan. 10, 1808, p. 26 ("philosophic gallantry"); May 9, 1813, pp. 299–300.

12. Dobrée, *English Essayists* (London: Collins, 1946), p. 30.

13. Laurence Stapledon observes that Hazlitt's "idea of conversation" also includes "the flex and reflexes of point of view towards a subject. Of conversation in this sense there is hardly an example before him": *The Elected Circle: Studies in the Art of Prose* (Princeton: Princeton University Press, 1973), pp. 101–02. Outside the essay tradition, though, there was one suggestive approximation: Johnson's conversation at times, as given by Boswell, the "dramatic play" of which Hazlitt admired (see 6.103). Hazlitt's model for his second, his "literary" style was Burke, who wrote "the most perfect prose-style" in English (12.10), unrivalled, in Hazlitt's opinion, for its expressive variety of modulation (7.303–10).

14. "An Unpublished Review by Charles Lamb," *MIQ,* 17 (1956), 353.

15. To learn how far Hazlitt has come from his youthful benevolism, and to be convinced that "sympathy" and "self-love" now appear very differently in the prose of this decade, consider such statements as these: "The sympathy with the art and purposes of man, as it were, irritates our own will, and makes us impatient of whatever interferes with it . . ." (19.80 n.).

"We set a value on things as they have cost us dear: the very limitation of our facilities or exclusiveness of our feelings compels us to concentrate all our enthusiasm on a favourite subject; and strange as it may seem, in order to inspire a perfect sympathy in others . . . men must themselves be *egotists!*" (11.277). "We hearken to no voice but that of our secret inclinations and native bias" (12.303). "They [mankind] avoid those who are in misfortune, instead of countenancing or assisting them. They anticipate the increased demand on their sympathy or bounty, and escape from it as from a falling house" (9.225). And the author of *The Plain Speaker* may not be sparing himself when he writes: "We find a set of persons who pride themselves on being *plain-spoken people,* that is, who blurt out every thing disagreeable to your face, by way of wounding your feelings and relieving their own, and this they call honesty. . . . Such is the fascination of what releases our own will from thralldom, and compels that of others reluctantly to submit to terms of our dictating! We feel our own power, and disregard their weakness and effeminacy with prodigious self-complacency" (12.349–50). "I believe," he insists, "in the theoretical benevolence and practical malignity of man" (20.343)—but it is doubtful whether the first adjective in this statement of belief can still logically refer to the theory of his 1805 *Essay.* At least Hazlitt seems now prepared to concede that self-love is more primal and elusive in human nature than he had imagined in his theory: "No one has ever yet seen through all the intricate folds and delicate involutions of our self-love, which is wrapped up in a set of smooth flimsy pretexts like some precious jewel in covers of silver paper" (12.352). Let it also be noted, though, as the rest of my chapter should make clear, that none of this "misanthropy" denies the moral nature of man, which is the ultimate cause of the will's obsession with self: "It is *ourselves* we cannot forgive" (8.118).

16. See 8.51 ff. (Paine and Cobbett), 12.336 ff. ("Sir Walter Scott, Racine, and Shakespear").

17. E.g., Watson, p. 136. James Ashley Houck, while not addressing the issue of impressionism, has recently emphasized the commitment of Hazlitt's criticism to "specific aims," namely, the "preservation" and "defense" of genius, including the "correction" of its errors as well as those of its age; and he quotes Hazlitt's warning that the critic must not only possess "enthusiasm" but must learn to "restrain . . . admiration," so that "reputation can be established on a solid basis" (18.51). This is an excellent statement of what remains constant in his criticism: see "Hazlitt on the Obligations of the Critic," *TWC,* 4 (1973), 250–58.

18. See Mario Praz, "Is Hazlitt a Great Essayist?," *English Studies,* 13 (1931), 5–6.

19. The first full articulation of the concept of *Kultur* (as distinct from "civilization") is in Kant, *The Idea for a Universal History,* in *Kant's Principles of Politics,* ed., trans. W. Hastie (Edinburgh, 1891), pp. 3–27; and for later modifications see Raymond Williams, *Culture and Society, 1780–1950* (New York: Harper and Row, 1958), esp. pp. 110 ff., 244 ff.

20. *HCI,* p. 167; Baker, p. 403.

9. PORTRAITS OF AN AGE

1. "The Place of Hazlitt in English Criticism," *The Profession of Poetry and Other Lectures* (Oxford: Clarendon Press, 1929), p. 94.

2. The number of essays and their sequence, to be discussed later, is that of the *second* English edition (1825), as given in 11.2-184. The one essay omitted from Howe's text is that on Cobbett, which Howe returns to its original (1821) place in *Table-Talk* (8.50-58). See Bibliographical Note, 11.2, and Patrick L. Story, "Hazlitt's Definition of the Spirit of the Age," *TWC*, 6 (1975), 102.

3. *Monthly Magazine*, 40.513–16 and *London Magazine*, 1.11–22 (introductory installments); Hunt, *LC*, pp. 148–76; and see Josephine Bauer, *The London Magazine, 1820–1829*, in *Anglistica*, 1 (Copenhagen, 1953), 85 ff. Laurence Stapledon, in *The Elected Circle* (Princeton: Princeton University Press, 1973), neglects the book's immediate antecedents, but I would agree with the conclusion that Hazlitt in *The Spirit of the Age* has "made something new; we might call it the portrait essay" (p. 108).

4. Leslie Marchand, *The Athenaeum* (Chapel Hill: University of North Carolina Press, 1941), pp. 234, 252; Gilfillan, *Gallery,* Everyman ed. (London: J. M. Dent, 1910), p. 109; Horne, *A New Spirit of the Age* (New York, 1844), p. iii. One great difference from Hazlitt is that these writers were all more biographical and fact-minded. Sainte-Beuve might have read Hazlitt's book and perhaps borrowed its subtitle for *Portraits Contemporains* (1832–33): see Lewis Freeman Mott, *Sainte-Beuve* (New York: Appleton, 1925), p. 262. The equivalent series in Baudelaire is in *L'Art romantique*, ed. E. Raynaud (Paris: Garnier, 1931), pp. 240–303.

5. Letter (Apr. 9, 1925) qu. in Howe, pp. 375–76. For Hazlitt and John Scott, see Bauer, p. 85; and for the probable date of the book's appearance, Baker, p. 433 n.

6. For the last three, the least common, of these descriptions, see, respectively, Cornwall B. Rogers, *The Spirit of the Revolution in 1789* (Princeton: Princeton University Press, 1949), p. 3; Sir Herbert Read, "The Problem of the *Zeitgeist,*" *The Tenth Muse* (New York: Horizon Press, 1958), pp. 317–20; José Ortega y Gasset, *Man and Crisis,* trans. Mildred Adams (New York: Norton, 1962), p. 45.

7. Schlegel, *Philosophy of Language* (1828), in *The Philosophy of Life and Philosophy of Language,* trans. A. J. W. Morrison (London, 1847), p. 420; see also pp. 158–66. Shelley, "A Defense of Poetry," in *Complete Works,* ed. R. Ingpen and W. E. Peck, 7 (London: Ernest Benn, 1930), 140.

8. Kermode, *The Sense of an Ending* (New York: Oxford University Press, 1967), pp. 5 ff.; and on "march of mind," see George Levine's Introduction to his anthology, *The Spirit of the Age* (New York: Free Press, 1967), pp. 1–15. On the relation to the French Revolution see M. H. Abrams, "English Romanticism: The Spirit of the Age," in *Romanticism Reconsidered,* ed. Northrop Frye (New York: Columbia University Press, 1963), pp. 27–28; and see his comprehensive study of Apocalyptic themes in Romanticism, *Natural Supernaturalism* (New York: Norton, 1971), esp. pp. 22–66. Erich Kahler remarks that in Romanticism *"the forward look engendered the new look backward,* the historical look": *The Meaning of History* (New York:

411

George Braziller, 1964), p. 168; and Kahler's account is also valuable for its way of explaining the later "degeneration of *historism* into *historicism*" (pp. 175 ff.). See also Hayden V. White, "Romanticism, Historicism and Realism," in *The Uses of History,* ed. White (Detroit: Wayne State University Press, 1968), p. 48.

9. *Man in the Modern Age,* trans Eden and Cedar Paul (New York: Henry Holt, 1933), pp. 6–8.

10. Park has fully developed this theme but, as he generously acknowledges (p. 89 n.), a similar emphasis on Hazlitt's antipathy to Coleridgean and other abstraction appears in my review article, "The Forgotten Self," *Partisan Review,* 30 (1963), esp. p. 304. Albrecht also observes that Hazlitt portrays his more "representative" contemporaries as "victims of abstraction" (*HCI,* p. 61).

11. Story, pp. 97 ff., first called attention to this definition, taking a hint from a note by Howe (12.400, n. 128). Negative connotations of "the spirit of the age" were not confined to Tories and other non-liberals: the traditional eighteenth-century phrase "spirit of the times" was often pejorative and did not generally connote "progress" or beneficent tendencies: see the examples in Park, p. 208, and note the contrast implied in the title of the Unitarian Gilbert Wakefield's pamphlet of 1794, *The Spirit of Christianity, Compared with the Spirit of the Times in Great Britain,* described in Story, p. 100. The change in usage parallels, and in part follows from, the shift in the philosophical sense of history from Voltaire's to Herder's—from godless, error-prone "times" to God-inspired Ages: see Herder, *Reflections on the Philosophy of the History of Mankind,* trans. (abr.) Frank E. Manuel (Chicago: University of Chicago Press, 1968), Pt. 2, pp. 81–82. Although I find it convenient to make frequent use of the term *Zeitgeist* in what follows, I am not assuming that there was much German influence (until Carlyle's time) on the meaning of the English term, although influence from the Continent was probably responsible for making the phrase "spirit of the age" more common in the 1820s (significantly, it is not to be found anywhere in Hazlitt before that time). See also Alfred G. Pundt, *Arndt and the Nationalist Awakening in Germany* (New York: Columbia University Press, 1935), pp. 50–85, 112 ff.

12. A favorite quotation from *Hamlet* III.ii.26–27; see 6.360, 19.35.

13. Hazlitt experimented with various arrangements: in the first edition the order of the first seven sketches was the same, but he had not yet clearly separated the major from the minor figures, and had yet to discover the wisdom of linking the Southey and Wordsworth essays and having them follow the essay on Byron so as to form the grouping I have described: see Geoffrey Keynes, *Bibliography of William Hazlitt* (London: Nonesuch Press, 1931), p. 82, and Story, pp. 102 ff.

14. Carlyle, *Life of John Sterling,* 2d ed. (London, 1837), pp. 69–80.

15. Irving and Coleridge are quoted in H. C. Whitley, *Blinded Eagle: An Introduction to the Life and Teachings of Edward Irving* (Chicago: Allenson, 1955), pp. 19–24, 39–49, and see Carlyle, "Death of Edward Irving," in *Works,* Centenary ed., 28 (London, 1904), 319–22. Hazlitt's other comments on Irving: 20.113 ff., 223 ff.

16. See John Stuart Mill, *The Spirit of the Age*, ed. F. A. von Hayek (Chicago: University of Chicago Press, 1942), pp. 2–6; and compare Mill, "Coleridge," *Dissertations and Discussions*, in *Works*, 4 (London: George Routledge, n.d.), 322 ff.

17. D. G. James so understands Hazlitt's criticism: *The Romantic Comedy* (London: Oxford University Press, 1963), pp. 264–65.

18. Albrecht observes that "all of Hazlitt's subjects dealt in the spoken or written word" (*HCI*, p. 59). Bentham's curious "jargon," the "monotony" and "voluntary" character of Godwin's prose, Coleridge's "prolixity" and his habit of "strewing with flowers" the devious ways of his reasoning, Irving's "extravagant metaphors," Scott's "bad and slovenly English," the "learned commonplaces" and mechanically "antithetical" periods of Mackintosh, the "logical apparatus" of Malthus that serves to conceal the "paralogism" of his doctrine—these are further instances of the decline or abuse of English idiom that Hazlitt finds characteristic of the age (11.15, 25, 33, 45, 67, 102–03, 107).

19. For further comment and for illustration of these themes elsewhere in Hazlitt's work see 20.92–96 (on opera), 143 ff. (on "the Dandy School"), 152–54 (on Beau Brummell). See also 6.162, 177; 1.281–82; 11.279; 19.73, 285.

20. "It cannot be concealed . . . that the progress of knowledge and refinement has a tendency to circumscribe the limits of the imagination and to clip the wings of poetry" (5.9). And he advises his son: "The best qualifier of . . . theoretical mania and of the dreams of poets and moralists (who both treat of things as *they ought to be* and not as *they are*) is in one sense to be found in some of our own popular writers, such as our Novelists and periodical Essayists" (17.94). See also 5.168; 6.121–23; and esp. 16.212 ff., 218, 268–69. A third prose writer who elsewhere wins praise from Hazlitt not unlike that given to Lamb and Cobbett, but with sharper rebukes for his "willful" and "Jacobin" egotism, is Landor: see 16.240–47; 19.105–07.

21. Robert E. Robinson, *William Hazlitt's Life of Napoleon Buonaparte* (Geneva and Paris: Librairie E. Droz, Librairie Minard, 1959), pp. 11–36.

22. Guérard, *Reflections on the Napoleonic Legend* (New York: Scribner's, 1924), p. 128. The change in English attitudes was largely motivated, as Hazlitt indicates in 17.313, by growing disgust with the Bourbon Restoration. Hazlitt would have been amazed to learn that even Wellington (though only in private, in a conversation of 1821), regretted the dethronement and exile of Napoleon: see Harold Nicholson, *The Congress of Vienna* (New York: Harcourt, Brace, 1946), p. 293.

23. Napoleon is quoted from August Fournier, *Napoleon I: A Biography*, trans. A. E. Adams, rev. ed. (London: Longmans, Green, 1912), p. 22 n., and from George Gordon Andrews, *Napoleon in Review* (New York: Knopf, 1939), p. 39. On the Legend, see Pieter Geyl, *Napoleon For and Against*, trans. Olive Renier (New Haven: Yale University Press, 1963), pp. 23–32.

24. [M. H. Abrams], "William Hazlitt," in *The Norton Anthology of English Literature*, rev. ed. (New York: Norton, 1968), 2.609.

25. For nineteenth-century views of Napoleon see Sidney Hook, *The Hero in History* (Boston: Beacon Press, 1955), pp. 14 ff., 60–66. Among Eu-

ropean contemporaries, Stendhal's sense of Napoleon (see Guérard, pp. 211–18) most clearly resembles Hazlitt's, and perhaps reflects, in part, their discussions in Paris: see Howe, p. 373.

26. Alexis de Tocqueville, *The Old Regime and the French Revolution*, trans. Stuart Gilbert (Garden City, N.Y.: Doubleday, 1955), pp. 206–10.

27. Since "progress" in Enlightenment theory was often conceived as an escape from the cycles of rise and decline that had overtaken civilization in Greece and Rome, it is not illogical that Hazlitt should have fallen back upon the cyclical premise: see Peter Gay, *The Enlightenment, an Interpretation: The Rise of Modern Paganism* (New York: Knopf, 1966), pp. 33–34. Only once before, so far as I can find, does Hazlitt indicate some acceptance of this view: the possible reversion of the modern arts and "taste" to "night and barbarism" is briefly mentioned, but not discussed, in 16.215 (1823).

10. CONCLUSION: THE FAITH OF THE CENTAUR

1. Howe, p. 367, quoting Robinson, 1.386. Information in this and the next paragraph is from 10.85 ff., 319–20 (Howe's notes); Baker, pp. 442–50, 464–69; Wardle, pp. 381, 391 ff., 428–40, 452–85.

2. For a Victorian's sense of a "new time" emerging in the early twenties see Harriet Martineau, *History of the Thirty Years' Peace, 1816–1846* (London, 1877), 1.370 ff.

3. Howe, p. 415 n. (quoting Coleridge); Carlyle, "Characteristics," *Works*, Centenary Edn., 28 (London, 1899), 31–32. One event which disposed Hazlitt to thoughts of happiness in his last weeks was the toppling of the restored Bourbon monarchy in the Revolution of the Three Days (July 27–29) in Paris. He had said (8.324, 373) that he "would like to live to see the downfall of the Bourbons," and he rejoiced (17.377, 429) in the abdication of Charles X as realizing this wish, although he still had fears of a future Restoration (see Wardle, p. 482). Yet even if this should come to pass, the event still proved, he said, that the impulse to Liberty is itself indestructible—is " 'the worm that dies not' " (19.334 n.).

4. The account that follows of Hazlitt's thinking about religion is adapted from my article, "The Faith of the Centaur: Hazlitt's Sceptical Triumph over Scepticism," *TWC*, 6 (1975), 85–96.

5. Jack, *English Literature, 1815–1832* (Oxford: Clarendon Press, 1963), p. 7; Robinson, 1.6.

6. See Marjorie Hope Nicolson, *The Breaking of the Circle* (Evanston, Ill.: Northwestern University Press, 1950), pp. 137–44; Franklin L. Baumer, *Religion and the Rise of Scepticism* (New York: Harcourt, Brace, 1960), pp. 90–95; Thomas Paine, *The Age of Reason* (London: Watts, 1938), p. 49.

7. *The Statesman's Manual*, in *Political Tracts*, p. 13.

8. *The Varieties of Religious Experience* (New York: New American Library, 1958), pp. 371–85.

9. Something very similar to this view, however different the contextual terms, is being suggested by C. E. Pulos, *The Deep Truth* (Lincoln: University of Nebraska Press, 1954), when he distinguishes the sceptically "ironic" but "sincere" awareness of Shelley's non-dogmatic idealism from the "deliberate

irony" of much German Romanticism (pp. 8 ff.); by M. G. Cooke, who, in
The Blind Man Traces the Circle (Princeton: Princeton University Press, 1969),
sees Byron's scepticism as generating a "counter-heroic" humanism, one that
"rebukes the desperate activity of the heroic no less than the desperate passivity of the idio-satirical" (pp. 181 ff.); and in the "quest" of the "speculative
life" and the bold "play of paradox" that James D. Boulger finds in Coleridge's later poems, consciously Christian though they are: *Coleridge as Religious Thinker* (New Haven: Yale University Press, 1961), pp. 201 ff.

10. See 4.238, 347; 5.47–56; 6.215; 11.267.

11. On the "privileged moment" in Romanticism see Georges Poulet,
"Timelessness and Romanticism," *Journal of the History of Ideas,* 15 (1954),
3–22, and his *Studies in Human Time* (Baltimore: Johns Hopkins University
Press, 1956), esp. 25–30.

12. George Gilfillan, *A Gallery of Literary Portraits* (London: J. M. Dent,
1910), pp. 109–11, 278 ("unhealthy heat"); Thackeray, review (1844) of
R. H. Horne (cited below), *Complete Works,* 25 (New York: Harper, 1904), 350.
Carlyle expresses his grudging respect in "Lord Jeffrey," *Reminiscences,* ed.
C. E. Norton, 2 (London, 1887), 251; and his earlier works, esp. *The Life of John
Sterling* and *The French Revolution,* contain more than a few echoes of Hazlitt.
Macaulay's stylistic debt to Hazlitt has been frequently noted, and Gilfillan
had no doubts that Macaulay "steals from Hazlitt" (p. 105). R. H. Horne, *A
New Spirit of the Age* (London, 1844), was perhaps the first to suggest the affinity of Dickens and Hazlitt (p. 19), and Dickens himself testifies to his
delight in Hazlitt in *Household Words,* 16 (1857), 477–80. W. D. Howe, "Hazlitt," *Cambridge History of English Literature,* 12 (New York: Putnam's, 1916)
cites Froude's praise (p. 197). Hazlitt's strongest literary admirer was probably Stevenson: "Though we are mighty fine fellows nowadays, we cannot
write like Hazlitt": "Walking Tours," *Virginibus Puerisque* (Harmondsworth:
Penguin Books, 1946), p. 146. And if Hazlitt had an intellectual disciple in
Victorian times, it was probably Walter Bagehot: see his and other testimonials cited in Howe, pp. 358, 422–23. George Saintsbury, constantly qualifying high praise with patronizing rebuke or condescension, may be said to
epitomize Victorian evaluations of Hazlitt: see his *History of English Criticism*
(Edinburgh: Blackwood's, 1911), pp. 364–75, and his *History of English Prose
Rhythm* (London: Macmillan, 1912), where again Hazlitt is praised for his "in
some ways, unmatched critical faculty" (p. 359). Hazlitt's strong influence on
American criticism is reviewed in John Paul Pritchard, *Literary Wise Men of
Gotham, 1815–1860* (Baton Rouge: Louisiana State University Press, 1963),
pp. 22, 105–11, 133.

13. G. K. Chesterton, *The Victorian Age in Literature* (New York: Henry
Holt, 1913), pp. 12 ff., 30 ff.

14. Augustine Birrell, *William Hazlitt* (London: Macmillan, 1902), p.
122.

15. See the discussion of possible but wholly unconfirmed influence in
David J. DeLaura, "Arnold and Hazlitt," *English Language Notes,* 9 (1972),
277–92 (there is "very little evidence of his reading in the Romantic prose-
writers": p. 277). Park stresses the critical affinity between Hazlitt and Arnold, but he places the emphasis on their solicitude for poetry (p. 1).

415

16. This and the equally influential essay, "The Study of Poetry," are in *Complete Prose Works,* ed. R. H. Super, 3 (Ann Arbor: University of Michigan Press, 1962), 262 ff.; 9 (1973), 163–64 ("personal estimate"). For the widespread academic impact of Arnold's criticism, especially in providing "rationale" for young and insecure English departments in America, see Richard Ohmann, *English in America* (New York: Oxford University Press, 1976), pp. 248 ff., 301.

17. *Anatomy of Criticism* (New York: Atheneum, 1969), pp. 8–29.

18. Much of what I say from this point on, I first said, somewhat differently, in "The Forgotten Self," *Partisan Review,* 30 (1963), 305–06. Although critical opinion after Arnold tended to minimize Hazlitt's importance or his durability as an exemplary model—a tendency that perhaps first takes a hostile turn in J. M. Robertson, *Essays toward a Critical Method* (London, 1889), who dismisses him as a "facile eulogist" (p. 81)—there have always been voices ready to defend him and even to nominate him as the supreme English critic. With some hesitation, H. W. Garrod did precisely that in "The Place of Hazlitt in English Criticism," *The Profession of Poetry and Other Lectures* (Oxford: Clarendon Press, 1929), pp. 94, 98–106. More recently, Henri Peyre has ventured the opinion that Hazlitt is the "truest," the "least unsatisfactory of all English critics": see his *Writers and their Critics* (Ithaca: Cornell University Press, 1944), p. 275.

19. See *Anatomy,* esp. pp. 343–54, and Frye's essay "The Problem of Spiritual Authority in the Nineteenth Century," in *Literary Views: Critical and Historical Essays,* ed. Carrol Camden (Chicago: University of Chicago Press, 1964), pp. 145–58.

20. Burke, *Attitudes toward History,* 1 (New York: New Republic, 1937), 213–16; and see the discussion in George Knox, *Critical Moments: Kenneth Burke's Categories and Critiques* (Seattle: University of Washington Press, 1957), pp. 70–80. Hazlitt's precedent, of course, though largely unacknowledged, can still be detected in twentieth-century practice. Judgments like his of the character of minds do not depend on cultural fashion, and lest the reader doubt that this is so, we might pause for a moment here to consider a striking instance—Hazlitt's account of Ben Jonson, as compared with Edmund Wilson's estimate. Wilson describes Jonson's "constipated genius" as a type of the "anal erotic"; and we find Hazlitt, like a prophetic convert to Freud, speaking of Jonson's "clogged" perceptions and "cramp manner," his "literal tenaciousness" and "excess of consistency," his "fastening on some one mark or sign by which he designates the individual . . . for fear of not meeting with any other means to express himself by" (6.38–45). Indeed, Wilson's essay "Morose Ben Jonson"—in *The Triple Thinkers,* rev. ed. (London: John Lehmann, 1952), pp. 203–20—is remarkable throughout for its unwitting coincidence with Hazlitt's critique. Bate (*Criticism,* p. 588) refers to Hazlitt as "Wilson's greatest predecessor." And Lionel Trilling has pointed out the strong resemblance between Hazlitt and another shrewd estimator of character, George Orwell: "George Orwell and the Politics of Truth," *The Opposing Self* (New York: Viking Press, 1955), p. 160.

21. Letter to the George Keatses (March 12, 1819), 2.73–76.

Index

417

"Rime of the Ancient Mariner," 45, 94, 310-11; compared with WH in philosophy, 46-47, 63-67, 88; on WH, 49, 55, 92, 343, 347; on power, 89, 95; dispute with WH concerning evil, 94-96, 391n.15; WH on "apostasy" of, 103-6, 113; compared with WH in criticism, 136, 204, 216, 370-73, 401n.5, 402n.9; on Shakespeare and tragedy, 189, 357, 400n.38, 404n.22; poetics of, 198, 204, 216, 225-26, 402n.9; *Biographia Literaria*, 204, 228, 321, 367, 391n.15, 401n.5 (WH on), 402n.9; on Milton, 215-16, 404n.22; on "fancy," 221; on Swift, 249-50, 407n.14; WH on thought and character of, 310-12, 348, 372, 401n.5; on WH's death, 343; challenged by WH on religion, 347-48; and Arnold, 366, 370; WH on *Remorse*, 396n.2; Walter Pater on, 402n.10
Collier, Jeremy, 248
Collier, John Payne, 400n.38
Comedy: WH's interest in, 231, 234; and the Romantic age, 233; WH's theory of, 234-39, 405n.5, 406nn.6, 9; types and periods of, 235-37; of "humour" and "nature," 235-36, 238-40; Restoration, 235-36, 243-48, 407n.13; "sentimental," 236, 248; of Shakespeare and Jonson compared, 240; decline of, 247-52; and the novel, 242-43, 258; and attitudes in criticism, 369-72; *see also* Wit
Condillac, Etienne Bonnot de, 61
Congreve, William, 244-45
Constable, John, 132, 143, 395n.15
Constable, W. G., 395n.13
Cooke, Michael G., 414-15n.9
Correggio, 137, 162
Courier, The, 312
Covent Garden, Theatre Royal, 167, 170
Crabbe, George, 303, 323
Criticism: estimates of WH's, ix, 164, 166, 197, 202-3, 211, 260, 363-75, 410n.17, 416nn.18, 20; WH on, 127-28, 160-62, 289-95; WH called "impressionist" in, 127, 133, 154, 163-64, 291, 366; WH's "character" method in, 161-62, 179-80, 183, 214, 368-69, 371-74, 403n.19,

416n.20; in WH's personal essays, 292-95, 299; WH and "public," 366-69
Crocker, Lester G., 391n.12
Cromwell, Oliver, 328

Dante Alighieri, 355
Dekker, Thomas, 403-4n.25
Delacroix, Eugène, 163
DeLaura, David J., 415n.15
Democracy: WH's theory of, 114-28; his definition of, 123; and intellectual culture, 295; and "equality" in Wordsworth, 319; in French Revolution and under Napoleon, 327-31; WH on tyranny of majority in America, 331; on future of, 331-35
Dennis, John, 396n.28
De Quincey, Thomas: on WH, 49, 50-51; on power, 90, 138; compared with WH as essayist, 270; on Shakespeare, 357
Descartes, René, 69
Dicey, A. V., 393n.38
Dickens, Charles, 7, 364, 415n.12
"Disinterestedness": WH's "discovery" of as "natural," 2, 11, 26-30, 388n.20; his father's ideal of, 18; and Godwin, 21-24; and WH's character, 35-36, 368n.39; and empiricist philosophy, 24-28, 53-57; and benevolence in WH's theory of imagination, 42-44, 58-61, 78, 85-88, 93, 98; and sympathetic functions of consciousness, 54-57; later qualifications of WH's theory of, 60-61, 285-86, 409-10n.15; in art, 161; in poetry, 205-6, 210; *see also* Imagination; Intersubjectivity
Dissent and Dissenters: influence on WH's thought and character, 3, 11, 13, 22, 36, 51, 77-78, 127-28, 159, 284; WH on mentality of, 6, 385n.28
Dobrée, Bonamy, 277, 406n.10, 409n.12
Donne, John, 222, 367, 371
Donohue, Joseph W., Jr., 181, 184; 400nn.22, 33
Drama: contemporary state of, 167-71, 248-49; WH on character in, 172-73, 175-83, 190, 193-94, 407n.13; on "prin-

Hagstrum, Jean H., 394*n*.1, 403*n*.19
Hale, J. R., 395*n*.10
Halévy, Elie, 394*n*.40
Haller, William, 384*n*.14
Hamilton, Anthony, 406-7*n*.10
Harbage, Alfred, 401*n*.41
Harris, James, 405-6*n*.5
Hart, Francis R., 408*n*.17
Hartley, David, 27,44,48,55,62,388*n*.22, 405-6*n*.5
Havens, R. D., 390*n*.10
Hayden, John O., 401*n*.3
Haydon, Benjamin R., 49, 134, 159, 344, 387*n*.42, 394*n*.7
Hayens, Kenneth, 399*n*.23
Hazlitt, Grace Loftus (WH's mother), 7
Hazlitt, Isabella Bridgewater (WH's second wife), 339-40
Hazlitt, John (WH's brother), 7; portraits by, frontispiece, 9, 16, 82
Hazlitt, Margaret (WH's sister), 5, 7, 17, 143
Hazlitt, Sarah Stoddart (WH's first wife), 80, 93, 266
Hazlitt, W. Carew (WH's grandson), 383*n*.5
Hazlitt, William (WH's father): ministry at Wem, 5, 17; education of, 7, 15, 17; WH's struggle for independence from, 10-11, 15, 19-21, 132; Puritan ancestry of and Presbyterian tradition, 12-14; Unitarian (Socinian) theology of, 12, 15, 17-20, 26, 350; WH on, 14-15, 30-32, 234; his faith in "progress of truth," 14-16, 33-34, 85; appearance of, 15-16, 401*n*.4; portraits of, 16 (by John Hazlitt), 139 (by WH), 141; in Ireland and America, 16-17; writings of, 17ff., 384*nn*.21-24; death of, 284, 342-43
Hazlitt, William:
—— *Life:* legend of his lack of intellectual development, 1-5; makes "metaphysical discovery," 1-2, 11, 386*n*.36 (see also "Disinterestedness"); his "consistency" of opinion, 1-4, 32-36; childhood piety and adolescent rebellion, 4-11; conflict and interaction of Boy and Prig in WH's mind and character, 5-8, 30-36, 46-47,

58, 78, 80, 118, 159, 174-75, 262-63, 280-84, 317, 331, 341, 363, 386*n*.39; at Hackney College, 11, 14, 21, 23-26, 30, 73; rejects father's "creed" and ministerial career, 14-15, 19-22, 26-29, 386*n*.36; period of Godwinism and philosophical studies, 22-26, 385*n*.32; inability after 1795 to write essay, 30-33; discovers deeper powers of imagination through poets of *Lyrical Ballads*, 30-31, 37-48; studies to become a painter, 31, 134, 141-42, 394*n*.6-7; his quest for expressive power and frustrations after 1802, 33-36, 92-93, 174-75; significance of Waterloo in his career, 34, 174, 387*n*.42; sexual habits, 35, 92-93, 387*n*.43; appearance, 36; reading in contemporary literature, 40-45, 292-93; experience of "contradiction" and abandonment of philosophy, 47-49, 51, 76-81; alienation from Wordsworth and Coleridge, 47, 88, 92, 94, 101 ff.; marriage and retirement to Winterslow, 79-80; launches journalistic career, 80-81; experience in the Louvre decisive for his criticism, 84-86, 128; despairs of his painting, 92; changes in his politics, 106-9; celebrity as a critic, 165-66, 197; Tory persecution, 197-99, 265-67; pessimism after 1819 and reaction against former beliefs, 265-70, 279-82, 289-90; separation from wife and infatuation with Sarah Walker, 266, 276; another "voice" and new awareness of himself in the personal essays, 270-71, 279 ff.; conflict of new and old attitudes in later works, 303-4, 317, 324-26, 331-37, 341-43, 358-61; European tour of 1824-25 and sojourns in Paris, 339-41; second marriage, 339-40; last years, 340-42; death and last words, 343, 363, 374-75; summary of his intellectual life, 361-63
—— *Works: Abridgement of the Light of Nature Pursued, An* (Abraham Tucker), 66; "Cant and Hypocrisy, On," 351-53; *Characteristics*, 285; *Characters of Shakespear's Plays*, 110,112,166,172-95,

189 ff., 194, 199 ff., 215 ff., 235, 244, 271, 283, 298 ff., 305, 345 ff., 353 ff., 360, 362; and Victorianism, 121; and tragedy, 189, 194-95; and poetic theory, 199, 201 ff., 401-2n.7; and Milton, 217 ff., 403-4nn.21-22; and comedy, 233, 244; and Realism, 270-71, 300; and history, 270, 304-5; and religion, 345, 353-57, 360; and later criticism, 363-66, 370-71

Rousseau, Jean Jacques, 25-26, 40, 44, 91-92, 152

Royal Academy of Art, 130-34, 146, 167

Rubens, Peter Paul, 145, 153

Ruggiero, Guido, 393n.37

Ruskin, John, 120, 143, 163, 364, 395-96n.22

Sabine, George H., 393n.35

Sainte-Beuve, Augustin, 302, 411n.4

Saintsbury, George, 414n.12

Santayana, George, 50

Sartre, Jean Paul, 203

Satire: WH on, 236, 241, 245-46; in WH, 282, 369-73

Scheler, Max, 56

Schiffer, John D., 395n.11

Schiller, Johann Christoph Friedrich von, 40, 193, 293

Schlegel, August Wilhelm von, 173, 189, 399n.23, 400n.38

Schlegel, Friedrich von, 201, 304, 401n.7

Schneider, Ben Ross, 24

Schneider, Elisabeth, 148, 386n.39, 391n.23

Science: and WH's philosophy, 51, 73; and art, 138, 156; and fiction, 253-54, 260, 262; and the familiar essay, 273; and the age, 315-16; and religion, 344-46, 349

Scott, John, 102, 272, 302-3, 397n.4

Scott, Sir Walter: WH on novels of, 257-63; on politics and character of, 315-19; also referred to, 81, 307, 327, 365, 408n.17

Sculpture, 146-47, 150, 156, 161, 163

Selby-Bigge, L. A., 385n.33, 388n.14

Self: in empiricist philosophy, 24-25, 28,

51-55; WH on nature and genesis of (self-consciousness, self-love, personal identity), 27-30, 54-61, 75, 100, 285-88, 292-99, 318, 409-10n.5; on transcendence of, 42-45, 128, 287; on will and passions of, 71-78, 88, 91-93, 96-101, 108; modern "abstraction" of mind from, 80-81, 117-18, 248-49, 305, 308, 319-20; his revaluation of, 85-86; and Buonaparte, 86, 329; experience of in art, 160-62; in drama, 178-79, 191-95; in poetry, 205-7, 227; in comedy and fiction, 246 ff., 259; in WH's personal essays, 283 ff., 288, 294-99; in culture of the age, 307 ff., 314-15, 322-24; and "self-knowledge," 311, 336, 349-50, 362; in religion, 348-49, 352 ff., 360; in literary criticism, 368-75; see also "Disinterestedness"; Intersubjectivity; Organic principle; Power

Shaftesbury, Anthony Ashley Cooper, third Earl of, 17, 396n.28

Shakespeare, William, 135, 161, 259, 285, 321, 374; and WH's psychology, 94; Coriolanus, 110-12, 169, 184; WH on genius of, 152, 176-77, 357, 399n.24; reputation of WH as critic of, 165-66, 175-76, 398n.19, 399n.23; on acting of, 169-73, 180, 397n.7; Antony and Cleopatra, 169, 180; Richard III, 169, 172, 183; Macbeth, 169, 176, 181-85; The Merchant of Venice, 172; Hamlet, 172-73, 176, 193-94, 307; character and passion in, 172-73, 176-81; Othello, 173, 176, 185-88, 400n.37; Richard II, 173; "design" in tragedies of, 175-85, 190-92; and Elizabethan tragedy, 175, 404-5n.25; King Lear, 176, 190-93, 195, 406n.7; Cymbeline, 177-78, 399-400n.26; tragic catharsis in, 191-93; and later English poetry, 200, 205, 208 ff., 219-22, 226-27, 404n.22; Venus and Adonis and The Rape of Lucrece, 221; comedy of, 238-40, 406n.8; character of Falstaff, 239; history plays of, 257; The Tempest (Prospero), 358; WH's spelling of name, 397n.3

Shaw, George Bernard, 166